The Vietnam War
IN AMERICAN CHILDHOOD

CHILDREN
YOUTH + WAR

The Vietnam War
IN AMERICAN CHILDHOOD

Joel P. Rhodes

The University of Georgia Press
ATHENS

Portions of chapters 1 and 7 appeared in *Growing Up in a Land Called Honalee: The Sixties in the Lives of American Children*, by Joel P. Rhodes (Columbia: University of Missouri Press, 2017) and appears here courtesy of the University of Missouri Press.

Athens, Georgia 30602
www.ugapress.org

Designed by Kaelin Chappell Broaddus
Set in 10.5/13.5 Garamond Premier Pro by BookComp, Inc.
Printed by Integrated Books International
The paper in this book meets the guidelines for permanence and durability of the Committee on Production Guidelines for Book Longevity of the Council on Library Resources.

Most University of Georgia Press titles are available from popular e-book vendors.

Printed in the United States of America
23 22 21 20 19 P 5 4 3 2 1

Library of Congress Cataloging-in-Publication Data

Names: Rhodes, Joel P., 1967– author.
Title: The Vietnam War in American childhood / Joel P. Rhodes.
Description: Athens : The University of Georgia Press, [2019] | Series: Children, youth, and war | Includes bibliographical references and index.
Identifiers: LCCN 2019018160 | ISBN 9780820356297 (paperback) | ISBN 9780820356112 (hardback) | ISBN 9780820356129 (ebook)
Subjects: LCSH: Vietnam War, 1961–1975—Children. | Children and war—United States—History—20th century. | Vietnam War, 1961–1975—Social aspects—United States. | Vietnam War, 1961–1975—Influence. | Children—United States—Social conditions—20th century. | United States—Social conditions—1945–
Classification: LCC DS559.8.C53 R46 2019 | DDC 959.704/31—dc23
LC record available at https://lccn.loc.gov/2019018160

Dedicated to the
Gold Star sons and daughters
of the Vietnam War

CONTENTS

The Vietnam War
IN AMERICAN CHILDHOOD

INTRODUCTION

> We were also always aware of the Vietnam War in our home. It was on the news every day so we saw firsthand how horrible war was. Because the horrible news was followed by such innocence, it made it all the more poignant to me growing up.
>
> —**MINNESOTA WOMAN BORN IN 1964**

"You're condemning this whole planet to a war that may never end. It could go on for year after year, massacre after massacre," Dr. Leonard McCoy argued, chastising his commander, James T. Kirk, in the *Star Trek* episode "A Private Little War." Broadcast twice in the science-fiction series's second season in 1968—first in February just days after the Tet Offensive began—"A Private Little War" is one of *Star Trek*'s several explicit allegories on the Cold War logic driving American involvement in Vietnam. Despite shaky ratings, *Star Trek* was a childhood phenomenon in the late 1960s, principally for the far-out gadgetry (phasers, tricorders, and transporters!) and exaggerated fisticuffs, but also for incorporating moralistic social commentary into fantastical situations, with storylines both comforting, yet cool, all of which translated seamlessly from Friday night television into imaginative play. Clearly, in choosing up sides for backyard battles, Klingons were the Soviets and the Federation was America.

In "A Private Little War," it is difficult not to recognize specific references to Vietnam. On the primitive planet Neural (Vietnam), the starship *Enterprise* crew finds the Klingons stirring up trouble again by arming "the villagers" (North Vietnamese) in their war of conquest against peaceful "hill people" (South Vietnamese). The Klingons hope to draw Neural into its sphere of influence with the supply of weapons, which although simple flintlock rifles, are far superior to any indigenous technology and will decisively alter the conflict's outcome. Captain Kirk is caught on the horns of a universal dilemma: obey the Prime Directive of noninterference, effectively ceding Neural to the slavery of Klingon authoritarianism, or arm the hill people with comparable weapons for a fight that will ultimately destroy their world for the sake of maintaining an intergalactic balance of power. Just like the United States in Southeast Asia, Kirk seeks to do the right thing in a situation without a satisfactory course of action.[1]

"I don't have a solution," McCoy acknowledges. "But furnishing them with firearms is certainly *not* the answer!"

"Bones," Kirk retorts, "do you remember the twentieth-century brush wars on the Asian continent? Two giant powers involved, much like the Klingons and ourselves. Neither side felt that they could pull out?"

"Yes, I remember—it went on bloody year after bloody year!"

"But what would you have suggested? That one side arm its friends with an overpowering weapon? Mankind would never have lived to travel space if they had. No—the only solution is what happened, back then, balance of power."

"And if the Klingons give their side even more?"

"Then we arm our side with *exactly* that much more. A balance of power—the trickiest, most difficult, dirtiest game of them all—but the only one that preserves both sides."[2]

Having finally made the unsettling moral choice to intervene, Kirk and McCoy's disillusionment in the final scene of "A Private Little War"—reflecting American weariness at the onset of Tet—is strikingly uncharacteristic of *Star Trek*.[3] "We're very tired, Mister Spock. Beam us up home."

For American children raised exclusively in wartime—that is, a Cold War containing monolithic communism turned hot in the jungles of Southeast Asia—and the first to grow up with televised combat, Vietnam was predominantly a mediated experience. A handful of these prime-time allegories notwithstanding, Walter Cronkite was the voice of the conflict and grim, nightly statistics the most recognizable feature. With his avuncular air of detachment, Cronkite concluded the *CBS Evening News* broadcast on any given night, as all network newscasters of the era reliably did, by tallying the most recent numbers in television's seemingly endless arithmetic of war. These "latest casualty figures put American battle deaths last week at 91, the South Vietnamese lost 216 killed," the anchorman reported in the summer when American troop levels first exceeded 300,000, "and enemy dead number 1,827, the second highest weekly figure this year." And that's the way it was, August 25, 1966.

Without Vietnam, the civil rights movement would have been "the sixties," but instead, as Lyndon B. Johnson "Americanized" the war in the spring of 1965, the escalating military commitment did, in fact, become America's most pervasive, and devastating, collective undertaking. The conflict's basic parameters had already solidified into the reality of Americans living in the nuclear age, and specifically into children's thinking about the Cold War after the Cuban Missile Crisis in October 1962. A useful way to begin appreciating Vietnam's place in childhood is by considering a broader developmental context. Most attentive elementary school children understood their country to be on some type of permanent wartime footing (U.S. defense spending under John F. Kennedy reached the highest levels in the postwar era) and themselves to be living in the shadow, if not the midst, of an actual war. Those younger than fourth and fifth grades took the words "Cold War" literally. With few of the cognitive resources necessary to tease out abstractions, subtleties of the Cold War—where ideologies, propaganda, foreign aid, and sanctions could be weaponized—made no sense whatsoever. After fourth grade, youth knew the country to be technically at peace. They tended to approach geopolitics more logically and appreciated some of the complexities of a conflict often waged by competing alliances, covert operations, and regional combat by proxy.

As U.S. involvement incrementally grew, Vietnam affected numerous changes in children's lives, comparable to the childhood impact of previous conflicts—chiefly the Civil War and World War II—whose intensity and duration also dominated American culture. Vietnam-era families, likewise, confronted home-front issues common to Americans in wartime. Several variances with direct bearing on childhood, however, make Vietnam distinctive. The typical father separation was shorter in length and more predictable given a serviceman's predetermined DEROS (Date Eligible for Return from Overseas). Having a father serving in Vietnam for a year-long tour was still a developmental factor, but some of the most problematic developmental issues observed in home-front children during World War II—when fathers were gone thirty-three months on average—either did not appear or were significantly diminished, except in prisoner of war (POW) and missing in action (MIA) families. Ironically, though, while preschoolers knew the least about the war and forged few memories, the youngest children of veterans were frequently those most negatively affected by problematic reunions.

Another striking difference is emotional difficulty. In previous wars, war wives worried over immediate home-front economic concerns surrounding how to make ends meet during separation. Vietnam-era spouses did, too, but they shouldered extra burdens keeping the family together and parenting for two during an unpopular war. Uncertainty and misunderstanding over America's war effort exacerbated a mother's usual distress as she struggled to reconcile a father's role in a national controversy. Compared with the circumstances surrounding World War II, during Vietnam the United States lacked unity of spirit or a collective war effort. Sacrifices were shouldered unequally by the population. Beyond life on military bases and adjacent communities, where conservative, pro-military attitudes held sway, views on the war were disputed. Most Americans appeared unconcerned with the price being paid by military families, and when people did speak up on Vietnam, it was frequently in protest. In this singular instance, at least, the Korean War appears to be a closer analogy. Although the relatively short period of hostilities in Korea prior to the armistice in 1953 did not have the same influence on the home front, the country also lost its taste for that undeclared "police action" as it dragged on.

Youth during World War II also retained with clarity into adulthood many of the proscriptive patriotic messages about U.S. rightness, why-we-fight, heroism, or sacrifice they were indoctrinated with during the war years. Conversely, in Vietnam-era children, those ideas are generally grounded emotionally rather than cognitively due to the power and immediacy, if not the sheer repetition, of television. Regardless of what preadolescents may have "learned" about the war, what they appear to have brought with them into adulthood are recollections of how the sights and sounds of Huey helicopters, men on stretchers with bloodied bandages, and odd little villagers in conical hats made them feel at the time. These unreasoned, emotive responses to televised footage bred a childhood ambivalence—although not necessarily of the "hawk" and "dove" kind—that endured in complicated notions about militarism and warfare.[4]

The ultimate depth of wartime experience followed closely developments in abstract thought—preadolescents grasp local circumstances before identifying with national life—as Vietnam's influence was directly proportional to the conflict's penetration of a child's proximal world. In this protracted struggle that took on the look of permanence from a child's perspective, adult lives were increasingly militarized, leaving few preadolescents totally insulated. Over the years 1965 to 1973, the vast majority of American children integrated at least some elements of the war into their own routines, most often through those common forms of television, war play, and to a lesser extent music. Parents, in turn, shaped their child's perspectives on Vietnam, while the more politicized mothers and fathers exposed them to the bitter polarization the war engendered. The fighting only became truly real insomuch as service in Vietnam called away older community members—neighborhood teenagers, lifeguards, acolytes, a teacher's son, a babysitter's boyfriend—or was driven home literally when families shared hardships surrounding separation from cousins, brothers, and fathers.

In seeing the Vietnam War through the eyes of preadolescent Americans—those born roughly between 1956 and 1970—I locate entry points where social and political changes from the broader adult world manifested in the separate sphere of childhood to become changes in the reality of children. Although a social and political historian of Cold War America, I too am a child of the Vietnam era. Born in 1967 to baby boomer parents, my birth is the product of a brief marriage perhaps incentivized by Selective Service's marital and parenthood draft deferments in the conflict's early years. My working mother with emergent antiwar tendencies and countercultural sensibilities raised me, along with my maternal grandparents, while my father served in Vietnam between 1970 and 1971. I may have older memories of growing up but none as vivid as his return. It was a Sunday night during *Mutual of Omaha's Wild Kingdom*, and the knock on the door came unexpectedly, unusual because I had not been told beforehand and we rarely received nighttime visitors. I opened the door and through the screen saw him standing in the porch light dressed in his khaki uniform. The overwhelming sense I had, and still do, was of being absolutely dumbfounded.

The year my father spent in Vietnam—having his letters read out loud or imagining I saw him on the television news—help frame my understanding of how children saw the war, of course, as do my memories of the aftermath. But historical methodology and sources mitigate against bias from my subject position. To study the broad range of childhood experiences during the Vietnam War, my work relies heavily on firsthand accounts collected chiefly through oral histories and archival collections. As a research strategy, I borrowed an approach from historian William Tuttle, soliciting stories from people about growing up in the sixties through a "Letter to the Editor" sent to hundreds of newspapers in all fifty states.

Nearly four hundred self-selected respondents provided childhood recollections of Vietnam. In addition to questions of sampling—since these points of view as a group may not necessarily reflect all children—there are also inherent limitations to remembered and imagined history. Memories can be selective and preferenced, honed over time and often in consultation with parents or siblings. Many who contacted me had clearly squared their stories with national, collective narratives on Vietnam, principally the mistreatment of returning servicemen. As historical sources, these recollections merit scrutiny, so to lessen problems of memory distortion and representation I supplemented oral histories with preadolescent letters at the John F. Kennedy and Lyndon Baines Johnson Presidential Libraries (similar correspondence files are, at present, still unavailable for Richard M. Nixon).

I am interested in not only the immediate imprint of Vietnam but also how children made meaning of the war based on their particular age. With a mindfulness of developmental and educational psychology, where appropriate I consider causal results that may continue to influence them as adults. The real cognitive and moral heavy lifting in our lives is done prior to adolescence, between the middle childhood ages of six and twelve, or as historian Howard Chudacoff says, the time when "children are really children."[5] Swiss biologist and psychologist Jean Piaget, whose pioneering cognitive theories on the processes of childhood learning are still the discipline's standard, identified these years as the "preoperational" and "concrete operational" stages of intellectual growth.[6] There is just no other period of life comparable in terms of the sheer volume of learning across the spectrum, from personality characteristics to basic acculturation.

Preoperational children make dramatic strides in language, basic classification of objects, and at least some symbolic thought. In remarkably receptive minds, learning unfolds uncritically at the unconscious level mostly through imitation and identification. The ability to manipulate relatively concrete concepts such as war and peace improves gradually, but they still stumble with thinking abstractly about notions such as democracy and justice. By the same token, perceptions remain predominantly egocentric in nature in that instinctively they assume all other people see the world from their vantage point. Yet, through a mutually supportive recipe of increased experience, learning, and maturation, by approximately ages seven through eleven children experience the adaptive changes Piaget defined as the concrete operational stage. Here logical and abstract thinking becomes more prevalent, and while egocentrism certainly lingers, children progressively appreciate other perspectives.

Extraordinary historical events, personalities, and forces can potentially have the greatest effect on those traveling between these sensitive Piagetian points. Depending on the developmental stage during which Vietnam was experienced—factoring in the force and duration of the historical moment as well—the war's impact molded this generational cohort in a number of fundamental ways. It is important, though, to exercise caution in making grand and universal claims of direct causality between what happened to a child in the 1960s and 1970s and explicit adult attitudes and behavioral outcomes such as political party affiliation or voting patterns. Clearly, there is significant plasticity in our development as earlier childhood experiences are regularly modified when we encounter later events at numerous points along our lives.

That said, there are tendencies and consequences traceable to the Vietnam War. Most immediately, the weaving of historical threads through the fabric of young lives commonly triggered relatively ephemeral changes in behavior and habits, recognized as "transitions." The most significant personal transitions in turn often guided permanent changes in children's "trajectories," leading them to consciously plot new courses toward a particular lifestyle choice or career in adulthood. So, too, did the intensified Cold War anxiety during formative childhood stages and the perplexing nature of the Vietnam experience tend to shape political socialization and moral development largely independent of factual knowledge. Hence, opinions and ideologies forged in childhood remain stubbornly resistant to later revision based on new learning, and like the first metaphorical layers of our cognitive and moral onion, are some of the last to be peeled away, or surrendered, as adults.[7]

The chapters are arranged around the general framework of those phenomena with the most immediate consequences for preadolescent children. Where applicable I give their voices the last word. In chapter 1, I begin the study broadly addressing childhood socialization to the Vietnam War—how youth acquired factual information, thoughts, beliefs, interests, and attitudes. This establishes a foundation for the rest of the book by identifying the two most significant agents shaping all children's thinking about the war—age and parenting—but also accounts for gender, race, and school, as well as popular culture influences in television and music. Chapter 2 continues to look at meaning making through normative childhood practices, specifically reading comic books and *Mad* magazine. While ostensibly a niche amusement at that time, perhaps as many as 90 percent of all 1960s children between seven and fourteen years old read comics. Moreover, besides television, this genre of youth-oriented literature dealt with the Vietnam War more than any other form of popular culture available in childhood. In chapter 3 I examine the increasingly militarized culture of manufactured war toys in the Vietnam era. Using the rise and fall of early incarnations of the action figure G.I. Joe as a case study, the chapter traces the martial toy craze in the early years of Vietnam and subsequent "anti-war toy movement." This small facet of the wider anti-war movement sounded the alarm on how the popularity of more convincing military toys and guns, set against the backdrop of relentless televised warfare, was intensifying childhood tendencies to play war with commercialized war toys aimed primarily at boys.

Chapter 4 begins to narrow the focus toward childhoods touched directly by Vietnam when older boys personally familiar to children and close relatives served overseas. I will also suggest how POW-MIA bracelets created fictive relationships for other children desiring this type of emotional connection. Chapter 5 features what I consider the principal aspect of Vietnam in the lives of children: fathers going off to war. Beginning with how military service—particularly draft and enlistment patterns—potentially influenced the timing and direction of career, marriage, and fatherhood, the chapter then explores the collective family crisis of father separation. Although 80 percent of military personnel in

Vietnam served in support roles, the narrative tends to disproportionately focus on children related to combat soldiers and pilots. Since the Defense Department did not collect data on family characteristics of servicemen, it is impossible to accurately determine the percentage of those whose fathers experienced combat compared with those in supporting roles, and typically younger children did not know what duties their fathers performed overseas. It is worth noting, however, that among the book's respondents and contributors there is a representational bias toward fathers in combat.

Similarly, my work did not lead to children with mothers serving in Vietnam. This is understandable considering that virtually all military women were nurses, and of the approximately four thousand female nurses in Vietnam, the average age was twenty-three years old, making them unlikely to be mothers. Still, while psychological and emotional displacements of father separation strained home-front families, the unintended consequence of female-headed households presented new domestic realities that helped fuel second-wave feminism. This chapter also explores the transitional months and years between reunion and reintegration. Commonly, even in well-adjusted households, family restoration was more problematic than veterans, mothers, and children expected. Here I will position Vietnam within the country's escalating divorce rate and number of divorces, as well as trace the development of secondary and intergenerational posttraumatic stress disorder (PTSD).

Although fathers are central to childhood, their chapter is proportionally smaller than the following treatment of two specific categories of father *absence*: POW/MIA and Gold Star youth. The reasoning is that having their father in Vietnam was generally a transitional change for children, while the latter prompted substantive trajectory changes into adulthood. In chapter 6 I concentrate on the semi-orphaned children growing up in POW and MIA families. Though the number of POW/MIA families was rather small—just under 600 POW and roughly 1,300 MIA when Vietnam ended—the length of separation (more closely approximating World War II) and the disproportional attention given them in our public imagination made these children a metaphor for a fractured country seeking to be whole. Chapter 7 covers the bereavement of Gold Star children. For an estimated twenty thousand American children, Vietnam devastated childhood, dislocating family cycles and burdening survivors with the Sisyphean task of understanding a father they never knew, making peace with his sacrifice to a rancorous cause, and keeping his memories relevant to future generations.

Chapter 8 shifts emphasis away from the United States to Amerasian children fathered by Americans, as well as Vietnamese orphans adopted by American families before and during Operation Babylift in 1975. The final piece,

"Aftermath," concludes by looking at how completion of the Vietnam Veterans Memorial in 1982 and perhaps more importantly the Internet opened the cultural space necessary for adolescent and adult children of veterans to form bonds of community while finally airing publicly their simmering private questions about their dads' place in history. In addition to the positive influences on veterans' children of being raised by strong and capable women, I will also suggest several broader developmental implications from being socialized to the political and ethical ambiguity of Vietnam. These range from moral relativism to deep cynicism, doubt concerning the notion of just war, pacifism, and generally lowered expectations of presidential efficacy, goodwill, and leadership in national endeavors.

Together, I intend these chapters to expand our historical perspective on children, childhood, and war. One of the book's principal contributions to the study of children, I hope, will be to raise the experiences of preadolescents during Vietnam to the level paid to childhood during World War II and the Civil War. This work will also continue broadening our perspective of "the sixties" as not simply something that happened on the West and East Coasts with maybe just Chicago and a couple Midwestern college campuses in between. And finally, looking at the war in the lives of American children will deepen our understanding of Vietnam's place in American history. It is said the war remains a great unending and arcane mosaic, consisting of millions of small, outwardly unrelated fragments. Each invaluable part can be studied in isolation, perhaps its meaning grasped. Yet how each fits into the whole defies comprehension. By using age as a category of analysis, I offer another modest piece to the immense puzzle.

CHAPTER 1

A Sort of Nebulous Sad Thing Happening Forever and Ever

CHILDHOOD SOCIALIZATION TO THE VIETNAM WAR

> I have 2 questions for you to answer. Would you please answer them? They are as follows: 1. Why are we in Viet Nam? 2. Why are we fighting in Viet Nam? P.S. After all it is their war.
>
> —TEN-YEAR-OLD CALIFORNIA BOY TO PRESIDENT LYNDON B. JOHNSON, JANUARY 12, 1967

Just over 3.4 million American men and women eventually served in Southeast Asia, which in a country with a population approaching 200 million meant the Vietnam experience can be thought of as two distinct realities: the harsh reality of jungle warfare for those overseas and, for the overwhelming majority of Americans, a more domesticated reality anchored nearly entirely in television. Regardless if families supported it, opposed it, or were simply bored with it, Vietnam—as seen on television—captured the nation's collective attention, at once seemingly so far away yet somehow the background context to virtually everything in the news. Since most American households featured just one television set, there was a campfire nature to congregating around its electric glow, with adults and older siblings controlling viewing habits of children (except on Saturday morning). Typically, whole families gathering during or after dinner to watch one of three network evening newscasts witnessed together their society's first extensively televised war in prerecorded segments and itemized body counts. In the 1960s, television's dominating presence felt like a virtual family member, a sort of third parent. And commonly television and parents operated collectively as the two most important, and mutually supportive, ad hoc agents for socializing preadolescent children on how to think and feel about the war in Vietnam.

Mothers and fathers watched nightly (and morning) news broadcasts with somber faces, discussing among themselves. But unlike the lack of communication surrounding the omnipresent threat of nuclear war, talk of Vietnam often happened in tones that were less muted around young ears. In many households Vietnam was a lively—if age-appropriate—topic of intergenerational conversation. Only when the more powerful televised pictures were deemed too shocking for the smallest viewers, or the conversations too upsetting, did adults turn the TV off. "I definitely had an awareness of the war on TV every night, if only the scattered snap shot images and understanding that it was a topic covered a lot by the news," a Kansas man born in 1967 recalled. Indeed, for many preadolescents, Vietnam seemed as a Kentucky woman born in 1963 remembered, "a sort of nebulous sad thing happening forever and ever" in the living room.[1]

Although the origins of political turmoil and conflict in Southeast Asia are grounded in the Vietnamese rebellion against French colonialism typical of the post–World War II era, American interests were more narrowly framed by the Cold War policy of containing the global spread of Soviet communism. A nationalist victory by the Marxist Ho Chi Minh and his army of Vietminh revolutionaries—operating under the direction of Moscow, the United States assumed—threatened to hand the Kremlin another communist triumph in Asia, further destabilizing the region like a row of wobbly dominoes. President Harry S. Truman had accordingly sought to contain Ho's revolution by effectively underwriting the French war effort, a multi-billion-dollar commitment Dwight D. Eisenhower continued even after France's humiliating defeat at the hands of the Vietminh in 1954.

Without its European surrogate to contain communism, and with Vietnam now partitioned Korean-style into two separate states by international accords, the Eisenhower administration embarked on a problematic strategy of building a stable, Western-style democracy in the newly conceived country of South Vietnam as a bulwark against communist North Vietnam. Through millions of dollars in economic aid and guidance during the 1950s, the United States fashioned a brittle government around an unpopular authoritarian, Ngo Dinh Diem, sending military advisers to train an army capable of protecting the regime from an indigenous insurgency, the Vietcong, revolting against American interference and Diem's misguided rule. By John F. Kennedy's inaugural, America was thoroughly invested in an intractable three-way civil war, defending the South from the North (backed substantially by the Soviet Union and People's Republic of China) who with their Vietcong allies operating below the seventeenth parallel were hell-bent on unifying the temporarily divided land as one communist country of Vietnam.

Still, in the absence of significant numbers of U.S. troops and casualties, relatively few in the generally apathetic public—certainly including children—paid close attention to such a remote Southeast Asian locale, even as Kennedy deployed counterinsurgency Green Berets to pacify the Vietcong and authorized the coup replacing Diem. It was not until the 1964 presidential campaign, almost two decades into U.S. involvement, that the Vietnam War began consistently warranting widespread attention and triggering social changes in the family lives of preadolescent Americans. Lyndon Johnson—whose Great Society expanded the federal government's responsibility for children—could no longer sustain South Vietnam without bringing substantially more American military power to bear, and in August 1964 the president maneuvered the Gulf of Tonkin Resolution through Congress for that very purpose. By authorizing Johnson to vaguely "take all necessary measures to repel any armed attack against the forces of the United States and to prevent further aggression ... including the use of armed force," Congress sanctioned the president's prosecution of this conflict directly from the Oval Office without the requisite declaration of war. Beginning in 1965, those necessary measures evolved into a strategy of gradual escalation, keeping the actions limited to Vietnam (not provoking World War III with the Soviets and Chinese) through a calibrated ratcheting up of military pressure in the unjustified confidence that at some future point, mounting U.S. strength would break the resolve of the North Vietnamese and Vietcong by denying them victory in the field.[2]

The proliferation of network news coverage paralleled the pace and intensity of U.S. involvement in the first several years of the war. The first full-time crews and reporters were stationed in Saigon during mid-1963, only after Buddhists immolated themselves in fiery protest of South Vietnamese religious repression. But in the succeeding twenty-four months, scores of correspondents and cameramen followed to cover the massive scale of American troops and supplies entering South Vietnam. Especially prior to 1968, network coverage largely appeared to be a drawn-out series of consecutive two-, three-, or four-minute visual segments. Taken in disjointed isolation, each was "timeless," meaning reporting and footage did not really depict a specific, important event but rather illustrated a handful of recognizable—and predetermined—narratives: "bang-bang" combat stories extolling the advantages American forces held in terms of technology, helicopter mobility, and raw firepower, or the human-interest winning of hearts and minds. As a result, daily coverage was often too brief or condensed to provide a consistent point of view. Cumulatively, however, when strung together, these "and-the-next-day-this-unit-forged-on-ahead-to-whatever village" pieces were framed—by accentuating the most optimistic elements and deemphasizing the most cautious aspects—in such a way as to make an extraordinarily convoluted story line sound quite linear.

With simplified reporting and emotional visuals, echoing some form of the official line from the Johnson administration and the military, television's narrative situated "our war effort" somewhere progressively along a trajectory between the heroic traditions of World War II and inevitable U.S. and South Vietnamese victory. At NBC, Chet Huntley and David Brinkley read the news and body counts without betraying any real sense of approval or disapproval of the war. Over at CBS, when Walter Cronkite spoke of Vietnam, his deliberately even voice inflections conveyed equal significance to all war news, landing him on a 1966 cover of *Time* as "the single most convincing and authoritative figure on TV news." Generally speaking, apart from Morley Safer's dramatic *CBS Evening News* report of a marine "Zippo raid"—burning the thatched huts—of Cam Ne villagers while on an August 1965 search-and-destroy mission, television newsmen lagged well behind print journalists in critical analysis of the government's intentions or the military's prosecution of the war.[3]

In his cultural critique of television in the Vietnam era, the *New Yorker*'s Michael J. Arlen observed how on any random night, families switching channels before prime time might find some combination of the following: CBS running "a three-minute film that showed a Marine company breaking off an unsuccessful engagement with some North Vietnamese (the Marines had been trying to get them off the top of a hill), that included a moving, emotional scene of wounded soldiers (ours) being helped, stumbling and limping, across a ravine, and that closed with a short interview with an out-of-breath, bright-eyed, terribly young Marine sergeant who said that it had been a tough fight but the Marines would push them off the hill tomorrow"; ABC reporting on a marine operation, followed by a statement concerning bombing in the DMZ, with the latest casualty statistics; and NBC airing a three minute clip of U.S. soldiers helping South Vietnamese (recently freed from the Vietcong) out of an air force plane. Back on CBS, South Vietnamese soldiers under a sniper attack were shown firing into a line of trees, with the voice of an American calling in choppers on the radio through the crisp rifle fire. "Then there were more scenes of soldiers, crouching and standing, firing toward the distant line of trees, and later, up in the sky, far in the distance, the two helicopters." Finally, a correspondent's voice-over narration concluded there had probably been three or four VC snipers in the trees, but as of yet no one could determine whether or not any of our enemies had been killed.[4]

Contrary to many popular recollections, television did not commonly focus on actual combat. Correspondents moved freely enough around troops without direct censorship, but cameramen were not allowed on bombing sorties in the sustained air campaign against North Vietnam and were only rarely permitted on search-and-destroy operations. Even after American soldiers launched the first offensive against the Vietcong just north of Saigon in June 1965 and later in the fall fought the North Vietnamese Army in the largest battle to date in the Ia Drang valley, most fighting in Vietnam erupted suddenly in small skirmishes at night or in extremely remote locations away from the camera. Viewers watched GIs waiting on an overgrown hillside for the signal to move up toward the sound of small-arms fire, which became louder and more intense. Sometimes machine guns, mortars and rockets—shaking the camera—tore through them. But as CBS's Safer would say, "another typical engagement in Vietnam. . . . A couple of battalions of the Army went into these woods looking for the enemy. The enemy was gone. There was a little sniper fire at one moment; three of our men were hit, but not seriously. It was pretty much the way it usually goes."[5]

Nevertheless, by 1966, as U.S. troop strength rose from 184,000 to 385,000 and the conflict emerged as the foremost world event, it was indeed as if every news story tended to become Vietnam. Networks supplemented the nightly news with special sixty-minute reports such as "Morley Safer's Vietnam." Walter Cronkite even frequently opened the *CBS Evening News* with "Today's Vietnam story in a moment." From half a world away, graphic videotape and unsettling depictions of the war's difficulties, hardships, suffering, and horror crept toward the very heart of the medium, intruding into the ordinary tempo of family life. The transition to color amplified the effect; as television historian Erik Barnouw eloquently points out, "mud and blood were indistinguishable in black and white; in color, blood was blood. In color, misty Vietnamese landscapes hung with indescribable beauty behind gory actions."[6]

While television's role in bringing Vietnam's visible face home is reasonably clear, exactly how it helped mold American perceptions remains more complicated, particularly before the Tet Offensive. These were the middle years of the decade when the majority of Americans supported the war. In November 1965 Gallup found a high-water mark of 75 percent of adults under thirty years old and 68 percent of those between thirty and forty-nine believing the United States was right to be in Vietnam. The real differences were between those favoring escalation, negotiations, or other nonwithdrawal options to achieve American objectives. There is a certain symmetry to public opinion findings in that developmentally preadolescents up to roughly third grade were likewise generally supportive of American involvement. Strictly speaking, common adult pro- and anti-war labels—hawk and dove—were not exactly applicable to younger children. Very few preadolescents would have been considered *for* war, and almost unanimously they condemned warfare as something extremely bad. As one nine-year-old Chicago boy put it to President Johnson, "Oh, by the way, did or didn't you stop the war. I really hope you did because I do not like wars."[7]

Until at least sixth grade, children almost universally demonstrated a basic ignorance, or severe misconceptions, about even the most widely known factual information. "What is the war like in Viet Nam?" another Illinois nine-year-old asked Johnson. "The only thing I know is that it isn't as bad as world war II." Another woman from Kentucky recalled that the most befuddling part of Vietnam to her way of thinking was hearing on the news how American soldiers were battling armed "gorillas" and laboring under that simian misperception for quite some time before finally seeking parental clarification. On hearing of tiger cages (small, subsurface concrete cells topped with ceiling bars to confine prisoners of war and political opponents in South Vietnam) a girl growing up on a Virginia commune nursed a grudge against the Vietnamese for animal cruelty. And a San Diego girl, on visiting her father at a Veterans Administration hospital, scouted around the facility to *find* the missing arms and legs of wounded patients she was told had been *lost* in the war.[8]

Several studies did seem to indicate that boys were better informed in regard to facts and military terminology, but even with the most rudimentary knowledge of Vietnam, pre- and early elementary school children were not equipped developmentally to conceptualize the complexity of issues required to make value judgments on the war. By piecing together scraps of information from television and parents, the smallest youth formed an appropriately simple picture of Vietnam. The United States was still at war with communism, but it was not being fought on American soil. "Our boys" were being sent "over there" to fight for "our country." And some of them would die. Victory and defeat were likewise subject to a simplified structuring of reality in the manageable scale of a child's mind. As one Missouri woman born in 1959 recalled, "every night they would give a count of how many people were killed, how many American soldiers were killed that day and how many Vietnam soldiers were killed. I remember thinking as a little kid well 'we won today' or 'we lost today' by the number of soldiers that were killed."[9]

This sort of preoccupation with Defense Secretary Robert McNamara's cold statistics often left children tremendously fearful of Vietnam. Whether given in numeric form next to the corresponding flags of combatants, displayed in graphs using little soldier figures, or spoken by the anchorman, television's weekly casualty figures were meant to provide the American public—conditioned to measure achievement numerically through batting or industrial averages—with a meaningful sense of progress. Still, the outcome was something far less than reassuring when NBC's Edwin Newman concluded a typical 1966 broadcast with "and against this background the battle continues and in it this week 274 Americans were killed, 1,748 wounded and 18 listed as missing. There is no end to the war in sight."[10]

Television's dramatic inclination toward "shooting bloody" footage, likewise, left children eager to see suffering stop. "I know that I had bad dreams from hearing about the Vietnam War on the news," a woman born in 1957 shared about how Vietnam sharpened a finer edge to her Cold War apprehension. "And dreamt of being under the cafeteria tables at school and having big cannonball looking bombs landing on the tables." "They still haunt me today," a Tennessee woman born in 1961 explained of how casualties being enumerated on screen first helped overcome some of her egocentrism. "It struck me as very strange and scary. I remember thinking: those are dead people." Young people motivated to write President Johnson poignantly expressed sincere hopes, as a nine-year-old from Alaska put it: "we can find a way to stop the war without the atomic bomb. I also hope that most of the people can be saved." A Virginia grade school boy concluded a similar letter to Johnson with, "I hope the war in Vietnam will end soon, to [*sic*] many of our boys are dieing on the battlefields. May God be with them."[11]

Yet neither should the youngest be understood as pacifists. Already instinctively capable of grasping war and progressively socialized to Cold War conflict, those capable of limited abstract thinking appear to have in varying degrees accepted, or at least tolerated, Vietnam—so long as the outcome meant swiftly scoring a decisive victory over their hostile communist enemy. "I know why we have to win the war," a New York boy advised the president in 1966, "because if we don't Britain, Russia, and Red China would say that we cannot defend ourselves and attack us." This patriotic wish to see America prevail over evil—a cognitive inability to comprehend beyond one-dimensional anticommunism—dominated younger children's reasoning about Vietnam. But it also opened many up to a worrisome possibility that on any given night those televised numbers would no longer add up in America's favor. "Too many people are loosing there [*sic*] friends, and families," an uneasy Illinois fourth-grader figured, and, as he explained to President Johnson, "we will soon run out of men to send. Then without men, Viet Nam will really get us."[12]

Like the Tet Offensive in early 1968 marked the Vietnam War's turning point both militarily and in terms of American public opinion, upper elementary school grades prompted an analogous developmental watershed for children's views and beliefs. Between third and eighth grade, preadolescents' overall knowledge of the conflict improved sharply, with nearly all this new factual learning coming from continued exposure to television and school. Throughout the postwar years, school-based citizenship training customarily oriented students (often heavy-handedly) toward a favorable—and patriotic—understanding of U.S. political and economic systems and Cold War foreign policy aims. Still, in the classroom, "teaching" time spent on Vietnam, and degrees to which viewpoints were expressed, was uneven, depending heavily on individual teachers and schools. Some classes objectively maintained large maps of Southeast Asia with students plotting newsworthy locations with colored pushpins. Others recited the previous night's television casualty figures out of habit for the class as homework. Under the guidance of more engaged teachers, students subjectively squared off in debates over American policy while veterans came as guest speakers.

In the proud tradition of the Lone Ranger, Lassie, and Mr. Ed, Batman took time off from his 1966 prime-time hit show on ABC to pitch the U.S. Savings Bonds and Stamps school program. From inside the Batcave, the caped crusader filmed a classroom plug encouraging students to buy bonds and give "important support to the cause of freedom and the men who fight for us in Vietnam." Investors in the war effort received a pledge card emblazoned with LBJ's picture and signature. By 1970, growing educational trends in "peace studies" also trickled down to some elementary schools, where teachers offered nonviolent alternatives to conflict resolution. Instead of simulating historical events, such as the Cuban Missile Crisis, as peace educators did in high school and junior high, elementary teachers could examine a fight on the playground to discern the causes and come up with ways it could have been avoided or worked out differently. Likewise, as part of a growing chorus of concern over the negative developmental impact of too much violence on television, school librarians recommended children's literature as an alternative to onscreen carnage. One such book believed to help young readers understand the nature of war was William D. Steele's *The Perilous Road*, a Civil War lesson in how wartime hatred divides citizens and how war makes otherwise good people do bad things.[13]

My Weekly Reader—known also as *Weekly Reader* at various times—continued to be a reliable and popular classroom primer for the nation's anticommunist foreign policy as well. This current events newspaper for public schools had consistently socialized thirteen million elementary students annually (two-thirds of all adults read *My Weekly Reader* in school) to the long, twilight struggle against Soviet communism. In younger, grade-appropriate editions, *My Weekly Reader* characterized the USSR as a "neighborhood bully" for its bellicose march toward world domination, a delinquent fast becoming too strong for free peoples to spank. Global maps tracked the ominous spread of "Moscow-controlled" areas—in red, of course—growing incrementally with each passing year while the number of besieged "free nations" shrank. A 1962 cartoon captioned "It's easy, just throw your weight around" showed the globe as a great trampoline. China's grinning leader, Mao Zedong, is waiting his turn nearby while Soviet strongman Nikita Khrushchev joyfully bounces around, landing on the Middle East, Berlin, Cuba, Vietnam, and Laos. A *My Weekly Reader* clarification pointed out how, in the case of Laos and South Vietnam, the Soviets were encouraging communist rebels to overthrow pro-American governments.[14]

Extensive coverage of the Vietnam War on the pages of *My Weekly Reader* mostly perpetuated this orthodox narrative, yet without the patriotic mobilization efforts from the Second World War. In a standard 1961 article, "Communists Threaten Southeast Asia," students learned that "the North Vietnamese aim is to overthrow the free government in South Vietnam and set up a Communist government in its place," and though it appeared the "Communist rebels . . . have little chance of success. . . . They are fighting a kind of war well suited to the jungle, mountain, and swampland of South Vietnam. The Communists hide in the jungle. They fight only when they think they can win." With the rebels currently "spread over half of South Vietnam," the government had "called on the U.S. for help," which America gladly provided to the tune of $2 billion in aid (money, food, clothing, and medicine). Additionally, the United States sent "military advisors, weapons, and troop-carrying helicopters to help push back the Red tide." Ultimately, *My Weekly Reader* concluded that "the U.S. wants South Vietnam to remain free. If South Vietnam stems the Communist tide, so may the rest of Southeast Asia."[15]

A 1962 cartoon, "Put 'Er Ther, Pal," reinforced those basic themes of American involvement. A soldier, whose helmet reads "South Vietnam," is sinking shoulder deep into a jungle swamp with a sickle and hammer staining the water's surface. In tall grass along the banks another heavily camouflaged soldier labeled "U.S. Guerrilla Aid" clasps the sinking man's hand to pull him—ironically—from the quagmire. Again, in language elementary students could understand, *My Weekly Reader* underscored how the United States was "keeping South Vietnam from sinking under Communist attack."[16]

One of the newspaper's most comprehensive articles on the war appeared in the fall of 1966. Broken into several panels, the article opened with a recognizable photograph of Huey helicopters picking up troops above four separate, contemporary newspaper headlines: "U.S. Air Strikes Smash Oil Depots at Hanoi," "GI's Scatter Foe after Hard Fight in Highlands," "Enemy Forces in South Put at 282,000," and "Units of Fourth U.S. Infantry Division Land at Quinhon." "These were some of the newspaper headlines this summer," *My Weekly Reader* observed. "They tell of a war that is being fought in Vietnam. They raise questions: What is the war about? Why is the U.S.—a country a half a world away—taking an active part?" The remainder of the article sought answers to these questions with straightforward comments concerning communist methods ("fighting a hit-and-run war") and U.S. methods (trying to beat the Vietcong at "their own game").

The same 1966 article also broached the subject of dissent, admitting for the first time that for all the matter-of-factness, many Americans remained unsure of the nation's direction in Vietnam. *My Weekly Reader* identified "Hawks" as those who agreed with LBJ or thought the United States should increase troops and bombing. "Doves" were people opposing direct U.S. participation and wanting to see troops removed before America started World War III. To both, the paper noted, President Johnson reminded his countrymen, "The U.S. does not want to conquer North Vietnam. It wants North Vietnam to 'let its neighbor alone.' Once North Vietnam agrees to this, he says, U.S. soldiers can come home." While *My Weekly Reader* remained mute on anti-war protest (as it had done with the civil rights movement), a 1970 article, "How Do You Feel about New Uses of the Flag?" did seek a measure of student opinion on some forms of protest. Alongside a photograph of activists carrying an American flag with a peace symbol over the field of stars, and another of protesters wearing Old Glory as a cape, the item explained how "some Americans are using the flag to express feelings for and against the Vietnam war. Other Americans are wearing the flag as hats, ties, and vests. Still other Americans are using the flag as picnic cloths and some as seat covers." Such uses sparked vigorous debate in the adult world, and *My Weekly Reader* invited students to similarly voice their approval or disapproval.[17]

To gauge cognitive improvements in the upper elementary school grades, political scientist Howard Tolley surveyed thousands of New York, New Jersey, and Maryland children in early 1971 concerning what they knew, and how they felt, about Vietnam. His attitudinal research found that of all variables affecting children's socialization to Vietnam—mass media, parents, school, gender, race, and income—age was indeed clearly the most important. Together with a strikingly better factual grasp of the war, logically based thought helped crystalize fairly definite viewpoints on Vietnam in a child's mind by sixth grade. While one in five third-graders did not hold much of an opinion, almost all fifth-graders expressed coherent sentiments. Among those with strong ideas, third- and fourth-graders—nine- and ten-year-olds—demonstrated the most *support* for the war effort of any childhood age group. Support waned incrementally in each succeeding grade toward adolescence. Indeed, fifth- and sixth-graders—eleven- and twelve-year-olds—showed the most *opposition* toward Vietnam, or at least the lowest tolerance, when compared with both younger preadolescents and even older youth, including adolescents. So within just a year or two of strongly backing U.S. efforts, the majority of fifth-graders surveyed came to believe instead that the United States had made a mistake getting involved with Vietnam. Fully half advocated withdrawal of American forces, even if it meant defeat. These results led Tolley to theorize that children developed the deepest feelings against the Vietnam War around ages ten or eleven.[18]

From a developmental perspective, Tolley's observations are consistent with the quest for cognitive equilibrium. When preadolescents make sense of their world using mental schemes currently at their disposal, they are said to be cognitively in a state of equilibrium. Nine- and ten-year-olds had a better, but still incomplete, comprehension of this particular war against communism, and it stands to reason they would be the most confident in simplistic acceptance. That is, until deeper perceptual understanding of Vietnam opened an uncomfortable mental door to doubt.

As thought increasingly permitted more sophisticated abstract and hypothetical reexaminations of their perspectives on issues such as U.S. foreign policy, the president, or the very definitions of victory, eleven- and twelve-year-olds found their reasoning disrupted in a vulnerable state of disequilibrium. The pronounced opposition to the war in Vietnam expressed by fifth- and sixth-graders probably reflects reservations and negative opinions developed during a preadolescent's natural drive toward reestablishing equilibrium. In this ongoing process of recovering equilibrium through which intellectual development occurs, all new experiences and stimuli related to the war would have been assimilated using advances in critical thinking skills to create new schemes and broader worldviews. I will argue later how reading those socially relevant comic books, which were undergoing their own reassessment of Vietnam by 1968, or acerbic satire in *Mad* magazine, probably facilitated disturbances in many children's cognition. Either way, developmentally, older preadolescents were encouraged to be discerning. They pondered the effectiveness of search-and-destroy; wondered how essential was a territory we briefly held before giving it back; questioned the veracity of casualty figures.[19]

Available evidence on political socialization toward the presidency appears to bear this out. It is doubtful children would have been influenced by two notable 1964 campaign television advertisements that ran only once yet still managed to frame adult perceptions of Johnson as the thoughtful peace candidate in contrast to the recklessness of Barry Goldwater. The first of those groundbreaking political "spots" focused on an innocent girl eating an ice-cream cone over the sound of a ticking Geiger counter. The most renowned of the pair featured a little girl picking daisy petals ahead of a nuclear explosion with the dark voice-over: "These are the stakes. To make a world in which all God's children can live, or go into the dark." Nonetheless, youth, whose emotional, and mostly imaginative, personal relationship with Lyndon Johnson still colored their formative political learning, kept faith with the notion of president as peacemaker. Even when adult anti-war venom and derision toward Johnson reached its ugliest—"Hey, hey, LBJ, how many kids did you kill today?"—preadolescents unequivocally understood the president's role to be dovish, making peace, not war, in Vietnam.

By 1966 considerable numbers were writing the White House expressing personal sadness about the war continuing, but also confidence—offering encouragement and compliments—in the president's ability to unilaterally end the fighting and bring the boys home. Collectively, letters reveal growing recognition of war as a regrettably regular hazard in international relations, dovetailing with a deeper appreciation for the presidency's diplomatic role in making peace (stopping this war) and keeping the peace (preventing future war). Many who expressed concern for Johnson's beleaguered and melancholy appearance attributed this to how heavy this burden must be for the only man on the planet capable of balancing world peace between Vietnam, the Soviet Union, and China. "I know that you are doing what you think is best for our country and for the benefit of the world," an eleven-year-old girl wrote. An eight-year-old New Jersey boy reassured, "I want you to know that I think you have a very hard job. Please keep your chin up and try not to let some people make you feel bad. I think you are a great President. I will keep praying for you every night. And I will pray for peace for all the people in the world." Another nine-year-old supporter in Maryland spoke for many with his belief, "I think you are doing the best you can to stop the war in Vietnam. I am sorry we have to go on living with wars. I hope this will be our last war. Please accept my best wishes in your very important job."[20] Any doubts about Lyndon Johnson—the so-called credibility gap between policies and military realities—appeared almost exclusively in those letters written by older youth struggling through disequilibrium, and in the final years of Vietnam when confidence in President Richard Nixon did begin to falter.

Childhood conceptions of death, in the context of apparently perpetual war, were likely involved as well. By kindergarten, as a child's maturing awareness of death allows for emotional bereavement, children can begin tracing causal connections between dying as the probable outcome of violence and killing. For several years thereafter, interest in this linkage grows, leading some, especially boys, toward a fixation on warfare as a means of voicing aggressive and hostile tendencies. The curiosity of preadolescents working through these thoughts was excited by Vietnam, similar to World War II. But in the sixties, hearing about violent deaths on the news became part of normal life.[21] "Night after night, I suppose I developed a morbid fascination with watching it," a Tennessee woman born in 1958 recalled.

> What I watched was unseen journalists right by the soldiers, recording for the news every horrible thing. Today they would have said this contains graphic footage and you may want to remove your children from the room. My parents didn't pay any attention to what I was doing and maybe they'd have let me watch it anyway. I can tell you I certainly didn't let my son watch the Twin Towers fall, for as long as I could. I saw our soldiers getting shot, sometimes their buddies dragging them off. I saw naked screaming children running. I saw monks sitting absolutely still like Buddha after setting themselves on fire in protest. Just a bunch of them, and they were covered with flames even over the tops of their heads, and they just sat upright and flamed. I saw Viet Cong get shot. Don't remember seeing napalm. You couldn't get any more up close than what these cameramen were doing.[22]

But around ten years old, again a tipping point in children's attitudes, when youth start realistically grappling with the concept of their own inevitable and irreversible mortality, fear of death cast Vietnam in a more threatening light. The conflict's length—"Viet Nam is lasting so long," a frightened fifth-grader lamented to Johnson—and the prospect of it sparking World War III led boys to worry that they were going to grow up only to die in it. "I wish there wasn't a war," a California sixth-grader wrote the president in 1968, because "in a few years I will be going to Viet Nam." "Even then," a man born in 1958 Alabama related, "I felt I would probably have to go there, and I did NOT want to!" In clarifying his own childhood aversion to the war, a rural Missouri man who turned ten years old near the conflict's end remembered no longer wanting to go to elementary school because, he came to suspect, "when you graduated you went to Vietnam."[23]

An eleven-year-old Pennsylvania girl writing Lyndon Johnson in 1966 began her letter with a comprehensive critique of the president's Vietnam policies gleaned, she said, from her sixth-grade class's frequent discussions. "We came to the conclusion that the U.S. should not be in Vietnam," she advised Johnson. "The U.S. is the only one fighting in Vietnam against the Communists. 80% of the South Viet Namese are on the Communist side. . . . Just because communism is wrong for the U.S., doesn't mean it's wrong for Viet Nam." But ultimately her reductionist conclusions were clearly grounded in the same fears of irrational, mass death to which all American children growing up in the nuclear age had been acculturated. "I know that many people say that the war in Viet Nam is good. But how many of those people would feel the same way if they were fighting in Viet Nam? In four years my brother could be drafted. I don't want him to go to Viet Nam. But maybe by then I won't need to worry about him. Maybe by then World War III will have started because of Viet Nam and all of the U.S. will have been destroyed."[24]

All this being said, after sixth grade a child's parents increasingly became the most influential socializing factor. Children continued to acquire mental images and familiarity with the facts about Vietnam from television. Among the oldest grade schoolers, however, Howard Tolley detected "a strong, predictable, positive relationship between children's views of American policy in Vietnam and the perceived opinions of their parents." This high level of agreement was also confirmed in hundreds of recollections collected for this study. It appears, then, that as more mainstream adults began questioning the war effort and expressing dissent after 1968, youth settled into patterns of shared criticism.[25]

Television's exact role in these public opinion shifts remains highly debatable, and many who thought coverage of Vietnam was slanted or prejudicial have cited this as a primary reason for U.S. failure ever since. But the Tet Offensive did provoke a new period of subjectivity in televised newscasts. The coordinated attack by the North Vietnamese and Vietcong on virtually every military base and city in the South during the Chinese Tet New Year starkly demonstrated that despite inflicting tremendous casualties on the enemy—strictly speaking, an American military victory—U.S. forces and the South Vietnamese regime they defended remained dangerously vulnerable. As much as anything, Tet images showing urban chaos, destruction, and American troops on the defensive provided inconvenient answers for an increasingly polarized nation demanding to know how much longer their troops would be stuck in this bloody quagmire. Perhaps Vietnam might go on indefinitely?

After Cronkite traveled to Vietnam in Tet's immediate wake, his first on-air expressions of personal doubt—that the United States might have to accept a stalemate—made CBS's February 27, 1968, commentary a defining moment in broadcasting history, reverberating all the way to the Oval Office. "To say that we are closer to victory today," the most trusted man in America editorialized, "is to believe, in the face of the evidence, the optimists who have been wrong in the past. . . . But it is increasingly clear to this reporter that the only rational way out then will be to negotiate, not as victors, but as an honorable people who lived up to our pledge to defend democracy, and did the best they could." Soon thereafter the tone of coverage noticeably changed as other television correspondents followed suit by subjectively suggesting what most of them already personally believed to be true: the deteriorating military situation was a colossal waste of blood and treasure. Anchors and correspondents abandoned the term "our war" in favor of "the war." World War II references were no longer used as guideposts to frame accounts of combat. Footage routinely showed GIs weary and weathered. NBC's Frank McGee even suggested on air that the United States was losing, while scrutinizing the specious logic of destroying Vietnam in order to save it.[26]

In practice, even if children paid less attention to television commentary of this nature, they unquestionably tuned into what their parents had to say about it. In those homes where educated or informed parents assumed a definite position on Vietnam, mothers and fathers actively engaged their children on the subject. Typically adults did so by promoting, consciously or otherwise, certain viewing, reading, and listening habits, while others cultivated opinions and perspectives in harmony with their own. A significant number of children from the Vietnam era in this study said they did not recall a time in childhood without the family talking endlessly about and debating the Vietnam War. "My first real awareness of Vietnam was the word 'Tet Offensive,' so I was ten or eleven before that war penetrated my consciousness," a Tennessee man explained. Children growing up on insulated rural communes—having no television but multiple parents—probably heard more than suburban youth. The transient nature of men living this lifestyle helped make Vietnam the only worldly issue consistently penetrating the communal reality of children, by visiting men sharing either personal war stories or how they were staying one step ahead of the draft. As a Kansas City woman born in 1957 underscored, it was practically as if childhood unfolded simultaneously to "the frenzied dialogue concerning Vietnam."[27]

Correspondence at the Lyndon B. Johnson Library tells a similar story. "In the past few months," a Massachusetts boy wrote the president in 1968, "I have heard so much about the war in Viet Nam and knew so little. I asked my father about the war and to explain it to me. My father told me it is a serious problem and I know you are doing a great job." "It has been a long argument in our family as to what started the war in Viet-Nam," an eleven-year-old boy in Wisconsin informed Johnson, as did a California grade schooler who confessed. "I have thought about the war and I think by sending small parties to Vietnam, we are loosing [*sic*] more men then if we were to call in all of our power, and if we had for it would become World War 3. I have talked to my parents, and they can't tell me if my idea is right or wrong so I decided to ask you."[28]

Tolley, therefore, determined that disapproval of an increasingly unpopular war appeared "with equal clarity in children." In tracking the nation's declining support, Gallup revealed a substantial post-Tet drop in the number of Americans believing the United States was right to be in Vietnam. By August 1968, 45 percent of adults under thirty years old and 39 percent of those between thirty and forty-nine (conceivably of parenting age) still agreed with the war effort. Yet those numbers fell to 36 and 37 percent, respectively, in September 1969, and finally to the nadir of 34 and 30 percent in May 1971. These statistics were virtually indistinguishable from Howard Tolley's survey of older preadolescents. "I knew 1968 was a year lost in time," a Connecticut man shared, "even at 8."[29]

If parents, often younger mothers and fathers who were baby boomers themselves, opposed the war, children identified with some semblance of various pragmatic arguments articulated in the adult world. Vietnam was peripheral to American vital interests. Funding of the war skewed domestic economic priorities, especially poverty programs benefiting African Americans. The draft was rife with inequalities. Two boys from Berkeley, California, were probably echoing their parents' anti-war sentiments in a letter to Johnson in 1967. "We feel very strongly against the 'illegal' war," the boys wrote. "You said while you were campaigning that you would try preventing further war in Vietnam, but now you're sending in troops and bombers. The war has not been declared war by Congress. You're spending money on 'illegal' wars that should be spent on the War on Poverty. You're spending money on sending in troops when most of the people in the troops get killed. You're actually 'double killing' you spend money on our troops, they get killed and more people are starving to death, so just think about it!"[30]

Honest disagreement might rest on morality, as well, grounded in pacifism or religious opposition. After all, as the activist group Another Mother for Peace's slogan went, war is not healthy for children and other living things. "My parents fought vigorously FOR civil rights and AGAINST the Viet Nam war," a Michigan woman explained, "and they were pretty candid about anything I dared to ask." In a 1967 letter to the White House, three Illinois children, in sixth, fourth, and second grades, began with, "No offense, Mr. Johnson, but we think that the United States should get out of Viet Nam. Of course there are reasons for this.... Maybe the people we are defending don't want war but would rather let the others take over peacefully. I would also like to tell you when there will be civilization. Civilization is when there are no more wars and everyone in the world gets along together. Think about this if you have never heard it. Please send your opinion on this, (good or bad)."[31]

Reflecting broader opposition to Vietnam among poor urban and middle class African Americans relative to lower- and middle-class whites, black children generally viewed Vietnam with more skepticism compared with their white counterparts. Due in some measure, Tolley hypothesized, to the Black Power movement and mounting resentment over racial disproportions in combat duty and casualties, black youth started opposing the war, and losing confidence in the president, at earlier ages. Indeed, his research seemed to indicate that white children ranked higher than blacks in every measure related to supporting Vietnam, except one—family involvement.

Over the war's first three years, African Americans made up 11 percent of the civilian population, yet during 1967 they accounted for 16 percent of draftees and 23 percent of combat troops. One-quarter of combat deaths in 1965 were black.

Percentages equalized as the war went on, but popular perceptions of blacks being disproportionally drafted and killed persisted. In the comic strip *Peanuts*, for instance, Franklin's dad was in Vietnam when this African American character integrated the comic in 1968. Tolley's statistical profiles, compiled from survey data, found that the child most likely to be an outspoken advocate for military involvement in Vietnam would be a middle-class, third-grade white boy with hawkish parents. The most vocal opponent of Vietnam: a middle-class, eighth-grade black girl whose parents disagreed with wars to contain communism.[32]

It is difficult to accurately trace parental preference in terms of what forms of popular culture adults wanted children to experience. Vietnam simply never inspired entertainment television programming and movies in remotely the ways the Second World War had with radio and Hollywood. In fact, although military programs proliferated in the sixties, the amusing or heroic martial life portrayed therein was nearly exclusively from nostalgic bygone eras: *Combat!*, *The Rat Patrol*, *Twelve O'Clock High*, *Jericho*, *McHale's Navy*, *Hogan's Heroes*, *The Wackiest Ship in the Army*, *Mister Roberts*, *F Troop*, or old John Wayne movies. The only exception set in contemporary times, *Gomer Pyle, U.S.M.C.*, somehow managed to ignore the Vietnam War altogether. And even when prime-time television belatedly got around to addressing the conflict during its last full year in 1972, Korea safely served as a surrogate on CBS's *M*A*S*H.*

Of those military-oriented television shows, only four were consistently popular—*Combat!*, *McHale's Navy*, *Gomer Pyle*, and *Hogan's Heroes*—and of these only *Combat!* was a drama. The rest, like *M*A*S*H*, were anti-militarist themed comedies largely parodying military life and war. Most of the era's military shows followed comparable military caricaturing, akin to the print cartoons *Beetle Bailey* and *Sad Sack*, and when taken cumulatively potentially imprinted preadolescent audiences with a somewhat compromised, if not diminished, impression of military efficacy. Any implicit messages were probably also bolstered in a child's thinking by mothers and fathers voicing approval through program loyalty, knowing smiles, and hearty laughter.[33]

Rare single television episodes, such as *The Twilight Zone*'s "In Praise of Pip" from the fall of 1963, where a distraught father exchanged his own life for that of his son, who was then dying in Vietnam, were probably negligible in shaping children's perceptions. At least three allegorical *Star Trek* episodes, however, are worth bearing in mind. Although not always straightforward, as one of entertainment television's only real treatments of the war, story lines involving Captain Kirk and crew may well have acted as thought-provoking catalysts in family discussions. Some scholars have suggested how even in episodes without obvious Vietnam overtones, Kirk's certainty when facing conflict on distant planets in contrast to Spock's ambivalence over the logic of war reflect arguments within the Johnson administration and the nation at large.[34]

Of the clear *Star Trek* parables, two are self-consciously dovish. Besides "A Private Little War," already referenced in the introduction, "The Omega Glory" is another anti-war commentary that aired on NBC in March 1968. On the planet Omega IV, the *Enterprise* encounters two perpetually warring camps of primitive savages, the Asian "Kohms" and Caucasian "Yangs." Dr. McCoy's research determines how the belligerents had at one point in the planet's distant history been advanced civilizations only to devolve through this endless war, which began for reasons neither side understood nor remembered. Only after the crew finally observes the Yangs' sacred rituals does an ironic truth become evident. In their "worship words" Spock and Kirk recognize a garbled Pledge of Allegiance recited by rote with an equally distorted preamble of the Constitution to honor tattered remains of an American flag. The Yangs are Yankees, the Kohms are communists. In true *Star Trek* fashion, as time runs out the captain, of course, convinces the Yangs to at last uphold the principles underlying the notion of "We the People" by making peace with the Kohms. Still, the didactic narrative left audiences with an unsettling prospect: what if America's Vietnam War, with no realistic sign of light at the end of the tunnel, doomed humankind to forever be locked in mortal combat at humanity's expense?[35]

Only a small fraction of preadolescents in the Vietnam era accompanied their parents in physical demonstrations of responsible criticism, handing out leaflets during neighborhood canvasses, joining mothers on petition drives, or riding on their fathers' shoulders along a march. Considerably more remember a definite desire to be older so they could join the protests. Often those aspirations are still closely, and maybe disproportionately, associated in memories with parental tastes for folk or protest music. It is a common misperception that protest songs were popular, or even commercially viable, in the 1960s. On the contrary, Bob Dylan, for instance, the most recognizable populist troubadour of cultural rebellion, had but four Top 40 hits, and his "Blowin' in the Wind" was the only song of protest to make it on the Billboard charts when Peter, Paul and Mary's version went to number two in 1963. Most topical folk songs by Pete Seeger, Phil Ochs, Buffy Sainte-Marie, or Tom Paxton were politicized in nature and did not find an audience outside coffeehouses in Greenwich Village or like-minded anti-war enthusiasts.

As with a family's single television, parents shaped childhood listening habits by controlling the record player and the dial of a lone car radio still dominated by AM's Top 40 format. Whether characterized as mainstream or "bubblegum," AM radio played what seemed to be a steady stream of Sonny and Cher, the

Monkees, the Lovin' Spoonful, the Beach Boys, the Turtles, Bobby Sherman, or the official (and apolitical) "sound of young America," Motown. Youth around twelve years old may have taken musical cues from elder siblings whose exotic tastes for FM radio's album-oriented rock music ran toward the Doors, Janis Joplin, Jimi Hendrix, or Jefferson Airplane. Generally, though, young parents just sang and tapped the steering wheel in time with the Association.

Yet, in many cases, children of the Vietnam era organize recollections around certain peace anthems and credit music with an integral role in shaping attitudes and interests toward Vietnam. "My parents apparently didn't hide much from us as far as politics, music and current events go," one such Georgia woman born in 1960 emphasized. "Having young parents [both nineteen at her birth] was definitely an advantage. . . . I was exposed to a lot of the great music of the time. But the most memorable was the Peter, Paul & Mary album with *Where Have all the Flowers Gone?* and *500 Miles* [the 1962 album *Peter, Paul and Mary*]." Above all, she underscored, "watching the war protesters with them on TV just made my 9 year old self want so badly to be 19 in 1969 so I could be old enough to get out there protesting the war!"[36]

"Being younger than the college kids who were in the protest marches," another woman born in 1958 Vermont echoed, "I studied what was going on from afar. I heard many adult grumblings about long hair and hippies, but I was impressed that people were willing to say that war was wrong and segregation was despicable. During the nightly Vietnam body counts on the national news I secretly cheered for those who wanted the insanity to end. I loved the music of Joan Baez [her 1968 anti-war album *Baptism: A Journey through Our Time*] and Pete Seeger and memorized their words." Like others who only dreamed of being whimsical "peace loving hippies," admittedly her anti-war activism remained confined to "throwing up an occasional peace sign" at school and "probably drawing a few here and there too."[37]

"Too young to participate in peace demonstrations," an Oregonian born in 1957 added, "I was in awe of students who took over administration buildings on college campuses. My one (pathetic) act of rebellion was to embroider a peace sign on a white T-shirt, and wear it defiantly in front of my dad. He was, and still is, a supportive parent, but he was not pleased that I was taking this stand and said several times that he was glad I wasn't older because he knew I would be 'one of those kids causing all the trouble.'"[38]

When parents, in particular those from the Great Depression and World War II generation, supported the war or at least remained noncommittal, children generally approximated their Cold War orthodoxy of America's role in the world. These fundamental attitudes and opinions, in truth, adhered fairly closely to folk singer Tom Paxton's 1962 sardonic line of lyrical questioning "What did you learn in school today, dear little boy of mine?" The United States must stand up to aggression anywhere, anytime, never rewarding a bully, to avoid the Munich mistakes that allowed Hitler to run amok in Europe. Presidents were inherently honorable, meaning Vietnam had to be a just and noble cause. "Our leaders are the finest men / And so we elect them again and again."[39] Serving one's country was a patriotic duty, as well as a distinct, and sacred, honor.

Early in the war a musically inclined eleven-year-old South Carolina girl tried her hand at songwriting, sending Lyndon Johnson an inspired, original song, "The Brave Soldiers in Vietnam." The patriotic lyrics were her own with handwritten music done in collaboration with her mother. She meant the song as a requiem for those who "gave their life" and "the ones still living" because, as she put it, "I feel like I am part of each one of the soldier [*sic*] that die on the battlefield."

> There are men in Vietnam they are brave soldiers.
> They gave there life for nation and neighbor.
> That is why I wrote this song in favor of the men that die at South Vietnam.

"So President," the songwriter stressed, "I love my country more than anything in the world. I obey and respect my country and President of the United States of America. When I grow up for my country I am eleven year old maybe you might think I am to [*sic*] young. But I'll do anything for my country even now. I'll do anything for my country and president. . . . I'll always stand up for those soldiers who die for their country. That is why this is 'The Greatest Country in the World.' Please let the President see this letter and song."[40]

Again, the availability of certain elements of popular culture typically reflected and reinforced hawkish, pro-military stances. The more conservative *Life* magazine, for example, remained generally supportive of the war effort despite its sometimes rather sobering photojournalism. Photo essays depicting the inherent costs of prosecuting the war to its successful conclusion from both standard military and human-interest angles—frequently cover stories—were a regular *Life* feature. Many of the still black-and-white photographs children recall were seen initially in parents' copies of the magazine. At the movies, John Wayne's 1968 *The Green Berets*, the only major motion picture about Vietnam prior to the "coming home" films of the 1970s, did well at the box office by projecting—although not too cleverly—the popular western/war story formula in the jungles of Southeast Asia.

Back on board the USS *Enterprise*, an earlier episode of *Star Trek*, airing in April 1967 when public opinion still supported the war, offered an interesting pre-Tet case for the sometimes dreadful necessity of going off to war. *Star Trek*'s stance on Vietnam evolved along with the national mood, and in "The City on the Edge of Tomorrow," Dr. McCoy goes back in time to Depression-era New York and in so doing inadvertently erases the future. To rescue the ship's doctor and restore their present reality, Kirk and Spock follow McCoy and eventually allow the captain's new love interest, Edith Keeler, to die in an automobile accident. It turns out that Ms. Keeler led a successful 1930s peace movement responsible for delaying American entry into World War II and therefore guaranteeing a Nazi (*Enterprise*-less) future. The hawkish message: despite Keeler's idealism and decency (not to mention Kirk's attraction to her), it is better her naive commitment to peace not be allowed to derail an arduous course of action history had nonetheless judged to be right.[41]

In homes where pro-military materials and messages received an enthusiastic hearing, Vietnam remained a mostly black-and-white issue. Dissent—but not always of the respectable Edith Keeler sort—was the most confusing part. As the mainstream press began paying attention to domestic unrest after 1965, most large-circulation print and television media fixated on the activism of groups such as Students for a Democratic Society to negatively frame the anti-war movement as unpatriotic and violent. Protesters and hippies were portrayed as scary, almost inexplicably so, and children accepted parental unease with, and condemnation of, these familiar folk villains. "I didn't understand why people were protesting the war," explained a Florida woman born in 1960. "I understood at a young age, the servicemen were just trying to do their job and serve their country. I suppose my parents must have enlightened me about this." The escalation of activism only aggravated a child's sense of alienation and confusion. Earlier mass demonstrations gave way to resistance—civil disobedience at induction centers and military installations—and eventually culminated in virtual rebellion after 1968, as seen in the Columbia University strike and the Weathermen's Days of Rage, with the radical wing of the anti-war movement igniting campuses and streets across the country. "As a child," a woman born in 1957 Kansas City made clear, "this contradictory nature of people using violence to protest the violence of the war created a lot of cognitive dissonance for me."[42]

Consider, however, that sources of "cognitive dissonance" and doubt were by no means limited to just radicalism and militancy as protest. Even in the most adamantly supportive households, among the most hawkish fathers and mothers, there were still ample shades of gray in child-rearing agendas and practices. The most commonly mentioned points of contention highlight how the war altered parental perceptions of traditional military service, which in turn tended to disrupt how parents communicated older ideas about soldiering and duty.

Military recruitment advertising in mass-circulation magazines—*Life*, *Newsweek*, *Sports Illustrated*—said nothing about the war in Vietnam, while downplaying broader patriotic notions of honor or gallant sacrifice on the battlefield. Instead, the recruiting pitch in other targeted publications—*Hot Rod*, *Electronics Illustrated*, *Popular Science*—concentrated on the individualistic opportunities for peacetime financial gain and technical training. On another *Star Trek* episode, "Let That Be Your Last Battlefield" from 1969, a disillusioned soldier fighting in a protracted and ambiguous struggle asked an *Enterprise* crewman, "Do you know what it would be like to be dragged out of your hovel into a war on another planet, a battle that will serve your oppressor and bring death to your brothers?" Moreover, by the early 1970s, when Vietnam veterans began appearing as prime-time television characters, roles were stereotyped as some combination of mentally unstable and criminal, usually playing opposite the good guys on police dramas such as *Hawaii Five-O*.[43]

Surely, Staff Sargent Barry Sadler's 1966 crossover hit "The Ballad of the Green Berets," and the military virtues the record celebrated, resonated with a far broader audience than did any protest music. Quickly selling more than one million copies and staying at number one on Billboard's Hot 100 chart for five weeks, the song's fallen hero makes a heartfelt and noble last request for his son to uphold the family's commitment to military service.

Yet numerous children still recognized a troublesome disconnect between parents' sense of duty in the abstract and reluctance to see their own sons serve in Vietnam. "The old WWII rules did not seem to apply—serve your country, no matter what," a Tennessee man born in 1957 came to understand. "The reality at home was this—most middle to upper class white parents, however philosophically they felt about the war, did not want their children to go and fight it," he explained. "They supported their kids in either joining the National Guard or helping their kids stay in school so they could receive deferments. As a 10 year old kid it looked like this—if you're poor, dumb or unaware, you allowed yourself to get in a situation where you could end up being drafted and possibly going to Vietnam. If you were 'smart' you found a way to stay away from this conflict."[44]

For another man, born in Missouri in 1956, dissension of this sort left the indelible memory of witnessing a heated quarrel between his parents from the family car's back seat in 1968. "Dad's a staunch Republican," he clarified by way of an introduction,

> and I can remember distinctly him and my mother having an argument about us boys, getting called up to the war. Dad served in World War II. He didn't think this war was a war. He thought it was a political war. He hated the war, and he

> thought it was a bunch of bologna, and it's not a real war, and it's just the politicians. And he said he did not want his boys in Vietnam. He made the statement that he would rather see us boys go up to Canada than fight in an unjust war. Now I'm like 12, and I'm listening to this, and that's shocking. Coming from my staunch, World War II veteran, Republican dad, because that sounds real liberal. And my mother, who always seemed to me to be the more liberal of the two, had a brother who died in World War II. And she was gung-ho. She said "these boys will serve if they're called. It's their duty. It's the right thing to do." And having lost a brother, you can see where she would be committed to the cause more than Dad, who didn't. But then Dad served, and maybe he knew the real stuff about war anyway, and didn't want his boys to be exposed to it. Who knows? But they split on that.[45]

"As a kid this complicated what it meant to be 'patriotic,'" the earlier man from Memphis continued, hitting directly on the key dynamic of childhood socialization to the Vietnam War. "My parents were from the depression-WWII generation in which serving your country in any capacity was a distinct honor. I was raised with these values," he shared in confidence. "Then came 1965 and you could feel the tension in the conflicting views." He continued,

> On the one hand our parent's generation held to the belief the U.S. had to stand up to aggression anywhere, anytime to avoid another situation like allowing Hitler coming to power in Europe. On the other hand, you felt the influence that this time it was somehow different—were we stopping communist advances in the world or getting in the middle of a civil war, in which was none of our business? Instead of helping a democracy, were we propping up a corrupt regime? It was difficult to know what was the reality of the situation. Very knowledgeable, responsible people were saying diametrically opposite things!

He concluded, "As I look back with some perspective, a person must find out for themselves what is right and wrong."[46]

CHAPTER 2

Why Couldn't I Fight in a Nice, Simpler War?

COMIC BOOKS AND MAD MAGAZINE

> I used to feel proud of my support for the war but things like this—first hand—really fog up one's thinking! Well, I'm sure of this—it's no longer Tony Stark's war.
>
> —*THE INVINCIBLE IRON MAN* **#68 (1974)**

Vietnam's challenges to traditional ideas of military service and patriotism, and the cultural confusion sown in television and child-rearing, regularly manifested in children's preferred reading materials and natural tendencies to play. The contested culture of war play will be examined more fully in the next chapter, but in continuing to explore how children made meaning of Vietnam, let us first focus on the pages of comic books and *Mad* magazine. With annual sales for an increasingly male readership topping 350 million by the early 1960s, it was estimated that 90 percent of all youth between ages seven and fourteen read at least some comic books. More importantly, aside from television, of all elements of popular culture readily accessible to preadolescents, comics offered the most treatment of the Vietnam War. This was, after all, the "silver age" of comic books, a watershed period distinguished from the "golden age" immediately surrounding World War II. Marvel's "flawed hero formula" reinvigorated the industry, after the doldrums of the self-censoring comic's code era of the late 1950s, and encouraged other major publishers to strive for social and political relevance on contemporary issues. And, again, within certain comic books and *Mad*, the resultant messages of uncertainty and outright misgivings over Vietnam probably played a meaningful *in loco parentis* role in shaping maturing ideas in many children while likewise reflecting and reinforcing cognitive dissonance throughout childhood.[1]

The smallest children, those pre- and beginning readers, tended to favor comics from Gold Key (known for its *Bugs Bunny*, *Daffy Duck*, and *Mickey Mouse* titles) and Harvey (including *Casper the Friendly Ghost*, *Richie Rich*, or *Sad Sack*) with each publisher selling nearly 25 million issues annually. Vietnam never intruded on these juvenile storylines as such, but anti-war sensibilities were inescapable nonetheless, coloring many of the extensive and tantalizing whole-page advertisements. Amid fabulous X-ray vision glasses, Sea-Monkeys, and too-good-to-be-true schemes promising prizes and cash, merchandise incorporating some semblance of the peace symbol was standard fare in Gold Key and Harvey titles by the early 1970s. As recognizable to children as it was ubiquitous, this design—a vertical line running through an inverted V inside a circle—was embroidered on groovy cloth patches fashioned into the shape of a policeman's badge (the Peace Chief) or an enlisted soldier's chevron (a Peace Sergeant), or replacing the stars on Old Glory (Peace Flag). Peace symbols were emblazoned, as well, on copper rings and belt buckles. "Army of Peace" dog tags came two to a chain, one with the symbol and the second with a dove. Some commercially available patches were adorned with variants of a disembodied hand giving the peace sign (an earlier generation's V-for-victory gesture). Others promoted the Woodstock music festival, or slogans such as "Stop War" (in the shape of a stop sign) and "War is not healthy for children and other living things." Posters (often of the black light variety) proclaimed "Suppose They Gave a War and Nobody Came," "Give Peace a Chance," and "Love a Hippie."

For elementary school age and older, war comics, proven staples among seven- to seventeen-year-old readers, were actually some of the chief culprits in promulgating misunderstanding. In the first years of Vietnam at least, the genre remained firmly grounded in the "good war" storytelling, if not actual battlefields, of World War II. Through characters such as DC's iconic *Sgt. Rock*, World War II just made for better reading with its clearly defined focus and glamorous ordnance. By comparison, Vietnam was merely tedious guerrilla warfare on a much smaller stage. Most war titles were understandably pro-military in orientation. Even when story lines slowly transitioned to the jungles of Vietnam, though, soldiers generally waged the same battle-tested, stereotypical comic book form of warfare from the previous generation: a sneaky Asian enemy (firing from concealment) ambushes an advancing American squad, leaving a downed member wounded in the open, before the extraordinary bravery of one GI saves his buddies. The ultimately victorious U.S. soldier—weary, but unbowed—was cast in sharp, melodramatic relief with an enemy whose lack of respect for life allowed for his zealous killing of injured GIs, civilian attacks, and torture.[2]

With a number of titles ranging from *Army War Heroes* and *Battlefield Action* to its *Fightin'* line (*Fightin' Army*, *Fightin' Marines*, *Fightin' Navy*, *Fightin' Air Force*), Charlton Publications dominated this particular market, unmatched among other publishers for its unapologetic embrace of Vietnam, as well as its prodigious output of war comics. On Charlton's pages, Vietnam was indeed depicted as a reasonable extension of World War II distilled through the anticommunist cold warrior style of John F. Kennedy. Alongside romanticized counterinsurgency stories, all titles, for instance, featured "educational" pages under the heading "Your Role in the Cold War." One such installment, "Are You Physically Fit?" in a 1962 edition of *Battlefield Action* echoed the White House's extensive publicity campaign introducing the President's Council on Physical Fitness directives. Some of the more polemical stories, similarly, followed the "education" of baby boomers who might be questioning Kennedy's call to bear any burden against communism. As the GI standing in the burning rubble of a village proclaimed to a Vietnamese boy on a *Fightin' Army* cover from January 1966, "Go ahead son . . . cry . . . your family, your village . . . wiped out by the 'Cong.' If we hadn't arrived when we did, they'd have gotten you, too! I wish all those who call us . . . whatever they do . . . I wish they could talk to me! I'd tell them why we're here!"[3]

In the story "A Tough War" from a 1967 issue of *Fightin' Army*, two eighteen-year-olds—one, a grubby sort of hippie and the other, a clean-cut all-American named Tom—receive notification of their eligibility for military service. "In their world few boys volunteer," a caustic third-person narrator warns. "They hang back, drag their feet, do everything they can think of to avoid serving their country." Not Tom, however, and after "growing into manhood more quickly than he ever could back home" during basic training, the handsome enlistee shipped off to Vietnam, albeit with lingering doubts. "It's a war no one wants to mention," the narrative concedes. "People resent it . . . they don't think it's worth being fought. Tom isn't so sure it makes sense either." Yet in combat Tom sees the true face of Vietcong brutality and truly comes of age. "The fools back home who burn draft cards or march in peace demonstrations are helping the Viet Cong," reads the conclusion. "They too are his enemies and he knows it now."[4]

Another Charlton title, *War Heroes*, depicts an even more pronounced retelling of a rather similar story arc in its May 1967 issue. The cover (always emblazoned with the Medal of Honor) shows a bright-eyed GI deflecting his sergeant's M16 rifle to stop him from shooting a Vietcong fleeing a burning village. "You've been drafted," the accompanying caption reads, "and sent to Viet Nam . . . but you still can't figure out . . . 'WHY?'" Inside, the first-person narrator, a naive draftee, Private Walt Andrews, explains why he kept the sergeant from shooting the VC (to which the sergeant had threatened, "Next time you pull a thing like that, you get the bullet, Andrews!"). His actions were based on pacifist misgivings and confusing letters from peacenik friends back home describing the VC as freedom fighters, not unlike "our ancestors were in the Revolutionary War." Torn between whom to believe—his sergeant or friends—Andrews later disobeys orders to throw a grenade into a hut on a search-and-destroy mission, and adding insult to injury, he freezes in fear without shooting the VC who escapes from inside. At this turning point, the sergeant forces Andrews to view sickening VC atrocities in the village so "You can write home to the bleedin' hearts and tell them how the Viet Cong fight a war!" After his moment of clarity, Andrews eventually shoots the VC who eluded him earlier. Having answered the question of "Why?" he severs all correspondence with his anti-war girlfriend and Vietcong flag–waving friends without "any doubts about whether or not they're on the right side." In signing off, Andrews makes it clear in no uncertain terms how "their kind of letters from home" are no longer welcome.[5]

As public opinion progressively turned against the war, however, the already niche market for pro-war comics shrank further. Most other war comics addressing Vietnam directly appeared to adopt either neutral or qualified antiwar perspectives. "We're the big guy fighting the little guy," one comic book artist admitted frankly of the industry's inability to generate reader empathy, "and the American has always been for the underdog." Even in some of Charlton's titles, young readers caught glimpses of ambiguities and frustrations experienced by American troops fighting a protracted guerrilla war. *Fightin' Marines* (later reprinted in *Battlefield Action*) sought to balance its hawkish tendencies by introducing a more dovish (though not cowardly) presence in the reoccurring odd-couple characters Sergeant "Shotgun" Harker, a hard-boiled, gung-ho grunt, and his make-love-not-war sidekick Private "Chicken" Smith. Another soldier in *Fightin' Army* pondered, as early as 1966, the illusive nature of victory when GIs had so much trouble distinguishing Vietnamese civilians from the Vietcong. "I had the uncomfortable feeling," he decided after a battle, "that we hadn't won a victory at all." Likewise, the October 1968 *Army War Heroes* story "This Crummy War" followed a GI complaining "we're wet, bug-bit, tired, and sick . . . sick of Viet Nam, sick of an enemy who won't stand up and fight. Sick of dying in Viet Cong tunnels, endless swamps, and impenetrable jungles." After one skirmish a lieutenant lamented, "Nine causalities? That's too high a price to pay for this stinkin' rice paddy . . . Why couldn't I fight in a nice, simpler war?"[6]

The changing tenor of Dell Publishing's *Jungle War Stories* followed these dissenting trends. Although the title's initial cover in July 1962 declared that "The Jungles of Africa and Asia Have Become Flaming Battlegrounds," *Jungle War*

Stories was, in fact, the first war comic devoted exclusively to Vietnam, which also makes it one of the war's earliest appearances anywhere in popular culture. Prior to its publication, Dell's comics traditionally appealed to a younger readership, but *Jungle War Stories* targeted older boys with pro-war sentiments framing the novel conditions of jungle warfare—guerrilla tactics, small skirmishes, and uncertain front lines—while justifying American involvement in the earliest stages of escalation. Most story lines concentrated on Kennedy's Green Beret advisers either helping the South Vietnamese army find the stomach to fight through displays of military prowess and superior leadership, or winning over villagers with acts of humanitarianism. Additionally, *Jungle War Stories* contained informational pages under the headings "Vietnam Battle Facts" or "The Enemy in Vietnam." A 1963 sampling characterized the black pajama-ed Vietcong as a "scrawny, unkempt 100-pounder who barely comes up to the average G.I.'s shoulders," but who is nonetheless a "cruel, cunning, and tough" adversary. In all, lessons children drew were fairly straightforward and clear. Although the United States had successfully contained communists by proxy around the globe up until now, Vietnam simply required a more hands-on approach. Not only were the stakes higher to make U.S. power credible, but moreover, the inept South Vietnamese military and ignorant civilian population appeared inadequate to defend themselves.[7]

Mirroring rapid Americanization of the war after Lyndon Johnson's introduction of five thousand marines in March, by mid-1965 Dell retitled *Jungle War Stories* as *Guerrilla War*, replacing Special Forces advisers with regular combat troops in leading roles. In *Guerrilla War*, however, victory became far less predictable, while stories depicting Vietnam's unique hardships appeared with increasing frequency. Soldiers tried in vain to draw an elusive enemy into set-piece battles, chased ghostlike enemies from village to sanctuary, wrestled with a fluid line between friend or foe, and doubted the reliability of their southern allies. A most curious special feature in the April June 1965 issue, "A Letter from Vietnam," looks to be a reprinted one-page message from "Jim" in Vietnam to his brother "Billy" back home. The soldier admonishes the teenager to make good grades, go to college, and avoid enlisting as the elder sibling had done. "I just don't want my kid brother," Jim hammers home in the last line, "to waste his life when it isn't necessary."[8]

In 1967 Dell also tried unsuccessfully to revive *Tales of the Green Beret*, a polarizing syndicated cartoon running for only a year in nearly seventy-five newspapers. Like its newspaper counterpart, the comic book version from Dell—announcing on the first cover "if we must fight ... we will win!"—disappeared after only a handful of issues, due to, as critics complained, its "bloodthirstiness." At this point in the war effort, one detractor wrote, "Why not sell hot dogs at car wrecks?"[9] *Tod Holton, Super Green Beret* was another failed comic book attempt to cash in on youthful fascination with the larger-than-life Green Berets, a theme explored further in regard to toy culture. But its silly story lines chronicling the exploits of a teenager who turned into a Special Forces superhero after donning his uncle's magical beret were nothing more than an outlying oddity lasting just two issues.[10]

Blazing Combat, from Warren Publishing, was easily the genre's most transparently anti-war title over a short four-issue run in 1965 and 1966. Its unvarnished stories of battle spoke directly to the horrors—not glories—of war, especially the capricious treatment of civilians by combatants on both sides. Most notably, the installment "Landscape" tells a war story from the perspective of an elderly peasant farmer perpetually caught between the Vietcong and Americans. Wanting nothing more in life than to grow rice in peace, the old man watches helplessly as communists "liberate" his village and recruit his son into their cadre. The subsequent U.S. "liberation" kills this son, and after the VC attempt to retake the village, GIs destroy his home and farmland in order to save it. Having lost his entire family to starvation, torture, and combat, the old man struggles to tend the rice paddy alone, only to be cut down himself in the crossfire of advancing VC and South Vietnamese forces. "Landscape" ultimately rankled the American Legion and enough other groups—who decried the story as subversive—to have *Blazing Combat* removed from many comic distributors' shelves, a backlash that probably explained the title's sudden cessation.[11]

Despite *Blazing Combat*'s anti-war influence on other war comic titles, the genre's overall treatment of the Vietnam War was, commercially speaking, poorly received and rather short-lived. Within just a couple of years, by the end of 1967, even steadfastly pro-war titles such as Charlton's *War Heroes* and the ridiculous *Tod Holton, Super Green Beret* were canceled. Dell's *Guerrilla War* (formerly *Jungle War Stories*) folded after only fourteen issues. Marvel and DC, the industry leaders by that time, also continued to steer clear of Vietnam—mostly. DC published five war comics in the era, but in only one, *Our Fighting Forces*, a war-anthology series, were soldiers fighting in Vietnam. Even here, it was the personal quest of Captain Phil Hunter, a retired Green Beret returning to Southeast Asia to find his missing twin brother, driving the 1966 story line, not the war itself.

Marvel likewise kept fighting World War II in its only war comic, *Sgt. Fury and His Howling Commandos*. In a lone 1967 "King-Size Special" issue, the elite commando unit—under direct orders from LBJ—inexplicably parachuted into Haiphong to take out a suspected North Vietnamese hydrogen bomb facility. Yet Marvel accounted for age progression by having Fury recruit his old World War

II buddies from their middle-age civilian lives, and after this one successful mission in Vietnam, the howling commandos returned home to the 1940s for good. Ultimately, while the overall lack of Vietnam-related comics corresponded to the country's changing attitudes, the war's effective disappearance from military comics abruptly around Tet likely sent mixed signals to preadolescents.[12]

Vietnam's complexity did not lend itself any better to the usually cliché-filled plotlines in superhero comic books, either. Although DC and Marvel reestablished superheroes as the era's most popular comic type, built primarily around vague Cold War orthodoxies, very few costumed crime fighters ventured all the way around the world to Southeast Asia. DC, with *Batman*, *Wonder Woman*, and *The Justice League of America*, only sent its flagship character, Superman, off to war, and then for only a single, brief "tour" in 1969. Superman historically had minimal or no involvement in World War II, Korea, or the Cold War, and DC's decision to incorporate Vietnam for a single issue was the result of actual letters the publisher received from young soldiers in the field complaining about his absenteeism. These letters were incorporated as a plot point within the Vietnam story, whereas it was the *Daily Planet* newspaper on the receiving end of such correspondence from GIs requesting Superman's help in fighting the communists. Consequently, Clark Kent temporarily enlisted as an army medic, eventually vanquishing (as Superman) the villainous King Cong, a brainwashed American soldier transformed into a giant creature by a mad Vietnamese scientist.[13]

Several of Marvel's popular superheroes—given their more contemporary and political orientation compared with DC—flirted only haphazardly with Vietnam. When not battling apolitical villains, Marvel routinely pitted its superheroes against generically communist bad guys threatening the American way in situations at once appealing to adolescents' tastes in science fiction, satire, and philosophy, but without alienating younger children drawn to colorful costuming and exaggerated action. Accordingly, in 1964, when Captain America awoke from his 1940s suspended animation, a mission took him to Vietnam, not to fight alongside U.S. troops as he had in World War II but to rescue a friend captured by the VC.

One of Marvel's longest-running superhero franchises, *The Avengers* (of which Captain America, Thor, and Iron Man are core members), confronted communist tyranny in the fictional country of Sin-Cong (a real river and city in North Vietnam) during 1965. But as a team the Avengers did not explicitly enter Vietnam until after American withdrawal. First, with the introduction of a half-Vietnamese character, Mantis, in 1974, and again in 1975 (the year South Vietnam fell) fighting the Titanic Three—communist supervillains in league with the National Liberation Front.[14] When Norse god Thor joined the fray in a 1965 issue, he did so as a combatant, despite being initially mistaken by villagers as a messenger from Buddha sent to defeat the communists. Although knocked briefly unconscious by mortar fire, Thor destroyed local Vietcong, decreeing (in vain, it turned out), "I shall return, and when I do, the hammer of Thor shall be heard in every village . . . in every home . . . in every heart throughout this tortured land."[15]

Even *Spiderman* touched on Vietnam, albeit through the characters of Flash Thompson and Frank Castle, both maladjusted veterans returning from war. After Flash, an old friend of Spiderman's alter ego Peter Parker, shipped out, Parker paused in one 1970 issue to wonder, "Which is worse? Staying behind while other guys are doing the fighting . . . or fighting a war that nobody wants . . . against an enemy you don't even hate?" The soldier's troubled homecoming two years later seemed a reasonable reply. In the 1972 issue "Vengeance from Viet Nam," Flash's return introduced comic-book readers to what would become the standard postwar caricature of Vietnam veterans as alienated from society by their service and otherwise maladjusted by guilt for taking part in the suffering of innocent Vietnamese. Frank Castle, or the Punisher, Marvel's martial vigilante character, made his debut in *Spiderman* comics during 1974 after serving five tours in Vietnam as a marine. Armed with various Vietnam-style assault weapons and grenades, the Punisher went on to wage a one-man war on crime in a number of his own comic titles. Additionally, Marvel's "Letters to the Editor" pages—with appropriately clever names such as "Letters to the Living Legend" (*Captain America*) and "The Spider's Web" (*Spiderman*)—sometimes served as evenly divided forums where pro- and anti-war readers debated these Vietnam story lines, or the lack thereof, as well as broader political issues.[16]

The singular exception, though, was *Iron Man*, whose origin story unfolded in the Vietnam War and was thereafter intertwined throughout the superhero's early life. Tony Stark, a wealthy industrialist and scientist manufacturing weapons for the military-industrial complex, toured Vietnam in a March 1963 issue of Marvel's *Tales of Suspense* to demonstrate his munitions for the army in a jungle setting. Wounded badly from a land mine, Stark found himself captured by Vietcong with shrapnel within inches of his heart and only days to live. In order to survive, Stark outwitted the VC by constructing a distinctive armored suit capable of keeping his heart beating, as well as affording tremendous strength and destructive powers. Once the communist captors were annihilated, Stark remained a fervent cold warrior, selling weapons to be used in the Vietnam War as the head of Stark Industries, while "containing" a number of communist villains—such as the Red Barbarian and Crimson Dynamo—as the superhero Iron Man.

Periodically, clashes brought Iron Man back to Vietnam, where his eventual victories highlighted American military efforts there as a force for good.[17]

That is, until 1968, when Iron Man underwent a marked conversion perhaps paralleling attitudinal changes in Marvel's writers and readership. Just as real-life recriminations of Stark's war profiteering and complicity in prolonging the conflict dominated the comic's fan forum page, "Sock It to Shell-Head," Iron Man lost faith in the war, struggling to reconcile his own role in it. Cold War themes virtually disappeared from the pages, and once student protesters targeted Stark Industries, he vowed to terminate his corporation's weapons research and development in favor of domestic pollution control and consumer goods. Yet Tony Stark found it difficult to overcome his past. When paying a hospital visit to a little girl Iron Man had saved in a 1973 issue, Stark was confronted by a nurse's stinging rebuke. "No amount of well publicized 're-ordered priorities,'" she scolded, "will wash away the Asian blood your weapons shed—not merely once or twice, but for a decade." On another 1974 trip to the bombed-out village of An Thoc—where he had been wounded a decade earlier—Iron Man lamented the devastation, saying to himself, "I used to feel proud of my support for the war but things like this—first hand—really fog up one's thinking! Well, I'm sure of this—it's no longer Tony Stark's war."[18] Coincidently, superpatriot Captain America endured a somewhat similar disillusionment. After failing to achieve peace in Vietnam, Cap temporarily renounced his identity (and Avengers membership) to wander as the Nomad, a man without a country, although the Watergate scandal, more so than Vietnam, seems to have motivated his estrangement.[19]

Stark's soul searching finally reached a climax in a 1975 story "Long Time Gone" in *The Invincible Iron Man*, published shortly after the fall of Saigon. Sitting in his office, Stark told his reflection in the mirror, "As Iron Man you beat the commies for democracy without ever questioning just whose democracy you were serving . . . or just what those you served intended to do with the world once you'd saved it for them. Vietnam raised all those questions . . . like: what right had we to be there in the first place?" During another flashback sequence (a frequent plot device when dealing with Vietnam) Stark recalled Iron Man witnessing "confused and weary American troops fight and die" while high-tech artillery he designed destroyed entire villages indiscriminately. Here, standing in the midst of one massacre Stark's weapons in part made possible, readers retroactively shared for the first time a glimpse into Iron Man's 1968 epiphany. It turns out that a tearful Iron Man had buried Vietnamese dead in a mass grave, "but the mound itself wasn't enough," the narrative line read. And thus while flying above them Iron Man decided, "It needs a tombstone! An epitaph! . . . Something so that someone coming after will know why the mound is there! So maybe they'll ask what these people died for!" With the laser in his right hand, Iron Man blasted the one-word inscription "WHY."[20]

In terms of annual comic book sales, Marvel's progressively uncertain and critical stance on Vietnam reached a youth audience of nearly 40 million by the early 1970s, second only to DC's readership at 70 million. *Archie* came in third among comic book publishers with 35 million issues sold each year, as well as a Saturday morning cartoon in the 1968 season. And although Vietnam had never been mentioned directly, in 1971 fans of *Archie Comics*—commonly preadolescents younger than Marvel readers—were blindsided with a provocative cover featuring Archie, Jughead, and Reggie standing at attention in the U.S. Army Induction Center under the bombshell "Archie drafted!?!" Inside the issue, the uncharacteristically serious "A Summer Prayer for Peace" begins with "The story you are about to read, is a story with a message for everyone! It is about the feelings and beliefs of many young men who are being drafted into the armed services of our country today, but in this particular case it happens to be Archie and his buddies—." Indeed, with only forty-eight hours to report to the army after passing their written and physical exams, Archie, Jughead, and Reggie quickly try to grasp the gravity of their situation on their walk home, an especially tricky proposition considering the Archies (a make-believe musical group with real Top 40 hits) were already organizing a peace rally for the next day.

Complicating matters, a long-haired, peace-symbol-wearing friend, Clyde, tempts the perpetually wholesome teenagers. To Clyde's question, "Do you cats want to go?" Archie replies, "Of course we don't want to go! Who in his right mind would want to go and maybe get killed?" "Then get with it, cats!" Clyde yells. "Protest! Refuse to go! Burn your draft card! . . . show our government that we no longer want to be used as pawns in a chess game for a senseless war by a few forceful politicians! I mean let's face it, you don't see the politicians risking their lives on a battlefield! So why should you?" With hands on his hips, Archie indignantly retorts, "It just so happens that we, the people elected them and gave them the power! Next time we won't! I think I can speak for my buddies, even though we are as much opposed to the war as anybody else—we don't intend to cop out! That's wrong!" The four continue to argue over how "two wrongs don't make a right," and how "violent wild protesting and senseless rioting" undermine respect for law and order. While they finally agree to disagree—Archie and Clyde exchange the peace sign as they depart—the conversation gives Archie an idea for a constructive, not destructive, anti-war song to "lay on them at our peace rally."[21]

At the demonstration, where the band performs before a huge crowd of colorfully dressed young people carrying placards with "Peace Now," "Love," or some combination thereof, Archie begins with,

> I'd like to thank all my brothers and sisters for coming to our peace rally, and we would like to play a special song we have written for the occasion! It's called *Summer Prayer for Peace*, but before we start I'd like to tell it as it is! . . . I'm speaking for the Archies, and it has to do with our country, the United States of America, the land of freedom! And with this freedom, we have the right to question and protest if we wish to! We have many growing problems in our country . . . and we are even engaged in a senseless war in which the Archies have been drafted to do our part! And we feel if everyone uses reasoning and works together it will be resolved, because this is the dawning of a whole new generation!

The song follows:

> Three billion people together forever
> Three billion people sing a summer prayer for peace
> Oh look—look around you, see what you have done
> Where's the world that got intended
> With love for everyone
> Sing, sing of freedom
> Sing a song of joy
> All together making better
> What some would destroy
> How will it end? How will it end? How will it end?
> Amen Amen A——men![22]

Curiously, the last panel contains a disclaimer bringing Vietnam's brief intrusion into the world of *Archie* comics to an ending even more abrupt, and puzzling, than the whole notion of the boys suddenly being arbitrarily drafted had been to begin with. "Readers—remember this!" the narrator says. "The Archies are still a year away from being drafted but this is the way it would have happened, this is not really the end, but a means to an end! . . . Don't forget to go to your local record store and look for Archie albums!" Alas, although the Archies did score hit records—"Sugar, Sugar" reached number one on the Billboard charts in 1969 and was in fact Billboard's song of the year—the slow and folky version of "Summer Prayer for Peace," released as a single in the spring of 1971, was not among them.

This finally brings us to *Mad*, a magazine for whom poking holes in the truths of the adult world, and by extension capsizing some of the very assumptions binding America to Vietnam, was stock and trade. *Mad*—in its heyday during the Vietnam era with annual sales at 2 million copies—was self-consciously apolitical. This meant that in skewering both pro-war and anti-war crowds, Alfred E. Neuman and company's absurdist satires were particularly influential developmentally in shaping the thinking of children's reasoning toward cognitive equilibrium. And regardless of a preadolescent's political knowledge or sophistication, *Mad* had a way of making children feel as if they were letting you in on the big joke.

The April 1969 cover, for instance, cast gap-toothed Alfred E. Neuman as Uncle Sam in a flippant reimagining of the famed James Montgomery Flagg World War I recruiting poster, yet instead of "I Want You," *Mad* asked, "Who Needs You?" In "A *Mad* Portfolio of Some Famous 'Protest Buttons' We'd Like to See Worn by Some Famous People," from a 1968 issue, Lyndon Johnson was pictured with a button reading "War Is Good Business Invest Your Son." The 1969 gag "Mad Look at Realistic Dolls" introduced Keen (Ken) sporting a long jacket that "comes complete with matching luggage and a one way ticket to Canada. Looks like Keen," the punchline read, "is making a *last-ditch effort* to keep from becoming a 'G.I. Joey'!"[23]

Mad's regular lampooning of the war effort intensified after 1968. A parody of *The Invaders* (a short-lived science fiction program on ABC centered on a man trying to warn skeptical earthlings of an alien conquest) brought the show's protagonist face to face with Lyndon Johnson at the White House. The president held the man up by the ears (poking fun at an infamous photograph of Johnson with his beagle) and lectured him (in the LBJ vernacular), "Listen, son! Ah'd lahk t' he'p you! But Ah cain't! Ah'm havin' enough trouble tryin' t' convince people t' believe Mah stories—about why we're in Vietnam—an' why we need higher taxes—an' why they should support mah Great Society—an' why they should love me—an' . . ."[24]

In similar fashion, the lyrics of "The War-Monger's Anthem" (sung to the tune of "More," the theme song from the 1962 movie *Mondo Cane*) played out below the cartoon depiction of a delighted Ares sitting atop a mountain watching GIs advancing in Vietnam on TV.

> War—Helps to the keep the pop-u-la-tion down!
> War—Means less people in the crowded town!
> War—Lets us try out new ar-till-er-y!
> War—Gives our soldiers foreign trips for free!
> War—Give us heroes who are strong and good!
> War—Gives us John Wayne films from Hollywood!
> War—Gives our TV newscasts more scenes of blood and death and gore!
> That's what Living Color's for!

As part of another 1969 spoof, "If Comic Strips Covered the Burning Issues of the Day," Sarge noticed Beetle Bailey had been wearing his olive-drab cap down over his eyes as if he had something shady to hide. On reluctantly taking off his hat, Beetle revealed a message printed on his forehead: "Get out of Viet Nam!"[25]

Despite its nonpartisan humor, *Mad* took particular pleasure in cutting President Richard Nixon down to size. Well before Watergate, Nixon's likeness appeared in the magazine twenty out of twenty-three issues (often with several pieces in each issue) between 1970 and 1972. "That Sinking Feeling," in 1971, showed the same photograph of Nixon—confidently holding his arms upward in victory—over the course of six panels. Each consecutive panel contained a chronological excerpt from a Nixon speech regarding his administration's successful handling of Vietnam, beginning with "I pledge to you the new leadership will end the war and win the peace" from the 1968 campaign. Ironically, every optimistic quote was juxtaposed with the Nixon figure sinking deeper into water until completely submerged in the sixth panel under the passage "If winding down the war is my greatest satisfaction in foreign policy, the failure to end it is my deepest disappointment."[26]

One especially potent 1971 pillorying in the wake of Nixon's controversial Cambodian incursion took the form of a self-described "satirical demonstration of how the present Administration widens the 'Credibility Gap.'" Nixon's public rationalizations for American troops entering Cambodia had *Mad* "wonder[ing] what it might have been like ... If Nixon Were President during Custer's Last Stand?" At a bogus nineteenth-century press conference following the sudden invasion of the Little Big Horn (Cambodia), Nixon replied to a reporter's question, "Our main objectives in this incursion ... and I use the word 'incursion' instead of 'invasion' because incursion doesn't sound as bad ... Our objectives in this incursion were to destroy SHIN ... Supreme Headquarters for the Indian Nations ... to cut enemy supply lines ... and thereby shorten the war." When queried about whether the U.S. military had accomplished its objectives at the Little Big Horn, the president enthusiastically responded, "I'm glad you asked that question! For the record, we captured seventy-nine arrows, thirteen bows, two totem poles, three peace pipes, six beaded loin cloths, a dozen blankets, five tomahawks, a bushel of feathers, fifteen bags of corn and twenty pairs of moccasins. There'll be a lot of cold, barefoot, hungry Indians running around." Follow-up questions regarding U.S. casualties prompted Nixon to observe, "Let me say this: as far as I'm concerned, one American casualty is too many! However, in a mission of this magnitude, we expected to suffer some losses—and we did! Mainly, General Custer and his men!" "But, Gentlemen," the president reminded, "I would like to add that the latest official body count of enemy dead is three hundred and seventy-seven!"—an inflated figure even Nixon acknowledged included "thirteen Indian ponies and a herd of Buffalo!" In fielding a final question concerning contradictory reports coming from Native American sources who claimed a decisive victory in the Little Big Horn massacre, Nixon concluded with, "Who . . . and I ask you this in all sincerity . . . who are you going to believe? Some savage Redskin—or your President?!"[27]

A regular sketch, "Hawks & Doves," pitted martinet Major Hawks against puckish Private Doves. A representative 1971 installment involved a company of soldiers on an overnight march and bivouac ordered by Hawks. After Doves convinced certain GIs to attach a lantern to their tents, Hawks drove up in a Jeep to observe the encampment at night, just in time to see a giant peace symbol on the side of a mountain illuminated by those strategically placed lanterns. Doves kept at it for years, always somehow thwarting Hawks's orders with a properly placed peace symbol, just as he did by secretly rewiring the major's elaborate new electronic war gaming table. There, in front of other brass, Hawks maneuvered the remote-control tanks, artillery, truck, and soldiers around the table until, thanks to Doves's work, all the pieces collided in the middle to form a large peace symbol with their wreckage. Such inversion of authority also flowed through the 1971 piece "The New Army," which depicted how the military now mollycoddled sensitive new anti-war enlistees by allowing them to sleep late, refuse orders, stop firing guns, and generally forego any discipline. The final panel, "The New Army appeals to the culture and vocabulary of the 'Now' Generation," portrayed a call-and-response marching cadence between a crusty old drill instructor and his platoon of long-haired, peace symbol–wearing recruits to the tune of "Sound Off." "You're cats who all dig the New Left!—*Right On!*—"You're cats who all dig the New Left!—*Right On!*—"Sound off!—*Tune in!*—"Sound off!—*Turn on!—Tune in . . . turn on . . . drop out . . . Right On!*"[28]

This notion of the new military experience paling in comparison to, say, World War II indeed found frequent expression in *Mad*. "Yessir, the Army has changed a lot in the past few years," a 1969 send-up announces. "To show you how big a change there's been," the narrator suggests, "let's look at some scenes from The War Movie of the Past . . . As Fought by the Old Army & The War Movie of the Future . . . As Fought by the New Army." In "The 'Platoon's First Invasion' Scene," an undaunted sergeant from the good war reassured a scared young private on an approaching landing craft. By comparison, in the second scene a spacey soldier (with pipe in his mouth) explained to a comrade that fear did not affect him because he was always stoned. Likewise, "The 'Long Night in the Foxhole' Scene" showed two homesick soldiers from the "old" army talking about the wholesome things they missed back on the home front. *Mad* contrasted them with two wistful soldiers from the "new" army (with flowers in their helmets instead of camouflage) ruminating on the times spent "spacin' out with a new chick every night, doin' what I wanted t' do when I wanted t' do it, blowin' my mind, sleepin' till noon, groovin' wild, crazy scenes" (and that, they qualified, had been in basic training). The final, perhaps most telling, panel, "The Heart-Rendering 'Lost Buddy' Scene," offered by way of comparison World War II GIs solemnly making sense of a fallen comrade's sacrifice with the understanding that he would have wanted them to follow in his heroic footsteps. Next to it, Vietnam-era grunts lamented a buddy who was also "gone." But, as one GI pointed out, he was not killed in action, just simply a deserter. "He chose to go that way," his lieutenant eulogized, "so he wouldn't have to fight a war he hated. Sure, I'll miss his anti-war speeches, and his freaky imitations of the General, and his flag burning! But don't mourn him . . . Remember him! And avoid fighting! He would have wanted it that way!"[29]

CHAPTER 3

Who Bombed Santa's Workshop?

MILITARIZING PLAY WITH COMMERCIAL WAR TOYS

The problem with war toys is that they grow up to become
violence toys . . .
They'll stop making war toys when we stop buying them,
Make love not war toys

—**PARENTS FOR RESPONSIBILITY IN THE TOY INDUSTRY**

Vietnam's interference in socializing children to the American way of warfare evidenced in comic book pages also affected the commonly overlapping landscape of war play, principally by militarizing the culture of manufactured toys. Just as titles such as *Army War Heroes* and *Mad* magazine bore the imprint of America's mounting distaste for Vietnam, those same renegotiations of traditional patriotism, heroism, and military service fueled a parallel rise and fall in the popularity of commercial war toys. "Because Vietnam was so complicated," a West Virginia man born in 1958 explained, "nearly all of the play combat I knew stayed in WWII. . . . Everyone knew who the good guys were and who the bad ones were. Unlike Vietnam, that war was just easier for kids to understand."[1] In this regard, the fickle relationship between consumers and early incarnations of the iconic action figure G.I. Joe can be seen as a case study. Joe's 1964 debut when the Vietnam War was being Americanized helped drive the growing prevalence of military-themed toys in the early sixties. Yet, as enthusiasm for the war waned, the plastic fighting man's association with Vietnam weakened sales, while at the same time sparking the subsequent "anti–war toy movement." These efforts against the militarization of childhood, in chorus with a much louder protest movement first resisting, then revolting against, the Vietnam War, eroded further an already deteriorating war toy market.

Throughout the early Cold War period, war toys for baby boomer boys—that is to say, playthings calling to mind military life, battlefields, or warfare broadly speaking—were relatively few in number. Part of this is because the acquisition of toys was not an everyday occurrence—given primarily just for birthdays and Christmas—meaning children comparatively did not own as many as today. These realities tended to heighten the sense of anticipation during the holiday season to a fever pitch when the Sears, JCPenney, and Montgomery Ward catalogs were endlessly poured over, studied, and marked up, which in turn has lent a romanticized timelessness and classic feel to the era's toys. More importantly, mothers and fathers were still heavily integrated into the toy-buying process, so the toys children received usually reflected traditional parental desires to train youth for adult roles. Understanding play to be the work of children, which makes toys their tools, parents chose age-specific and gender-differentiated toys they themselves had grown up with, meaning that many commercially available toys were marketed to endorse continuity in play between father and son, mother and daughter.[2]

Most war toys sold in the 1950s resembled pre–World War II toys of the genre in many respects: either commemorating history's epic conflicts by reenacting famous battles or, now in the age of television, imitating the action of western and space-themed programming. Miniature, multipiece plastic playsets ranged from the medieval Robin Hood and His Merrie Men of Sherwood to the Revolutionary War and frontier Fort Apache. Toy rifles—including Daisy BB guns—tended to encourage hunting and target shooting, although a number were framed as the preferred weaponry of the Wild West (Red Ryder) along with licensed pistols from such TV series as *Gunsmoke*, *Bat Masterson*, and *Wagon Train*. These six-guns commonly came as holster sets to complement cowboy costumes made up of chaps, vests, bandannas, and hats that, as *Parents' Magazine* reminded, well-adjusted boys needed to help them vicariously work through aggression. The Civil War's approaching centennial also brought "Blue and Gray" playsets, toy cannon, carbines, sabers, and uniforms from both North and South. World War II added still another theater of battle to war play by the mid-1950s, as boys refought the "Greatest Battle in History" with D-Day–inspired playsets and dressed up in khaki replicas of Dwight Eisenhower's dress uniform. Bags of inexpensive hard plastic green soldiers likewise restaged World War II battles but also began encouraging generic, pretend combat just for the sake of combat.

Generally, though, into the sixties, neighborhood war games typically involved considerable imaginative role-playing with creatively constructed arsenals and costuming. Though not exclusively sex-segregated, these confrontations lent themselves to boyhood tendencies toward outdoor play preferencing masculinity, competition, physicality, aggression, and construction. Boys *and* girls scrounged some basic uniforms and equipment from dad's World War II mementos or local army-navy surplus stores. Everything else was improvised out of whatever lumber, plumbing supplies, or hardware could be commandeered from in and around the garage. Backyard combatants staged elaborate battles wielding weaponry consisting mainly of machine guns fashioned from tree branches or two-by-fours, bazookas made out of drain pipes, and dirt-clod hand grenades. A nail hammered into a wood block served as the antenna for walkie-talkies. Foxholes dug deep enough to crouch inside were camouflaged with plywood, dirt, and houseplants. Tents populating vacant lot encampments and forts looked to adults like what they actually were, a mother's blanket hung over lawn chairs. Individual soldiers, of course, took responsibly for providing their own gunfire and bomb noises. But whether waged with store-bought military toys or do-it-yourself ingenuity, make-believe fighting still oriented children toward parental conceptions of how previous wars had been fought (and won). In a fateful cavalry charge, gunfight at high noon, storming the sands of Iwo Jima, or imitating popular fantasy television programs *Star Trek* and *Batman*, the ultimate victory of outnumbered "good guys" facing off against ruthless "bad guys" justified the winner's use of violence while validating his virtue.[3]

Then a veritable martial toy craze swept the country, beginning in earnest during the 1963 Christmas season, the first major gift-giving holiday to fully absorb the cultural impact of the Cuban Missile Crisis. Increasingly accurate-looking military weaponry and other related plastic models, often enhanced with machine gun, jet plane, or exploding sound effects, proliferated and sales surged. As a percentage of the total number of toys on the market—at least judging from the venerable Sears and JCPenney Christmas catalog "Wish Books"—the war toy genre rose from 5 percent in 1961 toward a Cold War–era high of 8 percent in 1965.[4] For a period coinciding with the first escalation in Vietnam, military-themed toys ranked among the toy industry's hottest commodities, particularly in the male demographic between ages five to twelve. In 1965 alone war toy sales in the United States totaled $70 million (or roughly the cost of recruiting, training, and equipping seven thousand soldiers for a year). And although a robust market for combat toys was clearly in place already—at least since Sputnik's launch in 1957—an intense television advertising campaign helped drive the retailing bonanza. Indeed, those commercials saturating Saturday mornings led more than a few Americans to wonder if a nefarious conspiracy orchestrated by manufacturers and broadcasters sought to deliberately militarize childhood on the eve of war.[5]

It appears far more likely, however, that manufacturers of military-themed toys were simply responding to market forces, specifically children's attitudes toward John F. Kennedy's can-do cold warrior stance. The emotional bond between Kennedy and preadolescents in the first years of the 1960s is distinctive, and the Kennedy presidency was central to their political socialization in regard to foreign policy. By following the commander in chief's television appearances closely, elementary school students had come to grasp what the Cold War meant: a long twilight struggle for world power between Kennedy (United States) and Nikita Khrushchev (Soviet Union). When asked what he remembered of the sixties as a child, a man who was twelve years old on the night of October 22, 1962, began his recollections with "Well, I can tell you I was watching the TV at home alone when JFK made the announcement on the Cuban Missile Crisis, standing at attention with my hand on my heart all the way through."[6]

Some sociologists even speculated on how demand for military toys reflected children expressing lingering missile crisis fears, pretending to protect their parents through backyard war play. To be sure, Kennedy's more nuanced approaches to containment—a "flexible response" based on calculating the relative degree of each particular threat—were lost on most children. Nor were many aware of the president's determination to make American power credible in Vietnam after the Bay of Pigs and the erection of the Berlin Wall. Yet, through Kennedy, youth increasingly understood how the jungles of the emergent Third World were the principal new battlegrounds against communism.[7]

As with the war comic titles *Jungle War Stories* or *Army War Heroes*, toy manufacturers initially continued to market historical and World War II–themed toys—just in greater variety and more realism—considering buyers expected the nation's role in Vietnam to play out along the basic American "war story" narrative reinforced through movies and television. The 1963 Sears catalog highlighted Remco's three-foot Mighty Matilda atomic aircraft carrier, as well as other World War II–style combat sets such as the nine-piece Paratrooper Kit with shell-ejecting tommy gun, cap pistol, two hand grenades, web belt, and jump wings. "Be a one-man junior army in the best equipped airborne outfit around," the description read. "You're all set for a midnight drop behind enemy lines with helmet, mess kit and canteen. You'll be a fearless *Paratrooper*."[8] (The first, and only, major parachute attack in the Vietnam War—Operation Junction City—took place in February 1967.) Other similar but scaled-down versions—the Fighting Sergeant Set and Combat Patrol Field Kit—were advertised along with depictions of children dressed in recognizably World War II olive-drab fatigues and mesh netting covering their helmet. Remco also retailed both a mortar and bazooka for destroying enemy pill boxes (a familiar World War II term for fixed fortifications).

Still, Kennedy's close association with the Green Berets' counterinsurgency operations and the novelty of Asian guerrilla warfare captured impressionable young imaginations, which clearly influenced the look and feel of many new commercially marketed war toys. Toy manufacturers began incorporating "jungle" themes into their combat collections aimed exclusively at boys: new camouflage patterns, berets, and accurate-looking equipment associated with the increasingly televised U.S. presence in Vietnam. Remco's Monkey Division for Jungle Guerrilla-Warfare line was introduced in 1963 with its own insignia: a monkey (clever wordplay capitalizing on a common childhood mix-up between gorilla and guerrilla) carrying an automatic weapon inside a green and orange triangle. Over the next two years, the Monkey Division offered a six-piece Jungle Combat Patrol Outfit allowing pretend soldiers to "Move out like a crack jungle veteran" with a bazooka, walkie-talkies, and helmet covered with distinctly Vietnam-style plastic foliage as camouflage.[9]

The line also sold a Monkey Gun (a 3-in-1 assault weapon), rifle-launched grenades, tent to conceal mortar emplacements, canteen, mess kit, and field phones. While some items appeared slightly futuristic and the cap-firing Okinawa Pistol was a deliberate World War II throwback, most realistic Monkey Division toy designs drew directly on Vietnam. The GI Combat Field Jacket (with pockets and grenade hooks) looked like body armor vests—colloquially referred to as flak jackets—commonly worn by American soldiers in the field. Likewise, the base of the Exploding Booby Trap and Mine resembled the Claymore antipersonnel mine used by U.S. troops since 1960. But when triggered the concealed device sent a grenade into the air that would detonate a couple of feet off the ground. This fearsome North Vietnamese and Vietcong weapon was known as a "Bouncing Betty."

"Your backyard becomes a jungle campsite," claimed another Remco advertisement as camouflage became standard issue on most basic combat sets, including a number of war toys heretofore depicting World War II. Sears began incorporating these types of foliage concealment patterns on its Ranger uniform costumes by 1964, and camouflage started adorning realistic rifles for "junior commandos." The Sears Paratrooper Jump Master Set, Leatherneck Set for Underage Marines, and Marx's Gung-Ho Commando Outfit adopted the new look at the same time catalog depictions of the Jungle Fighter Set featured children modeling camouflage face paint. "This all plastic military equipment will really put you in the role of an aggressive jungle fighter," the Jungle Gunner Set's ad announced. "Pull-back 23-inch machine gun is camouflage color and is mounted on a sturdy detachable tripod. There's more fire-power: 2 'exploding' grenades (use single-shot caps, not included). Polyethylene helmet has netting and sergeant's stripes. Use binoculars to sight advancing enemies. Flexible machete is your protection in close combat, can be used to 'cut away' underbrush, 'mark' jungle trails."[10]

Mattel's camouflaged Guerrilla Gun ("Attack . . . with barrel smoking. Fires 50 times in bursts or single shots . . . sounds real with or without roll caps") and associated Guerrilla Gun Poncho Set also brought a Special Operations Beret to war play in 1963.[11] The first appearances of berets—the symbol of the army's elite Special Forces—is a reminder of how abstractions and complexity generate less interest for children than do dramatic events and larger-than-life personalities. When Kennedy gradually increased U.S. assistance to South Vietnam, he had sent more than 16,000 military advisers, helicopter units, and five hundred Special Forces by 1963. These Green Berets were expert in counterinsurgency operations and the ways of unconventional warfare, a new breed of homegrown American heroes infiltrating, sabotaging, and effectively beating the Vietcong at their own guerrilla game. And while contemporary observers later claimed prisoners of war were the only heroes produced by the Vietnam War, the immediate popularity of Green Berets across comics and toys indicates this was not necessarily the case in childhood.

"Only Sears equips you to be part of the U.S. Special Forces—the most resourceful, most courageous fighting men in the world," the catalog boasted. Ostensibly compared to the Superman, Batman, and astronaut costumes on the accompanying page, "For brave fighters," only the new Green Beret Special Forces Outfit allowed you to "creep through your backyard 'Jungle' . . . then charge!" The accompanying illustration showing an armed boy wearing the camouflage coveralls posed in a fighting stance encouraged potential recruits to "wear your beret at a jaunty angle." For the youngest children Sears also carried Green Beret–themed pajamas so that bedtime might include, as the catalog suggested, a "Cadence Count to Dreamland." Despite Sears's claim to exclusivity, JCPenney's Christmas catalog similarly included its own Green Beret toys by the midsixties. Besides its version of the Special Forces Jungle Fighter Suit—displayed under the heading "boys will be boys"—JCPenney's Special-Forces Weapons Set came with all the gear you would need for "jungle survival" and "exciting special-forces activities."[12]

In 1965, after regular U.S. troops took over for Green Berets as the principal combatants in Vietnam (and in comic books), trends toward war toys "that look so real they belong on the battlefield" accelerated, increasingly reflecting the military equipment and ordnance identified with the war. A Commando Listening Post resembling a small satellite dish on a tripod made it possible to "track planes," "listen for snipers infiltrating your line," or hear enemies planning an ambush from a block away. The M16, fast becoming the military's standard service rifle, appeared in cap-firing toy form at middecade. "How's this for versatile firepower?" the 1966 Sears catalog asked, somewhat ironically given that a GI commonly referred to his real M16 as a "Mattel toy" because of its plastic components.

So, too, was the military's general purpose, belt-fed M60 machine gun replicated as Remco's Screaming Mee Mee-e rifle.[13]

As the sight and sound of helicopters became inseparable from the Vietnam War in the minds of Americans, toy Hueys and Chinooks—usually capable of only floor-bound movement despite battery-powered blades—were marketed in a variety of configurations. The Marx-A-Copter flew and hovered over a plastic battlefield accompanied by its special sound-effects record. What Aurora models lacked in action they made up for in realism with ten- to fourteen-inch scale replicas of the army's H-21 "Workhorse," the navy's Kaman "Egg Beater," the Hiller Hornet ramjet helicopter, the Sikorsky S-55 "Windmill," and the Piasecki H-25A "Army Mule." Perhaps the pièce de résistance of all Monkey Division–style gear was the One-Man Field Patrol Helicopter, carried exclusively by Sears in 1967. From this orange plastic backpack, arrayed with various controls, gauges, and flashing red and blue lights, a twelve-inch vertical rod extended above the wearer's head with rotating blades—a whirling helicopter rotor on your back. An acceleration lever adjusted the blade's varying speeds (using two D batteries) for simulating air mobile missions to "discover the mysteries of the jungle [and] penetrate behind enemy lines."[14]

With so much ferocious firepower at a preadolescent's disposal, it is little wonder a gung-ho Salt Lake City youth wrote President Johnson in 1967 volunteering for Vietnam. "I think you should send 9 thur [*sic*] 14 year old boys to War," he recommended. His logic rested on the promise that he and his third-grade friends required "no wisky, Play Boy eta. [*sic*]," because more than anything he emphasized, "We no [*sic*] how to play war" already."[15]

The military toy boom's peak corresponded with the 1964 introduction of G.I. Joe, a costumed, plastic soldier marketed by Hasbro as "America's Moveable Fighting Man." A boyhood equivalent of Mattel's fashion doll Barbie (five years his senior), the twelve-inch G.I. Joe gave preadolescent males the musculature of a flawless man's body, with a scarred face, Hasbro claimed, molded from a composite of twenty-three Medal of Honor winners. His jointed neck, shoulders, arms, waist, and legs allowed for infinite posing with a seemingly inexhaustible arsenal of realistic weapons he could manipulate using an opposable thumb and trigger forefinger. Upwards of thirty different uniform variations from all four branches of service could be purchased separately along with helmets, rifles, machine gun, sand bags, poncho, tent, field pack, and field jacket to be stored in a handsome footlocker with blank spaces for each new owner's name, rank, and serial number. The camouflaged Green Beret Outfit accessory package included a beret with Special Forces insignia, scarf, M16, grenades, and bazooka for manning an accompanying Jungle Outpost set.[16]

Joe's proud lineage can be traced back centuries in the toy world through cast-metal and later plastic miniature soldiers. But his real genius, and what immediately distinguished him as a watershed in childhood war gaming, was the shift in perspective downward from the child-as-general reenacting a battle by arranging little soldiers and armaments toward instead living the battlefield experiences of a singular soldier you dressed and posed: playing an ordinary G.I. Joe. To facilitate such inspired play, early G.I. Joes also came with basic training manuals on the proper poses for firing weapons, maneuvering hostile terrain, or throwing grenades. An official G.I. Joe Club—adding three thousand new members per week—also encouraged its enlistees to act out the daily adventures described in the club's comics (while entitling you to a personalized plastic dog tag, iron-on transfer, wall certificate, wallet-sized membership card, copy of the monthly club newspaper, and current G.I. Joe catalog).[17]

The popular dynamic worked so believably with five- to twelve-year-olds because, at least initially, the action figure represented a generic "every-soldier" character from World War II or Korea. Therefore, in a very conventional sense, G.I. Joe promoted intergenerational identification between boys and their fathers' wartime heroism or an older male relative's mandatory postwar military service. Hasbro offered no line of enemies for Vietnam-era G.I. Joes to fight. Pretend battlefields usually just pitted Joe against Joe in predominantly American versus German, Japanese, or Korean recreations. Television commercials highlighted as much, backed by male voices singing (to the tune of "The Army Goes Rolling Along"), "G.I. Joe, G.I. Joe, fighting man from head to toe on the land, on the sea, in the air." After all, the G.I. Joe experience was less about conquering a specified enemy than an affirmation of the values surrounding adult male military action and valor.[18]

Well on his way to being a "perennial fad" like Barbie, G.I. Joe was already by 1968 the best-selling single toy for preadolescent boys. Vietnam and the country's growing antimilitarism, however, drove the popularity of all war toys sharply downward, and along with them this particular warrior fell out of favor for the war's duration. On one hand, entertainment television programming, a reservoir from which young minds liberally drew raw resources for their imaginative play, was, as we have seen, polluted with largely comedic caricatures of military life or other distortions of those memorable good guy/bad guy story lines and personalities from World War II. Prime time's frame of reference, though—how TV depicted a soldier's basic appearance, demeanor, and actions—contrasted harshly with the actual portrayal of American troops on the evening news. "I remember really being shocked at how different this war seemed compared to what we had seen of the history of WWII," one woman shared. "The soldiers looked so much more beaten down."[19]

Maybe Morley Safer, who had so shaken Americans with his depiction of the Cam Ne incursion, spoke to these incongruities most clearly and directly. "I think," the broadcaster suspected, that "[viewers] saw American troops acting in a way people had never seen American troops act before, and couldn't imagine. Those people were raised on World War II, in which virtually everything we saw was heroic. And so much of it, indeed, was. And there was plenty in Vietnam, too, that was heroic. But this conjured up not America, but some brutal power—Germany, even, in World War II. To see young G.I.s, big guys in flak jackets, lighting up thatched roofs, and women holding babies running away, wailing—this was a new sight to everyone." As a Kansas man born in 1967 made clear, "adults just took Vietnam so seriously so I understood it to be [a] topic completely without humor, definitely not something that lent itself well to emulation through fun and games."[20]

Intergenerational bonding around military heroism broke down under the same strain of televised warfare. For World War II and Korean veteran fathers, purchasing G.I. Joe for children might still memorialize their own youthful military service. But unfortunately, this sometimes prompted comparative criticisms at the expense of U.S. soldiers currently in Vietnam. A Missourian born in 1958 recalled conversations about his father's distaste for "how Vietnam was being handled." In his father's opinion, formed during World War II, "we weren't trying as hard," the son explained. "Dad always said they never had enough men fighting and soldiers weren't trained right. I remember he would sometimes call them spoiled little babies and then go on about what he had to do when he was in Europe."[21]

What is more, a fundamental difficulty for adults seeking to socialize children with an action figure such as G.I. Joe—or Marx's knockoff, Stony "Stonewall" Smith—was that Vietnam presented far fewer World War II or even Cold War certainties on which to ground conversations. Given the fluid nature of the government's rationale and lack of conventional warfare, traditional concepts of patriotism and duty were being vigorously disputed in the adult world. Heroism became harder to define beyond risking one's life for a distant, vague cause, especially given the war's glaring asymmetry: the most powerful country in humankind's history against peasants on bicycles with single-shot rifles. Were U.S. troops fighting to contain communism or make the nation's power credible? Was South Vietnam a remote domino to be kept from falling or an invaluable ally requesting its freedom be protected? With few exceptions there was no territory really gained or lost, no dramatic campaigns, and no epic battles with the fate of armies and nations hanging in the balance. And, ultimately, who could say what winning would even look like—the protracted occupation of a wholly dependent client state? G.I. Joe's teaching role could be even trickier for young fathers reaching manhood during the Vietnam War. Whether men actually fought in Vietnam, opposed the war, or fell somewhere in between, most simply sought to distance their families from the atrocities, not introduce sons to a toy whose make-believe jungle battles constantly brought to mind this very real, and unsatisfying, military misadventure.[22]

Seriously hurt by Vietnam's declining popularity and intensifying public reaction against war-oriented toys, during 1970 Hasbro—fearing boycotts—reimagined the G.I. Joe line in the first of a decade's long series of transformations resulting directly from Vietnam. The fighting soldiers—given new flocked hair and beards—were repurposed into a G.I. Joe Adventure Team, big game hunters with kung-fu grip on safari, and scuba divers in search of treasure. Some Joes had been moonlighting as Gemini and Mercury astronauts or rescue frogmen for space capsule splashdowns since 1966, but the Adventure Team wore less military-looking "special adventurer uniforms" emblazoned with an "A" insignia (looking like a peace sign to anti-war observers).

Prepackaged playsets stripped *war* out of playtime in favor of *adventure* themes: Secret of the Mummy's Tomb (driving a six-wheel all-terrain vehicle), Mystery Spacewalk, Shark Surprise, Capture the Pygmy Gorilla, Fight for Survival (an arctic explorer and sled dogs), Eight Ropes of Danger (deep-sea diving for treasure versus an octopus), Secret Mission to Spy Island (wearing a black turtleneck), Revenge of the Spy Shark, and White Tiger Hunt. Six years later, in 1976, when war toys were making a post-Vietnam comeback, the adventurer was retooled once more, emerging as the modernized Super Joe, a futuristic fantasy warrior (albeit only an eight-inch one due to rising costs of plastic after the oil shocks) waging high-tech havoc on alien intruders with laser beams and rocket ships. Gone by this time were his cloth outfits, replaced by a molded uniform, and authentic military weaponry, supplanted by tiny science-fiction munitions. After a brief furlough between 1978 and 1981, Joe reemerged yet again under the highly influential shadow of massive *Star Wars* merchandising. For new cohorts of children with no memories of Vietnam, his otherworldly battlefield exploits against archvillain Cobra were now thoroughly estranged from the realities and values of military life. Post-Vietnam Joes have neither an identification with the service of fathers, older brothers, or grandfathers, nor any hint of all the unpleasantness from the sixties.[23]

The relatively small yet inspired "anti–war toy movement" undermining G.I. Joe's deteriorating footing on the home front was likewise hard at work denouncing all violent playthings. Since World War I, progressive organizations such as the Women's International League for Peace and Freedom (WILPF), War Resisters League (WRL), and Women Strike for Peace (WSP) had incorporated elements of anti–war toy activism into their comprehensive peace agendas. Historically these ethical campaigns to limit—if not abolish—the manufacturing, advertising, and sale of military-oriented toys were episodic and rather short-lived, ebbing and flowing in response to the proliferation of war toys commonly coinciding with American conflicts.[24] The Vietnam War energized those existing activist groups with an unprecedented sense of urgency, while giving purpose to newly formed ones, out of shared fears this militarized culture of commercial toys would further encourage American children to truly make a game out of war.[25]

In this way, an anti–war toy crusade developed—peaking in the late 1960s—as but one distinct facet of the broader anti-war movement. Most doves lending their efforts to the cause counted themselves among the idealist wing of the movement, adding maternal concerns to other pacifists, religious groups, and political liberals opposed to Vietnam on predominantly moral grounds. As the group Another Mother for Peace's slogan went, war is not healthy for children and other living things. This loose coalition of predominantly concerned mothers and teachers, bolstered by the views of Dr. Benjamin Spock and other child-rearing experts, sounded the alarm on how the skyrocketing popularity of G.I. Joe and more convincing military toys, set against the backdrop of televised warfare, urban rioting, and political assassinations, were magnifying conventional war play to unhealthy dimensions.

Most toy protest strategies were less direct and more discursive, taking the form of newsletters, newspaper editorials, petitions, coffee klatches, church and synagogue workshops, and PTA forums raising public awareness on the importance of play to healthy human development.[26] Since no one really knew for sure what impact Vietnam and war toys were having on children, activists participating in what was internally known within the wider anti-war movement as the "war toy debate" were probably most successful when opening dialogues with those holding divergent opinions. Here some of the questioning, challenging, and renegotiation of American conceptions of war and peace, and likewise, self-interest and social responsibility that defined the Vietnam era, echoed clearly within this focused dialectic over war toys.

For the better part of the twentieth century, periodic calls to "disarm the nursery" had generally failed to attract a wide public hearing because most adults accepted, or else tolerated, war play as something children have always done, some combination of developmentally healthy, patriotic, or simply harmless fun.[27] Many psychologists in the 1960s continued to maintain that gun and war play represented manageable releases for acting out a child's natural aggressiveness and hostilities. As Dr. Sirgay Sanger also observed, total disarmament of childhood was unrealistic given how forbiddance only led to fascination. In the absence of store-bought weaponry, the Manhattan psychologist argued, imaginative youth still found ways to create pretend guns. Parents often resented intrusion into what they believed to be strictly a private family matter best left to the discretion of responsible mothers and fathers. "What would be nicer than to sweep all war toys, indeed, all real life, war headlines into a closet and lock the door?" a father participating in a 1965 panel discussion for concerned parents in suburban New York asked rhetorically. "[Unfortunately] we have an obligation to our children to face up to the real and often distasteful facts of life."[28]

Others sensitive to the nation's mounting antiauthoritarianism insisted on being able to provide the tools necessary for training their children for honorable military and law enforcement professions. Some conversely worried how prohibition of war toys might condition preadolescents to grow up into unpatriotic adult draft card burners or pacifists. Toy industry representatives such as Jerome M. Fryer, president of the Toy Manufacturers of the USA, buttressed these concerns, suggesting that "the toy world is a duplicate of the adult world. We as adults are pretty bad. Our toy world is simply a replica of that. . . . The mother's groups are confusing the relationship of cause and effect. Toys don't create wars. Wars create toys. Unless you eliminate the adult activity, you can't stop the child from duplicating it. If you took away dolls, would girls stop having babies?"[29]

On the contrary, anti–war toy activists in the fields of child development and teacher education countered, mock violence *aroused*, not diminished, belligerent behaviors. They questioned whether children as young as four years old were already being integrated into the pretend world of bedroom search-and-destroy missions, dangerously below the ages of seven and eight when war gaming normally enters into play culture. Adherents of the "culture pattern model" also worried over whether war toy advertising on television—where real men suffered and died on the nightly news—amounted to unhealthy teaching tools perpetuating militarization.[30] These academic concerns and other legitimate questions resonated with fathers thinking the toy section of the local store looked more like Da Nang (the military's chief port of entry in South Vietnam) than Santa's workshop, and mothers finding their sons' ragged G.I. Joes strewn across the backyard, killed in action by bottle rocket, firecracker, and BB gun attacks.

By potentially glorifying war in the home, were military kill toys desensitizing boys to violence in the bargain? Spock, a converted ally to the anti–war toy cause, called on parents to instead surround children with predominantly constructive, civilizing, respect-creating influences. "We should bring up the next generation of Americans," he wrote in his 1967 revised *Baby and Child Care*, "with a greater respect for law and for other people's rights and sensibilities.

One simple opportunity we could utilize in the first half of childhood is to show our disapproval of lawlessness and violence in television programs and children's pistol play."[31]

Would pretend reenactments make war appear to be an inevitable part of American life? Dr. Judd Marmor, a professor of clinical psychology at UCLA, posited as much, noting in the *Bulletin of Atomic Scientists* how "We often hear it said that the military toys and war games with which most children grow up in our society are good for them—that they serve as outlets for their respective feelings. It may well be true . . . but they also prepare soil for psychological acceptance of war and violence." Julie Bloch of the Philadelphia-based Women Strike for Peace contended, "War toys teach children that war and violence are normal, socially approved forms of behavior. They educate for war." These were sentiments shaping Marty Cooper's song "Little Play Soldiers," a folkie anti–war toy tune recorded by the Kingston Trio in 1964 and the Brothers Four in 1965:

> Two little soldiers, their games are such fun,
> each with his helmet and little toy gun . . .
> . . . .
> Little play soldiers never know why,
> you love them and kiss them and then send them to die.[32]

And through their complicity in purchasing toy weapons and uniforms, or condoning combat play, were parents, in reality, modeling for children an implied endorsement of war? "When a parent gives a child an exact reproduction toy gun," an elementary school psychologist on that 1965 New York panel reasoned, "he is expressing his approval of this toy. Since there is only one way to use such a toy, the parent is by implication expressing approval of guns as a means of resolving disputes." "The more we take for granted that war is a fact of life," a troubled parent had added, "the more inevitable it becomes. We should not condition children to war by exposing them to toys of violence."[33]

Whereas organized public protests against the Vietnam War were, again, rarely factors for children, the individuals, homegrown organizations, and local chapters of national organizations working toward the disarmament of play represent some of the few meaningful ways anti-war activism actually manifested in preadolescents' lives. *The Toy*, put out sporadically between 1965 and 1967 by the group No War Toys (NWT), and the *Peace Education Bulletin*, first published in the winter of 1966 by Women Strike for Peace, functioned as the primary organs for disseminating the philosophies and educational undertakings of anti–war toy groups ranging from Creative Toys for Children to the American Society to Defend Children. In Minnesota a branch of the Women's International League for

Peace and Freedom distributed the booklet "Let's Train Them for Peace" as a resource for people involved in childhood education. A Minneapolis WILPF chapter constructed Christmas displays for a large department store window (with accompanying television interviews) in 1965. A year before, the wife of a Mennonite pastor put up similar displays of nonviolent toys and games in churches around the Twin Cities as part of the Women's International League holiday campaign with the Minnesota Council of Churches.[34]

Massachusetts women active in the nuclear disarmament movement took the name Voices of Women (from the antinuclear Canadian organization) to publicize the developmental consequences of pretend warfare. Their billboards on Boston's mass transit system reminded riders how war is sustainable in the adult world only because little kids are socialized to it through play. The WILPF in Newton, Kansas, placed posters in store windows requesting shoppers "Not to buy, give, or accept" toys glamorizing war. On the West Coast, a group known as the California Committee conducted parent and teacher workshops promoting peaceful play while the WILPF in the state distributed ten thousand anti–war toy leaflets in nursery schools, pediatricians' offices, and churches and on the streets during Christmas parades. The Committee for Creative Toys at Christmas hosted "A Fun Fair for Children" on the day after Thanksgiving 1965 in Hollywood to entertain participants of all ages with innovative toy displays, do-it-yourself ideas, a free expression area, puppets, sing-alongs, and clowns.[35]

Artists and intellectuals made similar anti–war toy messages accessible throughout popular culture. Al Capp's syndicated daily newspaper comic strip *Lil' Abner* and Walt Kelly's *Pogo* addressed the issues, as did Jules Feiffer's editorial cartoon work where, in one instance, Lyndon Johnson, believably dressed as Santa, hands out war toys as gifts to American children.[36] Although it took another generation to become evident, humorist Jean Shepard's essay "Red Ryder Nails the Hammond Kid," published in *Playboy* magazine, formed the sentimental basis for what became the classic movie *A Christmas Story*. Indeed, in his original short story for the December 1965 issue, it was a chance encounter with a little old lady sporting a "Disarm the Toy Industry" button that sparked Shepard's autobiographical ode to the BB gun.

Though only a small tributary of the anti-war movement, war toys also inspired several contributions to the era's protest musical genre. Besides "Little Play Soldiers," Mark Spoelstra's 1965 "White Winged Dove" lamented,

> I'm old enough now in this country to vote
> So I wrote me a song 'bout the white winged dove
> And a toy gun for Christmas in place of love[37]

The venerable Tom Paxton's sardonic "Buy a Gun for Your Son," which he first performed in 1965 on Pete Seeger's *Rainbow Quest* PBS television program in New York, predicted destructive trajectories for little boys well trained in martial play: "Place a weapon in his hand, / For the skills he learns today will someday pay." And by "pay," Paxton meant a decorated military career where, thoroughly desensitized to nuclear war at a young age, such boys will rise quickly through the ranks.[38]

Nonetheless, as NWT reminded its members, "this movement against toys of violence [wasn't] just some Pollyanna scheme of old lady Kindergarten teachers (many of whom are young and beautiful nowadays)." Some activists were made of sterner stuff. Carol Rich Andreas, a Detroit sociologist and mother, was one of the earliest to employ more direct action beginning in 1964, including strategically incorporating children. Both Mennonites, Carol and her husband Carl had lived with their three preadolescent boys in Pakistan working with USAID for five years before returning to the States, where they were surprised to see "how much children's games in America revolved around war." "Foreign children usually don't play war," Andreas told her neighbors. "They've seen too much of it firsthand." After writing an open letter to the nation's leading toy manufacturers, she and other members of the WILPF contacted advertisers as well as newspaper and television stations with related calls to replace war toys with playthings inspiring children to nobler causes. From there the Andreas family organized an informal toy exchange led by their sons inviting friends to turn in used war toys for donated construction sets, plastic models, and adventure figures. In conjunction with a wider campaign sanctioned by the WILPF, Carol continued community outreach with petition drives across her immediate Lafayette Park neighborhood aimed at both prominent toy makers and local merchants (securing 115 signatures to only two refusals). And while the national firms scoffed, Andreas's petitions convinced a drugstore and supermarket to eliminate military-themed toys from their inventories.[39]

Every March since 1964, VOW and WSP led protesters picketing the annual American Toy Fair's opening day in New York City (where manufacturers unveil what is new for the coming season). Toward the war's end, Vietnam veterans joined the ranks as well. In 1965 a dozen mothers handed out 2,500 leaflets denouncing war toys and accused those industry attendees crossing their lines of "exploiting the world's agony" in "the most cold-blooded fashion." This particular dustup apparently dissuaded Department of Defense officials from returning to the fair where they had publically congratulated toy makers on their accuracy and attention to detail the previous year. Later during the 1965 Christmas season, a woman dressed as Mrs. Claus picketed outside Macy's department store wearing a sandwich board reading: "I'm on strike against war toys."[40]

At the 1966 Toy Fair inside the New Yorker Hotel, women from Parents for Responsibility in the Toy Industry (PRTI), some with children by their sides, marched through the street and into the lobby. Adopting a *Mary Poppins* movie theme (after the 1964 film) for the demonstration, a few dressed as the magical nanny, and most carried black umbrellas taped with the lettering "Banish Hate Toys" and "Toy Fair or Warfare." Others distributed flyers reading "War toys teach cruelty and getting kicks out of hurting others." One of the PRTI leaders in full Mary Poppins costume, a thirty-one-year-old mother of two boys, unveiled her group's new "Dove of Good Practice Award" given to companies and stores promoting healthy and meaningful toys. "We're going to try to bring influence to bear," she announced, "on stores in our areas to let them know we're concerned about the psychological conditioning in war toys."[41]

PRTI, a New York City organization, later pioneered strategic boycotts, or "buy-ins" in language borrowed from the civil rights movement. For its December 1968 "Selective Toy Shopping Campaign," PRTI called on consumers nationwide to only do their Christmas toy shopping at stores displaying their Dove of Good Practice Award seal, which meant local volunteers had already recognized outlets for refusing to carry hateful toys. Besides shunning those stores without the dove, PRTI urged sympathetic shoppers to make a colorful event out of patronizing retailers displaying the award-winning seal, hence a buy-in capable of gaining publicity.[42]

College students active in the anti–war toy movement gravitated toward direct actions resembling tactics gaining notoriety in the civil rights struggle, perhaps seeing the deliberate violation of a toy business's "no trespassing ordinance" as an exciting, albeit relatively safe, form of civil disobedience.[43] University of California–Los Angeles students wearing "I'm a Creative Plaything" shirts marched on Mattel during the 1965 Christmas season.[44] Another group of students and faculty from Princeton's Theological Seminary peacefully protested the 1968 Armed Forces Day ceremonies at Fort Dix, New Jersey, where local children had been invited to join in such soldierly activities as (deactivated) grenade throwing, practicing bayonetting with broomsticks, and a simulated bombing of Vietnamese villages.[45]

While anti–war toy activities were commonly shaped by adult agendas and expectations, preadolescents sometimes demonstrated a great deal of agency as scripted actors in their own protests, picket lines, and marches. Steven Sándor John, a fifth-grader at the Bank Street School for Children in Greenwich Village, organized the Children's Peace Union in 1965 with a dozen or so of his classmates after he was denied membership in the Student Peace Union (an organization of high school and college students) because of age. Growing up in socially conscious households, the nine- to twelve-year-olds, mostly girls, making up the Children's Peace Union were, likewise, heavily influenced by Bank Street's promotion of the civil rights movement, often singing along with Pete Seeger on the way to school:

If you miss me at the back of the bus
You can't find me nowhere
Come on over to the front of the bus
I'll be riding up there

Prior to forming the CPU, Steven Sándor John, the son of Dr. E. Roy John, a World War II veteran and world-renowned neuroscientist, had already accompanied his father to several demonstrations against Vietnam and rallied with his mother, Vera John-Steiner, a March on Washington participant, for civil rights. With Holocaust survivors and victims on both sides of the family, the cause of peace helped mold his childhood. "As a very young child I decided to do something against war," he explained, including joining the War Resisters League as a junior member. "Specifically the war that was going on in Vietnam became very important to me and a few of my friends. Activism was very much a part of our milieu."[46]

The CPU purposely concentrated on war toys, using the issue as a fulcrum to broaden their budding political critique of the war, Cold War foreign policy in general, race relations, poverty, and other related problems then being held up for public scrutiny. "The Children's Peace Union," the credo spelled out, "is an organization of children, whose main purpose is to stop the sale of war toys. We also have a policy against the Vietnam war and for the promotion of civil rights. Membership is open to children of any race, religion or nationality. It is organized, composed and directed by, and of, children, with no adult support." Their logo's symbolism, likewise, reinforced the breadth of the CPU's programs. Inside a circular peace sign, the letters CPU were surrounded by the dictates "War Toys Kill Minds," "End the War in Vietnam," and "War on Poverty, Not on People."[47] "We thought we were going to put out anti-war ideas, we were going to try to reach other kids with ideas of questioning the dominant view of the war in Vietnam," John recalls. "Most of the kids at this time supported the war or really didn't have a clear stand, and I think part of what we tried to do was influence the children to question what they were being taught." Protesting war toys "was sort of our way of trying to find a children's angle, something that would be a children's issue related to this question of war in general and the Vietnam War . . . kind of a way for us to find an angle as children to somehow appeal to children on this question."[48]

Publishing the *CPU News* consumed the grade-schooler's time. The five-cent newsletter, circulated primarily to fellow Bank Street students and several other elementary schools (but also sold along Eighth Street), contained original poems, stories, songs, artwork, and essays highlighting war toys' role in conditioning children to be soldiers, as well as the glorification of militarism among boys. Traumatized from having ducked and covered during the Cuban Missile Crisis, one contributor penned a 1965 essay critiquing the continuance of routine civil defense drills in schools across the country. "The toy manufacturers 'helped' too," young commentators speculated concerning society's acculturation to war, "by manufacturing more and more, gorier and gorier, more warlike toys. Quite a few children, though, realize that war is not inevitable. What we must do, what [it] is our job to do, is to make more children understand that war is not a thing that has to happen, and not a thing to be taken for granted, and as a game. Peace is our one and only shelter." Most material sought to make Vietnam intersect with things preadolescents were interested in, with musings such as "Deliver us Dr. Spock—When Johnson wiggles his ears he's telling the truth. When he twitches his nose, he's telling the truth. When he opens his mouth he's lying." Coverage ranged from reports on the Spring Mobilization Committee's massive anti-war March on the Pentagon in 1967 to much smaller CPU activism and an interview with leaders from a comparable group outside New York calling themselves the Children's Union for Peace.[49]

"We were pretty radical I think in our outlook for the time," John believes. The *CPU News* "had cartoons about the war in Vietnam and stories about children in Vietnam because we wanted children in the United States to understand the situation of the children living under U.S. bombs in Vietnam." The young writers and artists "also wanted to raise some other issues about the society we were growing up in." Op-ed pieces focused on the discrepancy between military and War on Poverty spending, and often articles by black students with titles such as "Nixon's No Fun for Me Brother" incorporated racial analysis into anti-war arguments. "We were just a little group of kids that was very conscious of issues of racism and war," John continued. "We had an article in one issue about people on Indian reservations." In essence "we sort of wanted to raise the consciousness with kids on larger issues" by taking a stand against military-themed and kill toys.[50]

CPU News continued in print for three years between 1965 and 1968, maturing into an underground junior high and high school paper as its writers grew up, but members also embraced direct action in 1966. Akin to child activists in the civil rights movement who were developmentally drawn to protests focusing on local facilities most familiar and exciting in their lives, the CPU organized a series of pickets involving several Manhattan department stores. "The idea of a public demonstration was something we had picked up from civil rights demonstrations," John clarified. Many had protested with their parents, and the CPU expressly encouraged members to "participate, whenever possible, in demonstrations given by other concerned groups, such as: The Student Peace Union, The Congress of Black Equalit[y], etc." He noted, "The idea of demonstrations wasn't new to us, [and] we wanted to have our own demonstration that would be attributed to just kids on our issue."[51]

The first took place on May 14, 1966, outside M. H. Lamston's on Madison Avenue. Under the theme "War Toys Kill Minds," five children, including Sándor John, marched for four hours between Eighty-Eighth and Eighty-Ninth Streets carrying handmade signs proclaiming "Constructive Toys, Not Destructive Toys" and "War Toys Kill Minds"—which they also chanted—while distributing informational fliers linking war toys and Vietnam. Following a routine familiar to adult activists, print and television reporters drawn to the scene interviewed John and others at an improvised sidewalk news conference. Comments from onlookers varied somewhere between "Crazy kids!" and "You ought to be in school!" to "I'm with you kids" and "Good Luck!" Contributors donated $1.31 to the CPU cause and one child counterdemonstrator loudly mocked them with pro-war sentiments. In fact, "except for the ages of the demonstrators," the *New York Times* determined, "the pickets resembled the numerous marches and rallies to protest the war in Vietnam. There was the eagerness of the pickets, the quick appearance of hecklers and the general indifference of Saturday afternoon shoppers."[52]

Lamston's served as a precursor to larger pickets at FAO Schwartz and Macy's in the coming weeks. Over the next two years the CPU, working sometimes with as many as fifteen to twenty-five members, carried out probably six more at other toy stores. A flier promoting the "Demonstration to Stamp Out War Toys!" at FAO Schwartz advised potential recruits on "Ways that YOU can help STAMP OUT WAR TOYS" beginning with "a) attend this demonstration, at 2PM, b) Don't buy or sell war toys!, c) Picket stores, d) Organize antiwar toy clubs, e) Contribute to the Children's Peace Union," and ending with "Transportation help by parents will be appreciated." Besides CPU's "War Toys Kill Minds" buttons, original signage proliferated with each action: "Ban Toy Bombs," "War Toys Kill Minds," "Peace Not Pieces," "GI Joe Must Go!" and "Alfred E. Newman [*sic*] for President Before the World Goes Mad!" Activists also organized a war-toy bonfire in 1968, although those playthings burnt had to be bought specifically for the occasion since no CPU member actually owned any.[53]

"It didn't seem to us at the time that there was some sort of movement against war toys or anything like that," John made clear. "There was a movement against Vietnam and we were conscious that we were connected to that. We all went to the peace demonstrations against the war in Vietnam, that was part of our childhood, pretty much all of us did in the Children's Peace Union." And although he is unsure what impact the CPU may have had on reducing military toys and war play, he is convinced "taking the time to organize, to get a disparate group of people with their own personalities and proclivities, strengths and weaknesses together regularly and to plan events and to carry them out" were early experiments he still draws from. "I have continued to be active in radical politics and I think that the sorts of things that we did as kids were early phases in organizing. Most of the children in the Children's Peace Union eventually outgrew the toy angle," John reflected. "But we continued experimenting with our own political identity as very young people. Experimenting in some ways with different forms of activism in how to understand different issues, issues of women's rights, issues of the struggle against the war in Vietnam, a fight against racial oppression, in various ways we were becoming aware of all sorts of things."[54]

"As children," John concluded, "we were aware that in our view there were some very fundamental problems with the way the world was set up, in the society we were living in and with what we were expected to believe and we were trying to find a way from our own vantage point as kids to change that, that's what we were trying to do, and some of us sought over the following years to deepen our understanding of that and to remain, with whatever changes in the specifics of our outlook, loyal to those ideals of very young people throughout the rest of our lives."[55]

In addition to the CPU, some forty NYC students ranging from ten to fourteen years old calling themselves Students for Political Action staged several demonstrations against stores selling war toys before marching outside the headquarters of the Knickerbocker Greys, an exclusive military club for children, in February 1969.[56] Up the I-95 highway corridor, the Boston Bridge of Friends sponsored more than two dozen schoolchildren parading against war toys in front of the downtown Boston store W. T. Grant Company in July 1968 with the express purpose of ridding every Massachusetts store of violent playthings.[57] Further north, in Falmouth, Maine, children figured prominently in a September 1968 campaign by Payson Sawyer, a thirty-five-year-old toy wholesaler, to burn toy weapons in a ceremonial bonfire. One of Maine's largest toy distributors to chains, supermarkets, discounters, drugstores, and variety stores, Sawyer came to identify with the anti–war toy cause after Quakers approached him in the wake of Robert F. Kennedy's assassination. Publicly announcing his intention to stop putting toy guns on the market, Sawyer worked closely with local churches under the organization Toy Disarmament to burn roughly one thousand toy guns remaining in his inventory. Moreover, Sawyer recruited children to add their war toys to his fire. All youth dropping toy guns off at designated dumping locations received an official "I Turned Mine In" button and were listed on an official honor role of activists. "Certainly [war play] doesn't promote peace," Sawyer told reporters covering the events. "If the world isn't ready for disarmament . . . perhaps parents can disarm their children. . . . Perhaps we can start with this generation."[58]

The aforementioned No War Toys, originating in California in the fall of 1965, offers a particularly unique glimpse into not only how the war toy debate functioned inside the larger anti-war movement but also cross-pollination within the still broader dynamic of what is loosely referred to as "the movement" in the Vietnam era. As the United States grew more polarized, somewhere around six million socially conscious Americans mobilized to challenge the legitimacy of dominant institutions and conventions of Cold War society through productions of public political and cultural protest. This amorphous and diverse group was always in flux, a loose coalition of alliances with participants regularly dropping in and out. "Membership" implied an experience, a sense of solidarity and common purpose. In their attempts to persuade and ultimately educate the nation, movement activists on city streets, in public parks, and on college campuses sought to, in their idealistic eyes, make the world a better place. Ending the war in Vietnam was but one prominent issue.[59]

Twenty-one-year-old Los Angeles sculptor Richard Register positioned NWT as the logical ground floor of activism, attracting those already in the movement's sphere with the notion that replacing war toys with creative toys was the chief agent for sustainable social change. "If you want to change the world, start small," the NWT founder recommended. "Start with the child, for he is the father of the man. Start with his play because it is a promise of things to come. Remember this: the influence on an individual's personality is inversely proportional to his age: the older he gets, the harder he is to change."[60]

Register came to the movement seeking reconciliation on two conundrums from his youth in Santa Fe, New Mexico. Like so many in his generation, he grew up under the shadow of nuclear war in the 1950s, but family friends—physicists—working on the hydrogen bomb at nearby Los Alamos confronted the aspiring artist with a personally more profound cultural issue: individual creativity harnessed to the service of destruction. Vietnam's escalation equally challenged Register to ponder society's seemingly endless ability to perpetuate war despite organized efforts for peace. Though his I-Y deferment (unqualified for duty except in time of declared war or national emergency) kept him plenty nervous about Vietnam on a personal level, his thinking on the war, and militarism in general, finally coalesced on July 4, 1965. "Driving through a Los Angeles neighborhood," Register recalls of his motivation to dedicate the next three years to the peace movement full time, "there were flags flying everywhere in this particular neighborhood and a little child about four or five years old. This little boy was alligator crawling by himself with a machine gun and belt with canteen on, he was just playing war and having a great time between these American flags." Given that war toys were, by comparison, absent from childhood in the Soviet Union, Register embraced new insights. "I sort of self-cultivated, I guess," he remembers, thinking "maybe there's something in this.... It's a really powerful notion that we're indoctrinating the kids in a very informal, acceptable fun sort of way to think that war is actually heroic and fun." The key to succeeding where prior peace movements failed lay in socializing children to peace. "And so I started thinking no one is doing this that I know of, and thought it sounds like the sort of thing I could find support for in the anti-war movement, which was growing pretty fast then. I was on a mission."[61]

Unaware initially of the war toy debate or other anti–war toy activists, Register started showing up at southern California anti-war demonstrations to get the word out with balloons featuring a smiley face of his own design. This smiling face, soon to become the NWT symbol, looked remarkably, though unintentionally, like the ubiquitous 1970s icon (actually created in 1963). Yet Register chose it because he wanted something fun, not political with geometric symbols or letters. Smiley faces, usually in their parents' likeness, were some of the first things children drew, he reasoned, making the smile a universally accepted representation of happiness, confidence, and hope to children. "Everyone called me the happy face man," he explained. Fellow activists did not know what to make of this "sort of wild card character" or his balloons in 1965. "Here they were protesting death and carnage and it's like, 'hey, look here's the happy face guy, what's he doing here?' ... It really caught a lot of people's imagination and I managed to sell balloons like crazy." Based on the balloons' popularity, poet Shel Silverstein recommended Register hand out smiley buttons, too (after Silverstein purchased a sculpture from the artist), and introduced him to a nudist friend who in turn suggested calling the new effort No War Toys.[62] Soon flags and banners decorated with either smiley faces or the name No War Toys—on fifteen-foot-high poles carried by volunteers—flew along with balloons above local rallies.

Register's national appearance on *The Les Crane Show* (renamed *ABC's Nightlife* in the summer of 1965) raised NWT's profile significantly. The idea for an episode dedicated to war toys had been Register's, and after successfully pitching the concept to *Les Crane* producers, he was actually given wide latitude in its production. "The next day the phone was ringing off the hook," he recalls of the interview's impact. "Up until *Les Crane* I thought I was the only one, but it turns out there were a lot. . . . The American Friends Service Committee, Women Strike for Peace, War Resisters League all had somebody working on war toys. I found that out right away and they became really close allies." Together they bounced strategic ideas off each other, as NWT and these associated groups assumed central roles in protest activities taking shape every week or so, one right after another.

"We in No War Toys were right in the middle of it and very much welcomed and respected in the peace movement," Register said. "I was sort of a foot soldier in the other people's movements too, whenever they needed warm bodies, I'd show up even when I wasn't in on the planning phase or focusing on war toys." The friendship and patronage of Herb and Shirley Magidson, influential Beverly Hills activists whose wire-fabricating company supplied material for Mattel's toy cars and Helene of Hollywood's brassieres, further integrated him into greater civil rights and anti-war circles. Soon after a chance encounter—Shirley approached him in a post office to ask where he got the silk-screened No War Toys shirt he was wearing—the Magidsons' frequent events and numerous connections put Register and NWT in contact with some of the movement's most influential figures: Martin Luther King Jr., Huey Newton, Sal Alinsky, Benjamin Spock, Jane Fonda, and Bob Dylan. "He really liked the idea of focusing on toy weapons," Register thought on meeting the singer in 1965. And later that year, the activist appreciated what he perceived to be a war-toy reference in Dylan's line "make everything from toy guns that spark, to flesh-colored Christs that glow in the dark" from the song "It's Alright, Ma (I'm Only Bleeding)."[63]

Although NWT grew on California university campuses—the University of California–Los Angeles, UC Fullerton, UC Berkeley, Los Angeles State College, Valley Junior College, Los Angeles Community College, and the University of Judaism (plus a small chapter at Hollywood High School)—college students were not a natural constituency. As active membership topped one hundred, the group attracted some notable academics and artists: Spock, Erich Fromm (social psychologist), Carl Kline (child psychologist), Joseph Epes Brown (author), Isadore Ziferstein (psychiatrist), Jerome Frank (professor of psychiatry), Digby Diehl (writer and director of research for Creative Playthings toy company), Larry Moyer (filmmaker), Rod McKuen (poet), and Shel Silverstein. Young parents, however, mostly made up the rank and file.

By its peak in 1967 NWT branches had steadily taken root throughout metropolitan Los Angeles in Santa Monica, Fullerton, and Pasadena, further north in Fresno, and parts well beyond in New Mexico, New York City, Miami, Detroit, Tulsa, Santa Fe, Honolulu, Australia, Japan, and Vancouver, British Columbia.

Likewise, a national—and international—presence brought even more collaborations with the WILPF, Voice of Women, and Parents for Responsibility in the Toy Industry.[64] In the midst of such growth NWT briefly changed its name to No Death Toys in late 1966, ostensibly to encompass spy toys since children naturally lumped them together with military weaponry anyway. But it seems more likely the move was designed at least in part to distance them from the unpatriotic taint of radicalism already undermining the anti-war movement's credibility and effectiveness.[65]

Greater membership allowed NWT to periodically publish *The Toy* when funds allowed. With the look and feel of a typical underground newspaper, *The Toy*'s articles, essays, and artwork challenged activists to socialize children to higher-level thinking skills through play. "We do not believe it is harmful for a child to fantasize killing someone occasionally," their statement of purpose read in part, "but we do feel that repeating it over and over again with convincingly realistic weapons creates deep-seeded habit patterns and channels normal aggressions toward destructive rather than creative ends." Solving the world's manifest problems (today and tomorrow) required innovative and resourceful little thinkers, not more brutish soldiers, cowboys or Indians, pirates, spies, or gangsters. Accordingly, *The Toy* advised readers that all toys promoting killing or otherwise representing death were counterproductive—the more lifelike, the more objectionable. Posing hypotheticals, adults were encouraged to use common sense when determining what toys posed the greater threats to world peace in the hands of a preadolescent, a seemingly innocuous squirt gun, for instance, or those plastic grenades from Remco's Monkey Division. "There's a very powerful word if you stopped to think about called pretend," Register reminded. "Pretend means tending to do something before its actualization. So pretend is no joke."[66]

NWT evolved tactically as well, gradually steering away from physical protest in favor of activism focused on helping parents and children make those better toy choices. Besides selling merchandise—sweatshirts (golden ochre and beige) with the smiley logo, balloons, buttons, bumper stickers, and rubber stamps ("Don't Buy War Toys")—the organization maintained an active speaker's bureau in the Los Angeles area for interested PTA groups, Unitarian churches, free schools, or teach-ins. Volunteers regularly collected war toys and comic books for disposal, hosting summer toy exchanges where children traded in martial playthings for imaginative ones. Through Digby Diehl, the group cooperated with Creative Playthings to sell the toy company's "discovery" toys—mechanicals, musical instruments, laboratories, and so on—inspiring tactile learning. Creative Playthings, available in thirty-seven retail outlets nationally, in turn reached out to Parents for Responsibility in the Toy Industry, winning PRTI's initial Dove of

Good Practice Award. NWT also partnered with the Poor People's Corporation of Jackson, Mississippi, to sell handmade toys from African Americans losing jobs for registering to vote.[67]

In 1966, at the Magidsons' urging, NWT added its own line of simple and creative toys, making the plans for how to make them (not actual toys) available to crafty parents. They likewise published a popular book for young writers and illustrators. The book, deliberately left without a title so children might choose an appropriate name on their own, used a back-to-back format resembling cheap novels of the time. On opening the book from the front, a series of children's drawings appeared at the top of each page with blank spaces underneath. The reader thus assumed the role of writer, teasing out short stories below the pictures to describe whatever actions took place in the pictures. Flipping the book over vertically so that the back became the front, these pages contained brief scenarios—"you're coming home from school and thinking about what you'd like to do"—allowing writers to illustrate the narrative in the provided spaces. Praised by psychology and psychiatry professionals, the writer and illustrator books sold especially well for a time in art museums around the country.[68]

Whenever NWT supporters took to the streets, it was more often in staged public performances of play. Countercultural sensibilities ordinarily ran parallel to, and were often interwoven with, the movement's political activism, and NWT made an existential game of protest in gentle gatherings where adults and children acted out the group's values. Register never identified himself as a hippie, but he definitely looked the part and admittedly moved easily within hip crowds. Only after becoming politicized did he cut his waist-length hair and try to "look straight as I could" in order to be taken more seriously. As NWT's visionary core, however, Register's countercultural influences clearly shaped the organization's use of mirth and silliness as protest styles. Members built an adult-size treehouse in Hollywood with grown-ups and local boys alike climbing through the branches with hammer and nails, spontaneously fitting boards together until something took shape. An April 1966 event on Sunset Boulevard was promoted with the query "Feeling useless? Stymied by an overabundance of worthy causes to support? Try a No War Toys party and put zing back into your life. Join the cause that's enjoyable. Drink No War Toys punch and burble in the No War Toys Swimming Pool and generally carouse. Bring your favorite plaything . . ."[69] Another colorful member, artist William Brun, inspired a contest for the best kite designs to be flown alongside NWT balloons at various functions. He led similar efforts to fabricate a life-size rag doll (with the smiley face as its head and wearing a No War Toys shirt) while fielding suggestions about how to incorporate this mascot into the group's projects. On one occasion, when New York and Los

Angeles chapter members joined Women Strike for Peace and Parents for Responsibility in the Toy Industry at the American Toy Fair protests in 1966, the grinning rag doll was held aloft by those same activists dressed as Mary Poppins.[70]

Sandcastle-building parties developed into NWT's signature campaign. The easy-to-construct and impermanent edifices were perfect experiential expressions of family-oriented and noncompetitive play, emphasizing imagination and inclusion. For an organization perpetually operating on a shoestring budget, sandcastles were extremely economical, too. Just plant the banners on a beach, call the alternative *Los Angeles Free Press* for publicity, and let those armed with shovels and buckets make a party of it. The inaugural event in August 1965 on Venice Beach, organized by the Fullerton and Pasadena branches, brought out nearly one hundred—including a great many children—to erect what the *Free Press* immediately christened the world's largest sandcastle. Within weeks a twelve-foot-high castle rising from the same sand eclipsed the record. Colorful flags, banners, and balloons fluttered from its huge ramparts beneath Brun's kites soaring overhead. Curious onlookers came to gawk, some brought flowers, and many stayed for refreshments and groovy music. Thereafter NWT hosted annual, bicoastal festivities following the same basic format, but usually drawing larger crowds, and featuring bigger, more elaborate sand cities. After an event in Miami kicked off the 1966 summer season, folk singer Joan Baez (whom Register enlisted after attending a pacifist workshop with her) entertained nearly two thousand builders back on Venice Beach in August, less than a year before her performance at the Monterey Pop Festival. The Canadian Voice of Women later cosponsored three sandcastle events on Vancouver Island. In the spirit of these collaborations, NWT called on people all over North America to build castles in solidarity and send photographs to be published in *The Toy*.[71]

Though some allied groups answered NWT's call for more sandcastles, at least one organization played off this same humor-as-protest style in another way. The Committee, a San Francisco improvisational comedy troupe active in the anti-war movement, employed guerrilla theatrics made (in)famous by Yippie showman-activist Abbie Hoffman in collecting used war toys they planned to drop on the Pentagon by parachute. Their absurdist "bombing" campaign in February 1966—publicized with full-page ads in the *San Francisco Chronicle* and *Stanford Daily*—merged counterculture aesthetics with political activism, employing playful satire intended to invert the serious symbols of America's war effort. In this case they targeted the military's psychological operations during the fall and Christmas season of 1965 when American pilots had dropped thousands of toy bundles over North Vietnam to commemorate the annual Vietnamese harvest festival. The Committee invited Bay Area residents to donate war toys—making it a contest with cash prizes—best demonstrating wholesome American values for Vietnamese children. In due course, logistical difficulties dictated that the toy weapons were inauspiciously delivered to Washington aboard buses, but the Pentagon never mentioned the humanitarian toy drops in Southeast Asia again.[72]

By Richard Nixon's first term in office, with U.S. troops coming home and television coverage framing American involvement as winding down, the popularity and sale of military toys declined rapidly, falling toward pre-1960s levels. In 1970 and 1971 military-themed toy sales dropped fourfold to represent only 2 percent of the overall toy market, and war toys virtually disappeared from the Sears and JCPenney catalogs. G.I. Joe had accounted for nearly 70 percent of Hasbro's $25.5 million in sales in 1964, but by 1967 Joe's sales plummeted to $8 million and fell even further to $6 million after Robert Kennedy and Martin Luther King's assassinations in 1968. Retailers across the board noted parents' clear lack of enthusiasm for, and sometimes outright revulsion toward, "anything khaki."[73] The toy industry, cognizant of the bottom line, quietly acknowledged Vietnam's unpopularity as the salient factor in reducing the appeal of things associated with the military, including cowboy and Indian costuming. Anti–war toy activists claimed some credit as well. The martial toy genre traditionally sold very well during wartime. Sales figures in the late sixties and early seventies should have trended upward, not down. Vietnam may have made war and military heroes look less heroic to children, but many in the movement traced a direct causal relationship between their activism and such an unexpected reversal of fortune.[74]

Most of the movement's success was local. Major department stores in nearly every city where anti–war toy organizations worked were convinced to alter war-toy advertising campaigns or otherwise change policies on what weaponry remained in stock. Sears, the world's largest retailer, took the lead, removing toy guns from its Christmas catalogs and informing its 815 stores to stop advertising guns and "similar toys of violence." Other department stores all over the country de-emphasized toy guns, which meant not ordering them, while in New York Bloomingdale's and Stern Brothers took toy guns off their shelves entirely. As so many stores struggled to sell off military inventories, prominent manufacturers such as Marx began presenting toy lines—previously painted olive-drab green or camouflaged—in new garish—nearly psychedelic—colors. One toy manufacturer, Lionel, boldly challenged convention, foregoing their military lines in favor of trains, racetracks, and science and space toys reinforcing the company's principled new theme "Sane Toys for Healthy Kids." Even though Democrat John L. Burton's proposed legislation in the California State Assembly requiring labeling for toy weapons and military toys failed to gain traction, none other than Captain

Kangaroo himself, Bob Keeshan, bucked the commercialism of his network CBS by steadfastly prohibiting advertising for warlike toys and guns on his show.[75]

Just as the anti-war movement did not end the war in Vietnam strictly speaking, neither did the anti–war toy movement end manufactured war toys nor commercialized war play. What happened, however, is that both succeeded in large measure by fundamentally recasting these respective conversations. In the broader sense, 1971 marks the first time the majority of Americans came to share the movement's advocacy for immediate withdrawal from Vietnam, instead of negotiated de-escalation. Arguably the anti-war movement's work was done.

On the smaller war-toy front, while pacifist groups continued to incorporate nonviolent toys into their peace education initiatives, a number of other activists expanded the campaign's scope with their particular programs. Organized efforts to shield children from television violence, comparable to earlier apprehension over comic books, grew in direct proportion to sharp increases in prime-time television's depictions of violent themes. So, too, did other groups—consumer, environmental, and feminist—exert pressure on toy makers to eliminate deceptive advertising and any mechanically dangerous or otherwise offensive playthings. Parents for Responsibility in the Toy Industry cooperated with Women Strike for Peace and feminist allies in the National Organization for Women (NOW) against certain types of toys and advertising deemed sexist. In November 1971 those organizations picketed Nabisco's headquarters over its subsidiary Aurora's line of classic movie monster plastic models. Chanting "Sadistic Toys Make Violent Boys" and carrying signs reading "Sick Toys Make a Sick Society," the activists took issue with all eight ghoulish kits—Dracula, Frankenstein (by this time with glow-in-the-dark extras), Phantom of the Opera, Mummy, Wolfman, and so forth—but targeted two directly: the Pendulum and the Victim. The former, a plastic snap-together torture device, included a barely clothed woman figurine strapped in below the swinging pendulum. The female Victim (sold separately) was a likewise scantily clad doll that could also be eviscerated under the pendulum, locked in a hanging cage, or menaced helplessly by monsters in the series. Fearing a general boycott against the company, Nabisco quickly discontinued the Aurora series and with more protests—NOW also picketed the 1971 Toy Fair—other toy manufacturers made additional concessions, including Kenner, whose advertising voluntarily began showing girls in traditional male play settings.[76]

Together these concerted voices—and collective purchasing power—eventually helped bring people making, selling, and buying military-oriented toys closer toward the movement's way of thinking. Although NWT ran out of steam in 1969, Richard Register is still approached by men and women telling him how much his work affected their lives as children in the Vietnam era. When they say "you changed my life completely," Register stressed, "one of the stories is creating independent thinking—that's what was going on. A man who as a little kid had built giant sandcastles said he realized then he could do things. Or a little girl who had talked to the kids at her school and gotten them to swear off war toys that decided to become an actress." And while it is true that war toy sales rebounded after American involvement in Vietnam ended, manufactured war toys and how children played with them were altered in ways reflecting activists' pressure. Pretend battles were divorced from historical conflicts, or even realistic contexts, as markets increasingly shifted to otherworldly fantasy play and video games after the late 1970s. Linked with G.I. Joe's transformations, parents no longer purchased, nor did preadolescents dress up in, soldier and gunslinger costumes to wage the righteous American war story favored by previous generations on backyard beachheads or in family room gunfights. Conflicting adult feelings toward patriotism, American power abroad, and the military severed generational continuity in war toys, and within a few years after Saigon's fall, how children played war was mostly unrecognizable to adults.[77]

"The marching mothers were at the Toy Fair again this year," *Toys and Novelties* (one of the leading trade magazines) had reported in April 1966, "and a number of toy manufacturing firms adopted or continued campaigns against belligerent-type toys. . . . A real and vital issue is raised here," this editorial correctly predicted, "one that we would do ourselves a great disservice to ignore. . . . [We] suggest to toy manufacturers and retailers, individually and collectively, that what is required is that much deeper and much more searching consideration be given to the values inherent in the toys they produce and sell. These values may well differ from those of the marching mothers. But the underlying concern these mothers have for their children should be the toy industry's too."[78]

Arguably, the anti–war toy movement's work was done.

CHAPTER 4

One of the Most Agonizing Years of My Life

KNOWING SOMEONE IN VIETNAM

> A guy named Jack hung out in my grandpa's garage tinkering on cars. I liked him instantly, he joked a lot with me and called me "fink." But also because in the afternoons he'd get grumpy and have to lay down for his afternoon nap, just like me! I asked one day why a grownup napped, and my grandpa said it was because my "buddy" Jack had stepped on a landmine in Vietnam and needed to rest the metal plate in his head.
>
> —**MISSOURI MAN BORN IN 1967**

Early in the 1967–68 school year, Jerry Davis gave her fourth-grade students at Yorkship Family School, in Camden, New Jersey, a homework assignment writing letters to two homesick local men serving in Vietnam. After one of the soldiers, twenty-year-old Glen Williams from neighboring Cherry Hill, was killed at Chu Lai in November, Davis's fourth-graders collectively decided to honor the sergeant's memory by sending a Christmas message and packages to his comrades in the Fourth Platoon of Company A, First Battalion, Seventh Cavalry Regiment, First Cavalry Division.

These Yorkship parcels—airdropped while Fourth Platoon conducted search-and-destroy missions in the Que Son valley in November 1967—consisted of more than fifty pounds of "everything that wasn't nailed down," a greeting card signed by the class, and recorded audio messages offering both condolences and Christmas greetings. "We loved him very much [Williams]," a female student read into the microphone, "and think about the rest of you still in Vietnam often." "We loved writing to Glen," another girl added, "and looked forward to it every week and we knew Glen liked our letters." The tape also featured song selections from the school's upcoming Christmas play, closing with everyone singing "We Wish You a Merry Christmas."[1]

The men were so moved by the gesture they responded with a "thank you" letter written by Fourth Platoon leader Lieutenant Eugene Moppert, and signed by every member, including their hometowns. "I must close now as there is much to do before the patrol this afternoon," Moppert wrote.

> Thank you again for making our Christmas a lot brighter and reminding us that the folks back home are thinking of the boys over here.
>
> P.S. We assume that you are a school teacher (the signature on the cards) but are puzzled as to whether you are male or female. This became a topic of conversation within the platoon as none of us have ever heard your name before. We would like to hear from you again and perhaps you could send a picture of you and the kids? The boys were really tickled about the kid's signatures and decided to send their own.[2]

A couple dozen nine- and ten-year-old fourth-graders and the GIs of Fourth Platoon had adopted one another, although neither ever determined who actually adopted whom. Over the next four years, Davis's pen pal project took on a momentum all its own, eventually outliving Yorkship School and Vietnam—as students moved up to the next grades and soldiers rotated home—before eventually making its way to a collection in the Smithsonian Institution.[3]

The range of childhood experiences examined in the first three chapters were understandably most relevant and acutely felt when personal relationships with someone serving in Vietnam intertwined with young lives. Preadolescents' abstract-thinking skills develop outwardly from immediate experiences to comprehending local communities and finally national realities. Whereas adults can easily manage judgments based on intangibles, developing children require the more concrete. When asked what problems facing the world bothered them most at the dawn of the 1970s, only 37 percent of the quarter million children responding to *Life* magazine's reader's poll for kids said the Vietnam War. *Life* found the war ranked well behind the top three immediate childhood concerns—pollution, animal welfare, and drugs—which are findings consistent with political scientist Howard Tolley's surveys on attitudes toward the war.[4] The militarization of media and popular culture notwithstanding, Vietnam simply resonated most profoundly for those children who were acquainted with, or related to, a soldier. In small towns and on city blocks where everyone either knew the soldier or his family, children even remember taking it on themselves to watch Walter Cronkite a little more attentively and read newspapers at earlier ages.

Local papers routinely ran biographical stories about hometown GIs detailing their military occupation in Vietnam, civilian schooling, various honors, awards, and athletic accomplishments, as well as genealogy.

"My street was my world," an East Coast woman remembered, but eventually "it seemed like most of the older teen boys and fathers on my street were off fighting in Vietnam." "When we were growing up, Vietnam was a place 'over there' . . . a place that we thought little of," a West Virginia woman echoed. "Eventually though, we took notice as neighbors were going to 'that place' to fight a war that we knew little about."[5] It is interesting to note, however, that there did not appear to be consistent statistical differences in positive or negative attitudes toward the Vietnam War between children who recognized someone serving and those who did not. The only real variations were that the former tended to wish harder for the war to be over, expressed more hope for U.S. victory, and felt greater sensitivity to dissent aimed at servicemen.[6]

A significant number of younger baby boomers contributing to the book revealed how Vietnam's only enduring childhood impressions (and of the 1960s generally) were anecdotal associations with soldiers. Again, in regard to socialization, unlike youth during World War II, Vietnam-era children drew understanding more from emotions than strictly cognition, and often it seems these Americans organize their adult thinking about Vietnam around a handful of early—perhaps selectively poignant—memories. A California woman born in 1959, for example, whose father was recovering from surgery unrelated to Vietnam at a local Veterans Administration hospital recalled how "some of the guys on his ward were injured in Vietnam. My father would come home on weekends and bring along one of the soldiers. My mother put a stop to it eventually because some of them had PTSD and would wake up screaming. She feared this would frighten me. One boy was from Philadelphia, and he would always comment on the roses my mother would bring my father from our yard. One time she brought him a vase of roses too. He cried. My mother cried over that soldier all the way home."[7]

Another woman, born in Florida in 1960, traces her developing views on Vietnam through a series of emotional stories. "My mother's sorority had a project that I helped with: we packed care packages to the troops. That was cool!" she began, but then

> my babysitter's boyfriend who I was really close with was drafted and I was really upset. He came home to marry the babysitter and I cried through the whole wedding because not only was he going away, he was taking his wife with him somewhere. He had pulled my first tooth and she was our neighbor since I was 11 days old. Once overseas, he mailed my sister and I Oriental dolls in beautiful dresses

> that I treasured. (wish I still had mine) I remember our church always prayed for the servicemen from our area every Sunday. Sometimes they would be home on leave and come to church in their uniforms. They were so handsome! The older I got, the more confused about the war I was. It was a faraway place and people and especially children were dying. I was sad. I also didn't understand why people were protesting the war. I understood at a young age, these servicemen were just trying to do their job and serve their country.[8]

Reminiscences grounded in church fellowship are common, probably owing to war's jarring presence in this normally intimate sanctuary. "I was an acolyte," one man shared, "and became aware of the realities of Viet Nam when one of the older acolytes was drafted and then killed in combat."[9] "I was born in 1962," another midwestern man wrote. "I remember the boys from church who didn't come home, and I remember the ones who did."[10] Prayers offered for servicemen from the congregation were voiced more earnestly by these children, and they recall older worshipers adding merciful appeals that the fighting end before the youngest reached draft age. "I specifically remember one of the ladies at our church, who had 2 sons in the war, worrying about her youngest who was in high school," a Missouri woman born in 1958 explained. "She told my mom that she sure hoped the war would be over with by the time he turned 18. I liked knowing I was a girl and wouldn't have to be drafted to go to Vietnam. I didn't really know where the country of Vietnam was and it wasn't discussed in our school. Life at that time mostly revolved around my house and small town."[11]

"One memory that sticks out in my mind but did not register with me at the time as having any historical significance," a Tennessee man born in 1961 stressed,

> was when a young man, who grew up in our neighborhood, had to come back from Vietnam to bury his wife. She had been sick and died while he was overseas. Gary S. was like a son to my parents and apparently hanged around so much that other kids called him Mr. Mode [the family's surname]. He joined the Marines at seventeen according to my dad, and may have joined the Marines because of my dad. Dad used to tell him stories about being in the Marines. I recall being at Greenwood Cemetery in Knoxville on a very cold day, snow on the ground, and seeing Gary standing at his wife's grave site in his dress green uniform, shivering away. My dad took off his overcoat and put it around Gary's shoulders. Sometime later I remember finding all of Gary's medals in a garbage can in his parent's back yard. I took the medals home, but later felt guilty for taking them and put them back. I didn't tell my parents that I had found them, but perhaps I should have. My mom said Gary came back the most decorated sergeant in Vietnam. He came back wounded as well.[12]

In at least one case, a midwestern man, born in 1956, remembers drawing on the formative Kennedy assassination to adjust his perspective on the thousands of soldiers sacrificing their lives in Vietnam. From his small, hometown vantage point, he admittedly never "got" the relevance of the Vietnam War or thought much about it. Even when a young serviceman from the community was killed, the requisite funeral attendance left him unimpressed. Only when confronted with a flag-draped coffin at the funeral home did the war become real. Instantaneously his mind seized on the imagery of November 1963. "This is like Kennedy," he thought. "This is like Kennedy's funeral, and I solemnly understood the occasion, more broadly Vietnam, for what it was becoming for America; bitter, anguished, and bewildering. After that day, I followed events in Southeast Asia with grave concern."[13]

In elementary classrooms, the amount of teaching time devoted to Vietnam varied tremendously by school, individual teacher, and year. Few likely noticed one of the war's unforeseen consequences in education: increases in male teachers motivated to enter the profession as a draft avoidance strategy. For many students, the war was never part of elementary curriculums, and so school's role as a socializing agent is negligible. "I loved social studies. We often had current event topics and would have open discussions," one Florida woman born in 1960 wrote.

> I never thought about it at the time until I was a young adult, but do you know we never discussed Vietnam? I don't know if it was taboo in school or if it was late enough in the war it wasn't discussed. Again, once an adult I began to learn about the war, I started asking questions. One of which is why by the mid to late 70's wasn't anything in our history books? We didn't cover this in high school either and it made me angry as a young adult. I don't know what was going on in education or with the preparation of history books. It just seems weird to me.[14]

Wherever teachers addressed Vietnam, elementary school students who knew someone in Vietnam tended to approach war-related observances and assignments more purposefully and with greater sincerity compared with classmates without any linkage. Commonly these isolated memories of the war "coming to school" are what remains in their minds. "Oh yeah, yeah," a woman born in 1960 remembers of the curiosity other third-graders showed toward her brother in Vietnam. "I was the only kid with a relative in Vietnam and I kind of felt like big stuff. . . . I was kind of proud, especially the day when I brought an empty bullet casing he sent home for show-and-tell."[15] Often children from the era were particularly sensitive to teachers whose husbands or sons shipped off, and regulated their behavior accordingly. "In sixth grade we debated the Vietnam, er, War?" a California woman born in 1954 recalled. "I had to defend it and the teacher had a son who was serving there so she had mixed emotions.... Very interesting year, 1966."[16] Teachers requesting special supplications for soldiers by name during silent morning prayers—an honor usually reserved for astronauts and presidents—also made abiding impressions on grade schoolers.[17] So did standing behind your desk to honor a classmate's sibling or father when the principal periodically interrupted class over the PA system to announce such lists. And when former high school football stars were killed, normally festive Friday night halftime ceremonies took on somber tones. "The war became more real to me as a former high school student was killed there and we all knew his family," a rural Missouri man born in 1954 explained. "The school purchased a Planetarium in his name.... Seeing the plaque on it, with his name, made the war more real."[18]

On particularly special occasions, returning veterans—usually older brothers or dads—brought 35mm Kodachrome slideshows back from Vietnam. Several classes might gather together in the lunchroom or auditorium for the narrated presentations. "I vividly remember a first grade classmate's dad brought his slides to school," a Kansan born in 1967 offered. "The school library was packed, standing room only students and teachers, for the show. One hundred squirmy kids focused intently on the screen, waiting for pictures we assumed would look like the stuff we saw on TV. And waiting to hear heroic 'dad' stories. But what we saw were boys in green clowning for the camera. Tiny people no bigger than ourselves squatting on the roadside. Lush, exotic vegetation juxtaposed with a burnt orange wasteland littered in American garbage."[19]

A midwestern man's recollections of his class plotting newsworthy locations on a map and reciting the previous night's television casualty figures illustrates this dynamic. Born in 1954, he remembers his classmates "going to the world map each Friday and taking the pointer and pointing to Vietnam on the map (it had a large hole in it, where Vietnam was located, due to everyone doing the same thing) and giving a current event report which usually sounded like this: 'Yesterday in South Vietnam, American and South Vietnamese soldiers killed or wounded 125 Vietcong and North Vietnamese. There were 10 American casualties.' The fact is," he underscored, "many students forgot their assignment and would just go to the map and make up numbers about killed, wounded, prisoners, etc. Thinking back about it now, that was pretty pathetic. Making up those numbers back then seemed easy because you didn't know any people who were over there."[20]

The fourth-grade class at Yorkship Family School is a remarkable case study, not only because the teacher, Jerry Davis, is such an exception to the largely unrealized potential of how elementary school curriculums commonly approached Vietnam, but, moreover, for speaking directly to the transformative nature of connecting students with soldiers as pen pals. Sending and receiving weekly correspondence grew into cherished rituals deeply embedded in the cultures of both classroom and battlefield. Students wrote to their pen pals during designated class time, letters bundled together for delivery, while some also penned additional letters by night (and over summer break) to multiple soldiers. Mrs. Davis read all incoming mail meant for the entire class out loud and afterward pinned it, along with small memorabilia, onto a specially created bulletin board. Personal letters addressed to individual children remained just that. In Vietnam the men, likewise, might keep in touch with as many as three pen pals at once. After every mail call, letters from Yorkship were typically the first read, certain passages then reread or anecdotes shared with each other. Newcomers to Fourth Platoon, surprised to receive student greetings for the first time, were quickly integrated by old-timers. In the field GIs read letters by flashlight in foxholes, or by moonlight on beaches. Men carefully wrapped the letters, children's pictures, and cassettes (waiting to play them back at base) in plastic to keep them dry, stowing the items in pockets or packs as they traveled through the A Shau valley, Hill 270, Hue, and Khe Sahn.[21]

A few parents voiced reservations initially about the project's appropriateness, but Davis satisfied their concerns. "They'd come in and talk to me about it," she explained. "And I'd have to tell them, 'This is not about the war that's unpopular, this is about the men who are over there, and they didn't send themselves.'"[22] If there were any lingering doubts, Lieutenant Moppert's death in February 1968 solidified the bond but also guaranteed that Davis would be unable to shield her students from the realities of war. Moppert, a twenty-two-year-old from New Orleans, was killed by sniper fire near Hue during the Tet Offensive, and the news, broken gently to the class, left them stunned. "There was silence in the room," William Harrison remembered, "and then some of the girls started to cry. She tried to explain the best she could what that meant and how he died over there.... The day Mrs. Davis told us about Lieutenant Moppert, we were heartbroken. Most of us had never experienced death before, and it was hard to grasp."[23] Moppert's widow Sandra, however, understood the relationship clearly, and in June 1968 she and their toddler daughter made a pilgrimage to New Jersey to present Mrs. Davis's class with the folded flag that had recently draped her husband's coffin.

Just as Williams's and Moppert's deaths served as a catalyst, loss remained a central facet of the learning process. "If you send anymore mail . . . ." a platoon sergeant informed the class only days after news of Moppert reached them, "would you change the address to [just Platoon Sergeant]. The reason for this is there is always a [platoon sergeant]. If it addresses to one man . . . well I guess you can see why."[24] In writing to inform students of Sergeant Ed Frowner's death in 1969, a soldier advised Davis, "I've already written to my pen pal's about Ed's death but omitted any details. I shall leave it up to you to decide which parts of the story they should hear, if any." The facts of how Frowner, an African American from Alabama, died of shrapnel wounds to the chest followed, but for students the GI noted only that "Ed died easily, without pain and he 'went down,' as we call it over hear [*sic*], in a way of courage and bravery that I'm sure the kids would be proud of. Jerry, I will say one thing," the letter continued, "Ed did love those kids, probably as much as he loved his own family. There was never a day he didn't talk about them all for at least an hour and when one of the guys made a passing joke about it he was ready to pound him into the ground. He'd joke about anything but would stand for no comments from the other platoon about his kids."[25]

For their part, students heartily welcomed pen pals into the world of Yorkship Family School, sharing the most immediately important news of the day. Correspondence chronicled the seasonal rhythms of elementary school life with commentary on class holiday and birthday parties, fourth-grade fashion, Girl and Cub Scouting, spelling tests, athletic heroics at recess, fluidity of friendships, or class clowns acting the fool. Writers also offered insight into a more private sphere of brothers and sisters, pets, trick or treat hauls, roller-skating, and musical tastes increasingly inclined toward the Jackson 5.[26] Children were also quite inquisitive, a curiosity Davis stoked with factual learning and mapping. Not about the war as such, but rather mysterious jungle animals, monsoons, the comings and goings of the Vietnamese people (why they would rather celebrate Tet instead of Christmas), or the apparent absence of cats in Vietnam. "I never read the letters from the kids or corrected them," Davis later commented. "They went just the way the kids wrote them."[27]

Probably thousands of pounds of food and other items accompanied the letters, with Davis's husband paying all postage. Based on what they learned about soldiering, students organized collections of condiments (mustard, ketchup, and sugar packets systematically pilfered from restaurants) to improve bland C-Ration meals and Kool-Aid drink mix to make the water taste better. Delicacies such as fruit juices, pepperoni, cheese, canned goods, and saltwater taffy were boxed up. So, too, were scarce toiletries (soap, toothpaste, washcloths, and foot powder), books, cassette tapes, and camera film, along with original artwork and photographs of the senders. Ingredients for a full spaghetti meal allowed the men to cook a real feast in an ammunition box. Children donated their Halloween candy one year as well, filled boxes with Christmas cookies, and mailed Easter baskets with dozens of colored, hollowed-out eggs (thought to be the only Easter eggs in Vietnam). All student packages were considered communal property by Fourth Platoon.

"After writing and going to school and her talking about it," recalled Denise Knettle-Moloy, whose brother and brother-in-law were serving in Vietnam, "it was like a whole total different experience."[28] Developmentally, the difference may be explained in some measure by the project's powerful appeal to preadolescent moral development and specifically an ethic of care. Generally until around age ten, children govern personal conduct by concern over how external authority will punish or reward their actions. Afterward, children begin fashioning an autonomous sense of self where morality is increasingly grounded in mutual respect. "It was fun to write and receive letters," William Harrison related, "and a great feeling that a group of 10-year-old kids were able to brighten the days of soldiers with letters and care packages and actually make a difference in their lives."[29]

While boys mature ethically by progressively incorporating notions of rules and justice, girls more commonly tend to approach issues by thinking in terms of caring and relationships. Acquisition of this attitude of care in girls—although certainly not exclusive to females—usually coincides with fourth grade and may explain the immediate intensity of emotion between pen pals, but also how caring about, and for, others are vital starting points in integrating a healthy appreciation of social justice into adult ethics. "I don't think anyone envisioned we would have a lifelong connection," Kathy Cromie Gilbert reflected. Now a marriage and family therapist, Gilbert remains in touch with her pen pal Sergeant Brian O'Leary and understands the project as helping influence her personal and career choices. "It impacted my entire life, and I thank Mrs. Davis for it. It was the first time in my life I had a sense of being able to help other human beings."[30]

"A lot of it had to do with Mrs. Davis," Bill Harrison confirmed. "She was a firm believer that you treat others the way you want to be treated. She said if you learn nothing else from my class you'll walk away with that. We learned at that age a love of country, [to] respect the men and women in the service." He emphasized how the class's vantage point on Vietnam might make them different from other children. "We would never make fun of anyone who was in the service—a lot people did back then—it just taught us what America really is."[31]

Heightened empathy was likely reflected and reinforced by how generously soldiers reciprocated. "Those letters hit you in a way you can't explain," one GI observed. The pen pals lifted morale, and correspondence from Vietnam consistently articulated a mutual sense of responsibility. "It makes us feel good to know that there are more fighting for us back home than against us," another soldier penned. "I can't find any words in the dictionary to give you our thanks for the package you have sent us," a sergeant expressed. "We really appreciated very much for everything you are doing for us here. All of us are very proud to have a class like you to back us up here, and at least it makes us feel better to know that some one here back home, in the world of soft beds and white sheets is supporting us."[32]

Captain Harwood Nichols delivered a similar message in a letter Mrs. Davis read to the whole class in the spring of 1968. The company commander wrote,

> The news that reaches [us] here on the front is usually of a sordid and sensational nature and not one that leaves a warm spot in one's heart when he thinks of home. Your letters remind us that our country is growing and that the goodness of our memories is being passed on to others and what we hope we are fighting for is really there. The utter innocence and honesty of your children is enough to reconfirm any man's faith in the goodness of human nature and the future of America. Tell them to work hard and we will know that our hardships and losses are not in vain.[33]

"If people like the 4th grade class and Mrs. Davis," a serviceman noted, "were covered by the press as much as trouble makers, draft dodgers, and criminals you people would be making headlines every day. Thanks for being on my side." "Billy just remember no matter what people tell you," another GI added, "or whatever you see, or hear about your country and the men here helping to bring peace to this country, the United States is a great country and I hope you will grow up to be proud of it. I know I don't have to hope." Yet, like so much other adult thinking children were exposed to, there again was an accompanying air of dissonance in the letters. "I sure hope none of the boys," another soldier concluded, "have to go through an experience like this when they get older."[34]

Soldiers likewise sent tokens of appreciation Davis enshrined on or near the class bulletin board, a steady stream of insignia patches and pins, photographs, slides, newspapers, a bronze dog figurine picked up in Hue, and a hand-carved, wooden elephant. One GI shot a hole through a half-dollar, sent by a fourth-grader, because the boy wanted to wear it as a necklace. When a girl was hospitalized in the fall of 1968, the platoon passed the hat to send a dozen red roses from Hawaii, with a get well card fashioned from a C-Ration box. "If I come across some of those communist sandals the enemy wears," one soldier wrote, "I'll send you a set for a souvenir." Besides these tangible artifacts, storytelling made Vietnam come to life. "We were just kind of careful what we wrote to make sure it was fourth grade level," explained Sergeant Joe Meskaitis, dubbed Mosquito by Davis's class. "We just left the horror stuff back there." "I am in good health and spirits especially since yesterday was St. Patrick's Day," Brian O'Leary reported in March 1968. "Of course everyone wore green, not that it had anything to do with St. Patrick's Day because in the army we wear green 365 days out of the year." Students were also routinely introduced to sights and sounds peculiar to

Southeast Asia: nước chấm, an overpowering all-purpose fish sauce soldiers pronounced "nuke mom," which Vietnamese loved watching Americans attempt to eat; Montagnard tribesmen of the highlands, referred to as "mountain yards," in soldier's letters; mosquitos reputed to be man-eaters. "You know for a nickname like mine," Meskaitis once joked, "I think the buzzing bugs we have here in Vietnam would leave me alone—they don't!"[35]

In time, as pen pals became more comfortable with each other, letters got more descriptive. "Right now I have a dark tan from the waist up (There aren't too many chances to put on a bathing suit here)," First Lieutenant Robert H. Smith began one letter, which could have passed for a social studies lesson.

> Vietnam is a country with many different types of terrain. It is mountainous, flat, clear, jungles, big cities, very small cities, farms and everything. For the most part Vietnam is covered with jungles with trees as tall as 200 feet. There are many places that are very flat with no trees where they grow rice. The people are very short and usually very thin. Most of them are just a little taller than you people. Almost 100% of the people have black hair and it is usually straight. Very few of the children go to school and hardly anyone can write. The weather is different from yours. From Nov to May it is very hot and lots of moisture in the air and from May to Oct it rains almost every day. In June, July, and August it might rain 7 hours a day for a week at a time.

Smith's next passages presented the clearest pictures of soldiering any preadolescents were likely to receive.

> The life of a man in the infantry has a fairly hard life. He must carry with him all the equipment he needs to live on. He carries about 50 pounds of equipment with him at all times. Every man also carries a rifle and ammunition. On some days the men have to move long distances and walk through swamps and climb hills while other days they don't move at all. The longest I ever walked was 10 miles in one day. When it is raining the people sometimes stay wet for many days and when it is hot (over 100 degrees) the men are covered in sweat. There is always danger of being shot at but all in all it is not that bad. Each of the men does a lot of work each day and they usually go to sleep just after dark and get up before dawn. It may seem like a hard life but with everyone helping each other and all working together it is a bearable [*sic*]. The men are usually happy and as all people they only remember the good times. All in all I have enjoyed most of the time I have spent here in Vietnam. Many people have died here but all those who have died were doing a job that had to be done. Most of the people here don't want to be here but since they are they do the best job possible.[36]

A proposed field trip to Vietnam—a class idea augmented with the notion of bringing cats to Khe Sanh—never materialized, but the pen pals enthusiastically settled for several guest speakers. In March 1969, when the original cohort were in the fifth grade, twenty-three-year-old Joe "Mosquito" Meskaitis visited Yorkship Family School in fulfillment of an earlier promise to Lieutenant Moppert. Meskaitis had joined Fourth Platoon in early 1968 just after the first packages arrived, and during his tour he corresponded primarily with two students—Billy Harrison and Sandra Crissey—as well as Davis and the class. Sergeant "Mosquito's" arrival came as a surprise (ironically on a day Harrison was at home sick) and left students initially speechless. But excitement quickly overcame the class as they shouted his name and jockeyed for attention. Over the week he stayed in Camden (with the Davises), Meskaitis did a series of unplanned presentations for other classes—on water buffalo, snakes, tarantulas, Vietcong weaponry, and mountainside architecture—keeping students and teachers mesmerized. In testimony to the significance of his visit, one girl told Meskaitis she voluntarily sprayed her hair and wore her best shoes in his honor.[37]

Before war's end, Davis moved to Florida and transplanted the writing project to her new students there. Yorkship's pen pals, however, proved singular. "In over 41 years of teaching, I never had a class equal them," she noted. "They were just a bunch of unusual children."[38] Many, including Jerry Davis, valued the experience enough to keep letters and items safely tucked away, often in the same boxes used to store them as children. In 2014 Bill Harrison—Mosquito's pen pal—coordinated a donation of the collected letters and mementos to the Smithsonian's American History Museum. The resultant ceremony brought together a reunion of several 1967–68 Yorkship School fourth-graders and their families in Washington, D.C., most of whom had not seen each other or Davis in years.

No American communities were left wholly unaffected by Vietnam, nor any families with male members of draft age. The ubiquitous prospect of military service, a constant reminder with dramatic life consequences for everyone, permeated homes, forcing all family members regardless of age—even the most patriotic and civic minded—to seriously consider conventional responsibilities to one another, local communities, and the nation.[39] "The Vietnam War was discussed nightly for several reasons," a woman born in 1958 stressed. "One is that like most households we had one TV and the nightly news was something we all watched and of course was always a major topic on the news every day. Another reason the war was discussed was that I had an older brother that was graduating high school at the height of the Vietnam draft so the war took a very personal aspect in our household."[40] "Death counts on the nightly news" were one thing another woman born in 1960 recalled vividly, but her overriding thought on Vietnam as a child was, "Would my older brother be spared?"[41]

Because men remained draft eligible between the ages of eighteen and twenty-five, many remember how unsettling it was to helplessly watch adults sweat out a close relative's eight-year draft window. "What I do remember about the war was the draft numbers [Richard Nixon's "lottery" system of Selective Service begun in 1970]," a Minnesota woman born in 1958 clarified. "I have five older brothers. The first was in the U.S. Navy from 1960–1964, the second has asthma so he was exempt, the third is physically handicapped ... so he also was exempt, the fifth joined the U.S. Navy in 1971. But it was the fourth brother who every year anticipated the draft picks and how it would affect him. His birthday was always low on the list."[42] A child's sense of relief when a family member "missed" the draft seems to have been unequivocal. There is no available evidence to suggest youth looked unfavorably on relatives avoiding the draft through numerous deferments, conscientious objector status, or even extralegal means. Some witnessed protracted family debates, often causing generational friction, even ostracization, especially if one brother was already in service. Yet preadolescents appear to have been both incapable developmentally and unwilling emotionally to place abstract moral judgments over familial affection.

Ambiguity in parents' sense of duty in the abstract and pronounced reservations in offering their own sons to Vietnam, once again, complicated matters in a child's mind. Even fathers who were vocally proud to have raised sons willing to do their duty unlike those "long-haired commie hippies" protesting in the streets still outwardly expressed resentment over the prospect of their boys dying for nothing. "I think too that while my dad did serve in WWII," a woman born in 1958 believed, "the greater influence on their opposition to the war was the Korean War ('armed conflict') where they saw the futility of these types of armed actions."[43] "I had a cousin, who was older than me, who was drafted into the war," a Missouri man began when recalling how a specific conversation challenged his childhood conceptions of military heroism.

> He didn't have a father. His father died when he was a kid, my uncle. So my dad took on the job as his dad.... Before he left for the service, he came out to the house and dad sat him down and had a talk with him, and of course, I'm sitting there with big ears in the living room, listening to what they were saying. Just over and over, dad says "Jim, just get in there, do your job, shut your mouth, don't be a hero, and get home." Just get in, stay low, under the radar, stay low, do your time, and get out. He just said that over, and over, and over. He said "keep your eyes open, keep your mouth shut, keep your ears open, and just stay low."[44]

Waiting for draft calls still paled in comparison to the emotionally charged nature of home life when family members served a tour of duty. "Vietnam was a faraway place that didn't seem to concern me," a Pennsylvania woman explained of the intrusion, "until my oldest brother, right out of college and ROTC, was sent there. Everything changed—the war was brought home, in a big way." Childhood recollections on specific circumstances, such as, say, the actual departure, are inconsistent, ranging widely from proud to traumatized. A woman who was nine years old remembers the family driving her brother around town saying his goodbyes to friends and family before catching the bus, "sort of going around showing him off for the last time." A New Hampshire man described how "by 1970 my brother had trained in helicopter flying and was sent to Viet Nam to fly search and rescue duty. He had visited us before his deployment, and I was quite upset when he left. I remember spending a lot of time in the school councilor's [*sic*] office that day."[45]

The disrupting psychological burden of sending older brothers or cousins to war became the most prominent aspects of the Vietnam era for these preadolescents. While contemporary thinking on Vietnam may not have been statistically influenced positively or negatively by knowing someone overseas, childhood memories are notable for how often such thinking is understood to have directly shaped later adult judgments about Vietnam, war, and dissent. "What made it [my brother's leaving] worse," the New Hampshire man, born in 1958, clarified, "were the words of some vociferous anti-war types. They told me that they hoped he would be killed. To this day I have no use for this type of leftist, and nothing but contempt for them. Thankfully, he survived his tours, albeit with many stories, from that period." As a Missouri woman confided, "Vietnam protests were upsetting to me [because] my brother was fighting there, and not by choice. Even at a young age I could understand protesting the war, but not protesting, ridiculing, and mistreating the young men who were drafted into service."[46]

A Michigan woman's formative reminiscences of her brothers shipping out also reveal a key parental variable in how home-front children experienced separation. "I come from a family of seven children, six boys one girl . . . I am the girl," she explained. "Born in 1960, six out of seven, my two oldest brothers served in Nam, both came home whole. My strongest memories are of my Mother dissolving into tears each time she had to put them on a plane to serve. This was absolutely crushing for me. I thought my parents were rocks, we never saw them become that emotional."[47] Indeed, whereas children between six to twelve years old progressively find confidence in agency, preadolescents developmentally derive security in the knowledge that adults have thought matters through and are clearly in charge. Such uncomfortable perspectives on parents as these—not all powerful, reassuring and protective, but genuinely scared—intensified childhood distress.

"My mother was just terrified," an Oregon woman echoed of seeing her parents so out of character. "She tried to put on a brave front, but she was a nervous wreck during his entire tour. . . . Being 11 at the time," the woman, born in 1957, revealed, "I was far more interested in school and my friends, but I was concerned about the safety of my brother and I remember watching network television news every evening." Besides reduced length of service in Vietnam, television is the greatest difference in regard to family separation compared with World War II. Those network newscasts provided households a nightly window into Vietnam. Television was an unprecedented vantage point to follow the order of battles and draw a measure of tempered confidence (or skepticism) when enemy casualties far outnumbered American. Or a chance, in the most ardent hope of all children, to catch a glimpse of loved ones. "I recall the images broadcast on our new color TV," she continued, "especially the graphs on the Huntley-Brinkley Report, depicting the week's number of Vietcong vs. Americans casualties. They used the silhouette of a soldier, almost toy-like in appearance, and I'm not clear but I want to say that one soldier graphic equaled 10 deaths." She went on,

> My parents and grandparents were faithful followers of the evening news, and I remember as the weeks of my brother's tour dragged on, that the Viet Cong's casualties always far out-numbered ours. Even at 11 years old, I found that odd. I watched the news, I read the headlines and heard my family discussing the war and that graph simply did not make sense to me. While it's entirely possible the VC losses were consistently higher than the U.S., I wondered if someone was playing fast and loose with the figures and maybe padding them a bit. . . . For the first time in my life, I think I realized that America was not perfect, my parents didn't have all the answers and maybe, just maybe, everything wasn't always as it appeared to be.[48]

Television coverage also tended to present unvarnished reality with minimal parental censorship. Glued to the set themselves, mothers and fathers found it even more difficult to quash frank questioning concerning even the most dangerous and scariest aspects of what brothers and cousins might be going through. "My two brothers were there at the same time. My mother was a mess . . . about Vietnam," a Texas woman revealed. "I knew everything. My parents informed us about my two brothers everyday. Even the scary things."[49]

Worry marked the tempo of family life in countless homes. "My uncle was serving in the Vietnam War," a woman born in 1956 remembers, "and I worried about him every day and prayed that he would make it home safely. He made it home, but it was a long year." "I wish you could do something about the war," an eight-year-old Massachusetts girl wrote President Lyndon Johnson in 1967. "My cousin Philip is over in Vietnam. I love my cousin dearly and I say a pray [*sic*] for him every night. . . . Will you send me an address of some people fighting for our country. I have heard that there [*sic*] very lonely." Another anxious child writing to Johnson in December 1967 probably best articulated these emotions for other little brothers and sisters. "I'm only 7 years old," she began her holiday appeal to the "big daddy" in the White House. "That Chirtmas [*sic*] coming I should be happy. But Im not cause our family won't be together. My big brother is in Viet Namn. I am so scared something will happen to him I pray every night and while I'm praying I can hear mommy crying. Then I get scared. Oh please Mr Johnson please help me not to be scared. You can help me if youll [*sic*] only bring him home."[50]

Compared with Yorkship students, parents actually did most letter writing, faithfully composing several a week, if not daily. But at home children still eagerly assumed an active role in filling accompanying care packages with a GI's favorite foodstuffs, clothing, or newspapers from around the house. Entire families taped conversations about their day, played piano, or sang into cassette recorders, finally mailing them to the Army Post Office (APO). "I also recall my mother dictating into a tape recorder every day to them while they were gone, when the tape was full she would mail it out," the Michigan woman shared. "She also wrote to them each day. My oldest brother was drafted at age 20, returned 13 months later, then the next joined a year later so that he didn't get drafted, and served for three years. Both had experiences that to this day they do not speak of."[51]

It generally took seven to ten days for mail to reach the States from the field, so whole families waited intently for inconsistent correspondence and cassettes from Vietnam to arrive. Without World War II censorship, they devoured each page in order to glean precious detail about his whereabouts and safety. Many mothers likewise kept a large map of Vietnam hanging on the kitchen wall to track their sons' stationing throughout the country with homemade legends of stars, circles, and arrows. "I became familiar with all those strange names," a Pennsylvania woman reflected, "and faithfully watched the news with my parents every day. We anxiously waited for news; we never knew exactly where my brother was and letters from him were few and far between (sometimes they took weeks to arrive). It was one of the most agonizing years of my life. It was then that I really began to hate war and, in my opinion, very few wars since then have been justifiable."[52]

This is not to say life was always grim. Since preadolescents, particularly preschoolers, cannot emotionally sustain levels of concern and grief for as long as adolescents and adults, children sometimes incorporated elements of their Vietnam experience into familiar leisure and amusement routines more seamlessly than older siblings and parents. In one telling instance of preadolescent adaptability, a fourth-grade Girl Scout in Iowa became a local celebrity when her brother bought twenty cases of cookies during the annual sales drive in 1968. While taping the family's weekly letter to her nineteen-year-old brother, a marine serving his first tour in Vietnam, she had included in her portion a simple sales pitch: "Do you want to buy some Girl Scout cookies?" Several days later when the eleven-year-old got home from school, her mother greeted her with "Guess what?"—a surprise that initially left her assuming the worst. But quickly her mother allayed any fears by producing his newly arrived letter containing an order for twenty cases and a check for $120 ($100 for the cookies and $20 for shipping). "I just couldn't believe it," she told the local reporter. Besides ordering his favorite Mints (chocolate mint) and Savannahs (peanut butter), eight of her brother's buddies who heard his tape from home chipped in to order the rest, a total he guaranteed could have easily exceeded nine thousand more boxes if he would have asked around beyond his hooch. Regardless, the soldier's sales gave her more than enough "camper credit" to fund two whole weeks of Girl Scout summer camp.[53]

For Lisa Lehrer, a Minnesota woman who was nine years old when her brother left, Vietnam "happened" primarily around Sunday family meals on the farm. Since her mother's roast beef dinners after church had drawn family members and drop-in company for years, it seemed quite natural to record these gatherings on cassette tapes to supplement letters. The same setting doubled as the preferred venue when listening to his tapes sent from Vietnam. "My mom would put it on during suppertime," Ms. Lehrer, born in 1960 and one of three little sisters, remembered, "and we would forget the tape was even on. I'd listen back, and I recall hearing knives and forks clinking." More often than not her mom facilitated, either prompting participation at the table or else walking room to room after dinner holding out the microphone. "OK, who wants to talk to Danny?" "Now talk to Danny!" The family took turns addressing him as if in conversation, just as some individuals preferred to take the microphone into another room for privacy, a practice usually too awkward for the youngest because it seemed like talking to themselves.

On other afternoons Lehrer's mother laid the recorder on the table, essentially eavesdropping on the conversations. "So my brother was like a voyeur," she described. "There's one tape where my grandma is giving a recipe for rhubarb" and another "where my older cousin, a student at the University of Minnesota, is describing the campus protests, but emphasizing 'we just want [Danny] to come home.'" "Conversations were just things we would share at the dinner table about the things going on in our life on a daily basis," she clarified. Effectively the tapes were "a snap shot of normal life as if he was there around the table . . . which I think probably was nice for [my brother] to hear that life is—they're still on the farm—life kind of went on." In hindsight, she also now understands their beneficial nature on the home front as well. "I think with the tapes it gave my mom something to do," she reflected. "My mom was a go-getter, and I can only imagine because I have an eighteen-year-old boy now, and I can only imagine how she must have felt sending him off like that and just not knowing if he would come back. What you would do with that feeling? And so I think the tapes were one way where my mom felt like she could really do something."[54]

Correspondence to the APO only rarely contained heartfelt sentiments of the kind shared with President Johnson (or later historians). Children routinely covered the most mundane household and neighborhood goings-on: weather patterns, pet stories, how many teeth they had lost, Top 40 AM radio, baseball's pennant race, or how Captain Kirk escaped certain destruction (again) with only three minutes left in *Star Trek*. "I listened to the tapes over and over as a kid," the Minnesota woman recalled, "and he listened to them over and over in Vietnam." "I sang him a song once I learned at vacation bible school and talked about things that kids would talk to friends about." But "I never got like emotional because I just didn't get it," she admitted. The magnitude of his experiences

> didn't sink in to me . . . I said "I love you," "I hope you come home soon," it was kind of more of "I miss you thing." Listening was so much fun for me, kind of like reading a book, [but] you know I didn't really grasp the severity of what was going on or what my brother was facing at the time. I do recall watching the news and they would show footage of soldiers and I remember thinking "I wonder if I'll see Danny?" on the news running past in the jungle, but then you would see the body counts and it just didn't seem real to me at age nine.[55]

Soldiers, like those corresponding with Yorkship students, self-consciously kept story lines at age-appropriate levels for young relatives. Since letters and tapes arriving from Vietnam were meant to be read aloud by parents or listened to as a group, the chatty narratives highlighted extremes in rainfall and heat, strange flora and fauna (elephants and apes) in the part of Vietnam he was in, with a running update on how many days he was "short." Military matters were usually confined to slang terms and admiring descriptions of the awesome firepower America brought to bear, like the AC-47 gunship, which earned that particular aircraft the nickname Puff the Magic Dragon. Lisa Lehrer has kept a dozen tapes from her brother Daniel's tour between March 1970 and February 1971, and most demonstrate the intergenerational ways families listened and learned about Vietnam together. "Well, here comes a Cobra gunship," he recorded in 1970 over helicopter noises. "Now these babies are really something. You can hear it. Wow. Listen to that thing. Really smacking by. Boy, kinda nice when you hear those. Then you know you're safe. Charlie won't even stick his head up when he hears those babies because they really bring smoke."[56]

"What I hate is that it's starting to rain more," other tapes recounted over the course of several months.

> Never used to rain at all. Now it rains about every day, probably half hour or hour. But when you're in the field it rains just long enough to get soaking wet. Every night right before dark. Never fails, and then you have to spend all night laying in the mud with just a blanket. Wow. It's just, ugh. I hate it. But what do you do? [explosive sound]. The Saigon River runs right by our fire support base, maybe 800 meters from here. We're not supposed to, but the lieutenant gets a couple of us guys together, we grab our 16s and go swimming. It's kinda fun.... It's not all rough. But most of the time it is.
>
> Oh, one thing that will interest you a lot, dad, is the people over here, they don't use cars. There's very, very few cars in Vietnam. Once in a while you might see one, a real rich person might have a Dodge or Plymouth. The people around here, everybody rides motorcycles. Yamaha. Suzuki. Small bikes... But what they do—they pile the whole damned family on bikes. You wouldn't believe it. Here you see a bike coming along and you look and see one person, behind him two little kids, behind him will be mama, older sister. They get the whole family on one of those little buggers. How they do it I don't know but they sure do it. Not only that, they use them for a truck. They use those scooters—they'll pile four big bags of rice on the back fender and they're just balancing. The bike can hardly move. It's got to pick up momentum to get going. It's really funny.[57]

Besides sending unit insignia patches, soldiers shipped packages ordinarily containing handmade gifts from Vietnam—carved wooden and bronze animals, beaded jewelry, or colorfully dressed dolls—adding an intercontinental element to birthdays and Christmas. And while simple folk gifts may not have immediately overshadowed store-bought presents, some eventually became quite sentimentalized. Lisa Lehrer remembers one particularly exceptional parcel from Vietnam—a reel-to-reel stereo player bought in Saigon—she credits with helping "shape her beliefs" about Vietnam. She confided,

> Well then my girlfriend and I would get those reels out, and we figured out how to play it, and I'm sure my brother would have just died knowing that but we would like put on the Woodstock one [the 1970 album *Woodstock: Music from the Original Soundtrack and More*], the Woody Guthrie one with "1, 2, 3, what are we fightin' for?, oh I don't give a damn . . ." [actually Country Joe and the Fish's "I-Feel-Like-I'm-Fixin'-to-Die Rag" and "'The Fish' Cheer"] I remember playing that, I remember the words to that and oh kind of naughty, "give me an F, give me a U . . ." kind of went that direction and I remember we looked at each other and went "ooohhhh" like it was forbidden, but we would play his tapes, and so even though I was kind of at the end of that sixties era, the music, the things from the sixties really resonate with me, but like my brother is eleven years older than me, but it's the music that he and my sisters were listening to that really resonates with me.[58]

"There's something," the Minnesota woman concluded, "I don't want to say spiritual, but there's something that ties me to that era even though I was so young." Despite her inability to comprehend her brother's service as a preadolescent, when Lisa Lehrer listens to the tapes with a critical adult ear, the Vietnam experience comes together, and the music is put into proper context. The tapes are "just such an interesting picture of every part of the war because you hear it from both sides, it just really paints the whole picture for you." The last cassette her brother sent home is particularly powerful for its tone. "The tape is so emotional to me because you can tell that he's seen death," she explained of this turning point in her brother's depiction of war. "He came back from Cambodia, you can hear it in his voice, it's almost haunting."

"Well, the pointman saw two gooks and they fired, fired back," the cassette begins with her brother (by this time a sergeant) walking the family through the actions that were hardening him. "Everybody hit the ground, and the gooks left or crawled away from right there. And everybody got in line and we started opening up, reconning the area by firing the 60s. . . . By that time the whole company came over there and everybody was firing in there. And we thought, 'Well, they're either dead or gone,' so we got up and started sweeping the area. . . . We got about 20 feet from the bunker and these two gooks pop up from the bunker. God. Augh! And a couple of guys got hit pretty bad." Later, he admitted that he, too, had received the Purple Heart for shrapnel wounds in the leg, but it is clear he was losing interest in telling his family about Vietnam.

> Everyone was real nervous. Glad we're out of there. We got so everyone couldn't wait to get back to Vietnam! Compared to, between Vietnam and Cambodia, wow, there's no comparison. Like, we used to think Vietnam was bad when we'd

> run into five or six gooks, maybe once a month. Well, heck when you run into 10, 12, 15, or 25 of them every day, about three times a day, wow man, I was glad to get back here. I'm not even kidding. Suckers are all over up there. That's a haven for them. So that's why I'm glad to get back to Vietnam. But I'll be glad to leave here to get back to the world too, in six months, if that ever comes.[59]

When the day finally did come for relatives to get back, for all the anticipation, it is perhaps surprising how often homecomings turned out to be rather forgettable in a child's life, or when memorable, how anticlimactic. Many who contacted the author with recollections thought older brothers, uncles, and cousins effectively just reappeared, and from their stories it seems likely this was actually by design. One woman, born in 1960 in the Great Lakes region, recalled,

> I also remember vividly, when my brother-in-law returned from the war, we only received a quick phone call one day out of the blue. He was basically dropped off at a disclosed location and we went as a family to pick him up. No fanfare, no welcome home . . . just dropped off in a random location by himself. I also remember he returned in street clothing because it wasn't safe to wear your uniform for fear our country would do hateful things to you as a soldier. Even though he was drafted and had no choice but to serve, he was still in fear of being considered a "war monger."[60]

As Lisa in Minnesota related, "we knew when he was on American soil and that was comforting, but beyond that I don't even recall him coming home. . . . That's weird too I don't recall so much, because you would think I would remember. I know that my mom had wanted to throw a party or something and I think my brother did not want that, so maybe that was part of it. It would have probably been one of those things where my mom would have gotten all the relatives together and I think he just couldn't do it."[61] What began with childhood questions over her brother's unwillingness to be "welcomed home" properly crystalized by early adolescence into a sustainable skepticism. "Yeah, I think as I got a little bit older, I was kind of questioning the war," she continued.

> What are we doing there, you know he could have so easily lost his life, and for what, and I remember thinking, well first of all my brother would not talk about it at all when he came home for years and then he had these medals, he had a Purple Heart, and he got a Silver Star and a Bronze Star and he left them at our house, he never, he didn't take them with him, like he didn't want them. And it was always kind of curious to me, but my mom said, "Well, he doesn't want them, he's not proud." Well, I don't really know how to explain it. . . . I'm just anti-war now.[62]

The vast majority of these Vietnam-era children remember some variation of a happy ending to what a Pennsylvania woman had characterized as "one of the most agonizing years of my life." Yet for a sizable number, gnawing uncertainty culminated with the worst news imaginable. During the war, 1,400,000 Americans had someone in their family wounded and 275,000 had a family member killed. "Vietnam became more personal to me when my cousin went in 1967 and was killed," a Missouri woman underscored. "My dad and my uncle were vets of WWII so there was a pride in having him fight for his country but there was also a resentment knowing he died and people said it was for nothing. Four more people I was close to died in the war. I remember not wanting any to die but also didn't understand why."[63] Having familial involvement in the war may not have had an appreciable influence on views toward Vietnam, but in so many households where preadolescents had never experienced death, the war represented their initial socialization to loss. Often school-age children were away when parents received word, returning in the afternoon to find parents, neighbors, or people from church in their homes. The sight of mothers crying on the couch surrounded by friends while fathers clutched written military notification conveyed a nonverbal message. Later, churches might hold special services or mass attended by the serviceman's neighborhood, high school, and maybe college friends with extended family coming to pay their respects.[64]

In expressing anger, boys sometimes fantasied about getting out of school early to enlist in the military and avenge the fallen in Vietnam. One Georgia woman born in 1960 discovered new meaning and a measure of comfort in her parents' favorite Peter, Paul and Mary records when her cousin lost his life in Vietnam. "I absolutely hated the war," she revealed, "from my cousin being killed, overhearing my parents and seeing the news. . . . My feeling at the time was 'Why can't the President just stop it and bring the boys home?' We said our prayers every night and prayed an extra prayer for 'all the boys in Vietnam.' After my favorite cousin had gotten killed in Vietnam, I would play 'Where Have all the Flowers Gone?' and '500 Miles' [from the 1962 album *Peter, Paul and Mary*] on the stereo and cry and cry."

> Where have all the soldiers gone?
> Gone to graveyards every one
> When will they ever learn?

"Consequentially," she reflected, "I think this is exactly why I am so anti-war now. I am still pretty liberal and am against the [Middle Eastern wars] now. Just feel like we are there for the wrong reasons."[65]

Yet it is equally useful to consider how experiencing childhood loss can be, in fact, relative. Even when family members returned, and bonds of affection were renewed, Vietnam merely postponed adult lives and family cycles, whereas the war stole nearly two valuable—irreplaceable—childhood years. This remains an important distinction to make. Regret and resentment over older loved ones missing out on milestone Little League home runs or school plays are common recollections. But the sense of Vietnam's cost is sometimes much broader: soldiers not being able to share in the once-in-a-lifetime ages when kids really get to be kids. Like so many, Lisa Lehrer still ponders this uniquely preadolescent casualty of the Vietnam War. "The interesting thing was when my brother went to Vietnam I was nine but when he came home I would have been more like eleven," she stressed. "So I had kind of changed, probably going through early puberty. When he left he really used to roughhouse with me, but when he came back he really didn't know how to act. I think he just really didn't know how to handle me. I remember kind of having my feelings hurt a little bit about that.... Those years were just gone forever."[66]

Without any firsthand associations, the POW-MIA bracelet phenomenon allowed children a sense of agency to create fictive relationships, forging powerful and surprisingly durable emotional bonds with servicemen. As one popular aspect of a growing campaign to bring the plight of those listed as prisoner of war or missing in action to public attention, these nickel-plated and copper bracelets—engraved with a captured or missing man's name, rank, branch of service, and date of loss—gave youth "a guy" of their own to wonder about, worry over, pray for, and commemorate. The bracelets were the brainchild of college students Carol Bates, Kay Hunter, and Steve Frank, and their adult adviser Gloria Coppin in Voices in Vital America (VIVA). A conservative, Los Angeles–based student organization, VIVA searched for positive ways to support U.S. soldiers that might also counterbalance campus anti-war protests. In 1969 television personality, veteran, and soon-to-be politician Bob Dornan introduced VIVA members to both the POW/MIA issue and, just as importantly, the notion of wearing a bracelet as a constant reminder of their sacrifices. During those years before the National League of POW/MIA Families, when efforts to publicize the POW issue were still being carried out ad hoc by individual relatives, this VIVA chapter at what is today California State University, Northridge adopted the cause as their own. And in the plain brass bracelet Dornan wore—a gift to GIs from Montagnard tribesmen signifying solidarity—VIVA found a *raison d'être*.[67]

Having virtually no budget initially, they worked with a Santa Monica engraver willing to craft a limited run of 1,200 bracelets, made from materials donated by Gloria Coppin's husband, for a percentage of any proceeds the group might realize from sales. In actuality, VIVA had doubted whether anyone besides college students would be interested in wearing such unassuming bands, so the original plan was to seek donations and distribute them on campus for free. But when financial backing failed to materialize—members had even contacted Ross Perot and Howard Hughes—the decision was made to sell two versions: nickel-plated for students and copper aimed at adults. Only name, rank, and date of loss were inscribed at first because Bates and Coppin could not think of anything else to include. Prices were based on the cost of a student movie ticket in 1970—$2.50—with the copper bands going for $3.00 due to their perceived medicinal value helping overcome "tennis elbow."[68]

Although prototypes appeared in the fall, VIVA's POW/MIA bracelet campaign officially kicked off on Veterans Day, November 11, 1970, with a Hollywood hotel press conference. The thin metal bracelets immediately swept the nation, touching a nerve transcending binary politics of hawk and dove. "There was something about a specific name being on them," Carol Bates Brown, who served as national chairwoman, later explained. "People made a personal connection—'I'm watching out for this guy.'" The bracelets, to be worn until the POW or MIA's status had been officially determined, or the men returned home, allowed Americans a means of separating feelings toward policy makers from feelings toward soldiers. "Even those people who were against the Vietnam War could identify with us being held captive there—the torture and the mistreatment," former POW John "Jack" Ensch observed. "Nobody could argue that wasn't wrong. I think it was a collective learning experience for our society."[69]

Through distribution alliances with POW/MIA organizations, whereby local POW/MIA family groups sold VIVA bracelets on consignment, orders snowballed from 500 a week to 1,000, then 10,000 a week, and eventually at one point reaching 12,000 *per day*. At the height, Midway Stamping and Die Works, the engraver, employed 120 mostly college students and Vietnam veterans working around the clock. Steve Frank and Carol Bates dropped out of school to administer the program full time. Celebrities ranging from Bob Hope and John Wayne to Dennis Hopper proudly wore them, as did Sonny and Cher on their *Comedy Hour* television show. Sammy Davis Jr., Flip Wilson, and Princess Grace of Monaco found common cause with models and designers in the New York fashion scene. During the 1972 presidential campaign, bracelets even made strange bedfellows of candidates Wallace, McGovern, and Nixon. When John Ensch was imprisoned at the infamous Hanoi Hilton that August, he brought news to fellow POWs—tapped in code between cells—of how millions of Americans were wearing bracelets with their names on them. Indeed, by the time VIVA closed up shop in 1976, nearly five million bracelets were in circulation, and with those profits the group had disseminated innumerable brochures, bumper stickers, and buttons furthering POW/MIA awareness.[70]

Parents or older siblings usually gifted bracelets to preadolescents, either for Christmas and birthday presents or spontaneous purchases from vendors at local fund-raising events. Some often did so because children had expressed curiosity about what was around the adult's own wrist. What is this? How do you know this person? Others already familiar with the bracelet's message asked out of sincere desires to commemorate, frequently choosing men from their own state. "One night on the TV body count there was just one soldier killed that day," a rural Georgia woman born in 1960 who wore a band explained. "I remember looking at my dad and saying 'wow, just one, that's not bad, is it?' But then I thought how this was a name, a person. Vietnam became more personal to me, it became more real. I didn't think of it as political at the time."[71] "I knew that there were people who were for the war and people who were against it and that people were being killed, and MIA and POW, from TV," a West Virginia woman born in 1958 recalled. "I think probably what I felt then is different from what I think now.... I have a different perspective on it now. I don't think necessarily it was the right war for us to be in, but then I just remember thinking I was sad. My main object was just to support the person, and just to think about him and lift his name up, if that makes any sense."[72]

"Having people said to be missing was deeply frustrating, and rang an oddly deep chord in me," a Queens, New York, woman born in 1958 shared. "I was hopeful that wearing a bracelet would somehow allow a prisoner, or someone 'missing' to have an ally. Someone looking for them even if symbolically, demonstrative that he was/they were being sought after, and simply thought of... supported, 'looked for,' mattered ... even if from afar.... It seemed our society was mad at all serving soldiers," she continued, touching on this childhood agency. "Even then I felt it was way too broad.... Even as a youngster I liked to 'do' something about that which I felt might be 'unfair' or needed a voice/action. However at the tender age that I was during all that, I couldn't actually do much re: the war. Wearing a bracelet was an 'action' that I felt strongly about and was glad for the opportunity."[73]

Childhood meanings drawn from POW/MIA bracelets were amplified when preadolescents also had a close relative overseas. A twelve-year-old girl from Michigan composed a verse (set to the tune of "'Twas the Night Before Christmas") for the school talent show based on her empathy for POW/MIA families and separation within her own family. "I am a child of the sixties as I was born in 1960," she explained about how the song won a blue ribbon and thereafter has remained a keepsake. "I remember clearly the Vietnam era. My brother-in-law was drafted to serve in the Vietnam war just after he and my sister were married. I remember it as a sad, turbulent time, both in our household and in our city. . . . At the time I wrote this, most of my friends and I were also collecting the metal bracelets of MIA or POW soldiers."

'Twas the day before the next day, and all through the camp base
Not a soldier was stirring, you couldn't see a face
The men were all snuggled deep down in their beds
While waiting for the next day, which I assumed they would dread

When all of a sudden, with a boom and a flash
They arrived at their windows, just in time to see a crash
The fire on the crest, of the new fallen snow
Gave a luster of death to the men below [as an adult I now realize that snow didn't make sense]

While I was watching up in an airplane
I could see them all struggling, trying to rescue in vain
And then I saw one man, running about
His buddy was killed, as least that's what he'd shout

I tell you, this war was getting them down
You'd never see a smile, you'd just see a frown

Then one happy day, a letter came in
It said, "Hallelujah" to all of the men
The war was over, no worry, no fuss
Don't you wish that could happen to us?[74]

More often, though, in truth, children requested bracelets out of innocent, social imitation. They became fashionable and popular, a grade school and junior high fad, really, to be collected and worn—sometimes up to six an arm—with accompanying VIVA "accessories" like the frowning smiley-face button reading "P.O.W.s Never Have a Nice Day." Once around the wrist, however, the POW/MIA bracelet's grip took hold. Well beyond being merely a favorite piece of jewelry, these metal bands sentimentalized bonds of protective affection toward a stranger so far removed from their pleasant suburban life, a man precious few would ever really know. Besides his rank and formal, given name (unaware of what "for-short" or nicknames he actually went by) the only thing wearers knew was a date expressed in "3-11-65" format (the day Major Richard D. Smith went down in South Vietnam on the bracelet I have worn since childhood). Yet that was enough. For children still achieving abstract thought, "having" a soldier was Vietnam's entry point into their lives, not through any rational process but by egocentrically cultivating an emotional, and mostly imaginative, personal connection. Children chose accordingly to never take his name band off until he came home (requiring an application of clear nail polish to the underside lest your skin turn green). Sometimes commitment met hard childhood realities: forgoing swimming when pool rules dictated no jewelry; removing it to play basketball in PE class; or feeling utter devastation when you accidently lost it at the park.[75] Wearing the band meant commitment, a sanguine pledge ensuring Vietnam was never too far away, a daily reminder, buttressed by nightly prayer.[76]

"As a devout young Catholic and an altar boy," a Texas man who was twelve at the time shared, "I always included Sergeant Fitts in my prayers at Mass.... The bracelet always made me feel that I was somehow spiritually linked to him."[77] Many recall being preoccupied with concern for the man's circumstances, constantly speculating on whether he was hurting, unhappy, or lonely, and the same held true for his family. Does he have a wife or children who miss him? Since he was lost in December, did they celebrate Christmas this year? Hard to believe he has been missing almost a year. "I prayed for him. But it wasn't just prayers," a Washington State woman clarified. "I talked to John, imagining he could hear me: 'I'm pulling for you, John. Be strong.' One night I got a checkerboard out, set it up on my bed and said, 'OK, John, we're going to play checkers now.'"[78] Another woman from Illinois remembered how whenever she felt stressed, worried, or nervous, she rubbed his engraved name for comfort, which always seemed to help. "I thought (as did my family)," the Georgia woman born in 1960 said, "that I was a little strange to have such an emotional attachment to someone I never met but from reading the messages posted here ["Letters and Notes from Those That Wear the Bracelets"], I realize that I am just one of thousands."[79]

While hoping every day for a safe homecoming, youth eagerly searched weekly or daily newspaper lists of newly released soldiers and swapped status information with each other. One New Jersey woman born in 1958 still associates the war's last year with her bracelet, searching with her friends for the "names of returning POWs ... to see if 'our guys' had returned" and feeling "elated that 'my guy' had, indeed, come home."[80] She later elaborated, "That was our connection to that war that made it personal for us. I hate war today, but I don't know that it has anything to do with that bracelet. I think if anything the bracelet served to make me aware at a younger age that war has repercussions and that these guys were missing, that there were guys who were POWs. I don't know how aware I would have been, or how much I would have cared about it, if it wasn't for that bracelet."[81]

Those who received literature with their bracelet might also remember a clearinghouse where owners could send letters to the POW/MIA's family, and a few corresponded with the serviceman's children. "We just did this as something we could do in our own little way," a California woman born in 1959 explained. "I was too young to have a good understanding of what it was all about," but every week, in a nail-biting ritual, she and three older sisters (all wearing bracelets) consulted the *Los Angeles Times* to see if their boys were listed among the dead. And each week she breathed a sigh of relief when his name was not there. After her mother finally discovered an article listing him as being a POW, the girl kept the clipping, buoyed by knowledge that, although captured and facing unimaginable hardships, he had a home, Michigan, a real place where loved ones were surely counting the days until his return as well.[82]

Sometimes optimistic children harbored illusions about attending their guy's homecoming, daydreaming of traveling great distances to ultimately hand the bracelet over to its rightful owner. "I thought of him, imagined what he looked like, and had a fantasy during the time frame that the war ended," an East Coast woman remembers, "that he would be in one of the first groups of returnees, and that he would be stepping down from the plane(s)."[83]

Another California woman, twelve years old when she received a bracelet in her Christmas stocking in 1972, recalls feeling optimism on the eve of Operation Homecoming when American POWs were repatriated over a period of weeks between February and April 1973. "I was really excited," she later told a reporter. "I read the paper that came with it. And I just thought. I'm going to keep it on until he comes home.... They showed footage of the soldiers coming off the planes, and I always thought wherever he's flying into I'm going to be there and I'm going to give him my bracelet and I'm going to put it on his arm. That's how I always pictured it," she said. "But that wasn't meant to be."[84]

By the late 1970s, when most Americans resigned themselves to the reality that everyone who could come home alive already had come home, nearly all children took off their bracelets. Many mailed theirs with a brief note of thanks to repatriated men or their families at some point. Etiquette dictated one should never send the bracelet before a complete accounting had been made. When doing so many snapped it in two pieces, sending one half and keeping the other. Those continuing to wear the band in peacetime did so until it broke naturally or was lost. Sometimes bands were replaced with two or three incarnations bearing the same name. If the worn engraving became all but illegible, a few started wearing their bracelet only on special occasions, particularly Veterans Day, Father's Day, and the Fourth of July, or certain times of year between Memorial Day and Veterans Day. For other wearers, always eager to share the bracelet's stories if someone asked, the date of loss became something of a minor holiday in itself, the one time a year to put the bracelet back on in solemn remembrance. The rest, however, mostly tucked the bands away in shoeboxes and jewelry boxes with other childhood souvenirs and ephemera. And there they stayed for decades without definitive answers or closure—surviving countless moves from childhood bedrooms to college dorms, apartments, and homes in various cities—until the Vietnam Veterans Memorial opened in 1982. Moreover, the computer age sparked a renaissance for the old POW/MIA bracelets in the twentieth century's final years.[85]

CHAPTER 5

Mom Tried to Make It for Us Like He Wasn't Even Gone

FATHER SEPARATION AND REUNION

> My father is in Viet Nam. You might have seen him when you were there.
>
> —**FOURTH-GRADE GIRL TO PRESIDENT LYNDON B. JOHNSON, NOVEMBER 1966**

"As a small child I was very well aware that a War was going on," the daughter of a career airman, born in 1963, confided.

> My parents would always talk about things after we were sent to bed. But, our living space was so small that I could hear everything they talked about. At the age of 6, while living at Grissom Air Force Base [Indiana], I have my first memory of the effects of "War." There was a family that lived across the street from us. We used to go over there on the weekend for homemade ice-cream. When the dad went to Vietnam we would go with my Dad when he would help the mom with mowing, fixing house problems, etc. One night while in bed I heard Dad talking about our neighbor. His wife was notified that her husband had been captured and was a prisoner of war. I cried a lot during this time because I knew at some time my dad was going to be deployed.
>
> I asked my Dad many years later about our neighbor. He told me, with tears in his eyes, that the man did not survive. The big shock for him was that I remembered ALL of it.[1]

When daddies went to war, holes left in households by their continued absence deepened the cumulative family crisis, creating a much wider array of psychological and emotional displacements for preadolescent children. For career military families, separation from father—routinely overseas—was normative. Cruises and training were built into routine family cycles, so deployment in Southeast Asia was not necessarily understood as drastically outside a child's conditioned experience. When fathers were citizen-soldiers—draftees or enlistees—a tour(s) in Vietnam potentially altered the fundamental realities of childhood. These disruptive trends stemming from father separation—to include reintegration, the prisoner of war or missing in action experience, and bereavement—will be explored throughout the next chapters. Before examining such changes to a child's physical and social environment, though, it is useful to briefly consider the Vietnam War's statistical impact on marriage and birth patterns, family arrangements, and the roles of young women.

Once Lyndon B. Johnson brought U.S. power to bear in the cause of South Vietnamese independence, America's military buildup required substantial increases in draft calls, which jumped from 112,386 in 1964 to 230,991 in 1965, before peaking in 1966 at 382,010. Consequently, for the nearly 27 million baby boomer men who came of draft age between 1964 and 1973, the prospect of military service in Vietnam became the generation's preeminent consideration, informing very personal decisions about the timing and direction of career, marriage, and fatherhood. And, again, because the nature of selective service initially left men eligible between the ages of eighteen and twenty-five, life choices were subject to this tremendous uncertainty for the extent of an eight-year draft window. Around one-third of the armed forces in the Vietnam era were indeed draftees—1,857,304—and for untold numbers, conscription conceivably meant delaying by choice, or having military service postpone, whether to become husbands or fathers until later in their twenties. Early in the decade, 23 was the average age of an inductee, but as the war went on it fell to 21.6 by 1964 and 20.6 in 1966. Those with small children already may well have allowed anxiety over the impending letter from Selective Service to influence parenting styles. Moreover, since most draftees went to the army for two years—one spent in training and for 648,500 soldiers another year's tour in Vietnam—those families also experienced a disruptive absence. The remaining two-thirds of the military were enlistees, men who joined as a vocational choice or sense of patriotic duty, but frequently as a conscious alternative to being drafted. Increased enlistments corresponded positively to rising calls for inductions as draft-eligible young men—usually with higher levels of education—preferred to enlist in order to enter the military under more favorable circumstances.[2]

The preponderance of draft-eligible men avoided the military, however, by a convoluted number of legal and extralegal means inherent to the Selective Service system. Local draft boards classified all eighteen-year-old registrants as either available for service (1-A), exempted, or deferred. Those designated 1-A received preinduction physical and psychiatric examinations, and on passage they were required to report for service when the board determined who would be called in order to meet the Defense Department's monthly draft requests. Failure on any of the test's physical, mental, psychiatric, or moral components brought exemptions to slightly more than five million young men. Most commonly, potential draftees pursued a series of deferments to either delay or permanently avoid conscription, principally on the grounds of education, occupation, hardship, marriage, or fatherhood. Prior to Vietnam, these various deferments operated as the Selective Service's Cold War method of allocating human resources by utilizing the draft to "channel" manpower into civilian and military occupations deemed most important to national interest. For instance, male college students making progress toward their degree at a four-year institution of higher education were deferred from service until turning twenty-four. Even during the Kennedy years, when draft calls remained relatively low, the huge number of baby boomers easily outpaced the military's demand, and Selective Service's generous deferments continued to be quite manageable.[3]

Vietnam strained the system, quickly producing draft shortfalls necessitating adjustments to tighten up channels, which in turn appears to have produced several unintended consequences for family formation patterns and the timing of births. Marriage had briefly been a sufficient condition for deferment starting in 1963, but in the summer of 1965 Johnson signed an executive order eliminating those deferments for men who were married after August 26. What had been a noticeable trend in hastily arranged weddings accelerated as young sweethearts quickened their pace down the aisle ahead of the deadline. Nonetheless, Selective Service removed marriage deferments entirely two months later, announcing instead that all *childless* married men of draft age (regardless of when the nuptials took place) were still subject to the draft. Only husbands with dependent children now qualified for this paternity deferment. Together, these two middecade measures, coming unexpectedly but widely publicized thereafter, incentivized marriage and, later, the conception of firstborn children for self-interested men willing to manipulate the system with this draft avoidance strategy. There are, after all, statistics suggesting that similar to educational deferments—college attendance rates for men increased relative to women almost 7 percent by the late 1960s—marriage and paternity deferments positively affected decisions to start families. Marriage rates for twenty- and twenty-one-year-olds rose immediately by 10 percent between 1963 and 1965.

What is more, while the overall birth rate among young American woman was already decreasing rapidly, the number of firstborn deliveries to women in their early twenties jumped by 7 percent in the summer of 1966, roughly nine months after the policy changes. The year 1966 was also when fatherhood, marital, and hardship deferments were outnumbering student deferments almost two to one. As yearly draft calls began steadily declining in 1967, and family deferments were finally replaced by Richard Nixon's "lottery" overhaul of Selective Service in 1970, the Vietnam draft's causal relationship with marriage, and the number of children these families had (or subsequent birth spacing), becomes more ambiguous, just one of several cultural variables driving birth rates further downward by the early seventies. Still, any significant effects the draft had statistically on the fertility of women whose age approximated draft-eligible spouses would have also carried important consequences in the lives of their young children, including maternal education, mother and child health, child care provisions, and maternal participation in the job market.[4]

The Department of Defense did not compile data on family characteristics of servicemen in Vietnam, but contemporary studies suggest as many as 18 percent of white children and 28 percent of African Americans had a father or brother in the war.[5] Taking into account the young age of draftees and enlistees, a significant number of these children were preschool age with limited cognition or subsequent memories. They understood only that somewhere out there in the distance, an unknown man mentioned them affectionately, while requesting news of their exploits, in handwritten letters mothers faithfully read out loud.[6] For them, reunion and reintegration can be far more impactful than father separation.

Nonetheless, in families where fathers did serve, Vietnam was a perpetual and ominous presence, an ordeal testing each member's resilience, adaptability, persistence, and patience, regardless of age. Women, trying to compensate, adjusted personal orientations to revolve around preadolescent youth.[7] Separation and fear dominated individual lives as well as the interdependent, transactional nature of familial relationships. Many families experienced pronounced turmoil, while others faced only the most obvious hardships of not having a father around. Virtually all mothers and children dealt with their unique wartime situations through improvised trial and error, in their own ways striving to maintain stability and a sense of continuity with both subtle modifications and complex role adjustments to domestic lifestyles. Some families, just like some members, coped relatively better or worse.[8]

In these fundamental aspects, Vietnam-era families faced home-front issues common to other Americans in previous twentieth-century wars. Two relevant features with direct bearing on childhood, however, set Vietnam apart. Despite a recognized need for father figures in the successful navigation of early childhood cognitive, social, and emotional development for both boys and girls, the typical father separation in Vietnam was shorter in duration and more predictable given servicemen's predetermined DEROS (Date Eligible for Return from Overseas). Having a father in Southeast Asia for a year-long tour—twelve months for the army and typically thirteen months for marines—was still a crucial developmental factor, especially in the lives of school-age children who had known their dad before he left. During these last years when American children were raised by predominantly youthful parents abiding by well-defined, traditional gender roles—reliable, breadwinning fathers providing material support side by side with energetic and focused "stay-at-home" mothers—the man of the house was the parent still primarily associated with perpetuating such cultural ideals. Cold War–era researchers pointed to the paternal role in teaching delayed gratification, representing the principles and rules of society, and providing a masculine role model informing boys' and girls' sex role development (sexual identity formation in boys and the ability to develop healthy heterosexual relationships in girls).[9]

Conceivably there would be consequences from his absence. Yet some of the most troubling developmental effects scholars identified in home-front children during World War II—when fathers were gone thirty-three months on average—either did not appear or were greatly abbreviated. There is, for instance, little empirical evidence that paternal separation due to Vietnam, and the subsequent growth of maternal influence in the lives of preschool boys, produced the same levels of identification with mothers that led post–World War II experts to warn of feminizing tendencies and even sexual identity confusion.

Emotional difficulty is the other relevant variance. Whereas money was ordinarily the greatest concern for war wives in the past, Vietnam-era spouses felt the additional, special strain of a contentious war. Doubt and confusion about why America was fighting in Vietnam only deepened natural anxiety and fear. Comparatively, the country had no unity of spirit, nor was sacrifice borne equally. Civilians were not engaged in a collective war effort and had little stake beyond their own opinion. Outside insular military bases and surrounding communities, where pro-military and conservative views prevailed, attitudes toward America's war effort were at odds. At best people seemed largely indifferent, and from a family's vantage point it often looked like the only Americans concerned about Vietnam were those speaking out against it, up to and including a figure nearly synonymous with proper Cold War motherhood: Dr. Benjamin Spock. Watching protesters on TV and reading about anti-war marches in newspapers proved troubling, as did hearing questions of honest dissent from coworkers and friends. "I don't think we should be there," a navy wife told *Parents' Magazine* in 1967. "People don't talk too much about why we're fighting, but I don't know anyone who's sure we're right." Such disaffection bred bitterness, and a family's ability to function frequently rested on a woman's capacity to manage simmering resentment.[10]

The stories of one midwestern mother left at home with a four-year-old son in the early seventies speak directly to accommodating Vietnam's unpopularity with preadolescent thinking, and her own views as a twenty-four-year-old woman. "Yes, [my son] knew my feelings about the war—that it was wrong and we shouldn't be there—but I tried to make that a different deal," she reflected. "All the people he was ever around were anti-war people, those were the only adults he knew, and they were verbal, plus I couldn't help the TV being on. Even at that time he was aware that there were people who were very opposed to what was going on. He would worry, how could he help it?" So the key, she reasoned, was to disconnect people's opposition from his father being in Vietnam. "I made sure he separated his feelings for his dad from the war. 'Your daddy has to be there because the government is making him,' I explained, 'he has no choice, he didn't choose to go over there.' I always said 'he's a hero, he's doing good work, he's a super hero that nothing bad can happen to.' I had to. That was his dad, he loved him, so I couldn't have him associating dad with what people were saying about the war being immoral or soldiers being baby killers."

She specifically remembers shaping innocent questioning to satisfy this end.

> We saw Vietnam happen on TV every night for the first ten minutes of the news in the kitchen, people getting shot and loaded onto helicopters, and once he asked, "Well, Daddy won't kill anybody, will he?" I said no, he flies the helicopter that helps people, he brings wounded people into his helicopter and he takes them to safety, he takes Vietnamese, too—little children, wives, mothers, and old people—but not men because they don't know who the Vietcong is. And he knew what a Vietcong was, that they were the bad guys. He was curious one time when soldiers were going through the jungle, and I heard him quietly reassuring himself by saying out loud, "But, Daddy doesn't do that." "No, you're right," I said, "your dad's not there, he's always up in a helicopter . . ." and then, of course, we'd see the helicopters go down and crash. Another time he saw guns on helicopters and asked me if Daddy carried a gun. I said, "Well, I think so, they have to. If a bad guy comes up and Daddy has good people on the helicopter he'll have to protect them." My little boy also asked me once if Daddy dropped bombs, and I said no, but he pointed to fire coming out an aircraft. "Does Daddy do that?" "No," I answered, "he doesn't do anything like that."

"Always keeping it separated in his mind," the mother underscored, "made all the difference. 'Daddy's not there because he wants to kill; he does a job to help good people that are hurt.' So that's what he understood about his daddy in Vietnam. And that seemed to be OK with him."[11]

Renegotiating family dynamics—specifically reallocating daily household duties—meant that in order to "make the trains run on time" wives assumed unaccustomed stewardship responsibilities in a dual mother-father capacity. These behavioral changes on the home front, as unwelcome as they may have been, hastened out of necessity the undermining of polarized Cold War gender roles. The war fed into the era's gendered dialectic concerning the rise of female-headed households and declining male authority associated with second-wave feminism, or the more broadly vernacular term "women's liberation." Effectively Vietnam motherhood can be understood as an unintended—and disguised—catalyst for what feminists would soon refer to as an empowered woman's coming to consciousness. So, too, did children's acculturation to strong-minded and capable mothers lay groundwork for redefining America's paternalistic culture, and women's social roles in it, one individual life at a time.[12]

Younger mothers with preschool-age children, married to twenty-something draftees and enlistees, frequently moved temporarily back into the refuge of their parents' home for the assistance these familiar surroundings afforded. Older mothers of school-age youth, married to professional military men and feeling isolated from the civilian population, tended to stay within or near military communities, likewise for the inherent support system. Nevertheless, in either situation, taking over household financial management and budgeting—a real change for previously dependent wives—obliged some women for the first time to seriously ponder employment outside the home or continuation of an education. Adding an unforeseen layer of economic hardship, career enlisted men—even noncommissioned officers—routinely moonlighted with a second job to make ends meet, income that dried up when he went overseas.[13]

"My father was in the Vietnam War for a year and it took a toll on our family," a woman born in 1961 remembered, "and my mother had to get her first job, which my father wasn't happy about, but she had to feed four kids."[14] As female employment climbed in the Vietnam era, peak rates of women in the work force shifted from predominantly older mothers in the 45-to-54 age range to younger women between 20 and 24 years old, probably in part because of the war's impact on this demographic.[15] Economic decision making also routinely involved certain legal issues—selling a car or signing a lease—which in turn generated friction with the arbitrary limits of women's legal autonomy. It was frustrating for wives to realize they could not make personal property transactions without their husbands because titles and deeds were in his name.

The "double day" burden—paid labor compounded by unpaid household chores—got heavier with the scope of women's traditional domestic charge expanding as single wartime parent. Still cooking, cleaning, and clothing and running errands for children—all the while overseeing a child's physical health and social well-being—mothers shouldered more authoritarian roles as the family's principal arbiter of disputes and chief disciplinarian. Although an unofficial series of advice manuals for military wives, covering topics ranging from etiquette to child-rearing, were made available during the Cold War era, balancing discipline remained an endless, and anxious, source of second-guessing.[16] Am I spoiling the children to make up for their father's absence or being too strict because they feel sorry for themselves? Are misbehaviors deliberate or simply innocent symptoms of separation anxiety? Did I accidently cause my child's health, social, or interpersonal problems? A man who was in third grade during his dad's tour remembered his parents actually "had a pretty impressive" coordination in disciplining. "Mom would punish us when we misbehaved, but also told Dad about it," he said. "The two seemed to have worked out ahead of time that when he got home, he would punish us again for things Mom had already punished us for. Scarred by it . . . that's an understatement."[17]

Over twelve to thirteen months, however, mothers in many families reached disciplinary equilibrium. More confidence brought more flexibility in letting their own maternal sensibilities guide decision making. Instead of simply duplicating Dad's authoritativeness, mothers figured out how nurturing morale with love and comfort was more beneficial to children than strict adherence to rules. Wielding more carrots than sticks, mothers seemed to sense when children were feeling low. And on these occasions, spontaneously taking everyone out for ice cream spoke louder.[18]

Loneliness, guilt, and regret also tainted otherwise joyful children's milestones—walking, losing teeth, talking—as women witnessed an entire year of childhood development by themselves in the knowledge husbands had lost something they could never get back. To help preserve memories, whenever possible mothers encouraged children to write poems and keep diaries to share with their fathers, or else deliberately filmed "mental movies" of the kids growing up in their minds to be later "shown" and narrated by memory. Vietnam's unpopularity made this responsibility weightier still. If society did not appreciate their husbands' sacrifice, what must that mean for how people valued their role, or that of their children? Even in those homes where mothers believed the war to be just and right, feelings of being devalued led many to begrudge people around them, and sometimes their own husbands, too. "I see my neighbor and her husband in the garden and hear them laughing and joking," an air force wife confessed in 1967.

> I see the kids next door run to meet their daddy. Then my eight-year-old runs up in tears because someone was mean to him, and I want to comfort him, but I can't. I know he needs his daddy and I worry about being too soft. I feel mean, myself. What right has Sally got having her husband home? Why did Jim have to stay in the Air Force? If he really loved me, he wouldn't have done it. When that happens, I pack the kids up in the car and go to Burger Chef for supper and to cool off.[19]

"It's only once in a while at night that I realize how much responsibility I have," the mother of a marine's four children explained to *Parents' Magazine*, "then I get overwhelmed." She continued,

> One day, my husband phoned all the way from Saigon. I was so excited that I didn't know what to say. Before I knew what was happening, the call was over. I began to think about everything that I had forgotten to ask and I started to cry. I ran out and started poking in the garden so the kids wouldn't see. Then it was time to pick up Jimmy at nursery school. I was O.K. by then. I put the other kids in the car, picked Jimmy up and, nice and cheery, I told him about daddy calling. Instead of being happy, poor Jimmy was just like me. He's little, but his father used to do everything with him—took him fishing, taught him songs. Jimmy started crying too. "Why did he call when I was at school?" He couldn't understand that his Daddy had to call when he did. He kept it up all evening. Finally, I just snapped at him to be quiet. Then I felt so ashamed of myself that somehow I pulled myself together and got supper and afterwards took everyone out for ice cream before bedtime. When the children were asleep, I called my sister for advice. She thought Jimmy was losing his childhood trying to take care of me. That was too much. I never liked TV but I felt so low, I turned it on just to push my problems away for a moment. What did I see? Marines under fire in Vietnam.[20]

Baby boom mothers tended to deal with several layers of vulnerability. Deprived of their earliest married years, they also missed the youthful romance of just being teenagers in love or the exhilaration of hanging around the jukebox with friends, especially while contrasting abruptly grown-up parenting responsibilities with single, childless contemporaries from high school who nightly "skipped the light fandango" (to borrow a line from the group Procol Harum's anthem "A Whiter Shade of Pale"). Time and again, tensions also arose after having moved back in with family. Grandparents might still treat the young mother as their child or else forgot what it was like to have small children around. Generational relationships were strained as well, when in the search for appropriate father figures, grandfathers got closer to grandchildren than their mothers were.[21]

All these lifestyle changes required profound emotional adjustments, and feelings of satisfaction sometimes mixed uneasily with mood fluctuations, jumpiness, or dark bouts of depression. Women took comfort in immersive motherhood, or else they found other diversions, perhaps in returning to college or hobbies. "You learn to keep yourself on an even keel because you can't live at the height of worry. You just can't," a mother confirmed in 1967. "I try to manage to have something to do every day until I get too tired to worry. Keeping busy is the best way." Not infrequently, though, they "self-medicated" through alcohol or tranquilizers.[22]

As mother-child relationships quite naturally grew closer and more intense, preadolescents tended to trim behavioral sails to Mom's prevailing emotional winds. Children's dependency on their immediate environment heightens sensitivity to the temperaments surrounding them, and although every child reacted to the strain of adjustment differently—dependent, too, on developmental age—among numerous father-related responsibilities children inherited, they commonly acquired a heightened awareness of, and responsiveness to, their mother's moods, as well as her emotional needs and demands. Those younger than nine who were grieving over separation, but could not developmentally maintain sorrow for long periods, might mirror their mother's behaviors instead of exhibiting genuine despair. Elder children usually chose to suppress true feelings as a conscious strategy to not further upset their mother.[23]

Perceptions of their father might also undergo a series of revisions. Preadolescents mentally fashioned or reconstructed creative scenarios, perhaps of building model trains together or pretending to be asleep so he would carry you into the house after a memorable trip to the drive-in theater. Storytelling about good times—watching the Detroit Tigers win the 1968 World Series—were equally critical for keeping memories fresh. Yet thinking back to past bad behaviors that had required punishment from their fathers conjured up old feelings, making children relive guilt and shame. While some harbored undeserved resentment for fathers whom they suspected had deliberately chosen to abandon them by going overseas, far more fantasized about him, with glorified, heroic imagery out of proportion to reality. Youth frequently commemorated Dad by wearing military jackets or emblems of his service, and daydreamed idyllic homecomings.

Due to the relatively short DEROS period, when separation anxiety became symptomatic, it was usually through ephemeral behaviors. These customarily ranged from crying easily, nail biting, fear of the dark, nightmares, and delays in

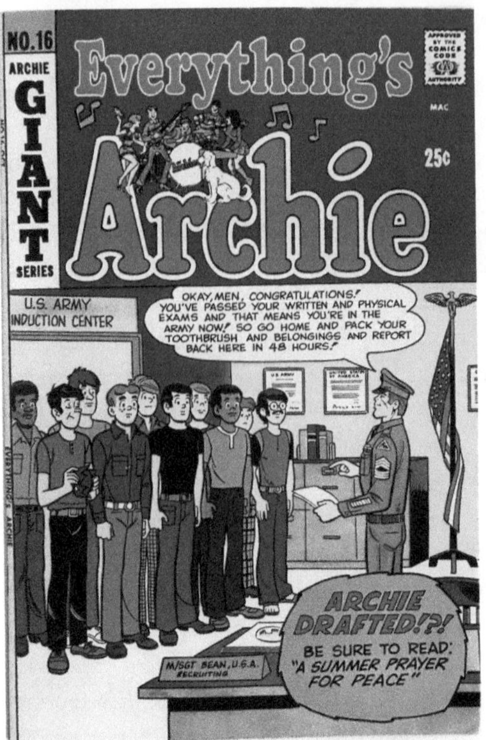

Everything's Archie #16, October 1971. In 1971 fans of *Archie Comics* were blindsided with the bombshell "Archie drafted!?!"

"Hawks & Doves," *Mad* #147, 1971. This regular *Mad* magazine sketch challenged children's thinking about traditional ideas of military service and patriotism.

Jungle War Stories #2, 1962. *Jungle War Stories* was the first war comic devoted exclusively to Vietnam, making it one of the war's earliest appearances anywhere in popular culture.

Sears Christmas 1963; Remco's Monkey Division for Jungle Guerrilla Warfare line was introduced in 1963 capitalizing on a common childhood mix-up between gorilla and guerrilla.

NO WAR TOYS

THE TOY 10¢

No War Toys Newsletter #4, Spring 1966. P. O. B. 69683, Los Angeles, California 90069 Printed whenever possible.

ERICH FROMM JOINS, PAUL G. HOFFMAN SUPPORTS NO WAR TOYS

Erich Fromm, famed psychiatrist and philosopher, joined NO WAR TOYS as a sponsor in March. Dr. Fromm is the author of many books, among them "The Forgotten Language," "The Art of Loving," and "May Man Prevail?"

Paul G. Hoffman also expressed his interest in NO WAR TOYS in a recent letter. "While it is quite true that I am very interested in efforts to substitute creative toys for the war toys which are so widely sold today, my position as an Under-Secretary of the United Nations prevents my sponsoring any outside activity. However, as a token of my interest, you will find enclosed a check for $100.00 made out to NO WAR TOYS, which I hope can be put to good use."

STATEMENT OF PURPOSE

ACTION IN N. Y.

WHAT IS A WAR TOY?

SPONSORS

CANADIAN PTA REJECTS WAR TOYS

The Toy was put out sporadically between 1965 and 1967 by the group No War Toys. Spring 1966.

Steven Sándor John, ca. 1965. As a fifth-grader, John organized the Children's Peace Union. His button reads "War Toys Kill Minds." Courtesy of Steven Sándor John.

When parents supported the war, children generally approximated their patriotic views. This original song, "The Brave Soldiers in Vietnam," written by an eleven-year-old South Carolina girl, was sent to President Johnson in July 1964. LBJ Library.

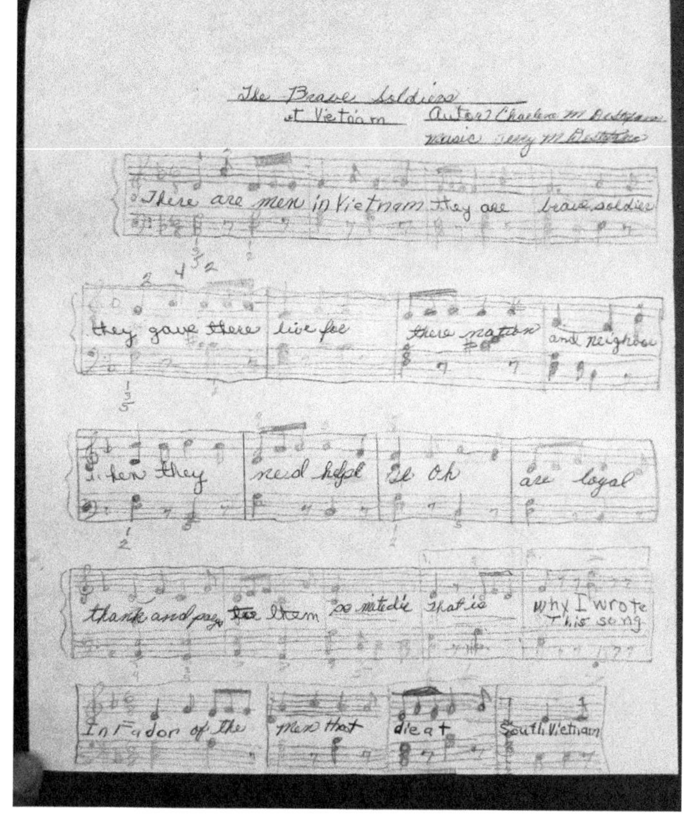

Letter to President Johnson written by a seven-year-old New Mexico boy. Younger children appear to have accepted, or at least tolerated, Vietnam, as long as the outcome meant swiftly scoring a victory over communism. LBJ Library.

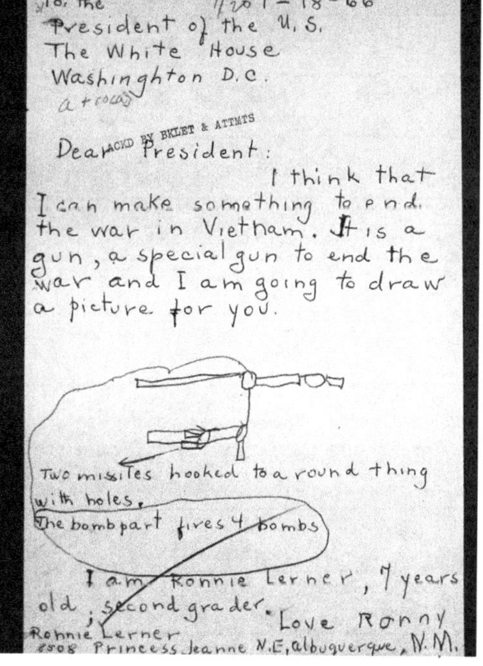
To the 1-18-66
President of the U.S.
The White House
Washinghton D.C.

ACKD BY BKLET & ATTMTS

Dear President:

I think that I can make something to end the war in Vietnam. It is a gun, a special gun to end the war and I am going to draw a picture for you.

I am Ronnie Lerner, 7 years old, second grader.

Love Ronny

Ronnie Lerner
8508 Princess Jeanne N.E, albuquerque, N.M.

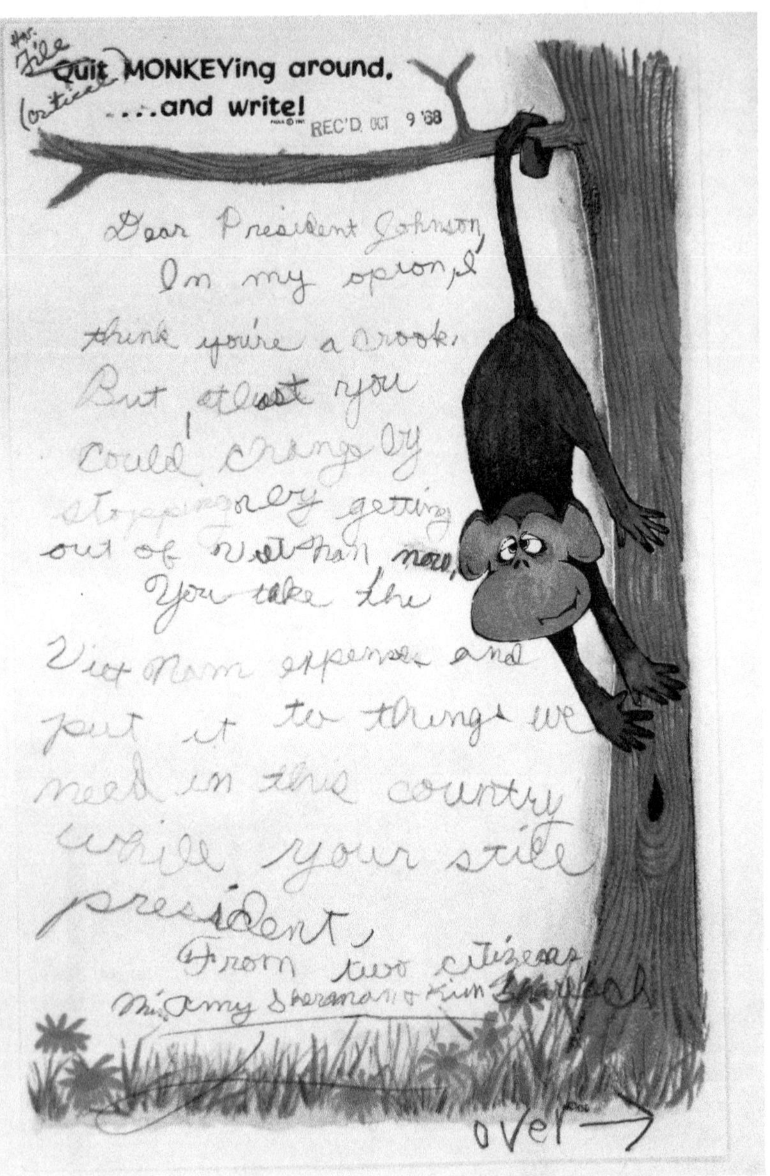

Hw.
File
(critical)

Quit MONKEYing around,
....and write!

REC'D. OCT 9 '68

Dear President Johnson,
In my opion, I
think you're a crook.
But atleast you
could change by
stopping, ery getting
out of Vietnam now.
You take the
Viet Nam expenses and
put it to things we
need in this country
while your still
president,
From two citizens
Miss Amy Sherman & Kim [illegible]

over →

Letter to President Johnson written by Illinois girls—thirteen and ten years old—in October 1968. As more adults began questioning the war and expressing dissent after 1968, youth shared their criticisms. LBJ Library.

Fourth-grade students at Yorkship Family School in Camden, New Jersey, and their classroom bulletin board decorated with memorabilia and letters from pen pals in the First Cavalry Division. Military History, Smithsonian Institution.

Sergeant Joe "Mosquito" Meskaitis visited Yorkship Family School in March 1969. Military History, Smithsonian Institution.

Returning veterans—usually older brothers or fathers—sometimes visited classrooms, and these memories of the war "coming to school" are common. Military History, Smithsonian Institution.

Staff Sergeant Franklin Ellinger with his sons Mike and Tim, 1967. Courtesy of Mike Ellinger.

Sons and Daughters in Touch, Father's Day 2010. Gold Star children gather at the Wall with their children and grandchildren. Courtesy of Gary Lee.

Lieutenant Eugene Moppert's widow presented teacher Jerry Davis and students at Yorkship Family School with the folded flag that had draped her husband's coffin, June 1968. Military History, Smithsonian Institution.

Many hundreds of thousands of families were eventually reunited with fathers, and these celebrated homecomings occasioned vivid flashbulb memories.

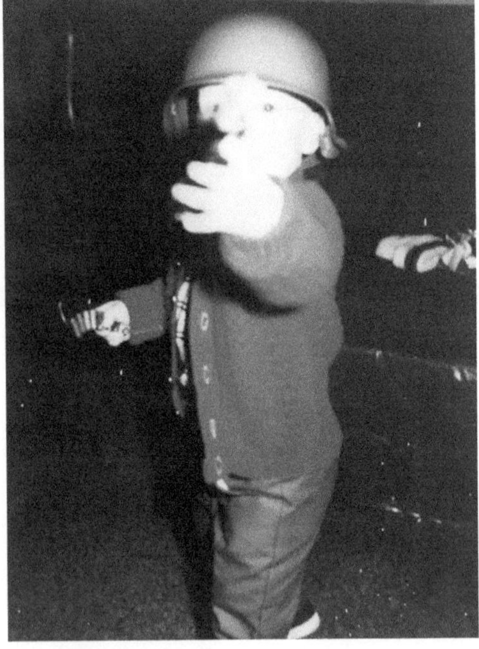

Christmas morning 1968. The popularity of manufactured war toys worried many adults that Vietnam was militarizing childhood.

William, Peggy, Charlotte, and Scott Duggan, Easter 1971. In response to seeing peace signs, Air Force Major Duggan good-naturedly had this necklace made. Scott wore it proudly in support of his fighter pilot father. Courtesy of Charlotte Duggan Priest.

GI Joe, *JCPenney Christmas 1973*. By 1970, Hasbro reimagined GI Joe into an adventure team because of Vietnam.

resolving normal developmental crises, to less subtle manifestations such as shyness, loneliness, social introversion, or rebelliousness. A California woman born in 1962 later learned from her mother that during her dad's last tour in 1966, "I was very fond of him when he was gone and I would have horrible nightmares and night rages that she couldn't wake me up from. She said I never exhibited those behaviors before or after." Some boys responded by acting too grown-up for their years, and girls recall developing "co-parent" relationships with mothers, almost as if the two were the same age. Others reverted to clinging too closely to Mom. After one father told his four-year-old son to keep a favorite easy chair warm while he was gone, the boy threw tantrums whenever anyone else (but the son) tried sitting there.[24]

Often those preadolescent boys who took being man of the house most seriously—entrusted with looking after Mom and any younger siblings—hastily retreated to Mom's lap quickest when requiring extra reassurance. Older youth suddenly withdrew to their rooms, eschewing play, friends, and schoolwork—perhaps due to a class discussion about the war—and while seemingly lethargic and standoffish, they were deliberately choosing self-imposed isolation as a means of governing feelings. Conversely, some purposefully acted out at school. One nine-year-old boy explained to his concerned mother quite matter-of-factly that although he was being given extra work by his teacher as punishment for repeatedly misbehaving, he gladly accepted the consequences for the attention and emotional release these outbursts afforded. In thinking back to her younger sister's troubles in elementary school, a woman underscored how "Mom had to go in, and they said, 'oh, the poor child is suffering because Dad's gone.' So I'm sure that it was all there except we wouldn't be aware of it in the same way an adult would be aware of it."[25]

Fear, though usually the least discussed, was nevertheless the toughest and most inescapable problem facing everyone. Considering the median age of soldiers who became casualties was twenty-two years old, very few children emotionally experienced a father being wounded. And prior to kindergarten, preadolescents struggle to understand death's irreversibility or consistently draw causal connections between war and death. That being said, youth sense danger much earlier. Preschoolers were more likely to be distressed by seemingly vague or irrational terrors, but by ten years old, with increasingly mature ideas about mortality, sons and daughters tended to wrestle with specific and realistic fears. "My dad served 2 tours of Vietnam," an Arkansas woman born in 1959 explained about how children began navigating these emotional transitions immediately on their father's departure. "The first time, I was in first grade (so 66/67). I remember family members were very upset. I didn't understand what was going on other than people were not happy. I stood up in front of the crowd and said, 'Wow, there sure will be a lot of tears tomorrow too.'"[26]

A California woman, the oldest of three sisters, noted a clear difference in how she reacted when their father returned to Vietnam a second time in 1970. She was nine years old during his first tour, and having been sheltered from TV news, she did not remember making a big deal out of seeing him off. "The second time was very emotional, though," she reflected.

> I knew he was going back, I had a sense there was a war there, I knew that when he came back from his first tour that he was damaged in some way, he was emotionally distraught, he acted weird, there was a lot of fighting and stress in the house. And so when he went back the second time we drove him to the airport, and I distinctly remember (so I must have been like ten or eleven) I sobbed uncontrollably in the back seat. I mean I literally could not stop crying, I could not make myself stop crying. Even though my family was sort of wishing that I could. They tried to turn on some rock music on the radio, they tried everything but I couldn't stop. I don't even know why I couldn't stop. I remember the song that was on the radio was "Jeremiah was a bullfrog . . ." [Three Dog Night's 1970 song "Joy to the World"]. That's what was playing on the radio when I was sobbing hysterically in the car, and also the Doors . . . The Doors were playing, I mean I remember the music because we were trying to get me to listen to it to stop crying.[27]

A Georgia man living near family in Virginia throughout his father's tour in 1967 and 1968, when he was nine years old, described how preparing for the inevitable ultimately did little to soften the blow. "My dad was career army and we traveled all over so it was generally accepted that he would [go to Vietnam], but my parents didn't talk to us about it, they knew what was going on and we all got to watch the news every night." Memories of the actual departure are lost to him, but he made clear how his dad's time in Vietnam "was quite a shock and one that I had a hard time dealing with. . . . When he left was when the news stories started registering," the Georgia man continued. "It was all relative and very hard on me. I was convinced that he was going to die . . . I became fairly antisocial . . . I ran away from home twice . . . had some difficulties in school . . . I had medical issues and it all went together to create a perfect mess that year out of me." When expounding on how Vietnam cheated him out of this year of childhood, he explained, "Absolutely, I had a lot of ill will toward the army in general, I was impressionable as the anti-war movement was really ramping up, and so I got a lot of that. I read an awful lot about Uncle Sam and his business." Yet, rather than feeling any resentment or anger toward his father or the army, "I more felt apprehensive that I would lose him. Yes, I thought about it every day, I remember being somewhat steeped in it if you will."[28]

"It was awful, awful in so many ways," the California woman continued. "He was gone and we missed him, and Mom was struggling to make it happen with three little girls in the house; we were always stressed out."[29] The mother of an eight-year-old girl in 1967 related how, after sending her daughter to bed early one night for refusing to eat dinner, the child lay crying into a pillow until her mom came by later to check in. Asked what was wrong, the girl first said her tummy ache hurt bad enough to make her cry, before finally confessing, "I don't want my Daddy to be killed." Another boy, six years old, who had been having a hard time sleeping for several nights in a row, attributed his insomnia to an overriding concern: "Will Daddy die?" God, his mother reassured at bedtime, watches over "the good guys" like his father. But the following week when a friend's dad was killed, he sought clarification. "Wasn't Sammy's father a good guy?"[30]

The experiences of Karen Spears Zacharias offer further insight into preadolescent coping given different adaptive resources available at particular ages. Just nine years old in 1965, Zacharias remembered she and her eleven-year-old brother being summoned to the living room at bedtime for a talk on the December night before her father shipped out. The whole notion of Mom and Dad *needing to talk* to them about anything struck her as an oddity since it was so unprecedented. What is more, her father began the decidedly grown-up conversation by declaring he thought they were both old enough to understand some things. (This specific vote of confidence relieved some residual embarrassment over childishly spilling cooking oil on her head while helping earlier in the kitchen.) Once both pajama-clad children nodded in the affirmative that they did, in fact, know who Lyndon B. Johnson was, Zacharias's father simply explained, "there's a country that needs our help, South Vietnam. President Johnson has asked me to go."

Ensuing questions prompted her dad's elaboration on Vietnam's geographic location and how he would be protecting the Vietnamese from communists. "Tears stung," Zacharias recalled, "not because I understood what communism was, or that Daddy would be in any danger. Simply because my daddy would be leaving me." Still fighting back those tears when her dad tucked her in, she at last admitted to being scared. Of what, he wondered? "That you won't come home!" "I'll come back," her dad comforted, "I promise." Good-nights and I-love-yous completed their farewell. "Grabbing my pillow, I sought to muffle the crying that grown-ups can control but children never can," she emphasized. "Daddy left early the next day, before the sun tiptoed over the horizon. He kissed me good-bye, but I barely woke in the predawn hours."[31]

Staff Sergeant David P. Spears returned home, a pledge reiterated in all his letters, for R&R (rest and recuperation leave) in the spring of 1966 while the family was stationed in Hawaii. He brought Vietnam with him in his changed appearance, his demeanor, and a singular story. "I studied the sadness on my daddy's face," Zacharias wrote, and besides appearing thinner and more serious, "he looked defeated. Tired. Plumb worn-out." One day in the kitchen he told of a Vietnamese girl blown apart by the Vietcong as a human booby trap to kill American GIs. Despite being bothered by the story, she remembered for the remainder of his R&R "Daddy didn't talk much of the war or of Vietnam. Other than the story of the little girl, I never heard him mention it again. He cleaned his gear, shined his boots, and grew sadly quiet as it got closer to the time when he had to return. He didn't make me any more promises," besides saying he would be home for good before her tenth birthday in November. "But this time I wasn't worried about his leaving. He'd come home just like he'd said. I figured he'd be home again soon enough. So on May 20, 1966, I barely woke at all when Daddy came in to kiss me good-bye. . . . I sat up and gave him a hug. He flipped off the overhead light, and I fell back to sleep, confident that there would be plenty of time for more hugs from Daddy." In regard to her birthday, "Daddy kept his promise, in a way. He did come back. Via airmail, in a cargo plane full of caskets."[32]

Whatever scary imaginings childish minds did not conjure up about the dangers lurking in Vietnam's jungles, television supplied on a nightly basis. Television's wartime coverage—most Americans' sole connection to Vietnam—was something of a mixed bag for children with fathers in the war. Graphic newscasts drove many preadolescents to hysterics, especially when showing men dying in areas where their fathers were known to be. Mothers, again, sought middle ground somewhere between regulating viewing habits and forbidding TV news programming outright, although most thought prohibition only increased children's anxiety. The Georgia man born in 1958 was one of the children who chose to limit TV on his own volition. "I remember seeing people dressed like my dad was dressed all bloody and dead, which did not do me any good," he recalled, "and I knew watching it on TV was not in my best interest."[33]

In other households, nightly news rituals can best be described as hopeful, a welcome part of domestic routines families settled into to help manage dislocation. Soldiers actually encouraged it. "Been watching any helicopters on the news lately?" a pilot wrote his preadolescent boy. "Maybe one of these days you'll get to see ole dad on the boob-tube. Not likely, but there's always a chance." The son, a Kansan born in 1967, remembered earnestly taking the advice to heart. "Every night's broadcast had a real sense of anticipation because it gave my mom and me a fresh opportunity to see him," he wrote.

> Being that little I guess I just naturally assumed Vietnam and the war were small enough that all soldiers knew each other and television filmed them all fairly regularly. The basic storylines were pretty much the same so I figured the "cast" must be the same each night too, maybe like a TV show? I can't tell you how many times I yelled "there he is!" whenever I saw any helicopter pilot. Mom did a pretty good job not squashing my enthusiasm. "Maybe you're right," she would say or "that could be him." I swore I saw him on TV dozens of times over the year which probably made me feel better. Only learned later on that I'd probably never seen him on TV after all, not even once."[34]

It was not uncommon for sons and daughters to feel self-conscious about how incomplete their family seemed compared with other more apparently stable homes. Whereas family separation became normative in World War II, families living in the civilian population during Vietnam—as opposed to the protective culture of military communities—were cognizant of how father absence set them apart. Feelings of inadequacy could, likewise, be exacerbated by recriminations of the war effort, which generally seemed to be harder on older siblings because people were more likely to vent anti-war frustrations at them for having a father in the war. "We moved to Indiana . . . to live near family while my Dad was in Vietnam," a woman born in 1963 confided. "This was the first time I had lived out of the shelter of military life. I was exposed to people who talked bad about our military and our president. It made me so angry and sad at the same time. I cried myself to sleep most nights, worried and scared that my daddy would not come home to us."[35]

Preadolescents filled in these emotional spaces left by father absence with whatever means and materials were most readily applicable to familiar childhood practices. Besides using TV news as a dinnertime portal into their dad's world, families carried out ordinary domestic tasks he still expected to get done. "Mom tried to make it for us like he wasn't even gone as far as daily activities," a man explained about finding normalcy in responsibility, "and we kept up the same routines as far as chores." Where fathers left unfinished home-improvement projects or other regularly scheduled maintenance, children "collaborated" in their completion (to varying degrees of success) in order to feel closer to him and garner his praise from halfway around the globe.[36]

War play sometimes reflected children's interpretation of what Daddy was doing over in Vietnam as well. Based more on recent photographs than actual memories of their father, boys might dress G.I. Joe in the same uniforms dads wore, carry the same weapons and equipment, or fly the same helicopter missions. "I am an Army brat and my dad was in Vietnam twice 68–69 and 71–72 though I only remember the second time he was there," a woman born in 1965 explained.

> I recall the "Wait til your father gets home" threat from my mother (she was left behind with 7 young kids). The only time my dad did call home was to demand that my older brothers fill in the tunnel system they had dug up on our hillside (we lived in rural Vermont) where we used to play war. We thought our model Vietnam war zone complete with Vietnamese hooch made from the old chicken coop was the best playground. My dad said he feared that his children would all suffocate in a tunnel collapse so he called home to threaten us with our lives (his bark was worse than his bite) if the tunnels and hooch were not down in 24 hours.[37]

Older elementary schoolers in later childhood gained an added sense of agency by developing a connoisseur's expertise on the Vietnam War through diligent study. In recollecting a nine-year-old's single-mindedness, the Georgia man who "read an awful lot about Uncle Sam and his business" highlighted how he "became a student of the war. It became a project for me. You asked if I became somewhat obsessed, well, I knew the name of every trail on the Ho Chi Minh Trail. I'm still very interested in Vietnam, but don't study it as obsessively anymore. When a story comes on I perk my ears up, but I probably not only already know the story, but know more about it than the author."[38]

Those progressing developmentally without a father figure also sought out psychological and emotional displacements through surrogate male role models. Mothers cognizant of the preadolescent's need for a masculine image—or else just somebody to take sons into public restrooms—encouraged traditionally male activities such as scouting and Little League or asked uncles, pastors, and male friends and neighbors to spend time around children. Grandfathers routinely stepped into this role of father substitute. "During his tour we moved back to my mom's hometown so her parents could help her with the 3 children," a woman wrote concerning this common recollection. "I remember my grandparents being over at the house a lot!"[39]

In yet one more family dynamic to be renegotiated, grandfathers working as proxy for their absent son or son-in-law—and with a natural tendency toward spoiling grandchildren anyway—forged relationships different than a traditional grandfather-grandson: "buddies." "My mom and I moved into a mobile home next door to both my grandparents and great-grandparents," a man born in 1967 recalled.

> I spent every day while she was at work with my grandpa (mom's dad) and you can say that he effectively raised me, at least in regard to "guy stuff." We tinkered on small engines, or the little Honda 50 motorcycle he gave me, in his garage together, and even as a little kid, I was responsible for fetching the tools he needed . . . so I had to know a crescent wrench or Phillips screwdriver. Or we hung out at the auto parts store or local garage or salvage yard, always telling me stories of fighting in the Pacific during World War II. His friends commented on how I sounded and acted like him and I was proud of that. Can't remember exactly when, but at some point I stopped calling him grandpa because it just didn't work anymore and I just gave him a nickname that stuck forever. I've honestly always felt like I was in a way born of that father too in my Vietnam years.[40]

Without, or maybe in addition to, a suitable male presence in childhood, innumerable children with fathers overseas appear to have written the White House on a regular basis. During the normal courses of childhood political socialization, preadolescents egocentrically cultivate an emotional, and mostly imaginative, personal connection to the president. To their thinking, the great and powerful president takes on a highly idealized character consisting of those benevolent qualities they find most satisfying about adults, and, more to the point, ideal parental virtues. In a sense, the president is what is popularly understood as a father figure possessing a dad's unfailing authority, wisdom, empathy, and strength writ large. If their letters at the John F. Kennedy and Lyndon Baines Johnson Presidential Libraries are any indication, preadolescents seem to have innately grasped something of the Great Society's paternalistic nature as well, meaning they regularly asked Lyndon Johnson for things—not so different from a real-life Santa Claus—far more frequently than they did with Kennedy.

Letters tend to approximate several schools of childhood thought. Many, like this fourth-grade girl, wrote, "My father is in Viet Nam. You might have seen him when you were there," probably referencing Johnson's surprise visit to Cam Ranh Bay in October 1966. Others are some variation of a fifth-grade boy's 1966 request, "Will you please send my friend's father home from Viet Nam?" Hundreds more mirror an upstate New York girl's plea. "My father is stationed at Bien Hoa Air Force Base, South Viet Nam," she penned in 1965.

> He is due to come home sometime in April of this year. I was born in San Antonio, Texas. My birthday is April 1st. I will be thirteen years old. Mr. President, would it be possible for my daddy to get home for my birthday. It is the only thing in the world I want for my birthday. Please Mr. President, my brothers, Billy 7, Paul 5, Tom 3 think our father is dead and will never come home. It's been such

> a long, lonesome year. I hope and pray God will help find a peaceful way to end the war in Viet Nam, so my daddy will not have to leave us again.[41]

Regular overseas communication was key to achieving a measure of wholeness. Whether folded into red, white, and blue-bordered airmail envelopes or recorded on cassette tapes bound for the APO, families kept one another integrated—as much as possible or prudent—into each's strange, new realities. "When I see that military families can now communicate with soldiers that have been deployed through e-mail and various other means, I remember that it was not always that easy with us," a Florida man, whose father left for Vietnam when he was entering first grade, commented about this vital lifeline.

> My mother and father would write each other, but during my father's second trip to Vietnam [1965] there was a time that we were receiving his letters but he was not receiving my mother's letters to him. He did not know why he was not receiving letters from my mother and it was getting him down. My mother was upset that he was not receiving her letters and got hold of whoever she could about it; the letters had been misplaced, when they were found all of them were delivered to my father. We would get a letter from him telling us where he was at that time and then we would hear on TV that the Viet Cong had attacked or that there was fighting there, [and] this would worry my mother. But usually he had moved to somewhere else by the time we got the letter.[42]

All domestic correspondence—whether schoolchildren to pen pals or relatives—followed similar patterns. Mothers (and grandmothers) and children mixed mundane, day-to-day goings-on (dentist appoints and mechanical issues surrounding family cars) with highlights (report cards and school photos) to paint reassuringly domesticated pictures. If anything, letters to fathers expressed more heartfelt sentiment. With preschoolers, verbal contributions had to be transcribed into a letter's overall narrative, which was actually less labor intensive than it may sound. As one mother pointed out, my son "didn't have a very big vocabulary so it was pretty easy." Novice writers usually added brief missives, while those more accomplished sent private letters directly to their dads without much maternal oversight. Where cassette tapes were the preferred mode, moms coordinated recordings with everyone encouraged to take turns speaking. "We would record us playing the piano, singing and talking about our day on cassette tape to send to my dad," a woman born in 1959 remembered, adding, "he said they were like manna from heaven."[43]

Fathers balanced tone and content, too, somewhere between observations on the beauty of the Vietnamese landscape and homesick, wartime stories (hopeful expressions of loving you, missing you, or being home for Christmas) that always stopped just short of revealing how close he had recently come to making his wife a widow. One California woman, twelve years old during her dad's second tour and the oldest of three sisters, recalled each girl receiving mail from Vietnam addressed to them individually. Letters to her and the nine-year-old were in his crisp penmanship, but those for the preschooler often consisted of mere scribbles because she could not read.[44]

"Everything in Phu Loi is just fine; if anything can be fine in Viet Nam," wrote an aviator in a series of father-son letters between July 1970 and March 1971. "Hi Man, It's me again. Glad to see the end of each day because that's just one less day until we're back together again," a July letter began. "Sitting here listening to machine gun fire in the distance—somebody is earning their keep and combat pay. The government is getting off pretty cheap paying $65 a month to risk your life over here—the longer I'm here the more I wonder if it's worthwhile." Yet the next paragraphs highlighted a dichotomy ordinarily residing awkwardly within all the pages. "It's your Dad here again—here it is midafternoon and I'm still in the same spot. Wish 'Charlie' (VC) would livin' up the day. If I have to die I hope it's not from boredom." "Can't think of any war stories to write about," the father reiterated weeks later. "Sometimes wish 'Charlie' would take a few pot shots at me just to make the days interesting. Not going to win too many medals at this rate but the chances of getting back home are about 100%."[45]

"Haven't got any idea what they have been showing on the news about Nam but it probably looks worse than it is—except maybe for Laos," he later penned in March near his tour's end. "Haven't been up there yet but from what I hear from other pilots our planes are sure taking a good beating. Hope you had a good birthday—sorry I couldn't send a present. There's nothing here to send a big boy like you, when I get home we'll go out and you can pick what you want." A few letters were also illustrated with the pilot's hand-drawn caricatures and humorous sketches showing the illogic of military life, which in the mind of a child seemed to help mitigate worry. How bad could things be in Vietnam if wartime was depicted in cartoon form? "Nothing happening tonight," another letter concluded. "Heard rumors the VC might mortar us tonight since they haven't hit us in over three weeks. No sweat—we got bunkers four feet thick just in case 'Charlie' gets a little ornery at night. Well, you be a good boy and drop me a line when you get a chance. Love ya much and always thinking about ya."[46]

Fathers likewise dutifully commented on minutiae from back home, knowing how anxiously families waited to hear his perspective on what they had been up to, and how his recognition and approval validated their experiences. "Grandma C said you've been wearing a pair of red baseball socks," the pilot wrote in July

1970, "even wore them to [uncle] Brent's game. Bet you really look like a big league player with those socks on. Maybe you can talk your mom into buying you a uniform." "Can hardly wait to get home and watch you swim," a different 1970 note read. "Bet you can swim better than your ol' dad." Several lines later the serviceman responded to a neighborhood bullying incident with fatherly advice. "Have you been putting any knots on Brian's head? For gosh sakes don't let him or anyone pick on you—just pop 'em in the nose. If they're too big for you to handle just put them on a waiting list and I'll help you in a few months."[47]

Telephone calls remained extremely rare. "My dad didn't call home very much from Vietnam because it was expensive," a California man born in 1961 explained. "It was a long-distance call. So we went months without hearing his voice." As a substitute, cassette tapes provided at least some interactivity. Dad addressed Mom primarily, either mentioning children separately or taking turns speaking to them directly. Excited youth instinctively responded to their dad's voice in imaginary dialogues, yet in some homes tape-recorded correspondence proved less successful if children became too emotional hearing his voice. Even so, cassettes allowed families to prerecord entire dinnertime or bedtime rituals. At the appropriate hour, Mom played the tape on which servicemen instructed children to get ready for bed, pick up their toys, and take baths, with the pause button on the recorder depressed while each step was accomplished. When everyone got into bed, Dad concluded the recording by reading a story, and in this way he tucked them in each night.[48]

Letters home from Vietnam were more passive by nature, almost akin to Mom (or again Grandma) reading a bedtime story. Many veterans' children remember feeling curious, and protective, about why some letters from Vietnam were addressed to them, while others only to their mothers. So, too, did youth find it frustrating when Mom edited out private "romance" passages in letters read to families. Just like cassettes, letters upset children at times, bringing apprehension and concern, especially when a soldier's balancing act failed to sufficiently mask the war's toll. "The war was changing him daily in a bad way," a woman born in 1961 revealed about her dad's correspondence, "[and] letters from him were full of bitter words, fear and worry."[49]

Accompanying gifts periodically lightened the mood, although fathers commented on how Vietnamese shops offered few toys as souvenirs and what little they carried were more appropriate for girls. Mainly, his letters served to sustain a hopeful presence until the impending homecoming. "I was sitting here thinking (something that comes hard for me) and you know next year you start going to school!" a soldier wrote his son in 1971. "At the rate you're growing you'll probably be finished with school before I am. Going to school is really something to look forward to, just think of all those kids you'll be able to play with and talk to. Wish I could start all that again! Don't know exactly when I'll be coming home.... Hope the weather is warm when I get there, sure looking forward to riding that train in the park and feeding the ducks. Be a good boy—remember I love you even if I don't write very much or often." "Sure seems like a long time ago instead of just a few months," a subsequent message ended. "Promised you the next time home it would be for keeps—may have to stay over here for 18 months but if that's what it takes to keep that promise that's what I'll do.... Better be ready for me because when I get home I'm going to wrestle the ears right off your head."[50]

"There is not a happier time than when a family member returns from war," stressed a southern man who was in the second grade when his dad abruptly came, in soldier's language, *back to the world*. "One day my mother just got a call. It was from my father, he was in New Jersey, he was home." Many hundred thousands of families were eventually reunited, and these celebrated homecomings occasioned vivid, joyful flashbulb memories with lifelong resonance. The exhilaration of suddenly seeing him standing on the porch or showing up by surprise at school—an intense compression of excitement, relief, and pride—was the singularly most gratifying event in many preadolescents' lives. "His second tour was around 68/69," wrote an Arkansas woman, born in 1959, of her dad flying home. "I remember watching him walk down the jet gate in full uniform and being so proud to see him. Dad was very sick with Hepatitis and went straight to the hospital for about a month. I didn't believe he was alive so the staff propped him up in front of a 2nd story window so I could see him."[51]

"For the most part I basically just remember not having a father around for most of my early years," a Vermont woman born in 1965 reflected on her father's two tours. What is more, she added, "being shy when he came home the second time [1972] and how proud I was of the cake we made for him to welcome the 'boss' home." One little girl presented her father with a handful of baby teeth she had lost the previous year, explaining her steadfast refusal to relinquish any to the tooth fairy until Daddy got to inspect them. She asked for only two things in return: a trip to Disneyland and no more spankings like Mom gave. A preadolescent boy constructed a cardboard box to leap from jack-in-the-box style when his father came through the front door. Young men such as he also frequently visited the barbershop for a shorter haircut prior to their dad's arrival.[52] When Christmas and birthdays fell just prior to the return, families might celebrate the holidays a second time, giving preadolescents two golden opportunities for studying the Sears, JCPenney, and Montgomery Ward "wish book" catalogs in the same year.

"When Dad returned from his first tour in Vietnam, he arrived at Standiford Field Airport [Louisville, Kentucky] still wearing his flight suit," a California woman shared.

> The airport personnel made him enter the terminal through the back door so he wouldn't upset the passengers or be called a baby-killer. I remember Mom and us three girls waiting just inside the big plate glass windows, watching each person walk across the tarmac, looking for Dad. Suddenly Mom flew around toward us and spoke quickly in a tone that made me know her instructions were very important. "Sit here, girls. Wait and don't move. I have to go meet your father at another gate." Mom's look was stern and fierce, but she wasn't mad at us. We sat wide-eyed for a long time, and finally there was Dad walking down the hall, Mom clinging to his neck. We ran and grabbed his waist, his knees, whatever we could reach according to our heights. He tried to hug us all at the same time with different hugs. Mom needed a certain wife-hug, Heidi a baby hug up in his arms, and Lori and I some little girl hugs. Mine came with a little respect attached since I was the oldest. Lori got the rough house since she was a tomboy and his favorite. We were so happy to see him.[53]

Beyond the immediate—albeit awkward—warm glow, however, the most significant developmental consequences were commonly shaped by bumpy realities of family restoration in the transitional months and years afterward. It is, again, a chief organizing principle in thinking about Vietnam's place in childhood to understand that while preschoolers may have known the least about the war, and carried forward the fewest memories of their dads' time away, they may have been the most negatively affected by any resultant crisis of unmet needs and unfulfilled expectations after his homecoming. Even in well-adjusted households, reintegrating the husband-father often proved to be surprisingly more problematic and less gratifying than veterans, mothers, and children anticipated. In truth, as counterintuitive as it might seem, the same reorganization strategies that helped families deal successfully with separation could most adversely affect readjustments. On the whole, families harbored unrealistic expectations about the process, and the time interval, for transitioning men back into domestic ranks. No one knew with any certainty how to coherently realign power and authority, revise divisions of labor, share home and family activities, or restore balance between loving husband and soulmate as well as fatherly caregiver and disciplinarian.[54]

Young children might be afraid of their fathers initially, particularly men coming on too strong, energetic, or enthusiastic. In some homes, youth grew anxious as his arrival drew nearer, insecure over the prospect of what effectively amounted to a stranger coming to live with them or what deviations in routine to anticipate. Consistent with the stressful child-father relationships historian William Tuttle noticed after World War II, Vietnam-era children, typically those of noncareer soldiers, worried about fathers upsetting stability established during his absence, whether in usurping their mothers' attention, assuming personal intimacies, or unfamiliar parenting styles. Older preadolescents, commonly with career military fathers, dreaded the possibility he would be disappointed in them after getting reacquainted. Far more often, returning servicemen did not live up to the hero imagery small children had elaborately built to enshrine him, a jarring and disappointing initiation to the gap between perception and reality. Those who idolized a great returning hero without really knowing him faced disillusionment or disappointment when he turned out instead to be a grumpy and fragile human being.[55]

We had a "big welcome-home dinner with hot dogs and a hot dog–eating contest," a Virginia man remembered about his dad's homecoming during the boy's third-grade year. "But before we left the table my dad had backslapped me across the room. . . . He was real ramped up, I guess. He came down after a while, but my father and I have had a very strained relationship probably from the day he got home from Vietnam on. I was not the strong, rambunctious boxing glove–type son, I was a hang-out-in-the-kitchen-and-draw-pictures, that sort of thing, son. We did not mesh real well."[56]

Veterans—dealing with multiple psychological and emotional adjustment issues—brought home impractical expectations of children—deportment, discipline, hair length—or sought to reassert a dominant head-of-the-house role more quickly than was comfortable. Those imposing military-style discipline, especially when mothers had been lenient or grandparents permissive, fostered particularly stressful child-father relationships. "It was an adjustment for the entire family with him home," a woman born in 1959 said of these new dynamics. "We could push mom much further than dad and had to rein it in with him home. Once before in the fifth grade I had been reading a book slyly tucked inside my textbook, when dad suddenly appeared in full dress uniform (he had surprised the kids with R&R). I remember thinking OH MY GOSH he has come to punish me for not paying attention. That was the power of being raised by a military man—you think he has eyes not only in the back of his head but across the world!" Overly judgmental husbands made mothers apprehensive, too. Women found themselves on the defensive accounting for household management, financial decisions, purchases, or child-rearing practices, and reluctant to surrender hard-won independence in these matters.[57]

Frequently, bonds between husband and wife were restored more easily and more quickly than those between father and child. To a child's thinking, sometimes fathers came back different, physically and/or emotionally. "When he came back, those were the dark years," the mother of a preschooler revealed. "Vietnam did not change him for the better." Numerous reminiscences collected for the book speak to children's anxiety about being around returned fathers, usually because they seemed sullen and estranged, or they behaved oddly. Again, similar to World War II, the sons and daughters of Vietnam veterans used terms such as "diminished," "solemn," "intolerant," "frustrated," "edgy," and "distant." When men withdrew, reluctant to talk about Vietnam, families often steered conversations clear of the war, a situation preadolescents found particularly puzzling. Why would parents remain silent on something as noble as military service, or as honorable as being a marine? And why did adults frown on expressing pride in your father's soldiering to others outside the family, in effect hiding his achievements?[58]

"When Dad got home, he was different," the California woman with rich memories of hugging in the airport also recalled about how rapidly their homecoming cooled off. "When we three jumped on him to tickle him in his chair, he growled and pushed us away. He turned mean. He got mad at the dog over an accident and threw it up against the wall. He broke a guy's nose at a party for making a comment about Vietnam. Mom tells how he woke up from nightmares in a cold sweat. All he could think about was going back over there, and that's what he did a few months later."[59]

One of the foremost readjustment issues centered on unlearning violence. Despite the increasingly recognized gulf between combat and civilian life among psychiatric experts and the Pentagon, particularly when soldiers traversed the two worlds literally overnight by jet, the military failed to provide training programs for peaceful reintegration equivalent to basic training's preparations for battle. Studies found that returning Vietnam veterans, both well adjusted and maladjusted, demonstrated elevated levels of aggression and hostility. These men also characteristically expressed deep ambivalence over the war, a lack of support by the country and the government, and problems communicating with civilians. With family counseling resources still scarce in the Vietnam era, mothers and children were the de facto first line of civilian immersion therapy.[60]

Usually this unfolded in embarrassing, isolated episodes that seldom appeared so quirky or harmless. Not fully comprehending Dad's problems with Fourth of July fireworks—flinching or hitting the dirt—for instance, are shared memories among veterans' children. One southern woman, ten years old when her father returned, clearly remembered his reaction to a tornado warning in their town. "Dad thought it was incoming fire and belly crawled across the room until he realized where he was. A few months later," she also revealed, "my brother walked up behind dad and tapped him on the shoulder. In an instant, he was flipped over my dad's shoulder on the ground with a foot on his neck. As an adult one of the things my dad told me about his experiences has really stuck out to me. He said it was hard for him to be around kids again—that they wouldn't have a grenade in their hand. Wow—how sad."[61]

Yet even if the stereotypical troubled Vietnam veteran can be overstated in American culture—and disputed statistically—an overwhelming majority of preadolescents successfully worked through rough readjustment periods by making necessary accommodations. Generally, these behavioral and attitudinal changes were by nature merely transitional. When new fashion or hairstyles appeared too trendy for their dads' tastes, girls had to forsake shorter "pixie" cuts (courtesy of the women's liberation movement) or vibrant colors and creative clothing patterns—purples, yellows, and reds—inspired by the British Mods and American counterculture. Though many boys after about 1967 yearned for longer hair, they settled for "square" haircuts (crew cuts in summer and just long enough to comb during the school year) mandated by Dad. Others reoriented their conduct, getting used to stricter discipline or reintroducing courtesy titles "sir" and "ma'am." Playtime had to be adjusted toward quieter, safe games (something other than pretending to be Batman and Robin, bath towels for capes and sapling trees for bat poles, with choreographed fistfights echoing shouts of "Bam!" and "Pow!").

When marriages failed to reconnect and ultimately dissolved in divorce, many sons and daughters who grew up as products of the era's broken homes understand their families to have been collateral casualties of Vietnam. The war played an unmistakable role in a surge of divorces, one of several that more than doubled the country's divorce rate between 1960 and 1980. As Richard Nixon reduced troop levels from the wartime high of 536,100 in 1968 to 475,200 in 1969, the divorce rate and number of divorces both jumped by 12 percent, with the United States setting the yearly record for number of divorces, previously held during another time of demobilization in 1946. By 1973, with virtually all troops home, the divorce rate—approaching 50 percent—likewise topped 1946, and annual divorces finally surpassed one million for the first time in the nation's history during 1975.[62]

The corresponding number of children involved in divorces soared accordingly, from an estimated 463,000 in 1960 to 630,000 in 1965, reaching 870,000 in 1970 and 1.1 million by 1975. Probably an equal amount were dislocated by parental separation each year. Regional variations not withstanding—numerically higher in the South and West, lowest in the Midwest and Northeast—this dramatic upswing statistically represented a threefold increase in American children affected by divorce between 1956 and 1976. Even though the experience of living in an intact two-parent family remained standard, divorce became an undisputed fact of life in the 1960s, broadening our definitions of family and the domestic context where childhood played out. Since almost all parents remarried, usually within three years, more and more children moved in and out of a variety of biological and blended family types.

Ultimately four out of every ten American children in the Vietnam era spent at least part of their childhood in a family headed by a divorced single parent—almost by definition a single mother. Principally because most divorces took place in the first six or seven years of marriage, children of divorce tended to be disproportionately preadolescents, and given the prevailing Tender Years Presumption, courts preferred to award custody of young children to the mother as a matter of course. And socioeconomic outcomes were challenging. Young divorced women and dependent children experienced declines in their standard of living—statistically much poorer than two-parent families—due to a single income earned from comparatively lower-paying clerical and service jobs and, because, in reality, primary judicial custody was rarely accompanied with adequate child support. In 1972 the poverty line for a female-headed household stood at $4,254. Children represented 36 percent of all white Americans, and 52 percent of all blacks, below this threshold.[63]

Coping with Vietnam-related divorces permanently influenced trajectory patterns toward adolescence and adulthood for these children. "Many of my friends' parents were divorced or single moms with no fathers even in the picture," a Missouri man born in 1962 observed. "Several people I knew that served in Vietnam divorced multiple times and their kids suffered as a result. Now take it to the next step the fact that so many of the children were from divorced families when they grew up they divorced too sometimes more than once even 5 times. So there was an impact if not directly but certainly from a societal perspective."[64]

A midwestern woman born in 1963 articulated this perception well in her overall appraisal of war's impact on divorce. "My parents divorced a few months after my Dad came home, I was 8," she reflected.

> I was thrust into the public world for the rest of growing up.... Life changed completely for me. My mother went to work. She became a very bitter woman. We moved a lot, so I never really developed any long-term friendships growing up. She was always looking for the man that would take care of her so she could live the "right" way. Unfortunately she made several poor choices in her search. She really wanted my siblings and me to be seen and not heard. We didn't talk

> about our futures, or what we wanted to do in our lives. We had happy times, but when we started developing our own opinions, my Mom couldn't handle it. I had very little self-esteem and I mostly read books and did my school work.

When discerning what the era meant from her childhood perspective, she underscored, "Really the one thing that I remember was Vietnam because we lived it. I didn't see things like the moon landing because they didn't matter much to my mother. I think that if I would've lived with my dad that would've made a difference."[65] Another man stressed,

> I don't ever remember a time when they were a couple, but Vietnam is the context for my earliest memories of him. When he returned I just didn't seem to be a priority, and we quickly drifted apart onto paths that we largely remain on to this day. I don't know how much, if any of a role Vietnam actually played in our estrangement. But the war became a very convenient organizing principal for explaining our relationship, an emotional short-hand I used to explain my situation in simplified terms to others as a kid, and probably myself over the years too. It just seems ordered, "Oh, my biological dad is out of the picture because of Vietnam, he came home and had a hard time adjusting to family life so he left. He seems to be a great guy, we love each other, but don't have any real relationship . . . never did . . . we're casualties of Vietnam." Everyone can easily understand that story. It's probably way too simple to even be true, but that's the narrative which has solidified into the truth as I see it. That's the Vietnam War to me.[66]

In extreme cases, development of post-traumatic stress disorder (PTSD) pressed families to the breaking point, with veterans' sons and daughters describing child-father relationships using words such as "anguish," "torment," "turmoil," "depression," "abusive," "controlling," "alcoholism," and "misfit." A number of them point, as well, to secondary or generational PTSD in mothers and themselves as key trajectory determinants in their adult inabilities to appropriately build friendships, sustain intimate relations, or maintain jobs. "As much as our parents tried to find some manageable outcome as a result of the war," a post on the website Daughters of Vietnam Veterans reads, "we are the bastard children of this mess."[67]

What combatants from previous generations knew as battle fatigue or shellshock, PTSD describes the diagnosis and treatment for an otherwise normal veteran's reactions to warfare's extremities. It has today come to involve exposure to other traumas outside the ordinary range of human experiences, but to Vietnam veterans PTSD generally stems from the intense feelings of terror or helplessness they experienced either witnessing or surviving violent carnage and death in Southeast Asia. The National Vietnam Veterans Readjustment Study (NVVRS) speculated that approximately 15 percent of veterans suffer from PTSD that began appearing within hours, or in other cases months or years, after returning to the world.

These men perpetually relive stressor events through vivid, uncontrollable memories and recurrent dreams—flashbacks—usually precipitated by some stimulus reminding them of their tour. Symptoms typically manifest in partial amnesia about the war, or deliberate avoidance of thinking or talking about Vietnam, with heightened arousal including sleep loss, unprovoked angry outbursts, difficulty concentrating, and a hyper startle response. Sensing danger where usually none exists and numbed to affection and joy, they struggle to relate to civilians, gradually detaching themselves from family and friends. When wives and children are exposed to veterans' PTSD, they also sometimes exhibit similarly persistent mood swings in rage, nervousness, and acute feelings of vulnerability recognized as generational PTSD. The Vietnam War thus transmitted—passed down—a legacy perpetually corroding collective family functioning along with each member's mental health and sense of self-worth.[68]

For more than two decades after Vietnam ended, in those veterans' homes disrupted by the condition, PTSD largely defined childhood's parameters. Alienated from fathers they simultaneously loved, admired, and feared, children dealt with emotional, verbal, physical, and sometimes sexual abuse in isolation. Many assumed they were somehow responsible for making family life so miserable and were convinced that if anyone else found out they would certainly incarcerate and/or institutionalize him. Dads could be emotionally withdrawn, or else physically missing, for extended intervals of time, yet even when he seemed most distant or preoccupied, family knew better than to ask about Vietnam. Volatility was the common denominator. One never knew what routine minutiae might set the PTSD off—loud noises, unpaid bills, a flat tire, the lawn mower not starting, anything really—but once triggered it was too late to walk back from the edge. Fathers lost control with wild-eyed, irrational mood swings and dangerous flashback episodes, particularly terrifying when involving weapons.

Regularly drinking too much and intoxicated, fathers sometimes left children places and forgot to pick them back up or else never arrived to begin with. "He was going to pick us up to go out for pizza," a woman born in 1962 confided, "and I just waited it out, and waited, and waited, and waited, and, of course, that never happened. You know things like that where you're really excited 'cause dad was gonna come home and we would do things like a family does and he wouldn't show up or he'd show up drunk." Families searched for ways to maneuver around the illness at home while projecting a guarded appearance of normality in public.

Try not to startle him and always reach out with long objects when waking him. Turn a blind eye to night sweats and tolerate inappropriate war stories as bedtime stories. Avoid family meals at restaurants lest Dad have another embarrassing eruption or pick a fight. His moods effectively dictated mothers' and children's moods and behaviors. It was like, one Vietnam veteran's child recalled, "being raised by PTSD."[69]

In her groundbreaking autobiographical *Thirty Days with My Father: Finding Peace from Wartime PTSD*, Christal Presley chronicled the odyssey through Vietnam's shadow from girlhood to adulthood. "For me, the word 'Vietnam' has never signified a country or even a foreign war," Presley clarified. "To me it has always been synonymous with my father and the undeclared war that raged within our home." By the time the Veterans Administration hospital diagnosed her father with PTSD when Presley was just beginning elementary school, she was already well versed in his symptomology. Prone to bouts of depression that kept him locked away in the bedroom, curled up for days at time, ultimately something mundane would make him snap at the drop of a dime. During the most intense periods he lost control of his temper and raged—shaking and writhing in anger—and frequently unlocked the gun cabinet to retrieve his rifle, kept clean and loaded. Then, cradling the rifle "against his chest like an infant and his pupils so dilated you could hardly see the whites of his eyes," Presley revealed, "he would march back through the house and out the door, but not before uttering a single sentence: 'I'm going to the river to kill myself.'" Invariably he returned unharmed, but while she wanted to believe he came back out of love for her and her mother, she came to fear it was hatred instead that drove him to torture them with these performances.[70]

"My mother and I protected him," she explained, "walked on eggshells, and did anything and everything not to provoke him. We knew no other way. I spent my childhood wondering if he was a bad person, a lousy father, or if the war really had made him what he was. 'It's not his fault,' my mother said. 'Not his fault. Not his fault,' as if she could convince herself the more she said it. 'It's Vietnam,' she always added, lowering her voice as if the word itself were unspeakable. We spent our lives hiding from that war, though it raged all around us." Just as the conflict boxed them in—emotionally and physically—against one another, childhood was whipsawed by searching for paternal intimacy and avoiding contact. Despite Presley's frustration with her mother because the woman could neither fix him nor fully protect the little girl from him—"Why am I always the one who has to fix things? Isn't that what parents are supposed to do for their children?"—the two developed a bunker mentality. (One of the reasons for her dad's failure to keep Vietnam in the past, she suspected, was her mother's well-intentioned penchant for memorializing his service in the shadow boxes she arranged with medals and other memorabilia or gave as gifts.)

Both mother and child cultivated close bonds over the years—best friends and confidants—in self-conscious alliance against him. "Sometimes I felt sorry for my father," she recalled, "and sometimes I wished he would die. And all the while I loved him.... I wanted to do whatever I could to help. I truly believed that if I loved him enough I could make him better. But he didn't allow me to do that. Instead, the sicker he got, the more he locked himself away from me. And the more I realized how powerless I was, the guiltier and angrier I felt." Once those fundamental connections between Presley's own behaviors and her dad's well-being solidified into preadolescent reasoning (notions reinforced by her mother's deep religious faith), the veteran's inability to master the illness only bred more resentment in his daughter toward herself, her mom, her dad, and God, a downward spiral intertwined with the onset of her generational PTSD.[71]

Complicating matters, there were sporadic times when Presley's father—who eventually received full disability insurance for PTSD—appeared healthy and home life seemed normal. "But as his mood swings became more and more frequent," she related, "I became more and more terrified of his unpredictability, to the point where, by the time I was eleven, I couldn't even acknowledge that there was another side to his personality." Family photograph albums from the period chronicle the shift. In early preadolescence, pictures deceptively depict a pleasant childhood; frequently father and daughter are seen spontaneously happy together. Then smiling ceased. "When I reach age twelve," Presley pointed out, "the pictures of my father and me together stop. We are separate after that, an invisible wall between us. I had reached the tipping point and pushed him as far away as I could. Retreating from him was the only way I knew to protect myself."

To help cover her tracks she began blocking out unpleasant memories as another defense mechanism while crafting elaborate subterfuge. "To me, 'post-traumatic stress disorder' was just a bunch of words. All I knew was that it had something to do with my dad's brain and he seemed to be going crazy. And I knew it was bad because my mom told me that if anyone found out how sick he was, they'd come and take him away forever—and they'd take me away, too, and she couldn't live like that. If he had to be that sick, I wanted him to have something everybody could understand. So I picked brain cancer." In the event he acted on those suicidal thoughts, Presley planned to tell schoolmates the gruesome details of how he succumbed to cancer, a plausible cover story offering the added value of sympathy.[72]

At school, Presley questioned whether her own brain was normal or freakish. She grew to an acute awareness of how her "weird" life indeed differed by comparison with that of schoolmates, even those who, she discovered, shared "it"—a Vietnam veteran father with problems. Still, she craved the understanding and acceptance from teachers and students she was missing at home, and she experienced emotional devastation anew when neither was forthcoming in the manner she hoped. "I was always on guard, ready for rejection, crying at the drop of a hat," she continued, characterizing herself accordingly as an overly sensitive young student. In turn she sensed that peers tended to shun her for that sensitivity, casting her as a loner in elementary school. Reckless behaviors—all symptomatic of growing up with generational PTSD—reinforced the outsider perception. Presley feigned illness frequently, ate poison ivy once, changed classmates' answers on tests so they would not score 100 percent, and stapled her hand to see how it felt. On one occasion she stole a neighbor's vacation photograph showing the family on a beach. After cutting their heads off with scissors and clumsily replacing them with her family's faces, she tried passing off the obviously doctored snapshot as her own at school. Even where opportunities to talk to others about her family situation presented themselves occasionally, she refused for fear people might not believe her, or if they did, they would judge the Presleys harshly. What if exposing her parents to scrutiny led others to lay the blame for her dad's problems solely at her feet? All through elementary school, she remained "constantly torn between the desperate need to tell my family secret and the fear of what would happen if I did, [so] I never let anyone get too close."[73]

Several other survivors shared their experiences for this project and also for the therapeutic benefits to be found therein. A southern man born in 1958 traced his ongoing depression to his dad's return from Vietnam in 1968 and revealed how "the scars and very heavy burden his brother carried started with my dad's service and lasted until the day he [brother] took his own life." The aging veteran lives with this son now, and the war resides there, too. "Dad breaks into a Vietnam story three or four times a day," he explained of how they work through two generations of PTSD. "Up to his dying breath he'll be trying to make up for the sins against God he committed in Vietnam."[74]

Another woman, Cathi Bond-Drake, whose Hispanic family moved between California and Colorado after her birth in 1962, was only four years old when her navy corpsman father returned from a second tour. To her mind, the idyllic childhood spent living with maternal grandparents disintegrated when she and her mother reunited with her dad on the West Coast. "My memories after that time are not good," Cathi recalled.

> I had never really seen him, and he had never really seen me. I was only eighteen months old when he left and when he got back he was really, really sick . . . he had

> PTSD so bad. All of a sudden it was like we were dropped off in hell. My grandma and grandpa drove away and left us there. I didn't know how to feel about it. I wasn't very old and I don't think I understood that we were going to stay there. My grandfather was really my father figure and I don't think it occurred to me that they wouldn't be back.[75]

Pleasant childhood memories are few and far between after the family's first holiday season—"my horrible Christmas"—that year in 1966. Her father was already a serious alcoholic and threatened to kill mother and daughter at gunpoint, setting off tumultuous periods of marital separation lasting until third grade. His full-time return to the family (now including a younger sister) escalated the drinking and precipitated more abuse and eventually molestation by her thirteenth birthday. "My dad tried to rape me," Cathi confided, "and my mother basically told him to lay off. She told me he didn't remember because he was drunk all the time, which was the standard line. After that our relationship really changed and I don't know if he, I'm sure there are a lot of things, he felt shame, he felt guilt, survivor's guilt, PTSD . . . I mean all of the above. But he became pretty distant after that and he kind of got hostile with me, started destroying my things."

Consequently, she, too, grew wholly dependent on her mother, exhibiting codependent tendencies and separation anxieties. "Mom was everything," the woman continued.

> She was the heaven and the earth, she was my safety, she was my only safety. I wouldn't go to sleepovers because I was afraid she might not be there when I got back. If I thought she was going to leave I would put her pillow and blanket by the front door, so if she left I would know. She always told me those were behaviors because I was insecure. And she never attributed any of my bizarre behaviors—well, I guess they weren't bizarre for what I went through—but any of my behaviors related to any of my experience with Dad, she never did and she never has until three years ago. She always talked about his PTSD but never acknowledged there could be any PTSD for me. We just didn't talk about Vietnam either, [and] I was trained at a very young age not to tell people what was going on in our house, so that added a whole level of secrecy to our life.

After a failed attempt two years earlier, Cathi's father committed suicide on January 19, 1981. "We always had this saying that Dad died in Nam but laid down in 1981."[76]

CHAPTER 6

God Bless Dad Wherever You Are

POW/MIA

> You and Michael are constantly in my thoughts and prayers—please don't worry about me or try to imagine what I am doing. Think of me only as being with you in whatever you are doing. My heart is filled with joy in knowing you are all well . . . I am glad that Michael knows that I am his daddy, but sad he doesn't know what a daddy is.
>
> —CHRISTMAS MESSAGE 1966 FROM NAVY LIEUTENANT COMMANDER WILLIAM TSCHUDY TO WIFE JANE AND SON MICHAEL, WHO WAS SEVEN MONTHS OLD WHEN HIS FATHER WAS SHOT DOWN

Vietnam's impact on the semi-orphaned children of men listed as prisoner of war (POW) or missing in action (MIA) and orphaned sons and daughters growing up in Gold Star families is metaphorically a foot wide and mile deep. Comparatively speaking, the number of POW/MIA families was rather small—just under 600 prisoners of war and roughly 1,300 missing in action at war's end—while it is estimated that 20,000 lost a father in Vietnam. Yet the weight of their unique childhood experiences altered the course of their lives the most, and these experiences remain central, I would argue, to a wounded nation's long road toward reconciling Vietnam as a country and people, not solely the war America lost.

If for no other reasons, circumstances surrounding POWs and MIAs are significant to understanding Vietnam and childhood because for most in the United States, the POWs return in March 1973 marked the end of the war. Poignant family reunions during Operation Homecoming not only represented restoration of particular families but also served as useful shorthand for unity in a divided land. Beyond the disproportional attention given them in our public imagination, moreover, for youth, a POW/MIA designation is a special category of father absence.

Considering that Vietnam War POW/MIAs were primarily officers and professional soldiers, compared with enlistees and draftees, these servicemen were older, married (four out of five POW pilots had a wife back home), and with children ranging in age from less than one year to twenty-five years old. Regular separation intervals might have been a fundamental aspect of military family life, but prisoners were held for a longer time than in any other American conflict. The average captivity lasted over five years for navy flyers and only slightly less for marines and the army. This unprecedented period exceeded the average year-long tour fivefold, and in fact more closely approximated family separation during World War II. Similar to World War II, the indeterminate and uncertain nature of waiting on the home front compounded and exacerbated usual adjustment patterns of Vietnam-era families to the separation from father. Mothers and children survived effectively in limbo, unsure if they were wives, widows, or orphans and never knowing how to plan a future that may, or may not, include his return or death, or both.[1]

When servicemen went missing in action, the notification experience initially resembled a routine familiar to those learning any relative had been killed in Vietnam. Wives were psychologically numbed on hearing the news, and children arriving home from school to find their mothers sitting in shock on the couch clutching the message instinctively knew it had something to do with Dad. Local papers ran stories about the MIA, and churches held special services. Homes filled with neighbors, aunts, uncles, cousins, his high school and college friends, as well as fellow aviators. And after these gatherings dispersed, families gradually settled back into some semblance of domestic routines, left alone to begin sorting through new realities.[2]

An MIA classification brought its own surrealism, though—as if he had just magically vanished from existence—one that went beyond cleaning out his dresser drawers or moving his old pickup truck from the driveway.[3] As shock diminished, MIA wives were increasingly driven to gather any definitive information about the circumstances surrounding his casualty. The Geneva Convention states that a country must announce the capture of POWs accompanied by a photograph, but North Vietnam rarely complied—only releasing its first official list of prisoners in 1970—meaning many MIA families waited months, if not years, without a reclassification from missing in action to prisoner of war. Air Force Lieutenant Colonel Carl B. Crumpler had been shot down in July 1968, a full two years before his wife Jane received a six-line letter he sent from the Vietnamese prison camp. "Now," she told *Time* magazine of that pivotal correspondence, "I can tell the kids 'When Daddy comes home . . .' rather than 'If Daddy comes home.'"[4]

The first evidence Sybil Stockdale, wife of Navy Commander James B. Stockdale, received about her husband's fate was an article in the Soviet newspaper

Pravda mentioning a downed American pilot misidentified as Captain James B. Stackdel, two months after he disappeared in September 1965. Only after his letters arrived in 1966, containing passages for their four sons, was she finally able to tell the children their father was alive. "I read over the messages he had sent to each of the boys," she explained in *Good Housekeeping*, and "I thought to myself, 'These are very precious, I must tell the children in the right way,'" by first sitting the youngest—ages four and six—down together before talking to the oldest—ages twelve and fourteen—individually.

"I constantly think of, love and appreciate you four boys," Commander Stockdale wrote from solitary confinement. "I am confident that you are helping your mother and doing your best at your activities. My thoughts deal not only with each of you but with plans about how we will enjoy each other and work together in the future and how I will help each of you achieve your goals in life. . . . I pray a good deal. Every night I remember each of you individually and I know you do the same for me. I live for the day of our reunion." Thereafter, Sybil Stockdale made it a point to always share information with the youngest boys separately first until they were old enough to join family discussions about their father. When Stockdale learned the North Vietnamese had finally released a picture of her husband, she feared her youngest boys might be upset seeing him suffering or hurt in the local newspaper, so she rose before the sun on the day it was published to judge the image's potentially negative effect firsthand. Based on the pilot's diminished appearance, she decided to show it only to the fourteen-year-old over breakfast while shielding the other boys until a more appropriate age.[5]

After exhausting every conceivable information source, wives commonly entered a period of depression lasting as long as two to three years. Intentional or otherwise, POW/MIA wives tended to live psychologically and emotionally walled off, keeping a low profile until disillusionment with the government's lack of progress on the POW/MIA issue compelled women and children to take leadership roles late in the war. "It is all a façade," Jane Crumpler, a nursing student, revealed about her family's apparently normal home. "The life behind it is terribly flawed." "Everyone says you're so brave, but you do your crying at night," the wife and mother continued in 1970. She stopped trying to blend into the social scene and eventually avoided going out altogether because the accrued pain of his open-ended imprisonment hurt worst after a night out. "I never forget it. I never stop thinking about him and what he's going through. It's just impossible to get it out of your mind." Marrying a fighter pilot had always been a risky proposition, but liminal widowhood was more than she bargained for, likening it to "a dark curtain falling over my life."[6]

"The worst times, were when I was out with other couples," another POW wife echoed about not really living. "That was when I really felt alone. When I stayed in my little woman's world, I was fine." During her husband's third year in captivity, depression came on less frequently, but still "I go to bed at 9 o'clock every night and I pull down the shade on that day. . . . I feel like I'm in a vacuum," she concluded, "a spectator on life. . . . God, get me through it and let me get the kids through it."[7]

"Each situation is different," Valerie Kushner, the wife of a noncombatant army doctor, shared with *Life* magazine in 1972, "and all of them are untenable." That said, a number of common stressors molded the POW/MIA home-front experience. Chief among these were self-generated or external pressures to maintain hope he was alive, and coming home, which often caused friction with relatives. Wives squabbled with in-laws over maintaining respectful appearances and in some cases moved out of their own parents' houses when children started calling grandparents "Mom" and "Dad." Various legal and monetary difficulties factored prominently as well. "It is strange," one wife observed in *Life* magazine in 1970, "but people think that the fact that your husband is missing is your only problem. They forget you are still living in a very real world and you have to put up with other very real problems."[8]

Besides unresolved marriage status, without a legal declaration of whether he was alive or dead, a wife could neither receive all unpaid military earnings or life insurance, renew power of attorney, conclude mortgage matters, nor probate her husband's estate. Constant tension and strain manifested in sleep loss, mood fluctuations, or suicidal thoughts. Some worried husbands would try to talk them into having another baby to make up for having missed their children growing up. Mothers wanting more children feared getting too old, or that wrinkles and weight gain (or loss) made them so unattractive that returning husbands might start new lives with younger, prettier, and more fertile brides.[9]

Each passing month added additional psychological and emotional weight from being such a public curiosity. Many wives resented violations of family privacy by people interested in their lives, finances, and sexual activities, including in some instances well-meaning correspondence from those wearing POW/MIA bracelets. One embarrassed wife recalled nosey churchgoers scrutinizing her family situation after one of her young daughters mentioned that her dad was a prisoner, a term the congregation naturally assumed meant jail. Another found judgmental neighbors' incessant questioning most bothersome. "Why aren't you 25 pounds under weight?" "Why aren't you crying constantly, withering away?"[10]

In time, most wives dealt with existential despair by consciously deciding to stop simply marking days and get on with living. The navy's Center for Prisoner of War Studies (now the Robert E. Mitchell Center for Prisoner of War Studies) began examining women's behavioral coping patterns when it opened in early 1972. Based on longitudinal observations conducted over the decade, researchers at the center's Family Studies Branch posited that wives' abilities to cope with spousal captivity—which in turn guided children's adjustments—were directly correlated with several important variables: the couple's background, her assessments on the quality of their marriage, his motives for going to Vietnam, and the family's preparation for separation. Of these, marriage stability appeared to be the most significant, while a serviceman's prior economic planning for helping his family handle long periods apart was a close second. Filing power of attorney, for instance, or setting aside monetary allotments minimized legal and financial disruption in the family's quality of life. Planning also fortified Dad's provider role against speculative resentment that he recklessly abandoned them.[11]

The more stable the marriage, the more likely wives' coping strategies revolved around establishing individual autonomy. The Center for Prisoner of War Studies discovered that better-educated women with employable skills—sometimes the least satisfied with military life or facing more legal troubles—dealt best with captivity through personal development and wage employment. Eager to prove themselves strong, and increasingly comfortable expressing anger over their circumstances, they embraced learning new skills, landed better jobs, and/or purchased new homes. One POW wife, for example, knew people meant it as a compliment, but she nonetheless chafed when friends said how impressed they were by her newfound competence, never doubting her own capabilities.[12]

It should be noted that in many households, a woman's individuality and economic independence was not mutually exclusive with maintaining emotional space for missing husbands. When wives expressed marital satisfaction prior to imprisonment, self-reliance commonly complemented maternal efforts to preserve family integrity as an allied means of coping. Mothers continued close involvement with relatives and in-laws—including living with or near his parents—stressing togetherness as an investment in their children, and all the while fostering hope for his eventual return.[13]

Sybil Stockdale's oldest son remembered,

> At one point while Dad was gone, Mom decided that we would not take any family pictures. She just said it one night at supper and we nodded knowingly as though that made sense. And she decided that she would buy no new clothes until Dad came home. There was also a point at which she decided that we should always have a small bowl of rice for supper and that's all to sort of share Dad's meager existence. These sound like strange . . . emotional kinds of things that really indicated how desperate we were to do something, you know, how we might live our lives in waiting.[14]

"All of us kids, we can still remember," Tony Cordero, four years old when his father was shot down in the summer of 1965, explained. "As we went to bed every night, Mom would stand in the hallway with all the bedroom doors open, we said our goodnight prayers and the last thing we said was 'God bless dad wherever you are.'" "I don't think I could have survived without the children," Mary Anne Fuller, navy wife and mother of four, related to *Life* in 1970. "I have them every night to fix dinner for, I have them to love. It must be so hard for my husband because he doesn't have them to touch, like I have."[15]

Wives with the least marital satisfaction before and during separation remained mired in loneliness, insecurities, and self-pity. A number took functional steps in psychiatric therapy, but mainly they gravitated toward dysfunctional behaviors offering immediate relief, whether smoking, alcohol, or medication. If husbands were also less educated and less mature, often holding lower rank, spouses tended to more easily close out his masculine role in favor of assuming dual mother-father responsibilities, while reassigning his tasks to other family members. Associated sexual politics were particularly tricky. Because they were unable to start over or remarry without a divorce, society expected them to remain faithful and celibate. These deeply frustrating conflicts—mixing grief and worry with guilt and shame—were not the topics of polite conversation, especially with civilian women who accused them of trying to steal their husbands. And while most quietly managed temptations, wives did receive divorces in Mexico and Haiti or else furtively dated without this legal step. In some cases women only kept wearing wedding rings to make their children feel better.[16]

Since most POW/MIA's sons and daughters were between five and ten years old when their dads went overseas, mothers played key roles in children's adjustment. Mature, stable, and well-adjusted fathers translated to fewer problems for preadolescents, but paternal influence was decidedly secondary. A clear and positive correlation existed between their mother's attitudes and ability to cope and how a child managed separation. While POW/MIA youth dealt with some fundamental issues shared by all home-front preadolescents, there are two major factors that affected how these children coped. The length of separation potentially opened more serious developmental issues. Again, most often mothers developed appropriate parenting strategies, some rather lenient while others more strict. "Sometimes I tend to be hard on my children because I don't want people to say, 'Well, they don't have a father and they are going to turn out to be brats,'" JoAnn Flora, an army sergeant's wife, commented during 1970. "I want to make sure that the children are what he expects of them when he gets back."[17]

Summative studies, however, detected in a number of POW/MIA families the same serious disruptions in healthy male psychosexual development found during the Second World War. Despairing mothers grew so dependent on children that the emotional manipulation used to control preadolescents created Oedipal sons whose resultant issues were frequently worsened by displacement problems when fathers returned. Opposition toward Vietnam among older preadolescents—eleven- and twelve-year-olds—and adolescents aggravated family tumult. Based on the center's surveys, in 1972 mothers feared that almost 20 percent of children suffered significant emotional problems during POW/MIA separations, and even in cases when counseling would have been advisable, few preadolescents received any.[18] "I, at one point, visited a counselor probably five years in," the oldest Stockdale son—by that time a teenager—recalled, "and the one piece of advice I remember was you may be better off just considering your father dead and gone, which, at the time, made pretty good sense to me, you know, after years and years of living with it."[19]

The "unknown" was another variable POW/MIA children faced, making separation harder to tolerate, even comprehend, compared with others with fathers in Vietnam. In one sense, it was socially awkward explaining to elementary school peers how no one knew whether your father was alive or dead. As a retort to being teased, the closest analogy might be comparing prisoners of war to jail inmates, not really a winning combination.[20] Almost as a rule, the children of POW/MIAs doggedly maintained hope, often despite mounting evidence to the contrary. But uncertainty gnawed at them constantly. Is he alive? How much hope can we genuinely have? How might he have died? Often older children refused to accept death's finality until seeing his body, while others reluctantly and painfully reconciled themselves to the inevitable.

Conversations suggesting their dad might not return were seen as threats challenging this faith, putting sons and daughters on the defensive. And just as children idealized absent fathers, often they grew overly critical of their mothers, mainly when her behaviors did not match their own convictions concerning his ultimate return. Many found the notion of the family moving on without him simply inconceivable, fantasizing that any loss of hope by individual members made the whole family liable for his death. In working through grief, boys constructed common rescue fantasies, whereby they enlisted in the military to save Dad themselves. "My daughter cried for two and a half years for her father," the wife of an air force sergeant captured in 1965 observed. "Finally, I said, 'Kid, shut up. He isn't here. What do you want from me?' It sounds very cruel, but after a while there is nothing you can do. Your heart is breaking as much as the kid's and she is just going to have to live with it."[21]

Here, fathers became "more remembered than real," represented around the house by rituals and fragments of memorabilia. An eight-year-old girl with few memories of her dad persisted in answering the family phone as his residence. A plastic 1/32-scale Revell model of his Phantom F-4 aircraft dangled from the bedroom ceiling (above a picture of him in his flight suit), a dry-cleaned Class A uniform hung in the closet, an official military head-and-shoulders portrait adorned her mom's dresser, and the *World Book Encyclopedia* stayed dog-eared to the Vietnam entry.[22]

Julie Kott, the wife of missing marine bombardier Captain Stephen J. Kott, explained to *Life* that of their three children—ages eight, seven, and five in 1970—"I think only [the oldest child] Stevie's scarred. The others want a daddy, any daddy, but Stevie wants his old one back." Indeed, older children with firsthand recollections endlessly retold a handful of the same cherished stories—about snowball fights, his sense of humor, or bouts of tickling—and concentrated to envision certain traits—eye color and physical features—that functioned to help define him in memory. Those too young to recall purposefully learned these stories secondhand. Having never known her dad, a preschool daughter and her paternal grandmother kept a scrapbook about the POW as a means of finding out about him while connecting with her grandma through shared memories.[23]

The Christmas holiday season—a means of marking another year of separation—presented special problems of sentimentality. Reminded of happier times, some mothers grudgingly went through the motions of putting up the tree or decorating to keep up normal appearances. "I don't bring Bill into Christmas," stressed the wife of navy lieutenant commander William Tschudy. "I don't feel Michael [a six-year-old kindergartener] should have to know all this, though I've told him about Bill. I don't want him to have to think of his daddy as something pitiful. To Michael, Bill is just a picture."[24]

"I answer all the questions, but I don't try that hard to remind my children of their father," Valerie Kushner echoed, referring to her four-year-old son with no recollection of his dad and an eight-year-old daughter's vague memories. "I refuse to say 'Okay, sit down, here's lecture No. 72 about daddy,' or 'Don't forget to kiss daddy's picture goodnight.' He comes up naturally in our conversation, frequently, but not daily. It's quite simple: the family is incomplete without him."[25]

Letter writing played a critical role in maintaining a paternal presence in all servicemen's families, yet for POWs, communication was more tenuous. Until 1968 letters from POWs held in Vietnam were scarce, and since mothers and children had no way of determining whether their correspondence reached him, families effectively wrote into a void, frequently penning multiple versions of the same letter.[26] The Geneva Convention mandated the exchange of at least two letters and four cards per month, but in practice North Vietnam allowed only one letter per month through the American anti-war Committee of Liaison. Small packages with sundry provisions—vitamins, medicine, tobacco, food concentrates, and photographs (no reading material, though)—might also be sent every other month through the Soviet Union.

Prior to 1968, when POW letters were more sporadic, those reaching home might be several pages long. However, by 1970 the North Vietnamese limited the prisoners' correspondence to seven lines on a four-by-six-inch form for easier censorship. Thereafter these short messages from Vietnam tended to come in haphazardly random bunches. Like other letters from overseas, POW fathers instructed kids to study hard, cautioned against watching too much television, or inquired whether someone had gotten their braces off yet. Usually, though, mail functioned not so much as satisfying communication but merely as tangible proof he was still alive on a given date. With so little to go on, wives tried to discern trends in his mental stability and physical condition by analyzing how clearly thoughts were conveyed or handwriting quality. "He is able, for example, to remember the dates of the children's birthdays, the fact that this one must be making his First Communion, this one must be in such and such a grade," Eileen Cormier, wife of an air force sergeant, said of the encouraging signs in one letter. "That is quite a feat for [a] man who never enrolled a kid in school."[27]

The Center for Prisoner of War Studies observed another coping method among wives and mothers—directing newfound agency into social activism. Women, usually without infants and preschoolers at home, got organized, first forming lines of communication with other POW/MIA wives before building grassroots groups on their shared anger with the military and government.[28] Per official government policy during the Johnson administration, POW/MIA families had largely stayed in the background. Throughout the 1960s the armed forces quietly supplied dependents with confidential information about missing men. But the complexity of imprisonment left families in isolated frustration, primarily because North Vietnam classified captured airmen as war criminals, refusing to negotiate their release or allow neutral inspections.

The turning point came in Richard Nixon's first years in office when families' mounting exasperation converged with presidential determination to strategically politicize POWs in hopes of rallying fading public support for the war after Tet. Encouraged by the administration's new public stance, Sybil Stockdale took the lead in facilitating communication between groups of POW/MIA wives already operating on both coasts. Her activism provided the impetus necessary in forming the National League of Families of American Prisoners and Missing in Southeast Asia, an advocacy organization made up of some 2,700 wives, children, parents, siblings, and close relatives, in May 1970.

With the release of POWs emerging as a linchpin in the basic framework for peace negotiations—a crucial North Vietnamese bargaining chip always tied to the timing of U.S. troop withdrawals—the issue gained a wider cultural meaning. The National League, always closely identified with Nixon's positions, spoke out with speeches, letter-writing campaigns, telephone banks, and even floats in local parades to keep constant pressure on both Washington and Hanoi. A soon-to-be universally recognized black-and-white flag—featuring a bowed POW, barbed wire, and guard tower, with the vow "You Are Not Forgotten"—came to symbolize the league's crusade. Their energy and urgency, in concert with other allied groups—as illustrated by Voices in Vital America's successful POW/MIA bracelet campaign—amplified public awareness. Newspapers featured editorials, radio and television programs broadcast segments, and stories ran in the foreign press. Private citizens undertook undercover missions. Congress consequently called for tougher demands on North Vietnam, the Pentagon began holding press conferences, and State Department officials finally met with POW families.[29]

In the war's last three years, thanks to the National League and Nixon, the situation of POWs and their families cut across military matters to become political and diplomatic tools occupying center stage in the national discourse over Vietnam. The conflict's unpopularity and associated feelings of disgrace made these predominantly navy and air force pilots and career officers arguably the first, and for a time the only, heroes Vietnam produced. And as Americans focused more intently on their imprisonment, mass media sentimentally framed this thorny geopolitical impasse around how it affected families, specifically childhood, starting with *Life* and *Look* magazines both highlighting children living without POW fathers in their 1970 Christmas season issues.[30]

The Paris Peace Accords signed in January 1973, formally ending direct American participation in the Vietnam War, allowed the United States to pull out its remaining troops in exchange for leaving the South Vietnamese government intact *and* the freedom of 591 POWs. The actual release reflected how delicate negotiations had been on the subject from the beginning. After the initial cease-fire agreement, Washington threatened to delay withdrawals unless Hanoi offered more cooperation identifying all Americans held in the North and by the Vietcong in the South. Ultimately, throughout the weeks of Operation Homecoming—phased in between February 12 and March 29, 1973—prisoners were at last turned over in groups, their release prioritized by length of imprisonment. Those handed over first had spent between six and eight years in primitive and inhumane captivity. What followed at Clark Air Force Base in the Philippines, where former POWs received processing and debriefing, was a patriotic outpouring—however brief—celebrating their repatriation. Still, despite North Vietnamese insistence that all prisoners had been returned, the United States suspected there may have been as many as 2,500 being held at war's end, considering that nearly 1,350 were still listed as missing in action and another 1,200 had been reported killed in action without a body recovered.[31]

"The day that Dad came home, we had been forewarned about Dad's injuries," James Stockdale's eldest son recalled,

> but standing there on the tarmac, when he came down . . . the steps, I remember just holding his featherweight frame in my arms. We were just sort of stumbling over our love for one another. . . . I remember the third night he was actually at home, he wanted to go and call the wife of one of the men who had died in prison. And we had about one of those to do a night for a couple of weeks. He felt it was his obligation to report what he knew about the nobility of men who had suffered greatly and had died of either injury or infection or, in a couple of cases, just a broken heart as he described it. We realized how close we had come and we maintained a fierce, loving allegiance to one another through to the very end.[32]

Differences in healthy emotional, social, and familial adjustment between reintegrating POWs and other returning Vietnam veterans are matters of degree, not of kind. The Pentagon and State Department did play a relatively more hands-on role in reintroducing former prisoners—with accumulated back pay—into postwar society, shielding them, and families, from public fanfare and media access as much as possible, so the process might unfold privately on their own terms. Otherwise, the principal difference setting POWs apart is the Rip Van Winkle nature of homecoming, or rather the culture shock of being dislocated time travelers. Never having set foot in a house where everyone now lived or paid such inflated prices at Montgomery Ward, men came back to the world woefully out of step with both radical changes in family cycles and wholesale redefinitions of American culture and society broadly understood as the sixties. Ironically, the most surprising feature to researchers studying POW reintegration was that while wives expected tremendous change in their husbands' personalities, aside from some basic reordering in the importance of certain values, that, in fact, had not been the case. Instead, husbands anticipated little fundamental change in wives and children, yet came home to quite a lot.[33]

Similar to homes disrupted by short-term Vietnam service, reintegrating POW husbands-fathers typically proved tougher and less fulfilling than expected. Extended separation created families significantly more female-centered than those of other veterans, and certainly more so than was still normative in America during these nascent years of second-wave feminism. Again, sometimes those same gendered reorganization strategies required to deal effectively with separation—closing out certain paternal duties—made readjusting especially problematic. The roots simply ran deeper, and the longer the separation, the more hesitant wives were to relinquish freedom and control, prone to framing husbands as interlopers in families functioning well without him. Tensions arose over whether, or how quickly, returning veterans could effectively reestablish male authority as head of the household in the face of these galvanized gender-role reversals. Uncomfortable with a wife's independence, former POWs had initial difficulty sharing domestic decision making and disciplining the children, leaving them feeling left out and unneeded as husband and father.[34]

Under some circumstances, a woman's emotionally trying and time-consuming activism on behalf of the POW/MIA cause became a bone of contention between husband and wife when the former judged such outspokenness to have been inappropriate. So, too, could strong bonds between preadolescents and grandparents filling in as father substitutes postpone restoration of father-child relationships. Veterans were reluctant to interfere with those emotional ties, and children found it hard making room for new membership in a grandpa-dad-child dynamic. Fully resolving the crisis in masculinity often took years, and observers noted that as late as 1976 POW families appeared considerably more matrilineal than most. Men had reassumed many, but not all, previously male roles, while wives still performed some family tasks commonly associated with husbands.[35]

A clear majority of POW couples kept marriages intact, and to a large degree by persistently renegotiating gender roles. Striking a mutually satisfying balance—restoring a meaningful paternal role while preserving maternal autonomy—proved crucial to bringing coherence to husband-wife, mother-child, and father-child relationships. Men came to accept wives more fully as equal partners, developing an appreciation for their self-reliance and greater respect for their capabilities. Women in intimate and longer marriages were the most agreeable to making these necessary postinternment accommodations.[36] Often couples came to believe the POW experience had given them a second chance. Absence had brought the two closer, and they moved forward determined to make up for lost time without taking each other for granted.

"The important thing was the kids," a former prisoner told researchers. "If either one of us fell to pieces, it might cause problems for the boys that would be hard to identify and take years to correct. The kids lived in euphoria for six months. I think they spent the next six months hoping I'd go away again." Marital bonds were indeed often easier to restore compared with parental. Prisoners came home to older and thus developmentally very different children. "The children will expect all problems to be solved and flowers to bloom in the middle of winter, once their father comes back," Valerie Kushner forecasted in 1970. "They won't be prepared for the shock of being No. 2 all of a sudden, they won't be the only ones to decide if we'll have hamburgers for dinner. My son loves the feeling of being my No. 1 boyfriend, but when Spank comes home I'm going to say, 'Go find your own girl, Mike.' It won't be easy for any of us."[37]

"My children have lived with this for so long that their father's return is going to be more of an adjustment than his having been gone," Eileen Cormier stressed. "What he has now is four children, no longer infants, whose lives are structured by school, and a wife who has now purchased her own home, who is unlikely to want to pick up and meander around the countryside with him as they did in the past."[38]

"Not all is perfect," Mike McGrath, a navy lieutenant commander captured in June 1967 flying his 179th mission over enemy territory, reflected.

> The few cases of problems I did hear about usually involved fathers (more senior officers with older kids) who were shot down when their daughters were approaching their teenage years. The father comes home after seven or so years, the daughter is now 18 or so, and the father starts laying down restrictions and laws for the daughter: put on a brassier[e], you can't wear that sexy outfit, no short mini-skirts, no black lipstick, no late hours at the mall, stay away from that punk kid with the marijuana, get better grades, do your homework, etc. You can guess the result.[39]

After arriving home, Air Force Lieutenant Colonel Kenneth North took his family to Disney World (opened in 1971), wondering the entire trip, "What would the North Vietnamese think of this place? They wouldn't believe it." Yet Colonel North quickly came to understand how far the POW's challenges went beyond just acclimating to the ordinary childhood schedules. "There is a world of rediscovery in this house," he clarified to *Time* magazine in the summer of 1973, "a father getting to know his wife and children, a family learning to be a family again."[40]

After six and a half years in captivity, North, who was forty-three years old when freed, described being reintroduced to four daughters, by that time seventeen, fifteen, fourteen, and eleven. "The kids are going 90 m.p.h. and I'm going ten," he related. "It's hard understanding a 17-year-old high school senior when you last saw her as a grade school child." The "shocks of re-entry" hit North early and often. "We've had dinner discussions when the girls used such vivid language that I was at a loss about how to clean it up," he joked, expressing equal surprise at his eleven-year-old's lecture on women's liberation. "She tells me how she is a person and has to be able to express herself." And even though he promised himself in prison long-haired boys would never be allowed in the house, North conceded, "well, they've come and they've stayed."[41]

Reintegration was about accommodation, he maintained, and that had to work both ways. "I don't want them to pity me, and I don't want them to think 'Daddy's home again and he's going to crack the whip.' I never want them to think 'Why doesn't he go back to Viet Nam'?" Often in his cell, North revealed, he daydreamed about someday sitting everyone down and insisting his girls recall absolutely everything he had missed in their lives. However, as he confronted stacks of family photographs commemorating bygone birthdays and assorted milestones, he had rethought the strategy. "I'm not going to do that. I'm not going to look back and feel sorry for myself. I say, let's go from here."[42] "In the case of my own two boys," Mike McGrath detailed,

> I was shot down when they were 2 1/2 and 3 1/2. They were 8 and 9 when I came home. Upon return, my wife and I discussed the kids. The youngest one was the perfect kid, no problems. The older boy was having behavioral problems. We knew he needed to be held back a year to mature. But, that might have been a disaster for his self-image. We made a decision. We bought a motor home. We took the boys out of school and travelled the states and Canada, hunted, fished, skied, golfed, explored wilderness areas . . . and rebuilt the family. I told the boys that the cost of this would be that after we moved (and I started postgraduate school) that they would have to complete the same grade they left. They bought in. We had a great seven months.

"I knew a secret," McGrath, who serves as historian for the returnees' organization NAM-POWs, concluded. "I knew that kids I had known who were held back a year were always bigger, stronger, smarter, etc. than the rest of their class. It worked. From that day on my kids got straight As. From there they got degrees in chemical engineering at Colorado University, electrical engineering at the Naval Academy, and nuclear engineering for the Navy guy. As predicted, they were great in academics, athletics, and personal relationships. Today they are ages 52 and 53 and have blessed me with six grandchildren with more A's and athletic accomplishments than I could have imagined."[43]

The Family Studies Branch of the Center for Prisoner of War Studies was actually unable to identify any significant links between either the gender, or the age, of children during separation and reestablishing satisfactory father-child relationships. Although some older youth and teenagers who kept their fathers' POW status hidden from peers due to Vietnam's unpopularity later dealt with complications stemming from ambivalence and shame, the two leading variables affecting reintegration were family readiness prior to captivity and abuses servicemen endured during internment. Those captured prior to 1969 generally suffered worse treatment than men becoming POWs afterward when conditions improved, partly as a result of the National League's efforts. The center concluded that the more taxing a POW's captivity, the more emotional and psychological distance to overcome with family, thus the greater residual bearing on childhood.[44]

Defense Department psychologists recommended wives and children not belittle the POW for odd behaviors, to be open and realistic about their feelings, and not to attempt to take his mind off the ordeal. It was deemed important for families not to treat POWs as mentally ill or returning heroes, but rather give them needed privacy and time. Again, a father's overall preparation for long-term separation likewise tended to alleviate emotional stress in children. Adequate legal, financial, and psychological contingency planning preserved in a preadolescent's eyes his critical role of protector and provider during the absence, insulating his masculinity from doubts that might otherwise have eroded those perceptions. Consequently, children renewed bonds of affection without necessarily having to rebuild basic levels of trust.[45]

Based on initial testing conducted in the first two years after repatriation, the center warned of POW children lagging profoundly below peer norms in personal adjustment (defined as self-reliance, sense of self-worth and personal freedom, feelings of belonging, and freedom from withdrawal or nervous tendencies) and social adjustment (defined as possessing social skills and social standards, freedom from antisocial tendencies, and healthy family, school, and community relations). Concern partly stemmed from almost 30 percent of POWs divorcing within the first year of returning (in fairness, not much different from overall divorce rates in the late Vietnam era). In reconstituted families, new stepfathers presented unique tensions that did not immediately offset harmful effects of prolonged separation and probably aggravated childhood problems.[46]

By the longitudinal study's conclusion in the late seventies, however, results indicated that POW children in reunited families had effectively closed the gap, improving in both personal and social adjustment to the point where significant differences compared with the general population no longer existed. Of note, where matrilineal environments encouraged independence and assertiveness during separation, some children demonstrated even better adjustment. Youth in reconstituted families largely remained behind for a few more years in coping with school and community relations, displaying nervous symptoms and withdrawal tendencies longer. But in reunited homes, as Dad's place became more established and predictable, the Center for Prisoner of War Studies determined that any significantly negative emotional and psychological effects the POW experience had on children were ephemeral, and this category of long-term father absence did not have enduring influence on family lifestyles.[47] For better or worse, developmentally these semi-orphans seem to have grown up very much like other Vietnam veterans' sons and daughters. "Of all the children I knew who were adolescents of NAM-POWs, none had problems to my knowledge," Mike McGrath underscored.

> In my experience as a Naval aviator who was at sea on combat cruises for as much as eight months at a time, separation of a father from the family was normal. Of course, after an eight-month cruise everyone is excited that Dad is home. After a couple of days, the kids are back to their normal school duties and friends. The couple settles down to normal activities. Dad can pay the bills and do the little repairs. Six months later, Dad will leave again on another eight-month cruise. Summation: Somehow it all works. When you have a strong marriage and a stable base for the kids, they excel. The separations, even the separation for several years in the cases of NAM-POWs did not severely affect the kid's development.[48]

Non-reunited families, those with husbands and fathers still missing in action, managed the tendencies and consequences of father absence less squarely. "The wives of POWs and those killed in action can run the full grief cycle," Peggy Duggan, wife of Major William Duggan and mother of two, told *Time* magazine in 1973. "But the MIA wife can never complete the cycle. You can only go 359 degrees, and then you start all over again." Families awaiting word on MIA husbands and fathers nervously studied each Operation Homecoming release list (as did those wearing POW/MIA bracelets) hoping against hope. These were anxious times, and each roster of names without resolution only intensified the pain. "I ran into the worst emotional bump when the lists of prisoners came out," Peggy Duggan revealed. "I was really expecting a big list. My antenna was up. Then I watched the P.O.W.s return on television. I don't know—I couldn't stay away—it was like a bird being hypnotized by a snake." Whenever contingents landed at Clark Air Force Base, Duggan bit the inside of her lip to keep from crying until Operation Homecoming ended altogether and the uncertainty marking the previous seventeen months since her husband was declared missing solidified into permanence. "The terror needs time to heal," Duggan reflected immediately after the last POWs came home. "I just cling to a fleeting hope. Maybe they were all murdered, but I can only hope they will find one of them in a cave somewhere."[49]

Although POW repatriation in 1973 ended Vietnam in the American mind, concern for a complete accounting of the remaining 1,300 MIAs proliferated politically and culturally, assuming, in the words of historian George Herring, "the power and mystique of a religion."[50] As part of the Paris peace negotiations, President Nixon had secretly promised North Vietnam more than $3 billion in reconstruction aid and $1.5 billion in commodities. But after Congress made payment contingent on North Vietnam accounting for all MIAs—which the Vietnamese either could not or would not do—America reneged on the deal. Given that most missing airmen were known to have died in circumstances making recovery nearly impossible, a full accounting is extremely problematic, but U.S. insistence on this solitary issue impeded normalizing relations and reconciliation between the two countries.

Resolution has also been delayed by the emotionally charged conviction among many Americans that some of the MIAs may, in reality, still be held as prisoners. Despite the Vietnamese allowing increased access and cooperation for MIA searches in the last generation—resulting in more than seven hundred servicemen's remains having been identified and returned—the persistent belief in men left behind and the commitment to bring them home remain powerful and controversial sentiments with a great deal of resonance in popular culture.[51] And while the country projected its collective search for postwar vindication and redemption onto the POW/MIA screen, for MIA children who waited, or still wait, for closure, prolonged uncertainty continues to inform individual healing processes.

Air Force Major William Duggan's daughter Charlotte was in junior high when her father went down on New Year's Eve 1971 during his second tour over Vietnam. Charlotte, born in 1959, returned to school in a civilian community a week later still in shock without having shed a tear. "Unbeknownst to me," she revealed of the encounter's subsequent impact on her life's trajectory, "my elderly seventh-grade teacher had also lost her husband during the Christmas break and the kids were naturally gravitating toward my sadness rather than to the teacher's. I walked into class and she said, 'Charlotte, have you had any word on your father?' I remember for the first time crying, and so, she said, 'OK students, pick up your feet, Charlotte's going to drown us with her tears.' I clammed up . . . and my trust level was gone after that." At that point, she remembered thinking, "OK, now I know I can't share my life with people because they won't understand . . . and it's taken me all this time to build back up trust with people."[52]

"After my seventh-grade teacher humiliated me," she continued, "my family pulled together as a unit and I stayed under the radar if that makes sense because I didn't have any trust and didn't quite know what to do with myself." Whereas youth in reunited families assimilated back into military or civilian communities fairly readily, children in non-reunited as well as newly reconstituted homes commonly viewed themselves and their families as outliers, somehow illegitimate compared with intact families in social settings. Children from MIA families, such as Charlotte Duggan, likewise characteristically suppressed childhood emotions as a coping method. Understanding outbursts to be socially unacceptable to adults anyway, displaying grief brought inherent risks at home and with peers. Mothers frowned on such behaviors, and already feeling alienated, deeply self-conscious, and inferior to other children, opening up potentially drew more unwelcome attention. "Those that knew me in the seventh grade," Charlotte said, "knew that Dad was shot down but I even forgot Mom bought a bunch of the POW/MIA bracelets. I guess I gave them out to all my friends in the seventh grade. I didn't [remember], I shut down emotionally, because it was easier to not have to deal with it. Later, people in high school were like, 'Charlotte, I didn't realize your dad was missing in action.'"[53]

While Charlotte learned to "play it close to the vest" in childhood, her mother and brother Scott, who was eleven when their father went missing, coped by "putting one foot in front of the other" more overtly. "I'm sure my mother and brother Scott talked more," Charlotte added. "I was not accepting. Scott dealt with it a lot better than I did." For Peggy Duggan social engagement and political activism served as a necessary outlet. Although she understood how other MIA wives and mothers gave up and moved on, she refused initially to, in her words, put up "any grave markers to her husband's memory" and stayed "nervously noncommittal about the future." "The only thing I can do is stay extremely busy in the daytime so that I just collapse at night," Peggy Duggan explained to a *Time* reporter in 1973. "I go to every dum-dum thing that comes along. I've been active before, but never with such hysteria. I cannot stand to think about it—if I relax, I cry."[54] Peggy served as an area coordinator for the National League and became involved in local community affairs, but most significantly she lobbied for changes in Texas law regarding MIA widow's rights.

Like most states, Texas law required a person to have been missing seven years before courts issued a death certificate, a real hardship for MIA wives trying to support families. Everything was in William Duggan's name. Peggy could not make property transactions, manage bank accounts and stocks, or probate the estate. Those living on military bases faced eviction. The Duggans at least had power of attorney but were unable to use it without proof he was alive, nor could the family enact his will without a death certificate. The air force sent only two-thirds of the major's service-connected paycheck each month, and the rest was deposited in a restricted savings account that could only be drawn on when the family showed cause. As Peggy told Texas legislators and reporters, America faced the disgraceful prospect of relegating more than one thousand veterans' families to welfare rolls if state laws were not enacted declaring MIAs legally dead when the Pentagon changed their status to missing and presumed killed in action.

Her advocacy on behalf of MIA families joined a larger chorus of predominantly female voices in the early 1970s urging Texas to prohibit sex discrimination in legal and financial matters with an equal rights amendment. After the state legislature ratified the federal ERA in March 1972, Texans had approved a state ERA later in November. Over the next two years, the act's core principle of equality launched several new statutes giving married women equal legal rights via comprehensive improvements to the Texas Family Code. Texas amended laws widely affecting family life, including insurance, banking, real estate, deeds, contracts, divorce, choice of residence, child custody, and disposition of property. As a direct result of Peggy Duggan's relentless urging and public pressure generated by her *Time* magazine feature, Governor Dolph Briscoe personally weighed in to assure passage of an emergency amendment regarding rights of MIA wives just minutes before the deadline in the legislature's final session in June 1973. With this law, Texas took the lead nationally in declaring an MIA legally dead on issuance of an armed forces death certificate, thus allowing widows immediate access to benefits.[55]

It appears likely that Peggy's encouragement of Charlotte's participation in the Miss Texas Teenager pageant was—like providing POW/MIA bracelets for classmates—a mother's attempt to draw her daughter out. From her mother's activist's perspective, the pageant, by extension, also presented the girl with her own age-appropriate platform for exercising agency. "I was Daddy's little girl," Charlotte recalled about the fulfillment she took from competing, "and that's probably why I gravitated into that pageant because what Dad used to do was, Mom would go out and buy me a new dress when I was a little girl, and Daddy would make me put it on and had me parade and twirl around in the room so he could see it. So that was important to me, you know, because that was like Dad watching me, instead of the audience.... I was reliving trying on a new dress and parading in front of Dad."

After winning the Miss Texas Teenager title in 1973, Charlotte—in pageant dress and tiara—frequently worked on behalf of the National League in area shopping malls getting petitions signed. And despite her reticence toward being an MIA child, she tentatively embraced this role. "It was my way of helping Dad. I was at a stage where whatever I could do to help Dad I was trying to do." At the national Miss Teenage America pageant in Atlanta, when contestants presented then-governor Jimmy Carter with something symbolic of their state, Charlotte took advantage of the occasion to keep focus on her father. "Well, we had gotten a cowboy hat for him," she said, "[but] at the last minute I changed my mind and I presented Jimmy Carter, I stood there in front of him, and said, 'I can't think of anything more Texan than my dad. Would you do me the honor of wearing my dad's POW/MIA bracelet?'" The attendant publicity around her simple gesture made Charlotte more uncomfortable, however, as did periodically negative antiwar reactions to her presence in malls. "As a kid that makes quite an impression," she confided. "So I pulled further and further into my shell. . . . I would smile at the world but was crumpling inside. You know how you can be in a crowd and be part of the crowd, but not be there—that was me."[56]

To a greater extent than POW families, and for far longer, MIA fathers existed imaginatively in childhood. Once he left for Vietnam, Major William Duggan, who flew hundreds of combat missions in Southeast Asia, lived and died in Charlotte's mind. "Dad was your epitome of the fighter pilot with the loudest stereo on the base, music blaring, fast cars, you know, crazy as a nut, typical fighter pilot," she emphasized. "My dad was just an overgrown child, never grew up, so he was a lot of fun to be around," Charlotte continued, illustrating her point with a story on how he escaped capture on a previous mission by being, to her preadolescent reasoning, the world's greatest at hide-and-seek. "It wasn't [until] after he was shot down, you know, subconsciously you make him into a God in your mind, and you forget that he is a human being, I mean, I've forgotten he had some serious alcohol issues as did most of the pilots."

"For three months prior to the visit from the military people," Charlotte remembered, "I would wake up screaming from nightmares that Dad was having a plane crash. And I saw a ball of fire. And I would wake up screaming and crying and I would tell my mom about it . . . so it didn't come as a surprise." But soon after his F4 went down over Laos, the recurring nightmares returned with her injured father and his navigator (Captain Frederick Sutter) trapped inside a cave, a curious twist since it was later learned that American POWs held outside North Vietnam were, in fact, sometimes kept in caves and bunkers. "That's why, vividly—and they haven't found anything—I feel like my dad lived and was a prisoner," she maintains. When pondering what he might be going through, she always envisioned a prisoner bowing behind bars, "but he was underground which was surprising to me in the dream. So I would say, 'Mom, he's a prisoner,' and somehow telepathically I felt like I was talking to Dad in my dream."[57]

"But I don't think he would have survived as a prisoner. He was too proud a man to do that. My dad died in 1977," Charlotte believes, when she was eighteen years old. "It was like all of a sudden my body shut down and I was just a shell and I can remember just leaving and walking the streets, and just walked because I just knew he had died, you know, it's like your dad died. And you go into shock and all you can do is just stagger and stumble around, which is what I did. He died in the fall of 1977, and you can't convince me otherwise of that. My brother keeps saying, 'Charlotte, he died in the plane crash.' They haven't found anything, nothing. We're still one of seven hundred families that have nothing."[58]

Prior to 1977 Charlotte lived as a self-described "goody-two-shoes" in the hopes this would somehow help her father. "Subconsciously," she said, "in my little brain I had it worked out that if I'm good Dad will come home." The ensuing mourning period over his "death," however, sparked adolescent behavioral problems and drug experimentation that followed Charlotte into adulthood. The first tentative steps toward reconciliation came from her mother's remarriage. Peggy had told *Time* in 1973 that she didn't think getting married again was a possibility. "It depends," she responded to the reporter's questions on the subject. "[Charlotte] Ann sanctifies her father, and I'm not sure anyone should ask to marry *us*. We still keep a home for Bill."[59]

Yet within a year or so, Peggy did remarry. "Mom was a lot more accepting than I was, and it's funny how it happened," Charlotte recalled.

> My mother's high school sweetheart is who she ended up marrying.... After Dad got shot down, he started coming around. I was not very nice [her younger brother Scott was more accommodating]. They got married right after Dad was declared dead in 1974. But I took it bad, and I remember the first time he came for a date, he had a nice suit on, and he had roses and [a] box of candy for my mom and I opened the door and I spit on him—I was not a very nice kid—ran out the back door to another friend's house and refused to come home for three or four days because I didn't approve.... I resented the fact that he was there to take the place of my dad.[60]

Though Charlotte and her mother never discussed the situation, in time the daughter's position softened as she joined the family in moving on. A mother's closure and willingness to establish new lives, usually signaled by remarriage, typically facilitated improved social and personal adjustment in MIA children, but not absolutely and certainly not overnight. These children, whose biological fathers remained absent, continued to struggle while the process of transferring trust and affection to the stepfather was underway. Many, like Charlotte, initially viewed stepfathers as nothing more than pretenders aiming to replace a hero, and as a result they acted out or withdrew. In these situations, lasting years, healthy coping hinged on reconciling children's need to maintain hope the MIA was alive with the need to build meaningful and lasting relationships with stepfathers. The stronger a child's faith in their dad's return, the trickier the evolution of child-stepparent relationships.[61]

"It takes a while," Charlotte now appreciates. "I had to see with my stepfather how much he truly adored my mother. When I started dating I would date people I thought had my dad's characteristics, or things I deemed my father, personality-wise, had; that's what I would look for in a man. [But] Mom didn't want to run the risk of losing another husband. She got with my stepfather—a well-grounded economist, a businessman, who didn't take any chances—nothing was left to chance, which was the exact one-eighty of my dad."[62]

CHAPTER 7

How Come the Flags around Town Aren't Flying at Half-Mast?

GOLD STAR CHILDREN

> Not a day goes by that I don't think of you and how different my life might have been.
>
> —TRIBUTE TO DAVID A. ACTON, SONS AND DAUGHTERS IN TOUCH WEBSITE

While the POW/MIA issue grew to nearly mythic cultural proportions in succeeding years, perpetuated with sporadic identification and repatriation of MIA remains, by contrast Gold Star children, whose fathers died during the Vietnam War, were harder to see and easier to ignore. Except when used by anti-war elements as visual symbols of Vietnam's cost, orphans remained largely invisible to the nation, to communities, and, moreover, to one another. The majority lost their fathers very early in childhood and possess few living memories of that brief time together. Studies conducted during the war determined that nearly 90 percent of servicemen killed in Vietnam were between the ages of eighteen and twenty-six years old, with 75 percent being between nineteen and twenty-three. For an estimated twenty thousand orphans of these young soldiers, Vietnam defined childhood. Loss painfully derailed a normal future they envisioned together as a family, replacing it with lifelong, uphill climbs to comprehend their fathers, make sense of his sacrifice, and keep those memories relevant beyond just storytelling and fading Polaroids. Gold Star child Jennifer Denard believes, "When a man dies for his country they say he paid the last full measure, but that's just not quite true. His children keep on paying" that terrific bill. "It's hard to explain what losing a father does to a family," offered another survivor, Karen Spears Zacharias. "Daddy's death is the road marker we kids use to measure our life's journey. Before his death, ours was a home filled with intimacy and devotion. After his death, it was filled with chaos and destruction."[1]

Wartime families instinctively recognized what the arrival of a military sedan or Jeep carrying two uniformed soldiers meant, and the flashbulb memories associated with its appearance are as powerful as they are similar. "I remember that day like it was yesterday," a California man began when recounting the marines in dress-blue uniforms—known colloquially as Angels of Death—delivering official notice that his father, Staff Sergeant Franklin Max Ellinger, had been killed in action. Seven years old in that summer of 1968, with a little brother three years younger, Mike Ellinger was sitting on the front steps as the men got out and walked right past him to knock on the front door. He neither saw nor heard the soldiers' sober conversation with his mother. Her scream told the story unmistakably.[2]

"We were eating donuts and listening to music," Stacy Swenck recounted of the day after Thanksgiving in 1971 when she, at twelve years old, heard about Major Robert B. Swenck. "An unmarked car pulled up in our driveway.... The men had only spoken a few words before my mother collapsed on the front porch. They carried her crying to the couch... mom sobbed; I felt shocked and numb."[3]

Tony Cordero was four years old when his father—an air force navigator aboard a B-57—died in 1965, but he was eight before the military declared the missing airman killed in action. Between 1965 and the discovery of the crash site in 1969, "every now and then there would be a knock on the door and air force officers would come to provide Mom with an update," Cordero remembered. "That might have happened two or three times during that period that Dad was missing. The last time was that proverbial knock on the door."[4]

Karen Spears Zacharias received word of her father Staff Sergeant David P. Spears's death the summer she turned ten years old in 1966. She recalled her brother, two years older, punching the wall and yelling, "Those Charlies killed my Daddy! They've kilt [*sic*] our daddy! I'm gonna kill them Charlies!" though Karen did not know then who Charlie was. "For years now," she shared in her pathbreaking memoir *Hero Mama: A Daughter Remembers the Father She Lost in Vietnam—and the Mother Who Held Her Family Together*, "I have tried to remember what happened next. But it's as if somebody threw me up against a concrete wall so violently that my brain refuses to let any of it come back to me. I supposed the pain is so intense my body just can't endure it. I recall only bits. Crying. Screaming. Hollering like a dog does when a chain is twisted too tightly on its neck."[5]

For the remainder of that day in the Ellinger home, women from their trailer community around Camp Pendleton were in and out with food and condolences. One spent the night with his mother, and the brothers heard her screams again punctuated with "God no, God no, why?" In the morning, she finally gathered them together, all hugging and crying as she explained matter-of-factly, "your daddy died in Vietnam." Zacharias had never seen her mother cry before, not even when her dad left for Vietnam, but on this day, she too heard her mom crying all night long, questioning God. The little girl had trouble falling asleep as well. "Getting to sleep is hard when you're worried about having your head cut off," she revealed about lying awake after trying to say her prayers. "It was a notion I obsessed over after I overheard some kinfolk discuss whether somebody had tried to cut off Daddy's head. From that moment on, for years to come, decapitation haunted my slumber. Avoiding dismemberment became my focus early in life."[6]

"The thing that was most frightening was that our mother was literally unable to help us," Stacy Swenck underscored. Seeing reliable caregivers incapacitated by powerlessness and depression was extremely traumatizing, as if the child's world had gone radically out of control. Sons and daughters, like the Swenck sisters, were unprepared for their mother's vulnerability, and it caused bewildering emotional discord manifesting to varying degrees depending on a child's developmental age. "She herself was so distraught that there was no one to talk to, there was no help coming from her at all, and no one else, either. We were like an afterthought. There was no adult, not even her sister or her mom and dad, who both were nearby, but no one knew what to do so they figured they needed to help her so she wouldn't, I guess, go off the rails. They were more worried about her. I think the idea was we were kids and kids will always be fine, they'll get over it."[7]

Hometown newspapers briefly elevated Gold Star families to near celebrity status, at least early in the war. In the intervening days leading up to the funeral, townspeople learning of a soldier's death in obituaries and small feature articles arrived at homes in waves, bearing casseroles and sympathies. Amid the commotion—which was often overwhelming—letters began coming: some sent by complete strangers, some from comrades still in Vietnam, and official communications from Lyndon Johnson or Richard Nixon. Childhood paused for the duration of the mourning period, which was, again, directly subject to developmental age. Although preadolescent views on death have matured by kindergarten, younger children, particularly preschoolers, emotionally simply cannot sustain feelings of grief for long periods of time compared with adolescents and adults. With play and television programming indefinitely suspended, children, unsure what to do with themselves, studied social cues from adults who seemed to mainly sit around for hours drinking coffee and smoking cigarettes, trading "remember when?" and "what if?" stories. Small children innocently sought comfort in regularity and often got back into accustomed habits much quicker than older siblings and parents. Karen Spears Zacharias found it difficult to determine exactly what her seven-year-old sister comprehended, sitting quietly with her dolls, stopping only to stare at their mother periodically or else reach over to hold her hand.

Adult behaviors were particularly confusing to decipher, however. "I don't believe there is anything more troubling to a kid than to see a roomful of grown-ups cry," Zacharias wrote. But perhaps saying "I'm sorry" was worse, she came to believe. As adults paid their respects, few lingered long enough to talk with children, but all apologized. To her reasoning, asking for forgiveness in this manner was a common childhood punishment meant to demonstrate contrition for misdeeds. She had no concept of how to respond to adults apologizing when they had not wronged her. After all, she thought, no one was sorrier than herself.[8]

For Mike Ellinger the funeral remains a handful of vivid recollections: a closed flag-draped casket, twenty-one-gun salute, his heart physically hurting. "Mom," he wondered on the quiet drive home, "how come the flags around town aren't flying at half-mast?" Compared with Ellinger's concern that his father's funeral passed unrecognized, Zacharias experienced a tremendous display of respect. As the funeral procession drove along the rural Tennessee route between church and cemetery, bystanders spontaneously stopped in solemn reverence to honor the fallen. Farmers working the field placed straw hats over their hearts, people standing in their yards and shopkeepers in front of stores bowed their heads, senior citizens sitting on their porches rose, and others saluted.[9]

Besides being profoundly struck by the first dead body they had ever seen, most Gold Star children only remember ordinary and disconnected particulars, such as shopping for formal, uncomfortable new clothes or how certain floral arrangements appeared. Other memories such as Stacy Swenck's center on already recognizing the emptiness so many eventually accepted as the contours of home life. "I took my two little sisters, ages six and nine, downstairs to the basement and kept them there," she remembered. "We stayed quiet and listened, forgotten in the confusion. For two days we made sandwiches and stood apart, watching. People brought us food for a few days, there was a funeral, and then we were left alone. Mom stopped crying and walked around the house with a distant stare. A dark silence occupied our house for a long time."[10]

Families quickly realized that after giving a husband and father to the country, once a soldier—in military terms a "sponsor"—died in Vietnam, dependents were, indeed, in many respects on their own as civilians. Zacharias noted how after the funeral an army representative came to see her family one last time to finalize paperwork regarding death benefits and receiving Social Security. Up until then, her mother had never shared the subject of any military visits or telegrams with the children, yet from overhearing adult conversations they sensed her mounting frustrations. "Mama was crying lots now," she recalled. "Seems like every time a telegram came, she got mad and cried some more, but she had quit yelling at God. Instead she just started cussing out the Army."[11]

Tensions with the military inherently arose from suddenly facing bleak financial prospects and eviction from military communities. Families were eligible for Dependency and Indemnity Compensation (DIC) payments, as well as the standard $10,000 serviceman's life insurance (which 98 percent carried), various educational benefits, loan privileges, and medical care. In the early 1970s these DIC benefits rose to $167 per month to widows for the lowest-ranking enlisted men and up to $426 per month for widows of the highest-ranking officers. An additional monthly payment of $20 per child remained constant regardless of rank. Even with modest survivor benefits under Social Security, though, the lowest DIC levels left widows and orphans financially strapped below poverty levels, while also deincentivizing remarriage since all DIC eligibility terminated immediately. "I don't have my own memories of my dad," Jennifer Denard, only two years old when he died in 1970, shared. "What I have is memories of my mother crying all the time, what I have is memories of my mother not being taken care of."[12]

In homes too numb for families to effectively communicate their sense of loss, members distanced themselves from death. Isolation and denial dominated these childhoods. Although living in the same household and mourning the same man, a naturally awkward reluctance to meaningfully discuss death or grieving—acerbated by this particular time of war—choked off intergenerational communication. Many mothers—out of some combination of stoicism and despair—never purposefully or adequately explained anything about their daddy's death, conversations that could have comforted or else corrected misperceptions and outright absurdities in immature thinking. Sons and daughters—out of some combination of fear and embarrassment—never brought themselves to ask.

Childhood was a scarier place now, and death made preadolescents acutely sensitive to the very real prospect of further abandonment, either physically losing another loved one or alienating their affections. Both were terrifying and unacceptable prospects. Gold Star children discovered how even the most innocent curiosity about their fathers caused immediate distress for people who did not want to be reminded. Accordingly, they adopted a broad and fundamental rule: talking about their dad, his death, or Vietnam made Mommy sad, and they grew up trying never to be the source of more anguish. As Zacharias remembers, "Daddy's last instruction to me was to stop crying because it upset Mama. I tried as best I could to do as Daddy had asked. But what he didn't know then is that

Vietnam would upset a lot of people. I learned at an early age to handle the burning things in life with mitts of silence."[13] This coping strategy satisfied few, instead sowing deep-seated guilt, antagonism, doubts, and bitterness toward the surviving parent.[14]

Consider first the basic questions of fairness from a child's perspective. A father's seemingly infallible authority and invincibility is the foundation on which developing self-worth is anchored. His violent death at the hands of an amorphous enemy shook children's faith in what they thought they knew about the world and themselves. Bad things happening to good people developmentally defies understanding without the capability of abstract thought. This is what Karen Spears Zacharias meant by the literal observation that no one was sorrier than her. To many preadolescents' immature moral reasoning, they were to some degree actually to blame. Despite being increasingly able to conceptualize causal linkage between war and death, until around ten years old children think egocentrically. Ethics and personal conduct—telling right from wrong—are largely governed by punishment and reward. "It seemed reasonable to me that if salvation resulted from repentance," Zacharias explained of her imaginative culpability in his death, "then certainly the reverse was true. The unrepentant would not go unpunished."[15]

In her guilty mind, she fixated on an incident after a Christmas church party the night before her father shipped out for Vietnam. He had playfully snatched the bag of treats she brought home, laying claim to a prized chocolate football wrapped in gold foil as the only candy he wanted. Rather than allowing him to have it, Karen selfishly devoured the chocolate, offering a malted milk ball in substitution. "If my father had come home from Vietnam alive," she reflected, "I probably never would have remembered any of this. But as a child I believed the reason he died was because God was teaching me a lesson."[16]

Whenever her mother wailed "why me?" Karen's natural inclination was to absolve her by explaining God had taken Sergeant Spears as the penalty for a *daughter's* childish refusal to share. Yet she shouldered the awful secret alone. "Being the daughter of a dead man made me feel dirty on the inside, as if I had done something so wrong, so nasty, so unforgivable that God's only recourse was to take my daddy away," Zacharias decided. "That intense hatred seared a hole in my heart so big nothing eased the pain. Not that anyone was necessarily trying. Mama certainly never tried to talk me through my confusion. She was too busy trying to salve her own hurts. Linda, Frank [her siblings], and I never ever talked about Daddy or how much we missed him."[17]

Opportunities for honest conversation outside the home were equally limited as self-consciousness and an inherited determination to keep up appearances handicapped youth in social settings. Many were the only fatherless children in their communities and felt lonely and odd in elementary school. Peers occasionally teased them as well, and they were left out of events that involved dads, or else they attended functions like father-son sports banquets alone. After Zacharias once explained to an inquisitive classmate that she did not have a father, her mom angrily scolded her for saying such a thing. You have a daddy, she was reminded; he just is no longer with us, so always tell friends he is deceased. The girl bridled at how sanitized that sounded and grew angrier at her father and God for having been placed in this uncomfortable situation.[18]

Replying to the question of what Vietnam meant to her, a San Diego woman born in 1959 whose father had died (unrelated to military service) when she was in the first grade, responded, "I felt very 'different' because all the other kids had both a father and mother at home. [But] as the Vietnam War churned along, more and more kids became like me. I remember when a student wouldn't show up for class for several days, the teacher would tell us that (name's) father was killed in the war. Be extra nice to him/her when he/she returns.'" Children nevertheless learned to recoil from all types of public recognition, sensitive to teachers' and classmates' otherwise well-meant expressions of sympathy. Perpetual apologies over an endless state of being pitiable only brought unwanted attention while adding additional layers of shame for the child. "After he died, my sister's teacher blamed her misbehavior on our 'broken family,'" Stacy Swenck remembered. "No wonder our mother taught us to not tell anyone and to pretend that we were a fine, normal happy family."[19]

"There wasn't any guilt per se," Tony Cordero clarified, "but I grew up, and I think this is a common denominator, with a lot of good friends, and girlfriends, who didn't know anything about my life story." And that included his high school football coach, a veteran navy corpsman in Vietnam. "I remember telling my girlfriend one time, as a senior in high school," he elaborated. "I told her that having a boyfriend-girlfriend relationship in high school made me think of my dad a lot, and she kind of laughed it off. It was one of those efforts of testing the water, dipping a toe in to see what it's like, what kind of response you get if you tell somebody you thought about your dad who was killed in a war. Kind of like a snail sticking its head out of its shell. If you don't like the temperature, you get back in your shell."[20]

"Soon after his death," Swenck shared, "I remember running into Mom in a dark hallway and her sharp intake of breath as she said, 'You look just like your Dad.' I stood there, guilty, in the middle of the floor. I couldn't help being a reminder of sorrow. Did I remind everyone of Death, my face an omen of the grief Death brings? What else could explain the averted eyes, the painful silences from both friends and strangers when the news was told?" It was as if "a dark cloud descended on our house," Swenck recalled, "and I don't know when it lifted, maybe never." To her, this cloud mostly demarcated childhood's boundaries growing up in California. "There was never any fun, and there was never any idea that this should be fun, and it isn't. My mother was like a ghost in the house. There was never a time when that cloud was lifted for any reason. I have pictures, not long after it occurred . . . within a year or two later. . . . I have pictures of myself sitting in Key West [where they were visiting her aunt] like there's no smiling happening, just the picture of depression. And those are just snapshots of me taken on the beach. We were just shell-shocked."[21]

Mothers commonly closed out his presence, emotionally and physically, as their primary coping strategy. All material objects once belonging to, or referencing, Dad were soon stored away. Fewer and fewer photographs adorned the walls before disappearing entirely. And little was done to privately or publicly honor or remember him, either by commemorating the gravesite or even celebrating his birthday. Anyone growing up after World War II knew heroes fought for only good causes, their deeds celebrated, not removed. These purges could feel like a part of the child's heritage or birthright was being eradicated. Perceptions of the Vietnam War might be significantly prejudiced in the process. Everything appearing on the nightly news and in daily papers, especially after the Tet Offensive in 1968, reinforced the lesson that Vietnam was an ugly word. And similar to other Vietnam veterans' children, Gold Star youth found it difficult to clearly distinguish between their father the soldier and the war's unpopularity, or the government policies targeted by protesters. The major difference is children did so in an emotionally repressed environment threatening to instill a sense of indignity associated with a father's military service. "Back then we had to shut off our feelings," Denard pointed out about trying to reconcile the disagreement. "It's like a big secret that when your dad dies in Vietnam you don't talk about it. Unfortunately, the children bore the brunt of that."[22]

Oddly enough, World War II orphans experienced feelings of estrangement and alienation growing up, too, but, as Zacharias wrote, "I learned at a pretty early age that the death of soldiers in Vietnam didn't invoke much concern from others. Truth was, nobody really seemed to care that [we] were growing up without a father. . . . Like the multitude of Vietnam veterans who were returning home to empty airports, our family had no one around to embrace us or tell us that they appreciated our sacrifice."[23]

Gold Star children were also deeply ambivalent about the anti-war movement, with some feeling personally vulnerable to its growing rage. "There was nobody sitting beside me explaining that the protesters burning effigies of U.S.

soldiers or shouting obscenities about the Vietnam War weren't angry at *my father*," Zacharias continued. "The more virulent the protesters became, the more shame I felt over my father's death. I feared telling anyone about Daddy's death." To a child's thinking, if those opposing the war spit on American soldiers because they were thought to be baby killers, then by extension protesters would equally hate a murderer's daughter or son. It was safer to remain mute. "For much of my life," Zacharias revealed, "I was embarrassed and conflicted over my father's death in Vietnam. I thought he should have known better. All those intelligent people protesting the war certainly seemed to know better. Why didn't Daddy? It was a question I pondered almost daily as I listened to Walter Cronkite's latest war report and heard the growing casualty numbers during dinner each night."[24]

Developmentally, it appears that preadolescents up to roughly third grade (generally supportive of American involvement by nature and less cognizant of public discord), as well as older children approaching adolescence after sixth grade (secure in a cognitive equilibrium supporting the war), had fewer questions about why their dads were in Vietnam. Some knew what their fathers did in the war or some details of their service, but many did not. Still, people who were in these two age groups at the time their fathers were killed have subsequently maintained more confidence in the understanding that Dad was a soldier doing his job, fighting bravely and giving his life for freedom, and thus deserving of honor. For those in the middle grade-school years, however, whose attitudes and feelings toward Vietnam were still subject to reestablishing cognitive equilibrium, unresolved questions about their fathers' deaths emerged as a chief socializing agent.

"As I grew older," Swenck explained, "I came to hate the Vietnam War and blamed the government, even though I had no idea about the war's causes and avoided any mention of it. I became a rebellious teenager, transforming hurt into toughness. I grew bitter in my ignorance. Hating the war helped when I had to tell someone my father had died fighting there. Joining in the belief that it was a bad war made it easier to get along with others who hated it, which was most everyone I met. I did not know then that my father had been a hero."[25]

"One of the things I think any survivor wants to know and feel," George Casey, retired general and former army chief of staff, believes, "is that their loved one's sacrifice isn't going to be forgotten and there was a time I wasn't sure whether my dad's sacrifice was really appreciated." Certainly not all homes closed Father out, but whether in private or as members of more expressive families—who solemnly preserved his legacy—preadolescents yearned for his presence in their lives. "I didn't know how to say 'Hey, mom, tomorrow is the day dad was killed,'" recalled Jennifer Denard. "I was so desperate to make my dad a part of my life that any time we would get a new calendar that I would flip forward to June and circle June 6, just circle it.... I wanted mom to know that I knew it was coming, that even though we didn't talk about it, it was on the refrigerator circled."[26]

"There was never a time for me personally," Tony Cordero reflected, "and I assume I can speak for my siblings [his mother was three months pregnant with child number five when his dad went MIA], that dad wasn't present.... I remember in elementary school always telling my friends that I was going to enlist in the air force when I turned seventeen," he continued. "I think that was a kid's way of articulating a tribute to my dad. I wore my Cub Scout uniform and if I can remember my rationale at the time, I wanted to be in uniform like my dad. I never kept a picture of him everywhere, [but] he was never secluded or sheltered or anything like that. I knew he was there, I was always thinking about him, but our good friends and teachers may not have known the rest of the story."[27]

With each passing year through adolescence into adulthood, Gold Star children predictably sought more meaningful understanding of their fathers. Beyond just impersonal vital statistics, they required subtle particulars and qualities that had made their dad uniquely a person. Since circumstances conditioned them to be incurious, preadolescents had to cautiously navigate their searches or else cause more generational friction, particularly in reconstituted families after mothers remarried. What some mothers potentially did not realize, or appreciate, was that they had already lived a life (at least a few years) with him, yet their children had not. "One of the key things is for the parent, the dead spouse is just a dead spouse," Swenck made clear. "For the child it's part of you, your parent is literally part of you and when that has died, part of you had died. The parents can go and find another spouse and grieve in a normal way but a child's grief is different. And my mother never really understood that."[28]

Speaking for many with no memories of Daddy, Sharrie Downing, only two years old when he died in February 1968, explained the lifelong dilemma this way. "I have an outline of him and would just like to get it filled in." "I used to dream about him," Jennifer Denard similarly reflected. "I always knew the outline of the man, the basics, how old he was when he was killed, I knew what he looked like, where he'd grown up, but it was just a sketch.... I really didn't know the man, I wanted to know what was his favorite cake and what color were his eyes, I wanted to know what he smelled like.... I knew how he had died, but I didn't know how he had lived."[29]

During the Vietnam era understanding remained largely restricted to a handful of stories passed down by older siblings, aunts, uncles, and grandparents.

Many also nurtured secret illusions that fathers were not really dead and might miraculously reappear in their lives. Tony Cordero pointed out how Gold Star families from the Iraq and Afghanistan conflicts nearly always get a body back, a relative advantage compared with Vietnam. Missing men lost in remote jungle crash sites have left families perpetually wondering, "Is he going to be coming around the corner one day?" "When I played football," Cordero continued, "I always wondered, always looked out of the corner of my face mask, if somehow mysteriously everybody got it wrong and he managed to escape or get home and find his way to my high school football field. I'd walk off the field after practice someday and this guy who looked like me [would] say, 'Hey, I'm your dad.'" He later said, "Even now, I wonder what it would be like for Dad to be with my children, or to have a beer and watch a ballgame together." "For months," Stacy Swenck wrote, "I imagined my father showing up at my classroom door to take my hand and walk me home. Even now, I still wonder if his spirit will ever visit me in a dream, giving me guidance I still long for."[30]

After Karen Spears Zacharias's mother briefly remarried, she experienced the first of what became a recurring lifelong dream. Sergeant Spears comes to the front door and, without knocking, walks in, announcing, "Honey, I'm home!" Karen then runs to hug him, but insistently he asks where her mother is. Stomach churning, she evades his questions with, "I love you, Daddy. Why have you been gone so long? We thought you died. They told us you died." He describes how the army identified the wrong guy—the exact thought she had had all along. After pressing her about his wife, Karen finally reveals, "She's out with another man. She didn't know. She thought you were dead." As she tells it, "That's when I wake up, and I never find out what Daddy thinks about Mama being with another man. The dream leaves me feeling horrible. I'm angry with daddy for dying and leaving us. And I'm angry with Mama for being unfaithful to my father."[31]

The most functional families effectively managed bereavement by preserving a central space for fathers—both as men and as soldiers—in domestic life. For these widows, children were his last living representations, and onto their preadolescent shoulders many mothers placed immense obligation—and attendant guilt—to carry on a fallen soldier's name, identity, values, and aspirations. This approach was significant because it appears for children growing up under such circumstances, the lengthy process toward reconciliation began in childhood. "I had to grow up, really faster than I thought I would," Mike Ellinger observed. "As the oldest I had to become the man of the house." Already close, the relationship between Mike and his mother Carol grew "damn strong" after Sergeant Ellinger was killed in action in 1968, and Mike readily credits her with single-handedly being his "backbone" ever since.[32]

Though both mother and son believe Vietnam to have been a "useless war," she instilled through discipline the same integrity, honesty, and character associated with both parents' beloved marines (the couple had, in fact, met in the corps). Regularly, her parenting style deliberately evoked memories of Mike's father. Pointing out the physical resemblance or how much Mike reminded her of him often served as positive reinforcement. Punishment, or at least the threat of negative consequences, also incorporated certain paternal lessons from the past. By harking back to the spanking Mike had once received from his father for disobediently riding his sparkling Stingray bicycle (green with white banana seat) through mud puddles, for instance, Mom later reinforced the importance of respect and care for one's property.[33]

Earlier than most—around 1970—Mike also met other Vietnam War orphans through Carol Ellinger's activism in the organization Gold Star Wives. Up until then he had never known peers whose dads had not come back from Vietnam, but Mike thought befriending others as a child was a godsend that remained a profound influence on his coping abilities. When his mom went to college, she left him in charge of the evening latchkey routine: completing household chores, preparing meals, cleaning the dishes, homework, and getting himself and his little brother to bed. In short, Mike says, it was under her direct guidance, in the years after 1968, that he came to really learn "who the Ellingers are." Protecting that legacy also required her faithful nurturing of the natural athleticism and passion for baseball (more specifically, the Los Angeles Dodgers) passed down from father to son. On the diamond, with Mom in the stands—or working games as the only female Little League umpire around—Mike transcended loss, nine innings at a time. Somewhere, he thought, his dad was watching. Ultimately, similar to many who overachieved to make up for their fathers dying so young, he dreamed of being a major leaguer until injuries in high school dictated another career choice. Given the circumstances, his family's history in the marines made that a logical option, and Carol left the decision strictly up to him. But in the end he chose to walk a different track, simply unable to bear the thought of putting her through another military funeral.[34]

For countless others of the estimated twenty thousand Gold Star children, reconciliation—or what is considered healing—did not begin in earnest until adolescence or early adulthood. Frequently this process began only after years of reckless, dysfunctional behaviors and/or "self-medication." A persistent fear of abandonment that followed them from childhood manifested as difficulty with people leaving or searching for father figures. In some cases, teenage pregnancies and failed marriages early in life were predictable results of misplaced love and affection found lacking in childhood. Many had to overcome resentment, if not outright anger, toward their parents, their siblings, and God, which tested faith and alienated family members. "Daddy's death made me so angry I just wanted to go out and kick someone's ass," Karen Zacharias admitted. "Anybody's ass. I wanted to spit in God's face and tell Him what a pathetic mess He'd made of things. I didn't realize then that most of the mess was manmade." Stacy Swenck's younger sisters both had anger issues growing up, too, but she, as the oldest and at the onset of puberty, was most rebellious. "I don't remember having a conversation with my mother about it as a child," she shared. "But she sent me to a psychiatrist when I was fifteen so we must have talked at some point, but only in terms of what's wrong with you, why aren't you getting over it, you need to get fixed. . . . It was not unspoken, it was clearly about Dad."[35]

"Vietnam was the mystery," Cordero made clear.

> I didn't know where the damn place was, much less why we were there or what he was doing. But I know one of the things that hardened me was my sympathy for others who lost their parents. I remember one specific situation, a guy I went to elementary and high school with . . . his dad died of a heart attack unexpectedly. I was talking with him after the funeral and he didn't know my dad had died so many years before that, and when you talk about getting cheated, it was this bit of emotion that kept me from feeling overly sympathetic to others who lost their mom or dad. A friend of mine might lose a parent at twenty-five years of age, and they had all that time with their mom or dad. In the back of my mind, my emotion is saying, "Well, welcome to the party. You got twenty-five years. I got four."[36]

"I avoided it for most of my life," Swenck confided.

> When I was in my thirties I got divorced. I had a very tumultuous first marriage, and I went to seek counseling during that tumultuous time and the lady suggested that I might have some trauma surrounding that. My mother sent me to a psychiatrist after he died, and that was the first I heard of PTSD and they told me I had it. I was sixteen at the time. . . . I just thought, "You stupid fucker, what do you know." I was just bitter and angry, I got in trouble, I hung out with the wrong crowd, I was rebellious, I smoked pot. I did drugs, it was the seventies, I was a bitch, I was nasty to everybody. You know, that was my teenager years.[37]

Some combination of milestones in the life of the nation, or individually, usually precipitated the initial steps toward meaningful resolution. For many the process coalesced around the Vietnam Veterans Memorial Wall opening in 1982 or reaching the age when children realized they had outlived their fathers. The final chapter returns to these subjects, but for now Karen Spears Zacharias probably captured most eloquently the sentiments of fellow Gold Star children of the Vietnam War in her book's final observations: "I have come to terms with a harsh history, as a daughter and as a citizen of a free nation. I don't miss my father any less with each passing year. I am simply more aware of all the life he's missed," she wrote. "Grief is a journey with a beginning, but it does not have an end, not in this life anyway."[38]

CHAPTER 8

Yes, I Am My Lai, but My Lai Is Better Than Viet Cong!

VIETNAMESE ADOPTEES AND AMERASIANS

When I grow up my father will be very old. But I'll have a job then and a lot of money. So I will find him and take care of him. He'll need me then.

—NINE-YEAR-OLD AMERASIAN BOY

In seeing the Vietnam War through the eyes of preadolescent children, there is a last reality yet to consider. Not all American childhoods were confined to the continental United States. American soldiers, construction workers, embassy officials, and numerous civilian contractors fathered upwards of perhaps four hundred thousand illegitimate Amerasian children with Vietnamese women, although no exact number has ever been determined.[1] American families also adopted another three thousand or so Vietnamese infants and young children, including some Amerasians, through the controversial Operation Babylift in the frantic spring of 1975 and several early adoption agencies.

For the most part these relatively few Vietnamese adoptees, after tenuous beginnings in an exotic land, grew up in predominantly homogenous, middle-class homes, acculturated to speaking English, eating McDonald's food, watching Saturday morning cartoons, and going to elementary school. The childhood concerns most meaningful to their lives centered on emotional and psychological tensions inherent to straddling cultures. Preadolescents coping with a sense of being incomplete—common to foreign adoptees—grew up alienated from both American and Vietnamese culture. Operation Babylift altered how parents acquired families as well. Caught up in the rush, couples already pursuing adoptions conceivably accepted available Vietnamese children as an expedience rather than continuing to wait. Others may well have made spur-of-the-moment decisions to adopt children when under normal circumstances they probably would not have. And with standard adoption protocols temporarily circumvented, some lacked the fitness and commitment to be parents.[2]

By contrast, Amerasians left behind in Vietnam after 1975 largely raised themselves far outside the scope of a recognizable suburban-oriented childhood. A marginalized and despised minority in one of the world's poorest nations, there is a tragic sameness in the Amerasian experience, to borrow a phrase from urban historian Gilbert Osofsky. As many as half may have died as children, either among the two million civilian casualties of the war or thereafter from abandonment, disease, or suicide.[3] The rest survived preadolescence, malnourished and mistreated, before finally arriving in the land of their fathers decades later as adolescents and adults through the United Nations Orderly Departure Program and Amerasian Homecoming Act. Amerasians and adoptees are physical, often uncomfortable reminders of the war for both Americans and Vietnamese. But just as their emigration has been variously interpreted as something between benevolent or selfish steps along America's path toward reconciliation, these fractured perspectives add needed texture and depth to our historical appraisal of Vietnam's consequences for children, more specifically the process of immigrant acculturation, constructions of identity, and refugee policy.

America's military withdrawal in 1973 left South Vietnam to fend for itself against an intensifying communist onslaught. An already flawed government and economy further corroded, paralyzing our former ally for the last two years of its existence with runaway unemployment and inflation, plummeting morale, political unrest, and rampant corruption. In the United States, public notice of Vietnamese orphans appears to have grown in inverse proportion to America's presence in Southeast Asia. In short, national concern for the welfare of the Vietnamese people generally, and particularly children, took on a sense of urgency only in the early 1970s as military involvement ended, reaching a climax during Operation Babylift. Estimates in 1973 placed the number of orphans in South Vietnam at slightly under one million. Of these, it was believed that three hundred thousand resided with grandparents, aunts and uncles, or other members of their parents' extended families. Nineteen thousand lived in nearly 130 orphanages recognized by the government's Ministry of Social Welfare (MSW) in and around Saigon, with another five thousand in approximately three dozen unregistered shelters. The balance existed as vagrants traveling rural areas in small packs. Though these figures were only educated guesses, statistics had clearly been trending sharply upward as uncertainty surrounding the U.S. departure intensified civilian displacement. Most children had been orphaned by the loss of one or both parents in the hostilities, while others were abandoned for combinations of increased poverty, homelessness, parental self-preservation, physical handicap, or injury. Often neighbors or strangers who found them dodging urban traffic or wandering dusty orange roadsides brought them in, a convenience in a land without systematized birth certificates.[4]

The MSW alleged that Amerasians made up only 4 percent of South Vietnam's orphan population, but aid workers noticed comparable upticks in this demographic, too. American soldiers had commonly subsidized Amerasians, either directly by supporting mother and child or indirectly by patronizing the vice trade in which many mothers worked. When GIs went back to the world, women lost the financial resources to care for Amerasians, and in many cases they married Vietnamese men who no longer wanted half-American children around. Another important variable, and one cutting to the heart of subsequent international adoption disputes, was the ambiguous nature of what "orphan" meant by American definitions. In Vietnam rational mothers and fathers often temporarily placed children in orphanages as child-care repositories—effectively foster homes—while traveling the countryside as either refugees or soldiers, or otherwise until economic prospects improved. Contrary to American assumptions, it did not occur to Vietnamese that by leaving children they permanently relinquished parental rights. Bar girls brought their Amerasian youth to orphanages as a means of protecting them from that lifestyle, and the government customarily used the shelters for the children of political prisoners. To Vietnamese, children are not considered orphans if they have a living relative, so untold thousands of these wards were not strictly speaking orphans because the children would be reclaimed by parents or extended family once conditions stabilized. "If Mother is Lost," Vietnamese said, "there is Auntie; if Father is lost, there is Uncle."[5]

Orphanage life in a war-torn, underdeveloped country was predictably grim. The vast majority of young residents were less than nine years old, the age at which facilities routinely turned out all but the most physically or mentally handicapped. Because black Amerasians made up a disproportionate percentage of orphans in some locations, for cultural taboos discussed later, those accommodations became racially segregated. Whether run by Catholics, Buddhists, or secular relief agencies, urban orphanages tended to be better equipped, staffed, and supported compared with their rural counterparts, but really just by varying degrees of spartan-ness. Although perpetually overcrowded, shelters remained stark and unadorned, devoid of Western childhood clutter: nothing to decorate the walls, no toys, no books, no crayons. What little furniture there was consisted of a few cribs, beds, and crude—dangerous—metal playpens for the smallest, and dirty floor mats for the biggest. Orphans wore the only set of clothes they owned, and by placing bedpans under the playpens, the need for diapers and cleaning might be greatly reduced. Everyone ate from communal bowls and shared utensils staff reused for each meal.[6]

Preadolescents were charged with providing care and watching over toddlers and infants. Hunger, however, precluded play as many lacked the energy to sit up for long periods of time, and some as old as four had never learned to walk. With children piled four to a bed or playpen and left there for days at a time, supervision consisted of nothing more than swatting swarming flies, hour after monotonous hour. Disease—congenital and communicable—ran rampant, just as natural and man-made disabilities were commonplace, whether polio, blindness, deafness, cerebral palsy, tuberculosis, heart defects, cleft palates, or napalm burns. Foreign observers openly worried as the mortality rate in South Vietnam's orphanages approached 80 to 90 percent in extreme cases.[7]

Since the Ministry of Social Welfare possessed neither economic means nor the infrastructure and expertise to adequately administer basic child welfare programs, support for only those officially recognized orphanages ranged from one to three dollars per child per month, scant outlays shrunk further by the country's inflationary spiral. In the absence of comprehensive governmental aid, orphan care in South Vietnam fell to an ad hoc collection of some twenty international relief agencies and various volunteer or religious humanitarian groups—UNICEF, CARE, the World Health Organization, the Red Cross, Save the Children—laboring, mostly in vain, to pick up the slack. Much of their limited funding was, in time, underwritten by the U.S. Agency for International Development (USAID). Reflecting American interest in assuming a broader role in the mounting Vietnamese refugee and orphan crisis, Congress ultimately appropriated $5 million in the Foreign Assistance Act of 1973 for USAID to channel—along with $2.5 million of its own funds—into building and improving orphanages and day care centers, as well as initiating other programming officials hoped would shore up childhood nutrition and health in a post-American South Vietnam.[8]

Concerned Americans nevertheless judged the nation's belated response to Vietnam's neediest youth to be shamefully inadequate: too little, too late both in terms of expenditures—probably pennies on the dollar of what was needed—and taking responsibility for the fate of Amerasians. For some, stirred by seemingly endless lines of filthy and bleeding little refugees shown on the *CBS Evening News*, private adoption came to be a principled solution. Yet prior to 1975, the number of Vietnamese children adopted internationally by non-Vietnamese grew only modestly, from just below 400 in 1971 to nearly 500 in 1972 and more than 700 the next year, with the United States accounting for about 75 percent. The initial obstacles discouraging prospective parents stemmed from how little enthusiasm American adoption agencies and social services demonstrated for Vietnamese children, and how little presence they had in Southeast Asia. Couples who mulled the decision over for months were often told that if they really desired a racially integrated family, there was an abundance of available African or Native American babies to adopt, and if it absolutely had to be Asian, then Korea probably presented the best option.[9]

More than anything, however, vagaries in Vietnamese and American adoption laws kept these figures depressed. Americans seeking to adopt Vietnamese youth during the war had to satisfy South Vietnamese as well as American federal and applicable state laws. This required mastering (in different languages) out-of-sync mechanisms with multiple moving parts, which operated semiautonomously with divergent priorities, duplicated procedures, and expectations having little in common. And while by 1975 the two countries moved haltingly toward streamlining red tape and applying statutes more liberally, the complicated and misunderstood processes involved in bringing a child from overseas remained exasperatingly expensive and time consuming: two years, more than $1,000, and only if the child did not die in a war zone before then.

On one side of the Pacific, Vietnamese ideas about adoption had not fully solidified. Just as with the definition of "orphan," adoption was a Western concept relatively new to Vietnamese culture. Comparable to other Asian countries, South Vietnam only began legally recognizing the institution after decades of war with France and the United States overwhelmed the family's or village's ability to fulfill traditional child-rearing roles. In codifying its first adoption laws in 1960, South Vietnam drew from conservative and in some cases outdated principles grounded in the Napoleonic Code. Adoption was a practical matter: a rare, last recourse based solely on legitimate need and potential value for the child's welfare. Both these questions required tangible proof in a Vietnamese court. One adoptive parent needed to be at least thirty years old and no less than twenty years older than the adoptee. Married couples were expected to have been childless for a minimum of ten years. Moreover, any surviving relative, legal guardian, or accountable organization must approve the transaction before children could be legally designated "adoptable." As a matter of course, South Vietnam frowned on out-of-country adoption and summarily opposed mass adoptions. The Ministry of the Interior reviewed all duly processed requests on a case-by-case basis, applying these criteria strictly in rendering a verdict on whether children left Vietnam. Given low priority among the beleaguered government's other headaches, individual adoption claims commonly dragged on for a year, earning the Vietnamese a bad reputation in the States for arbitrary delays and obstinance.[10]

On the other side, American adoption laws varied by state, and each successive bureaucratic layer had to be navigated before the U.S. Immigration and Naturalization Service (INS) issued a visa to legally enter the country as an immigrant by adoption. Under the era's immigration laws, once citizens located a potentially adoptable orphan in Vietnam—usually through the news media or painstaking word of mouth—those approved as suitable parents filed the necessary petition with the INS regional office nearest their home. These forms were accompanied by substantial documentary paperwork including, but not limited to, birth certificates, marriage license, detailed financial statements, police clearance statement, and processing fees. If successful, routinely within six weeks to three months, the INS granted immediate relative status to foreign adoptees, exempting them from the country's numeric immigrant quotas. Federal officials also mandated whatever medical examinations, vaccinations, and treatments for infectious diseases were deemed necessary to raise the child's physical condition to required standards, typically another three months of fairly intensive health care for the average orphan. Still, the most daunting steps in the INS process of securing immediate relative status stipulated that parents physically travel to Vietnam at their own expense to meet the child, privately arrange adoptions through a Vietnamese lawyer, and accompany new sons or daughters back to the United States.[11]

When more American mothers and fathers started making the journey, however, mounting concerns over the prospect of civilian casualties compelled the Americans and South Vietnamese to relax protocols, allowing parents to instead designate a proxy—a representative—to facilitate adoption requirements in both countries. Seven voluntary organizations operating in Vietnam—Holt International Children's Services, Traveler's Aid—International Social Services of America (TAISSA), Friends of the Children of Vietnam (FCVN), United States Catholic Conference (USCC), Friends for All Children (FFAC), Pearl S. Buck Foundation (PBF), and World Vision Relief Organization (WVRO)—eventually served on parents' behalf in what many referred to as the "mail-order" process. These U.S.-based adoption agencies—all authorized by the Ministry of Social Welfare—worked for several years in conjunction with, often supporting, Vietnamese orphanages while managing international adoptions for Americans as well as families in Australia, Canada, Germany, and England. Later, South Vietnam—at the U.S. embassy's urging—permitted intermediaries to handle all adoption proceedings, even allowing some children to leave the country prior to the paperwork's completion when escorted by agency staff. In 1974,

1,362 international adoptions were finalized in Vietnam, and the pace in the first months of 1975 already looked to eclipse that.[12]

Improvements notwithstanding, the anxious waiting period—seemingly one step forward and two back—severely tested all parties involved. Always cognizant they were in a literal race against time, adoptive parents invested considerable material and psychological resources during months of planning and preparing for their child's arrival. Through the intermediary organizations, mothers and fathers frequently supported children living in Vietnamese orphanages with lifelines of money, food, and supplies. Emotional attachments naturally developed as through regular correspondence and photographs parents learned the adoptee's name, personality traits, and bits of background. Informal communities of adoptive parents organically grew up nationwide as families sought each other out for advice, insight, and moral support. Consequently, pre-Babylift orphans reached America somewhat better prepared. To help connect or familiarize children with strange, absentee benefactors, many orphanages displayed letters, cards, and pictures arriving from the States. Those with adoptions pending were taught English words, specifically "mommy" and "daddy" to identify the faces on Polaroids, and to recite what the letters said.[13]

Deteriorating circumstances by 1975 convinced desperate Americans already in the adoption process, along with those still pondering the prospect, as well as agency workers in Southeast Asia, that time had at last run out. South Vietnam's inevitable collapse came abruptly, so much so even the communists were left surprised. First across the highlands and then the coastal cities, the final military campaign by North Vietnam and the National Liberation Front that spring turned into a rout, leaving in its panicked wake a complete breakdown in the rule of law and massive dislocation. As communist forces swept south—pitched battles erupting behind fleeing refugees—the United States watched helplessly a world away. Fresh rumors circulated daily depicting an impending bloodbath amid chaos, with untold thousands of Vietnamese civilians slaughtered at the hands of communists, and Amerasians singled out for mutilation or torture. Officially the United States resigned itself to standing down due to war weariness and worsening unemployment and inflation problems at home. Yet this nightmare scenario created the basic circumstances for the mass airborne evacuation of South Vietnamese children known as Operation Babylift, a gamble that, while overshadowed historically, unfolded parallel to one of the lowest points in modern American history, that humiliating embassy rooftop helicopter escape when Saigon fell on April 30.[14]

For better *and* worse, Operation Babylift expedited the adoption process. Between April 2 and May 7, with the South's governmental approval, 2,547 preadolescents flew out of Vietnam on forty-six government-sponsored and privately chartered flights, loosely coordinated by USAID, in consultation with the INS, Defense Department, and the seven adoption agencies. The United States ultimately processed 1,945 children for adoption, of which 91 percent were under eight years old, 57 percent were male, and 20 percent Amerasian. Though the postwar carnage never materialized in ways Americans envisioned, Operation Babylift briefly took on a momentum and logic of its own, fueled by the outcry of parents in the adoption pipeline and perpetuated by "adoption mania," a fresh public demand for Vietnamese orphans, sweeping the country. Sympathetically framed media coverage of the Babylift piqued public imagination in ways similar to Operation Homecoming in 1973, primarily because, like returning prisoners of war, rescued war orphans gave bitter defeat a relatable, humanitarian face and, moreover, held out redemptive promise in the Vietnam War's eleventh hour.[15]

That being said, trouble and tragedy plagued Operation Babylift from day one. Working in a constant crisis atmosphere to get every abandoned child out, it appears the overseas adoption agents on the ground in Vietnam were a collection of dedicated true believers with honorable intentions, handicapped by amateurishness and haste. The field of overseas adoption was only beginning to be professionalized, and regardless of its organizers' commitment to child welfare, this ambitious undertaking suffered chronic disorganization, inadequate oversight of bureaucratic procedures, and logistical failures. All of these conditions created the original space for an ongoing debate over the true nature of Operation Babylift: was it an altruistic gesture to save legitimate orphans from suffering under authoritarian oppression, or a self-serving kidnapping to convince one another, and the world, that Americans had not simply abandoned the Vietnamese? Most media reporting, covering the dramatic flights first as a national story before focusing on anecdotal accounts of localized adoption families, rang sentimental and impressionistic. Critics—editorialists, social workers, historians, educators, clergy, doctors, and demonstrators on both coasts—characterized it as social imitation, contending that any racial obligation to save Vietnam's children (as opposed to, say, Nigerian Biafran orphans) only became fashionable in 1975. Others also speculated about whether this was a cynical political gambit to generate favorable public opinion toward South Vietnam when most people no longer cared.[16]

The idea behind evacuating orphans en masse had been on the minds of some agency administrators working in Vietnamese orphanages for some time. Securing requisite exit permits from South Vietnam and entry permits into foreign countries was an issue, but arranging transportation proved most prohibitive.

There simply were not enough available seats on planes scheduled to leave Vietnam to accommodate all eligible children and escorts from all competing agencies. Within the small international relief community, word of their dilemma reached Ed Daly, whose World Airways, reputed to be the world's largest charter airline, was already operating at Tan Son Nhut (Saigon's primary airport) moving refugees and food supplies. The prospect of such a daring mission appealed to Daly's maverick (and self-promotional) sensibilities, and on April 2 a World Airways DC-8 cargo plane used for hauling rice brought fifty-eight children and twenty-seven adults to San Francisco without permission from Vietnam or the United States. Daly's unauthorized flight made front pages and evening news broadcasts nationwide, and the resultant public uproar—thousands called their congressmen and various federal agencies—sounded alarms in Washington. The next day, April 3, President Gerald Ford responded to this sudden demand for a coordinated federal effort by announcing that USAID would take the evacuation out of private hands by overseeing Operation Babylift.[17]

All seven international adoption agencies received notification and eagerly accepted invitations to participate. But the inaugural Babylift flight under USAID auspices, a C-5A Galaxy having just offloaded its inbound weapons cargo at Tan Son Nhut, crashed immediately after takeoff on April 4, killing 78 of 228 Vietnamese children aboard. The first successful planeload landed in the United States later that day carrying several injured Galaxy survivors. In general, the bigger, better established, and broadly experienced organizations—USCC, WVRO, and Holt—managed Operation Babylift more capably. These agencies possessed solid administrative infrastructure and professionalized staff, which translated into the planning and logistics, coordination with social services, and familiarity with adoption protocols necessary to deal with such a high volume in a compressed period. Holt, perhaps the most proven of the seven, had been arranging hundreds of adoptions in Vietnam for more than two years and during the Babylift processed children in a relatively organized and efficient manner, finally leaving the country on April 6 aboard a privately chartered Pan Am 747 with 374 children. Conversely, the smaller, less seasoned—FFAC and FCVN—lacked administrative and procedural expertise, making for a sloppier exit with repeated mistakes. Along with Holt, FCVN and FFAC accounted for more than half of all Babylift evacuees.[18]

The chief logistical failing, from start to finish, was identification. At this crucial juncture, the singular link between every child's two lives, their two identities—Vietnamese and American—were carelessly mishandled. The depth and accuracy of documentation varied wildly. For each of the nearly four dozen flights, agency and orphanage staff compiled passenger manifests. Next, individual adoption dossiers had to be cobbled together with whatever combinations of records existed—name(s), birth certificate, photographs, medical records, South Vietnamese government paperwork—all in varying degrees of completeness. These so-called files (consistently not much more than disorganized scraps of forms or sometimes nothing) then were collated with adoption papers—identifying destination country and adoptive parents—for those pending cases. "Three, six, nine babies would be left in front of the agency, mothers begging us to take them," a USAID official in Saigon explained of the conditions. "There were large sheaves of paper and batches of babies. Who knew which belonged to which?"[19]

Under any circumstances, compiling records would have been extremely problematic, but children commonly arrived at orphanage doors, irrespective of the reasons why, with incomplete or no background information, some without names. Many were known only by the temporary orphanage or nursery name they had been given until adoptive families picked a permanent one: Western (Brian or Elizabeth), biblical (Matthew), classical (Socrates), or else inane Vietnamese phrases.[20] Guidelines initiated midoperation to correct these increasingly glaring irregularities—instructing agencies to at minimum provide name, birth date, place of birth, and confirmation of adoption—failed, and may have unintentionally incentivized staffers to fabricate biographical information, or pressure parents already approved for adoption (domestic or foreign) to accept a Vietnamese child immediately instead.[21]

Even when dossiers were relatively comprehensive, there was no systematic processing coordination across the Babylift entities involved in physically handling children. Some agencies issued ID wrist bracelets and tags around the neck corresponding to dossiers, but those might be easily misassigned, lost in transit, or traded and collected by preadolescents. Onboard amenities were likewise uneven. Planes provided seats or else padded areas where children shared space with carry-on luggage, blankets, supplies of formula and diapers, and volunteer escorts. Packets got switched, and paperwork was scattered by play, ruined by leaking diapers, or crushed under foot over the long trip. Infants stowed in low-sided cardboard boxes, either belted into seats or secured underneath, had to be moved periodically for feeding and diaper changes. Some did not get returned to the correct boxes where their dossiers were attached. Toddlers were likewise switched when volunteer "laps"—weary adults assigned carrying or holding duty—got confused. On landing, required INS forms that needed to be completed with information matching dossiers often were not.[22]

Administrative failures to consistently identify Babylift evacuees often highlighted the culturally contested nature of what it meant to be orphaned. Many were legitimate, documentable orphans at some point in the adoption process. Older youth, a few having already met prospective adoptive parents, grasped what was happening, and many clearly welcomed it. Others, though, later confirmed they lived in orphanages while mothers worked out ways to care for them but refused to believe she meant to put them up for adoption. Younger children struggled to make sense of events, increasingly unable to communicate with unfamiliar English-speaking adults but cognizant of traumatic memories surrounding being left behind at the orphanage: how they had clung, cried, and begged mothers not to go, the ensuing separation anxiety, and families periodically coming back for visits. Any number—including a handful of Cambodians—never resided in orphanages yet could not articulate where they had been separated from family, in what refugee camp they were found, or even their parents' names, knowing them exclusively as Má (mother) or Ba (father). Healthy, well-fed, and educated boys and girls occasionally appeared on Babylift planes, too, obviously not abandoned but more likely from middle-class Saigon families with the wherewithal and connections to smuggle them out. Officials never determined exactly how many of the 2,547 Operation Babylift children were *not*, in fact, orphans by American legal standards. Estimates ranged widely from at least 10 percent to nearly 60 percent.[23]

One in five evacuees ended up in other countries, but the rest were processed through three reception centers in the United States at the Presidio in San Francisco, Long Beach Naval Complex, and Fort Lewis, Washington.[24] Agency representatives accompanying the children retained legal custody until adoption, bypassing visa or passport requirements by invoking emergency "parole" powers in U.S. immigration law. This distinction provisionally paroled individuals, as opposed to being technically admitted, into the country for urgent humanitarian reasons. The military otherwise coordinated all logistics. At the Presidio, the chief point of entry, where President Ford and the first lady ceremonially greeted the first planeload, service personnel handled triage, housing, feeding, transportation, and security. Much of this was accomplished in collaboration with the Red Cross (which supplied diapers from Walgreens and clothes from Sears), a small army of civilian volunteer laps or babysitters, and medical staff from the nearby University of California–San Francisco. Around 15 percent required hospitalization for serious disease or injury, but most commonly suffered from multiple ailments the orphanages had been unable to address: poor nutrition, vitamin deficiency, ear infections, pneumonia, lice, worms, intestinal parasites, typhoid, anemia, conjunctivitis, boils, fungal infections, scabies, and tooth decay.

There were nine recorded deaths during processing, seven of which were infants younger than twenty weeks old.[25]

The federal role ended once Babylift children left these facilities and the various agencies took over housing and care for them during the interim while completing adoptions. Parents expecting orphans already assigned to them had watched this last leg of the journey from Vietnam with pronounced trepidation, especially after the C-5A Galaxy disaster, when media did not immediately specify what agencies had been involved in the crash. A few later compared the intensity of emotion to the day John F. Kennedy was assassinated. Those in the early stages of the process who received phone calls explaining that instead of having to wait weeks or months, a child was available now, scrambled to procure basic childhood amenities virtually overnight in homes unprepared for children. Others just becoming adoptive parents during Operation Babylift completed few of the typical protocols required—referral, screening, reference check, home visit, and follow-up—for adopting American children. Equipped with perhaps nothing more than the Department of Health, Education, and Welfare's proscriptive pamphlet "Tips on the Care and Adjustment of Vietnamese and Other Asian Children in the United States," they confronted adjustment issues and medical problems because they were unprepared to be parents.[26]

Vietnamese children arriving at their final destination—at times in the company of random airline passengers recruited as volunteer escorts—commonly came in tears, dazed, and clutching prized possessions or sacred mementoes: creased family photographs, a U.S. military unit patch, or donated toys and crayons from the reception station. The adjustment to adoptive families, both as a child-rearing dynamic and an agent in acculturation to American life, was a period defined by transitional changes in childhood behavior and habits to cope with adoptee culture shock, often lasting years. For verbal adoptees, the language barrier presented immediate, critical obstacles. Disoriented, many spent their initial days in reception stations and new homes hunting for anything familiar: geographic landmarks, faces, and, moreover, Vietnamese-speaking adults. Without access to interpreters, nothing about the surreal experience was explained.[27]

Adoptive parents, likewise, searched for translators—rare commodities in local communities—and in those families fortunate enough to provide one, even for a brief visit, adoptees told their stories. Much to parents' dismay, children often responded to news of what had happened by forcefully shaking their heads "no" and pleading to be told when and how they would be taken home. After these initial interpreted conversations, family members labored largely in isolation to communicate, through tedious fits, starts, and nonverbal means, until preadolescents developed language skills in total immersion. The mother of one five-year-old related how the little girl initiated a routine whereby she moved around the house touching objects and saying their names in Vietnamese. Family members responded by pronouncing the corresponding English words, including numbers for counting.[28]

"My sister," an adoptee recalled of greeting her American family, "who's only eight months older than me, has always been and still is a foot taller than me, so she was five, but she was HUGE compared to me! So I just remember getting off the plane and her coming over and swinging me around! And I didn't know English at the time, but I remember mom saying 'Carrie, put her down!' It was all very overwhelming. They were very excited and there was a lot of energy, and of course, I had no idea what was going on."

At home, the family ate dinner together at the table—a curly-haired Jewish father, a blond, blue-eyed mother (both over six feet tall), and two daughters—before getting ready for bed. The woman explained,

> We have a tape recording of me and my sister in the bathtub, and I'm speaking in Vietnamese. I had it translated and I'm saying, "I'm going to wash my mother's hair." So I'm pretending to wash my mother's hair. And the next memory is that night, too—they were trying to have me sleep with my sister, because they were told that the family (in Vietnam) all sleeps together. But when it came time to go to bed, I tried to make a break for it! I tried to run to the front door and get out of the house—all very traumatic—and I think they were surprised. I just think that was the point at which I was really scared and didn't know what was going on. . . .
>
> And even in the bathtub translation, you can hear me saying (to my adoptive sister) "Oh, your dad is coming into the room." So I knew these parents were her parents, but I certainly didn't say, "Oh, this is our dad." And I think I just blocked out a lot, because I really can't remember making the transition from that to speaking English a month later. They said I was pretty quiet for about a month, and this was early May. And by the time I started pre-school in August, I was more verbal than my sister. I made a major turnaround—I completely stopped speaking Vietnamese.[29]

Inability to verbally communicate potentially made bonding that much trickier. Mothers' and fathers' recognition of, and appreciation for, children's unique personalities were delayed. Boys and girls remained distant without anyone listening or responding to, or connecting with them. For the significant number of Babylift adoptees suffering acute orphan syndrome—failure to thrive due to intellectual, emotional, and physical deprivation—attachment issues grew deeper, and they fell even further behind their chronological age in cognitive and moral development. Basic cultural illiteracy tended to exacerbate misunderstandings as well. Vietnamese did not like being touched on the head, for instance, and resented being called with the "come here" index finger gesture, a summons used only with dogs in their culture. Adding another cross-cultural element of dissonance, of the 173 black Amerasians involved in Operation Babylift, only 20 percent were placed in African American homes. Often adoptive parents expected gratitude and felt indignant when adoptees failed to express any appreciation. Forgetting that biological children typically do not verbalize thankfulness, either, parents unrealistically assumed the incredible sacrifices being made on an orphan's behalf guaranteed a special rapport, or at least an expressed sense of indebtedness, from children who were not conditioned to say "thank you" in any language.[30]

Adoptees discovered American childhood on a myriad of at times curious and amusing fronts. Former street children from Saigon often appeared fearless, until encountering grass, trees, and hills. Likewise, neighborhood war play was frightening, as the sight of pretend soldiers dressed in camouflage patrolling vacant lots kept panicked newcomers inside. Cold weather or air-conditioning were novelties, as were stairs and elevators, holding a hamburger or hot dog to eat, and cute stuffed animals (Vietnamese equivalents appeared scary by contrast). Fifteen hours and the international date line removed from Vietnam time, schedules got turned upside down, inviting nighttime play and daytime sleep. And then there was television. Either squatting on the floor or resting on couches, children were simply spellbound, particularly by cartoons where slapstick action transcended words, and they physically tried to interact with programming. Most adjustment issues, however, could be moderated when adoptive parents acted purposefully with patience and sensitivity, although abandoned children, unaccustomed to supervision, usually resisted being disciplined by adults. The keys, successful mothers and fathers progressively understood, were twofold: avoid kneejerk assumptions that all disobedient and naughty behaviors—spitting out spinach at dinner or throwing a tantrum at the grocery store—were deviances attributable to being a Vietnam War refugee, and resist culturally derived inclinations to break down their Vietnamese-ness as rapidly as possible. Parenting black Amerasians also usually meant mastering ethnic questions before addressing race.[31]

Name changes are prime examples. Nearly all adoptees were given white, middle-class American names. But many incorporated the child's heritage or family into a middle name. The Vietnamese order names by cultural importance—family, then individual—which is in reverse compared with the West. The hope was that during the transition adoptees would take comfort in using their

Vietnamese identities but eventually choose to go by their American names. Many families similarly began preparing for a day when adoptees might want to learn about their Vietnamese birthrights or perhaps someday return to their homeland.

To overcome immediate discomfort learning new American cultural elements, parents often allowed for choices and the time to adapt at children's own pace: chopsticks or silverware, rice and soups or macaroni and cheese, sleeping on floor mats or in beds. The mother of an eight-year-old Amerasian girl, adopted in Connecticut, kept nước chấm—a popular Vietnamese fish sauce used as a condiment—on the table for every meal after discovering it made American foods taste Vietnamese. While converting the girl to Christianity, the family also permitted her to fashion a traditional Vietnamese altar in her bedroom using a hand towel from the kitchen over a foot stool and arranged with mirror, picture, and little Buddha she brought from Vietnam.[32]

Regular household routines and school helped facilitate assimilation. Siblings and classmates might be initially gentle and deferential with adoptees, but subjection to normal teasing, horseplay, and schoolyard justice functioned as social acceptance. After less than a month in her home, a preschool adoptee demonstrated keen interest in following two older brothers to elementary school, laying out favorite outfits on her own each night as Mom did for them, and packing a paper bag with crayons, pencil, and coloring books each morning. Judging her readiness for this next step, the family enrolled the girl in nursery school, where exposure to games, music, art, and interaction with peers hastened her mastery of American attitudes and practices.[33]

A woman who was four years old in 1975 remembered the excitement of picking out new clothes for the first time. "The shoes were a whole funny story, too," she reflected, "because the social workers had told my adoptive father that I had never owned a pair of shoes or had shoes in Vietnam, and that I probably wouldn't like wearing shoes. And after the first day I spent with my adoptive family, they couldn't get me to take off my shoes! I was just obsessed with these red shoes."[34]

When youth stole food from the pantry and hoarded it under their beds, stayed hidden outside for hours, hit anyone trying to be affectionate, or avoided policemen—behavioral concerns clearly traceable to wartime experiences—some parents studied the root causes to come up with teachable opportunities. In one Missouri family, Melissa, a timid and fearful girl since arriving in 1973 before the Babylift, greeted all adults by rushing up and clutching them around the knees, to the point where the mother and preschool teacher found it easier to simply carry her everywhere. After talking with Vietnam veterans, though, Melissa's parents learned how lunging and clinging to adults' knees was common among Vietnamese children. Orphans, in particular, idolized American soldiers and had figured out that those children who got to soldiers first received candy and attention. This knee-hugging greeting was a tactic having little to do with shyness, and once the family appreciated its purpose they deliberately taught Melissa, whose birth name had been Ngoc-Lon, that there was enough affection, and candy bars, to go around.[35]

As soon as the couple announced intentions to adopt a second Vietnamese girl, Melissa became uncharacteristically sullen, acting out destructively at home and preschool. In consultation with teachers, the family decided that orphanage life had conditioned her to be anxious toward competition of this kind. Older orphans perceived, rightly or wrongly, an American preference for cuter—and whiter—children, thinking these were the first ones adopted. Nuns operating Catholic and Buddhist orphanages also reinforced a belief that parents only wanted younger children. Accordingly, orphans interpreted delays in the adoption process as adoptive parents having chosen a more attractive and smaller child instead. This is why adoptees routinely lied about their real age, claiming to be younger than they actually were. The girl felt threatened, fearing she was being traded in and would soon have to return to Vietnam. Once the family convinced Melissa otherwise, she still worried over the new arrival taking her bed, so they allowed her to help pick out the sister's new bed, after which her behavior returned to normal.[36]

On April 29, 1975, a class-action lawsuit filed on behalf of evacuees by San Francisco attorneys in conjunction with the New York–based Center for Constitutional Rights called for a halt to all Operation Babylift adoptions. Working as the Committee to Protect the Rights of Vietnamese Children, the lawyer's principal argument in *Nguyen Da Yen, et al. v. Kissinger* (Secretary of State Henry Kissinger) centered on growing evidence suggesting that at least 1,500 children were, in reality, ineligible for adoption in the United States due to inadequate or falsified documentation, no signed release from birth families, or invalid releases signed under duress. Though some adoption cases might be valid, plaintiffs conceded, Operation Babylift violated the Paris Peace Accords' proviso stating that the United States "shall not intervene in the internal affairs of" South Vietnam, in addition to three articles in the Geneva Convention calling for civilian refugees to be transferred back to their countries and reunited with families as soon as hostilities ceased and for war orphans to be cared for by people of "similar cultural tradition" whenever possible.[37]

The lawsuit sought the constitutional right of due process for adoptees by keeping each individual case open under active INS review until concerned families in Vietnam could be notified to reclaim their children. The problem was that virtually no Vietnamese knew about U.S. lawyers trying to represent their interests, and the new Hanoi government sent ambivalent signals. Both the Provisional Revolutionary Government (the communists' rival government to the South Vietnamese regime) and Hanoi protested Operation Babylift—declaring kidnapping an illegal attack on Vietnam's sovereignty under the Geneva Convention—and called on the United Nations High Commissioner for Refugees to oversee repatriation. Yet other priorities kept the Vietnamese government from pressing the issue in 1975, or from officially sanctioning the International Red Cross's offer to use its Central Tracing Agency in unifying families.[38]

When some Vietnamese birth mothers living in refugee centers operating within the United States eventually came forward, many filed custody claims in state courts independent of the class-action suit. A handful of evacuees were returned to birth families without legal recourse, but adoptive parents ordinarily refused, leaving children caught in the middle without a satisfying outcome for anyone. Together these various custody battles challenging Operation Babylift adoptions were simultaneously litigated across the nation's court system, with the original class-action suit evolving through multiple hearings, delays, appeals, and counterappeals (in the same San Francisco federal courthouse as Patty Hearst's trial). Comparable to modern custody decisions, judgment hinged on discerning "the best interest of the child," but arguments reflected that profound missionary impulse within the American character. How capable were Vietnamese of caring for their children? Was it better to grow up in American affluence with adoptive families or in Vietnamese poverty among biological relatives?[39] By 1976 judges had awarded custody to a dozen or so individual birth parents, but overall the intractable lawsuit ground to a halt. The court ultimately decided it was beyond its capabilities to handle what was more appropriately more than two thousand separate cases. Thus, all but a handful of Operation Babylift adoptions legally stood.[40]

In satisfying INS residency requirements for foreign adoptees, most waited another two years to become naturalized American citizens. Acculturation, to whatever degrees of completeness, defied such standardization. International adoptions are challenging under ordinary conditions. Adoptees experience psychological distress from dislocation and culture shock, and while not normative, neither are emotional and developmental issues uncommon among Operation Babylift children. Problem placements were reported and adoptions failed. State social services had to remove a number from adoptive homes and relocate them elsewhere, sometimes for physical, emotional, or sexual abuse. Others estranged themselves from adopted families. And many exhibited depression and patterns of dysfunctional behavior—eating disorders or continuously seeking substitute families—well beyond preadolescence. Unlike other Asian immigrants congregating in insulated, ethnic communities, Babylift adoptees were also often raised in smaller towns as the only Asians around, alienated and acutely aware of how they stood out and what they represented to neighbors in post-Vietnam America.[41]

A woman who was three years old at the time of her adoption remembers,

> As a child, I struggled with severe nightmares which would cause me to scream, sweat, and even sleepwalk on occasion. My mom described my scream to be so horrific that it would sound like someone was physically attacking me. When I was awake, I would even get upset if I heard the sounds of a siren from a fire truck or even the sound of a tea pot whistling. She said I would become hysterical, then run and hide under the kitchen table or my bed. The nightmares continued until my young teenager years when I began seeing a psychologist who helped interpret my dreams. He said my dreams were so detailed, and I knew so much information, that many of them were probably actual things I had experienced as a baby prior to arriving at the orphanage. They began to subside after working through my fears.[42]

Despite everything, the majority of Babylift children, and those adopted prior to 1975, appear to have had relatively happy childhoods, and adoption's impact on their life trajectories has been generally positive. The most relevant variable influencing successful acculturation and healthy, well-adjusted adulthood was age at adoption. Infants and toddlers without memories of Vietnam settled into adopted life with fewer difficulties compared with preadolescents with concrete experiences prior to Operation Babylift. Those adoptees old enough to remember life in Vietnam, observed journalist and author Dana Sachs, "seemed more likely to have trouble adjusting to their new situations overseas. They knew, most clearly, what they had gained by leaving, but they knew what they had lost as well."[43]

If there is a common denominator among older youth, it is the disputed nature of identity. Perhaps this explains why so many Babylift children consider themselves Vietnamese adoptees rather than Vietnamese Americans. The most obvious conflict was grounded in never sensing a genuine belonging in either culture. "I have had a great life from the outside looking in," one man made clear. "But if you were to see me from the inside out, you'd see hate, anger, frustration, denial, low self-esteem, racism, prejudice, shame, and betrayal. For the longest time growing up I hated being different-looking from my friends. I hated the way others teased me, even though I had white parents like everyone else."[44]

To become American, in a land where the host culture devalues an immigrant's culture, children grew up increasingly disassociated from Vietnam, unable to comprehend the language or relate to its values, specifically honoring ancestors and traditions. The assimilated know Vietnam only through books and the Internet today, while the less assimilated are further isolated. "This story almost sounds too good to be true," another articulated, "because it is. I spent many years battling ADHD, learning disabilities, mild depression, and abandonment issues. I was just one of many growing up American. We woke every morning in a world that sometimes didn't welcome us or give us a chance or the respect we deserved just because of the color of our skin. Some fought back while others took the pain. I still dream of seeing my birth parents to thank them for life, a clean slate."[45]

Adoptees indeed work equally hard to reconcile gratitude for their birth parents' sacrifice and contentment for having been adopted into privilege. These feelings resided uneasily with doubt that staying in Vietnam amounted to a death sentence, and resentment over whether they may have been better off staying put. All invested extensive time and energy since childhood managing this balancing act with constructive coping strategies. Taking responsibility for life by agency seems to have been most effective, while allowing incompleteness to shape one's life, the least. To bridge substantial holes in individual histories and solve life's pressing mysteries, adoptees reconstruct workable personal narratives by connecting random fading memories, educated guesses, and whatever factual information still exists. Support groups such as the Vietnam Adoptee Network (VAN) together with sites such as adoptvietnam.org and Vietnambabylift.org have enabled many to answer some questions, and in the last generation adult adoptees are making pilgrimages to Vietnam—where the Galaxy crash site is an honored stop—leaving no stone unturned to make meaning, find family, and reintroduce themselves to a birthright.[46]

"There's no clear-cut answer to that," an Amerasian woman responded when asked to discern Operation Babylift's meaning.

> It's hard to explain what I would want to convey to you. If you look at my early memories, there is all this chaos about leaving at age four. And now the chaos has been put to rest; there's healing and peace. I mean, on one hand, I lost my language, my culture . . . my roots. Maybe it would have been okay if I'd been a rice farmer and not had the benefit of an upper-class upbringing. Not that I would have it differently, because this is how my life turned out. But this probably wouldn't have been my choice. Ironically, if I'd stayed [in Vietnam] through the Orderly Departure Program, I would have been allowed to come to the U.S. with

my birth mother. I don't know. There's a different pace in Vietnam. Their culture is just so rich . . . the family traditions and the lifestyles. There's a loss there.[47]

Operation Babylift represented only a fraction of the nearly 130,000 Vietnamese evacuees from Saigon in April 1975, the first wave in a mass exodus swelling later in the decade by fleeing boat people. Although some Americans leaving in the final evacuation brought their Vietnamese wives and biracial children out with them, most people in the United States only discovered the existence of Amerasian children through television and print media's emphasis on this particularly poignant category of orphans. And for a moment amid the chaos, their troubles weighed heavily on the American mind, as journalists highlighted the startling population of abandoned Amerasians, including toddlers, living in squalor on Saigon's teeming thoroughfares. National fascination and concern proved ephemeral, however, and just as quickly Amerasian stories were drowned out by the greater cacophony accompanying America's last days in Vietnam and then silenced altogether by the country's postwar amnesia. The U.S. government did not have a repatriation plan for servicemen's children comparable to France's when that colonial power left in 1954; instead, as a matter of policy, they avoided the embarrassing issue with benign neglect. Countless GI fathers probably never even knew they had a son and/or daughter still in Vietnam if the pregnancies occurred at the end of their tours. Only a few private philanthropists and charitable organizations such as the Pearl Buck Foundation took much notice. That is, until a photograph from *Newsday* in 1985 rediscovered Amerasians, and with the accompanying groundswell of popular support, these American children finally left for the United States, forming the last wave in the Vietnamese diaspora.[48]

Not that Amerasians had been a particularly well-kept secret to the American presence in Vietnam. Post–World War II occupation forces in Japan produced thousands of Amerasians, as did the Korean War. Dating back to the Filipino Insurrection, illegitimacy was simply a by-product of any American military footprint in Asian countries. Vietnamese Amerasians became more visible to soldiers as the war went on, growing up in villages near American bases and neighborhoods where servicemen frequented. They appeared distinctly American and were accordingly hard to miss. For a variety of genetic reasons, physical features in Amerasians tended to manifest three-quarters American and one-quarter Vietnamese, with possibly 25 percent fathered by African Americans. Like all Vietnamese children, GIs were fascinating to Amerasians, and wherever soldiers traveled, preadolescents swarmed around these physical giants requesting candy, money, or cigarettes. Groups routinely pilfered through base trash and jockeyed near helicopters at takeoff and landing to feel the wind. Some platoons and whole units adopted individual boys as mascots and provided care for the homeless. Schools and playgrounds built to win hearts and minds attracted Amerasians by the score.[49]

A significant proportion of Amerasians were products of casual sex with prostitutes, and too often rape. Rear areas supported active social scenes with abundant access to alcohol, drugs, and prostitution in dance clubs, bars (often de facto racially segregated), and brothels. Prostitution was unlicensed, controlled by South Vietnamese political and military corruption, and pervasive. Poor, displaced farm girls from rural villages, most between fifteen and twenty years old, supplied the demands of a military force, in which almost four out of every five soldiers were support, not combat troops with greater opportunities for fraternization. International relief workers in 1969 estimated, though probably overstated, there may have been as many as a quarter million prostitutes and bar girls working in South Vietnam, noting that virtually every bar in the country had at least one pregnant woman employed there.[50]

Later studies conducted with the mothers of Amerasians in the Orderly Departure Program suggest instead that the majority, maybe the vast majority, of biracial children were products of some form of relationship between parents, often genuinely affectionate. Among mothers interviewed, 12 percent claimed to have been married to the father, and 81 percent cohabited for periods lasting from usually less than one tour of duty to, in rare instances, seven years. According to 64 percent, American fathers supported the family while in country, and 11 percent continued to do so after returning to the States. Over half of these women expected the family to immigrate to the United States with him, and despite those expectations rarely materializing, eight out of ten still viewed the father in positive terms a decade later.[51]

These figures are almost certainly subject to memory distortion and, moreover, need to be distilled through the idealized, imaginative narratives mothers and Amerasians fashioned concerning family life. Their emphasis on stability and continuity may reflect comparative improvements in a Vietnamese's standard of living when associating with Americans. Installations were magnets for young women, who migrated to work on site as maids, laundry girls, seamstresses, secretaries, and clerks, or in off-base markets, food stalls, fruit and drink carts, and bars. When socializing occurred, Americans treated women quite well by Vietnamese standards, spending money on entertainment and gifts local men could not afford, especially U.S. civilians employed by international companies or contracted by the government. Tens of thousands of American construction workers operated in South Vietnam, earning five times the average GI paycheck and staying for years, not months.[52]

Consider also how the nature of paternal commitment was subject to a young father and mother's interpretation of relative cultural constructions of "girlfriend," "temporary wife," and "wife." Some women sold themselves outright as "rent-a-girls," living with Americans for a flat weekly, monthly, or yearly rate that went up if they spoke English. Far more often couples developed emotional bonds, frequently living together as circumstances and regulations allowed. Yet whereas GIs recognized the relationship as casual—boyfriend dating girlfriend—Vietnamese women misread that American distinction, instead understanding all long-term relationships to be serious and, as such, equivalent to marriage.[53]

Any paperwork involved contributed to the confusion. Despite no official prohibition on fraternization, the military and government discouraged it procedurally. Soldiers needed to file local cohabitation papers (Vietnamese common-law marriage certification), or women might be arrested for prostitution. Even if a GI wanted to get married, the lengthy, cumbersome process involved multiple levels of military, INS, and South Vietnamese bureaucracy.[54] Enlisted men first had to receive permission from their company commander before women underwent medical exams and security checks. After the requisite waiting period of three to four months—when chaplains customarily warned how war brides would not be accepted back home—women securing South Vietnamese clearance to leave were required to do so within forty-five days of their wedding. Officers faced fewer obstacles, but still, nearly one-quarter of all applicants withdrew from the process. Most of the rest simply finished their tour prior to completion. Again, although actual certificates were a rarity, Vietnamese women generally viewed all official forms filed at any administrative level as tantamount to marriage. Even without qualifying documentation, she referred to him as husband and thought of herself as wife, when in reality she was just a temporary one.[55]

Perhaps as much as anything, mothers deliberately grasped at whatever measure of legitimacy these familial arrangements extended to *con lai*—half-breed—children. So long as women continued some semblance of a relationship—however contrived or fictive—Amerasians were valued, or at least not hidden, and occasionally even welcomed into the mother's family.[56] Although obviously shaped by economic necessities as well, in cases where couples separated, some mothers managed a sort of informal visitation and child support from GIs. Departing soldiers routinely passed temporary wives off to buddies at tour's end, and mothers purposefully settled into a domestic lifestyle with another American, which might also result in additional half-siblings by several servicemen.

A single, twelve-month tour assured that almost no Amerasians remember living together with both biological parents, unless fathers re-upped for a second or third hitch. Still, this basic maternal drive to socially validate the family, even after fathers rotated home, resulted in two resonant emotional commonalities found in Amerasian childhood. Mothers gifted to children modest keepsakes—unit patches, dog tags, photographs, correspondence, or music cassette tapes—left by departing fathers. More significantly, she passed down, almost as a bequest, variations on the same story. In one, the child's father intended to reunite the family by returning to Vietnam for good as a civilian after the war. The other, more popular, involved mother and child immigrating with him to the United States, an invitation she had ultimately chosen to decline out of family loyalty.

By framing these remnants of her own unrequited aspirations as an Amerasian's legacy or inheritance, Vietnamese mothers hoped to fortify children developmentally. So regardless of the veracity of those marriage statistics or the truthfulness of these stories, both constructs congealed into reality in preadolescent minds. Amerasians took comfort in what effectively became sacred talismans and mythologies, since they served as timeless evidence of a father in America still wanting and caring for them.[57] Yet as an organizing principle in childhood identity development, such a rich and pervasive fantasy life was not particularly healthy or constructive, meaning much of what Amerasians subsequently built on top of it remained out of plumb. The alternative, though, growing up as *bui doi*—the dust of life—was grim.

It is important to be cautious of sentimentality about the *bui doi*, a pejorative term roughly analogous to the harshest American racial slur, and also overly generalized assumptions about Amerasians, with whom the expression is usually associated. Socioeconomic and cultural differences existed in their childhoods, but all were marginalized, first by family and community when American fathers left, and afterward in a chiefly de facto sense by a repressive political system in communist Vietnam. In this traditional family-centered society, patriarchal lineage is the foundation of individual identity. "A child without a father is like a house without a roof," says the proverb, and each family member's sense of self-worth and livelihood is predicated on legitimacy. And just as all extended members benefit from a family's reputation—for instance, improving one's marriage or employment prospects—everybody shoulders dishonor.[58] Personal conduct is often guided by the importance of maintaining the appearance of paternal standing.

Amerasians—biracial and illegitimate offspring of foreign enemies—were anomalies threatening family continuity by stigmatizing past and future generations. Irrespective of how mothers felt about Amerasians, or any steps taken to legitimize their relationships with American fathers, these children disgraced them. Vietnamese bias naturally assumed impropriety, casting all women who had sex with Americans as lower-class prostitutes. Under such damning conditions, after giving birth some mothers left Amerasians at the hospital or at orphanages, while others sold them. Later surveys estimated that 93 percent of Caucasian Amerasians were raised by their mother, but only 77 percent of black Amerasians. Although some families supported mother and child, rejection was customary. Even when Amerasians could physically stay in the home, they and their mothers grew up emotionally ostracized from relatives so as not to stain the all-important family line.[59]

A Vietnamese man living in the United States related,

> In our family we called women who married or went with Americans "bar girls," and in school we made fun of Amerasians, saying "Your mom is a whore." All the Amerasians were very poor, and on the street would be kicked and beaten, and their mothers called whores—worse if the kid was black. Some tried to deny they were mixed—they'd say, "Oh no, I just have darker skin," or claim they had some French blood way back in the family.... One Amerasian girl told me that every day when she went to school people would line up along the road as she passed, saying "Your mom is an ugly whore." She said she'd just put her head down in shame.[60]

More broadly, Vietnamese society reinforced Amerasian marginalization. Given the country's homogeneity and color consciousness, mixed-race outliers likewise encouraged social instability that threatened cultural continuity. Growing up in Vietnam "I told them I was Vietnamese," an Amerasian woman recalled, "and they laughed and said Vietnamese don't have brown hair and blue eyes. I would tell them my eyes were a disease and they would laugh and tell me it was a disease from Americans." While Vietnamese adoptees were adjusting to American childhood, *con lai* experienced decidedly more spiteful racial prejudice and discrimination, especially those fathered by African Americans. Darker skin was associated with the primitive, tribal peoples in the mountains—Montagnards—and Vietnamese easily folded their racism into learned American forms. "I only went to school up to second grade," an Amerasian of African American descent remembered. "The students don't like black skin, they hate it. They like to play with the fair-skinned people. They never let me forget I was black and that I had no father. They always called me names and made me ashamed, so I stopped going."[61]

Already targets of racism and classism, Amerasians were disproportionately singled out for political discrimination by communists as a suspicious sort of people threatening Vietnamese nationalism. Reunification Day, April 30, 1975, when North and South Vietnam became one nation, is a nearly universal flashbulb memory. "The end came so quickly," a mother commented. "Panic everywhere, and fear. Guns and South Vietnamese army uniforms thrown out into the streets. Most terrible of all, rumors that the Viet Cong planned to kill all Amerasians and torture their mothers, pulling out their fingernails. Some said that all Amerasians would be tossed into the sea." Women destroyed or altered birth certificates in the crisis atmosphere that drove Operation Babylift, burning all documentary evidence of American parentage. Photographs and letters with a father's complete name and U.S. address were lost forever. Active preschoolers were sequestered indoors for weeks at a time, and women attempted to lighten or darken skin color or shave off the blond and red hair of those that could not stay hidden.[62]

Although government policies never approached the violent persecution imagined, within the victor's multipoint program for peaceful reunification—rebuilding Vietnam's infrastructure and agriculture while weeding out corrupting American influences—the treatment of Amerasians was largely ad hoc based on local officials' sensibilities and attitudes. Amerasians were identified, along with other potential collaborators and troublemakers, by a bureaucratic "household registration" census. Those unable to prove their loyalty for police during the interrogation portion of the process joined former South Vietnamese soldiers and administrators—without due process—in some combination of provincial jails or reeducation camps to receive communist indoctrination. Since most preadolescents did not comprehend, mothers were typically incarcerated first, leaving confused and frightened children abandoned for arbitrary and indeterminate lengths of time.[63]

Eventually, most former South Vietnamese deemed corrupted and undesirable—including perhaps as many as three out of four Amerasians—were relocated to designated New Economic Zones (NEZs). Communists populated these undeveloped lands, located in desolate jungle areas mostly near the Cambodian border, with "surplus" labor to address Vietnam's food shortages through a system of government-imposed collectivized agriculture. NEZ residents were given a parcel of land to clear and farm with a portion of the crops going to the state. Yet most workers, certainly Amerasians from liquidated orphanages, had never farmed, and given the land's poor quality or the life-threatening animals, snakes, and malaria, they subsisted on the margins of survival, more exile than comrade. "We lived in the NEZ from when I was 9 years old until I was 16," an Amerasian woman recalled.

> A terrible place; I cannot describe it! We were always hungry. I worked in the rice fields all day. There were leeches in the water. We were very poor. In the NEZ, the communists hated Amerasians. At meetings they always talked bad about us. I felt like KILLING them . . . ! And the other kids taunted me all the

> time, "You are *my lai* [Amerasian], you are *my lai!*" So I yelled back at them, "Yes, I am *my lai*, but *my lai* is better than Viet Cong!" For this the police were going to jail my mother, but in the end they released her because there was no one else to take care of us kids.[64]

The state expressly prohibited adult Amerasians, and other ethnic groups, from military service, higher education, government work, and certain industrial jobs, but contrary to popular belief, it apparently did not systematically deny schooling to children. Instead, taunting and anti-American indoctrination discouraged regular or sustained attendance, leaving the majority with only a few years of formal education in the elementary grades. School was the earliest awareness of being physically different for Amerasians raised insulated from anticipated communist reprisals or else in rural areas where family and villagers tolerated them without harassment. Peer teasing, both good-natured and cruel, about their height and facial features bred discomfort and self-consciousness in preadolescents. Rubbing the coarse hair of black Amerasians was dehumanizing, as were popular schoolhouse insults (sung more for the rhyming quality in Vietnamese than any literal meaning). "Amerasians eat potatoes and beg," children chanted. "They eat in hiding because they're afraid of ghosts," or "Amerasians have twelve ass holes, if you plug up one, gas and shit comes out the other eleven." That "was an old singsong the kids would call out whenever I walked by them," an Amerasian confided. "They would shout and point at me with sticks and call me the stupid American. Why didn't I go back to my country? I learned to run very fast whenever I had to go out of my home."[65]

"I went to school for five years," an Amerasian woman echoed. "That's where I found out that I wasn't Vietnamese, that I was Amerasian. The other students let me know. I was the only Amerasian in that school, and they always put me down, make fun of me. . . . Even when I quit school and went to help my mother at the market, people would insult me. Vietnamese don't like Amerasians. So many times I wished that I was Vietnamese, so people would like me."[66]

To survive abuse and beatings, others fought back, gaining reputations as troublemakers. Teachers looked the other way, for the most part, either ignoring Amerasians completely or blaming them as discipline problems. The nationalist curriculum likewise seemed an indictment on their existence. All students learned the glories of Ho Chi Minh and the evils of America, either in written lessons for older children or via patriotic songs in the lower grades. "Every day they (my teacher) talked bad about Americans and said things like, 'America is rich only because it steals and makes wars,'" another Amerasian related of the institutionalized scapegoating. "I couldn't stand it when they talked about my father."[67]

Whether having been expelled or kept home by protective mothers, or as dropouts of their own volition, Amerasians grew up outside normative school-age experiences. Without formal schooling they tended to be friendless throughout childhood, which developmentally precluded healthy socialization and hardened an outsider identity. Moreover, Amerasians were prematurely forced into the job market as child labor, where negligible education and prejudice (against both mother and child) relegated them to the most menial or exploitable work. Amerasian youth regularly subsisted in a transitory lifestyle, alternating between periods living with mothers or extended family and homelessness. Almost four out of five lived in the rural countryside, and when on their own, Amerasians hired themselves out for laboring in rice fields, fishing, and gathering firewood or other natural jungle products. Town markets offered legitimate curbside vending opportunities—selling fruit and scavenged merchandise—alongside illegal moneymaking schemes as beggars, smugglers, prostitutes, and petty thieves. Life on the street as a child, among adult criminals, drunks, addicts, and mental and physical casualties from the war, placed Amerasians at a disadvantage in the primitive competition for sleeping space and food left at restaurants and garbage piles. Gangs eventually recruited many, offering protection, acceptance, and a place to stay in exchange for a percentage of their income. All too often the price of membership in a surrogate crime family might also involve periodic jail time, alcohol or heroin abuse, or torture and death at the hands of rival gangsters.[68]

In postwar Vietnam, where a decade of fighting left nearly a quarter of a million disabled, a million widows, 25 million acres of farmland devastated, and 1.5 million farm animals dead, poverty, famine, and disease touched everyone. But Amerasians were among society's poorest and most vulnerable, and consequently one of the most adversely affected by punitive U.S. economic policies. As the inexperienced communist government struggled to reorient the South's failing economy, America handicapped it further by defaulting on nearly $5 billion in promised reconstruction aid and commodities. Reluctant to normalize relations with Vietnam until a full accounting of MIAs had been made, the United States likewise extended the wartime trade embargo against the North to include the entire nation and froze all Vietnamese assets in the States. Americans were also prohibited from sending money to Vietnam, which effectively cut off humanitarian aid as well.[69]

"I always lived in Long Xuyen," a twelve-year-old Amerasian boy explained.

> I went to school for only one year. My classmates called me names; sometimes they beat me up or threw rocks at me. But still, I liked school, and felt sad when I had to quit because we had no more money. . . . Every day I left our house early

to search for plastic bags to collect, clean and re-sell to the vendors. It was messy. I had to crawl underneath houses sometimes to get them—but then the people in the house would get mad and dump hot water on me. So then I would just look through the garbage piles. By the end of the day I could earn about 5 piastres [about 12 cents] to give to my mother. But I was always alone all day.[70]

Predictably, hardship and degradation in childhood adversely affected socialization and had profound causal developmental results. In spite of their American physical appearance, Amerasians acted basically Vietnamese in personality and habits. Researchers later posited that family stability was instrumental in determining the degree to which conditioning reinforced traditional Vietnamese qualities in Amerasians. When consistently raised in affectionate, protective environments by mothers or either biological or surrogate caregivers (stepfather, grandparents, extended family members, foster parents, or community members), children "appear[ed] to embody values and attitudes which are manifest in their behavior and are essentially those of the broader, Vietnamese culture." Polite and respectful of authority, their positive attitudes about family standing or education, for instance, remained strongly Vietnamese. A maternal presence in child-rearing was the optimal situation developmentally, but children under some type of surrogate care fared comparatively much better so long as adults were dependable. Often older men—grandfathers, usually—formed particularly warm and nurturing paternalistic bonds with Amerasian youth.[71]

Those raised in less secure socioeconomic circumstances, with erratic or inattentive caregivers (single mothers, abusive stepfathers, or foster families) did not "reflect traditional Vietnamese values and behaviors at the same level," American researchers found. Particularly if a communist father figure had fought against the United States, Amerasians' "daily lives may well have lacked the kind of structure and discipline inherent in the traditional family or school environment. These differences are manifest in their expressed interests, expectations and behavior and [played] a fundamental role in how they interact with and are perceived by others." One Amerasian recalled being raised by a woman who found him in the market. "She was good to me," he pointed out, "but her sister, my aunt, and my aunt's husband, they hated me. They were jealous that my stepmother loved me. They despised me because I was Amerasian. They made my life miserable, and finally I ran away when I was still pretty young." "Most of the hurt I felt came from my family," another Amerasian man remembered. "My aunts loved me, but their sons insulted me all the time. My second and third cousins were cruel. They tell me, 'You're a bastard, you don't have any father' and things like that.... Coming from my family, this hurt me very much, and many times when I was alone I would cry over this. I spent much time alone rather than face these difficulties."[72]

Having been sent to a NEZ, an Amerasian man related how childhood conditions worsened when his guardian became involved with a local official. "We were very poor, and my aunt had to work very hard," he said, "but soon after we got there my aunt fell in love with the Communist village chief, a former guerrilla soldier. We moved into his house, a thatch hut with a dirt floor. His position made life easier for my aunt, but very difficult for me. He was a former guerilla soldier, and he hated me, hated my American blood. He beat me, he tortured me with pliers. He even threw me down a well and almost drowned me. My aunt didn't say anything, she was afraid of him."[73]

Streetwise but undersocialized due to limited family bonding, children did not benefit from appropriate social behaviors being modeled in the classroom, nor did they derive normal feelings of competence or confidence from school, either. Their sense of identity was shaped less by the positive reinforcement associated with being a "good" student and more by a defeatist "can't do" mentality continuously reinforced through classmates and family denigrating their ambitions and dreams. "When I was a boy, I didn't know that I was half-American," a light-skinned Amerasian revealed, "but when I got older, some children in the neighborhood were very mean. . . . When I make a mistake, they say, 'You do that because you're Amerasian. You're not the same as Vietnamese people. Your father fought against the Vietnamese government.' They tell me, 'You are not the same blood as me. You have to go back [to America].' I don't like that, I hate it."[74]

"When they were little, they didn't react the same as other children," a Catholic nun observed. "They were quieter, more simple, and more honest, and usually very obedient because they had such low self-esteem. They were teased by other children so much that they didn't like to interact with them. They had very little self-confidence, and when they grew up, they remained the same."[75]

Life conditioned Amerasians early to feeling unwelcome, and accordingly they adopted natural defensive posturing in social interactions as a coping strategy growing up. Seemingly aloof or guarded to others, Amerasians tended to internalize accumulated psychological weight, which in turn made them prone to adjustment problems and dysfunctional behaviors unusual in Vietnamese childhood. Besides lacking motivation in school, they managed moods and impulses poorly—inclined toward temper tantrums, lying, and defiance—avoided or delayed confronting problems, and had difficulty trusting. Adolescence exacerbated many issues. Often Amerasians displayed age-inappropriate behaviors as teenagers, frequently acting much younger as in playing with dolls or coloring. Boys exhibited significantly more hostility, and with greater need for attention, they developed substantially more disciplinary problems. Girls became sexually active earlier with a greater likelihood of promiscuity. Self-harm—burning and cutting—and attempted suicide were common to both. "All my life people despised me, they called me a 'bastard,' a 'nigger,'" one man shared. "I didn't care about myself. I wanted to die. So I took a razor and slashed myself all over. People see my scars and they think, 'Oh, he's a tough guy, he's a troublemaker.' They might judge me. But it's not like that, I just wanted to die. I tried to kill myself four times. All my life has been sad. I never had a father's love, only a mother's, and that was not enough for me."[76]

Even among the most maladjusted, positive identity development in all Amerasians inexorably ran parallel to, and at some point intertwined with, the search for their father. Only a random few managed to salvage contact information or random mementos, but out of a few artifacts and mothers' storytelling, children constructed exaggerated American fantasies. In contrast to the austerity of their world, Amerasians imagined a fatherland depicted in glamorous movies and advertising, where idyllic families lived in clean, white suburbia. Compared with cruel stepfathers, pretend American men—honest and dependable—still intended to be loving husbands and attentive fathers. Preadolescents might love and respect mothers, but mother does not have the principal status of father in Vietnamese culture, and children deluded themselves into thinking that scenarios about being a part of a family in the United States somehow conferred social rank on them. Many wore their fathers' dog tags through childhood. Others kept his picture on the Buddhist alter with incense. If they knew where he had been stationed, Amerasians sometimes haunted the deserted remnants of a base for years, daydreaming about father-child reunions in this physical setting.[77]

A small number of Amerasians left Vietnam among the boat people, a term broadly used to describe nearly two million postwar Vietnamese refugees, but referring specifically to those fleeing by sea in 1979. Thousands of boat people perished during the dangerous escape, and in a humanitarian response, forty countries, under the United Nations' sponsorship, created the Orderly Departure Program (ODP) in 1980 to resettle them in the West. Although a few Amerasians also applied for ODP placement, several inconsistencies in U.S. immigration policies, and the absence of diplomatic relations between the two nations, meant there were no protocols for admitting them into the United States. Early guidelines allowed Amerasians born in Southeast Asia to emigrate to the United States, but the State Department balked at accepting accompanying family members. A 1982 Amerasian Immigration Act later accepted Cambodian, Laotian, and Vietnamese children, but without a consular apparatus, the law could never be implemented in Vietnam.[78]

The chief stumbling block involved citizenship. Neither country recognized Amerasians. The Vietnamese basically considered them American, and the United States classified them as Vietnamese, except the tiny fraction already issued birth certificates or passports before 1975. Under American law, all other Amerasians had no legal claim to U.S. citizenship. Immigration codes at the time offered nationality to children born abroad when one parent was an American citizen, but illegitimate children were specifically excluded unless paternity could be legally established by legitimation prior to their twenty-first birthday. The prevailing standard for legitimation required an "identifiable" father to legitimate them through affidavit or other documentation. For Amerasians left with nearly no information about their fathers, and thus no real proof beyond physical appearance, legitimation was practically impossible. On occasions when names and addresses survived self-imposed purges, many soldiers had inserted "do not contact" notations in their service records. As a result, only a handful out of two or three thousand Amerasians trying to legally enter America under the ODP between 1980 and 1987 had fathers willing to extend them citizenship.[79]

The aforementioned 1985 photograph in *Newsday*, a metropolitan New York daily newspaper, coupled with Vietnam's eagerness to use Amerasians as a means of opening diplomatic dialogue, eventually forced America's hand to develop more systematic repatriation. France had dealt forthrightly with these problems in the 1950s by creating a nonprofit Federation for French Children in Indochina to coordinate comprehensive legal, material, educational, and job assistance for its soldiers' offspring. Twenty-five thousand were ultimately relocated and financially subsidized throughout France to foster assimilation. French citizenship was granted to all, including those not recognized by their fathers, but children kept the option of Vietnamese citizenship on turning eighteen. Yet American objections to implementing some variation on this French plan had always reflected the State Department's cautious approach to overhauling immigration law or extending dual citizenship.[80]

That is, until the *Newsday* photographer's pitiful image of Le Van Minh, a severely handicapped boy begging on Ho Chi Minh City (Saigon) streets, inspired a separate ODP just for Amerasians. Urban Amerasians had for years gravitated around the Ho Chi Minh City neighborhood near the Ministry of Foreign Affairs, primarily to raise their visibility among tourists who might help them reach America. Reunification Park, which faced the Ministry, became known as "Amerasian Park" for the hundreds living there, and many of these first photographs of Amerasians in American newspapers were taken here. The photograph of Minh, published around the world, particularly resonated with

Long Island high school students who petitioned Congressman Robert Mrazek (D-N.Y.), a Vietnam veteran, to intercede. Mrazak's Amerasian Homecoming Act (AHA), passed in late 1987 in collaboration with fellow veteran Congressman Tom Ridge (R-Pa.), authorized preferential resettlement of all Vietnamese American children born between 1961 and 1976, and their immediate relatives, at U.S. expense. The key was finally accepting Amerasians as immigrants, based primarily on physical appearance (as the Vietnamese had long contended), but bureaucratically classifying them as refugees, which meant eligibility for better entitlement benefits, more legal protections, and exemption from stricter immigration numbers.[81]

With the State Department acting as gatekeeper of the registration and screening process, the AHA operated in conjunction with ODP and for the most part remained indistinguishable from it. Despite pent-up demand, the number of applications was relatively modest as the AHA program got under way in 1988, when the youngest Amerasian participants had turned thirteen years old and the oldest was only twenty-six. Part of the initial hesitation to use AHA stemmed from a stipulation allowing only one relative to accompany Amerasians to America, often leaving young people to choose between mother, siblings, or spouse. In 1991 AHA rules were relaxed, allowing immigrants to bring blood relatives as well as spouses. Rumors likewise limited early participation. Since police in rural Vietnam had been charged with disseminating AHA information, many Amerasians suspected a ruse: a communist plot to finally round up Amerasians for expulsion, reeducation, or worse. Many simply waited until they received letters from other Amerasians safely resettled in the United States before initiating paperwork at local police stations. Yet, after a slow start, annual departures for America quickly rose from four hundred to nearly ten thousand at the program's peak in 1991 and 1992.[82]

The AHA unintentionally cast Amerasians in an unprecedented role, no longer reviled children of dust but rather coveted golden children to Vietnamese seeking a means to escape communism. Competition within families grew fierce, including strangers claiming to be long-lost relations, and members attempted to outdo one another with gifts and guilt in the hope of being chosen to travel together to the states. Relatives physically fought over Amerasians, and relationships ended in jealousy and resentment among those left behind. Once the United States accepted physical appearance as adequate proof to immigrate and allowed multiple accompanying family members, the AHA also incentivized a thriving and corrupt black market for Amerasians. Wealthy families recruited, bribed, or in essence purchased the youth, who then claimed them as relatives in the AHA process. Often hired "prospectors" sought them out in the rural countryside or urban "brokers" arranged meetings. For several years, Dam Sen Park near the Amerasian Transit Center in Ho Chi Minh City functioned like a fish market as the affluent competed for Amerasians with offers of gold, cash, meals, clothing, or attractive daughters for marriage. In an era when the average yearly Vietnamese income was $150, the going rate for an Amerasian reached $2,000 to $4,000.[83]

"One day I was walking home," an Amerasian remembered of the introduction to the AHA, "and my foster father come [*sic*] outside and tell me to pack my clothes, that I was going to live with another family. I thought I was going to help this other family. Then I saw my foster father and mother wearing new clothes and fixing their house. I did not know what was happening because no one told me. Later, I figure out I had been sold so that the new family could get a ticket to America. I was their ticket to America."[84]

These "fake families" paid for the requisite documents to be forged and the bribes necessary at every bureaucratic level to keep paperwork from getting "lost" or delayed. Sometimes, though, Amerasians, just as opportunistically, arranged their own purchase or exploited the situation. A savvy Amerasian might come to terms with the highest bidder but never show up for the AHA interview or else reveal the scheme to officials before making themselves available to another family. Wholesale corruption eventually ended significant American support for the program by 1993, but in the first five years it is estimated that in addition to the approximately 30,000 genuine Amerasian immigrants, probably 80,000 phony relatives and con artists entered the United States with them illegally under the AHA.[85]

Prior to arrival, AHA participants spent a mandatory six months in the Philippine Refugee Processing Center attending orientation classes, English classes, and vocational training. From there federal, state, religious, and nonprofit agencies contracted to facilitate their resettlement to several dozen "cluster sites" concentrated primarily in California, Texas, Pennsylvania, and New York. Since most Amerasians immigrated as "free cases"—meaning they had no American sponsor or family in the United States receiving them—cities were selected based on available social services. Under special refugee status these included government entitlements such as Medicaid and food stamps, job placement, and housing assistance for periods that varied state to state.[86]

American realities, however, clashed immediately with American dreams as the AHA's momentary golden luster wore off. Safely on U.S. soil, fake families no longer had any use for Amerasians, defaulting on promises and subjecting them to all manner of mental or physical abuse, as well as abandonment. So, too, were public benefits inadequate to offset the disadvantages of vulnerable children whose average age was only seventeen. Low-income healthcare did little for preexisting physical and emotional problems and job training was largely irrelevant for youth with limited education, illiterate in two languages, and unable to speak English. Thus relegated to the lowest paying jobs—and recognized as neither Vietnamese in the non-Amerasian expatriate community nor American by society—they tended to instinctively became ghettoized again in low-income apartment housing in depressed and crime-filled inner-city neighborhoods.[87]

Composites of the Amerasian experience in America drawn from various contemporary studies depicted an adolescent living in a single-parent family with his or her mother and half-sibling as "free cases" in a midsize U.S. city. Unsure what to expect, Amerasians stayed hopeful. Enrolled in school, they struggled to catch up academically while learning English. And despite some manageable problems—missing grandparents back in Vietnam or getting used to routines and time management—youth made good-faith efforts to successfully adjust. Certain elements of acculturation were, in fact, fascinating: seemingly unlimited books, games, toys, and television; multistory buildings; shaking hands; having enough food to eat. Children particularly enjoyed the freedom to go outside and play after years of being sequestered inside or disregarded in childhood culture. Rural Amerasians often never developed a sense of simple numeric calendar time—opposed to the Vietnamese calendar's "Year of . . ."—and had limited concepts of distance or space. One man unable to pinpoint his exact birth date, for instance, began celebrating his birthday for an entire week. In school, students often found geography and social studies most interesting. When comparing life in Vietnam and the United States, Amerasians usually cast their two worlds as largely mirror opposites: projecting favorable feelings associated with one place as reflections of unfavorable feelings toward the other. Much had been lost in leaving behind Vietnam's human relationships—understood to be more affectionate and authentic—or the language, food, and weather, yet something was gained in educational and job opportunities, freedom, and relatively less discrimination.[88]

Self-conception developed fairly tentatively. Overall satisfaction in the United States seemed to be inversely proportional to expectations. Higher—that is, unrealistic—expectations diminished happiness while more modest aspirations translated to contentment. Fathers remained paramount to the equation. Strong correlations existed between how mothers felt about fathers and a maturing sense of self in the new country. In the majority of homes, Vietnamese mothers expressed warm, or at least positive, sentiments, not in the hope of rekindling their romance but to assist in finally establishing the father-child relationship.

"What will I say to my husband if I see him?" one mother told officials. "I will say, 'Hello, long time no see. I am very surprised to meet you again. I come because my son wants to see you. I don't want to make trouble for you if you're married. That's the main thing. I don't want to make trouble for you . . . but you see my son, for a long time he misses you. I just want my baby to see you and call you father." Here, children likely shared her outlook—stubbornly enshrining that idealized image—and often grounded their self-identity accordingly. Of these children, 41 percent considered themselves American, 38 percent Amerasian, and only 17 percent Vietnamese. Those identifying as American reported far fewer adjustment problems and performed much better at school and work. Conversely, when mothers harbored negative feelings toward fathers, youth internalized anger, bitterness, and antipathy, with a mere 4 percent thinking of themselves as American, 30 percent Vietnamese, and 58 percent Amerasian.[89]

Consequently, immigrants generally prioritized the search for birth fathers above all else, despite probably more than half of them not knowing anything about him, including his name. The AHA, however, having been opposed by many veterans' groups, had no provisions for reconnecting father and child. In fact, the Pentagon and Veterans Administration initially blocked access to basic military records in the interest of veterans' privacy. A 1990 district court ruling in favor of the British organization War Babes—formed by illegitimate children of American soldiers and English mothers during World War II—eventually ordered the Department of Defense to open these files for children seeking to identify their fathers. In specifically including Amerasians, the court found a child's right to know about genetic histories or potential inheritances, and the psychological need to authenticate his or her identity, outweighed a father's right to privacy. Still, cooperation from the National Personnel Records Center meant little for Amerasians lacking rudimentary information. Most came to rely on the Red Cross's tracing service or private individuals to solve these mysteries.[90]

Long odds notwithstanding, even adult Amerasians maintained childlike naivete, to the point of expecting fathers to have been waiting at the airport in anticipation of their arrival. "I have my father's picture, and I will find him," an Amerasian son stressed to officials. "I will just knock on the door and when he opens it, I will ask, 'Father, do you recognize me?'" "I'm always watching on the streets," an Amerasian woman explained. "Maybe that way some day I'll see him. His face will be my face." "When I see my father," another offered, "I am afraid he will not understand me, because I speak Vietnamese. But I will ask him, 'Do you love me, did you miss me, because for a long time we have not seen each other.'"[91]

Best estimates place the number of Amerasians who actually found their fathers at only 2 or 3 percent. On the infrequent occasion entities such as the Red Cross made contact—considering probably one-third were already deceased—men were apprised of the circumstances, but the decision to reciprocate was left solely to him. For many the revelation of paternity arrived as a complete surprise. Usually those that knew, or suspected, had long since rationalized leaving it in the past or maybe carried this emotional weight as another facet of survivor's guilt. A few feared child-support requests. Regardless, contact threatened too much disruption, and typically biological fathers rebuffed the intrusion outright or pursued legal action. When meetings took place, brief encounters were extremely awkward, tense, and fruitless, with rejection characteristically the final outcome. The Red Cross thought that in the 3 percent of cases where fathers had been located, only 3 percent of those successful searches ended in a happy reunion. Just a single meeting, though, confirmed a father's existence, which offered some measure of vindication at least. "Amerasians seeking their fathers just want to know for a fact that they have a father," a researcher concluded. "If the dad won't see the kid, then that kid knows he's everything bad anyone ever said about him in all the years he was growing up . . . [but] the minute they have a real dad . . . they are no longer the dust of life.'"[92]

By the first decade of the twenty-first century, with normalized relations between America and Vietnam, and in the wake of 9/11, resettlement under the AHA dropped to below one hundred per year before effectively ceasing. Probably only several thousand Amerasians remain in Vietnam, those who for whatever reasons failed their exit interviews or decided to continue a life they had already carved out. Though poor, they experience less prejudice and political discrimination, but they persist in thinking of themselves as different. Those in the United States, now in their forties and fifties, work to manage this exceptional immigrant experience. Likewise, they are predominantly socioeconomically disadvantaged on the whole. Perhaps half of them remain illiterate in both Vietnamese and English, mired in low-income jobs and housing, and are not U.S. citizens. Amerasians are the only foreign-born Americans required to file for naturalization and pass the citizenship test as immigrants. Periodic lobbying efforts to grant blanket citizenship come and go, including a failed Amerasian Naturalization Act of 2003 introduced by California congresswoman Zoe Lofgren and Texas congresswoman Sheila Jackson Lee.[93] The question of proving paternity remains the principal obstacle.

As did many other children from the Vietnam War cohort, Amerasian sons and daughters have formed organizations such as the Amerasian Fellowship

Association to build community and foster support. In 2009 they began a tradition of gathering at the Wall to pay respect on Father's Day. Dysfunctional behaviors are all too common and many remain suicide risks, but developmentally the traditional Vietnamese belief in karma gives them some common ground with other veterans' children. Amerasians make meaning of their circumstances and cope through this perspective. In their view, some transgressions in a previous life account for the Amerasian condition. Once that karmic debt is paid, life will be greatly improved next time around.[94]

AFTERMATH

> I was born in 1965 . . . and I asked my mom when I was about 12 why I had no memories of Vietnam and she said, "We have never had a war in your lifetime." How 'bout that?
>
> —MISSOURI WOMAN

For forty-six years, a trifolded American flag that once covered Lieutenant Eugene Moppert's casket hung in a hallway near the auditorium of Yorkship Family School, in Camden, New Jersey. Despite routine repainting and additional plaques and other awards being added along the blond brick wall since the 1960s, Moppert's small memorial remained untouched, rendered effectively invisible by time. Mounted behind glass on a red background inside a wooden frame, a small inscription read simply, "Lt. Eugene Moppert, Killed Feb. 26, 1968." Yorkship students and teachers gradually forgot over a generation, or two, the story of why and how such an artifact came to the elementary school. For years, everyone casually walked past the flag without a glance or care. Adults recognized the date as being from the Vietnam War, but who could say anymore if Moppert had been a former student, teacher, or parent?

Then in the summer of 2014, Bill Harrison and Kathie Cromie-Gilbert, classmates in Mrs. Jerry Davis's 1968 fourth-grade class, approached Yorkship Family School requesting Moppert's flag as the centerpiece in a donation to the National Museum of American History at the Smithsonian. The flag, Harrison and Cromie-Gilbert explained to administrators, once physically represented a special relationship between a classroom of ten-year-olds and their GI pen pals. Some students had stayed in contact with their soldier since the sixties, although now mostly by Facebook messaging. In one case, Wendy Strang Rooney became a teacher because of Davis's inspiration, creating her own student pen pal assignment with American troops in the Middle East.

"As an adult I would wonder about that flag," Harrison shared, "wonder if it was still there, wonder if it was all real." At their former teacher's suggestion, he finally rejoined the flag with a collection of letters, photographs, and keepsakes exchanged between these correspondents in order to preserve their story in the museum's Vietnam War holdings. On November 14 of that year, Mrs. Davis, eight of her former students and their families, and army veteran Joe Meskaitis and his two granddaughters, one the same age his pen pals were during Vietnam, came together again at the Smithsonian to officially present Moppert's flag and the rest of this Yorkship School collection. "We knew this story needed to be told," Harrison underscored. "Even back then, I knew this was something special that happened, because I kept my letters from my pen pal all these years despite moving several times." On the project's influence he reflected, "I look at the Vietnam War differently from most people. Most people think, well, any war is not good, but there was a purpose for it at the time and these boys were fighting for freedom and I just feel that, when I look back I have a different perspective. I'm not one of the protesters, I was one of the ones standing up for the boys." Meskaitis determined, "It was something we looked forward to and we must have made an impression on them." Indeed, the Yorkship Collection at the Smithsonian is today both a memorial to and historical evidence of how a few American children saw the Vietnam War through the eyes of distant friends in the Fourth Platoon, Company A, First Battalion, Seventh Cavalry. And "who knows?" Sergeant "Mosquito" pondered. "One day, someone's grandkids may want to look it up."[1]

In examining the Vietnam War's historical imprints on American childhood, I have tried accounting for relative causal effects on various aspects of adult life—again, how such unique childhood perspectives on Vietnam may influence later outlooks, values, or interests. Several broad observations emerged. As the Yorkship School collection at the Smithsonian clearly demonstrates, children from the era want to claim a legitimate place within the Vietnam experience and have their voices considered in our national conversation about Vietnam's stubborn grip. "What I remember," a Kansas City woman explained, "is the Vietnam War as 'background' context to everything and in the news every single day (body counts, campus protests, political debate, etc.). In 1975 [when] the last troops were leaving Saigon, it truly marked a milestone. I realized that practically my entire education occurred simultaneously with the war. It was then that my childhood seemed really over, both literally and figuratively."[2]

Demographer Landon Jones observed how children in the Vietnam era "had less agony—but also less ecstasy." Many look back with frustration, feeling cheated, as if their involvement in one of the country's most pivotal moments is less interesting and more forgettable. Being socialized during an intense time when so much of adult culture was in flux, they were more prone to confusion and ambivalence, but with fewer resources available for making meaning of inconstancies transpiring in the adult world. Those politicized in a passionately polarized nation often purposefully followed politics with sincere interest, but they were politely dismissed as cute, but not serious. They are hesitant to understand themselves as having been legitimate historical actors with agency, and thus they remain less inclined to consistently appreciate the validity of their experiences or those developmental influences that make Vietnam extremely relevant to our lives as well.[3]

Not surprisingly, veterans' children even tend to miss the consequences of a seismic but disguised shift in the very ground beneath childhood: confident mothers as strong female role models. Most are conditioned to mistake second-wave feminism for sensationalized spectacles of "women's lib" or "bra burning." In reality, Vietnam motherhood illustrates how behavioral changes in women paved the way for attitudinal changes. Women successfully took on dual mother-father roles in keeping families together, during both a father's wartime service and the frequent single parenting that came afterward, due to divorce, severe PTSD, or death. They were clearly liberated women, before activism popularized the term.

Vietnam galvanized Cold War fears common to American children in the post–World War II years, intruding into childhood as a scary televised presence. Growing up acutely afraid of this living-room war during formative developmental stages and political socialization appears to have manifested primarily in trust issues. This is Vietnam's chief developmental implication. Unlike adult and adolescent distrust of governmental policies and intentions, or a particular politician's duplicity, children in the Vietnam era had a difficult time reasoning through political and ethical ambiguity. Families neither adequately explained nor controlled a seemingly permanent series of confusing events: televised cruelty, adult trepidation over military service, or the prospect Vietnam might eventually claim little boys as well. Instead, parental socialization offered only more confusing questions, while prematurely introducing preadolescent minds to an odd concept: cynicism.

Prior to Vietnam, preadolescent Americans appear to have held the presidency and the president—easily the most recognizable public person for children—in unanimously high esteem, an infallible "benevolent leader" associated in childhood thinking with the paternal qualities of protector, power, honesty, and inherent goodness. The notion of the president, deliberately or unwittingly, being capable of disaster was largely incomprehensible. Vietnam likewise altered that dynamic. And while Watergate's role will be better understood as materials become available at the Richard Nixon Presidential Library, besides eroding trust, the war also lowered children's expectations in American leadership.

Compared specifically to the certainty of children in World War II—acculturated to pride, unity, and patriotism—Vietnam contributed to tendencies toward relativism, making for starkly different adult views. Aside from memories of Cronkite, body counts, and helicopter sounds, there simply do not seem to be many absolutes. Support or opposition developed around ages ten and eleven endures, meaning Americans will not reconcile with Vietnam anytime soon.

"My brother came home safely," an Oregon woman, born in 1957, shared, "although his experiences changed him in ways we weren't to know for years to come. I haven't burned down any buildings in protest, but I have participated in anti–Gulf War rallies. I pay my taxes but worry that the money is spent on military spending instead of food and health care. I've taught my children to try to make the world a better place. I've been deeply proud of my country and deeply disappointed, too."[4]

"Vietnam was a major part of my life for the first 13 years or so," a Florida man emphasized. "It was my impression that the attitude in Tallahassee towards the military was different than it was in the military towns and bases that we lived. I learned that I was somewhat more pro-military and conservative in my thinking than a lot of the people I got to know. I still am."[5]

"Unlike a number of people who have [written to you]," an Arkansas woman, a veteran's daughter, echoed, "I am not a political or social liberal. I believed then and believe now that servicemen rise to the call of their country and their commander-in-chief. No American citizen should ever denigrate the serviceman. I am much prouder today of how Americans have received veterans coming home from Iraq and Afghanistan. Thankfully, in that respect, it's a different world from the 60's."[6]

"I look at the current war(s) from the perception of how Vietnam touched my family," a woman born in 1959 concluded. "Not the politics but the personal toll it takes on Americans. I see the support the troops get from Americans today and wonder if and when that tide will turn—based on how my father was treated coming back from war in the 60/70's. I notice how the flags that flew so proudly after 9/11 are gone and how people have moved on to the latest and greatest news item."[7]

A rural Missouri man's lesson is an appropriately poignant metaphor. "Our neighbor's son was killed a week or so after he was drafted and sent to Vietnam," he confided. "I was upset and worried about his death and the fact that he had to go! But as a child I was more upset that his car sat in a field and fell apart. His parents had bought him a graduation car that 'I wanted' a 1960 black and white red interior white top convertible Chevy Impala! It was awesome . . . After [he] was killed his parents parked the car in the field behind the house and trees eventually grew up through it. Every time I drove by it for years it became my 'sense of death' reference." This wasted Impala became for him "a sad memorial" to Vietnam, a lasting childhood reminder that "Life is not fair!"[8]

The completion of the Vietnam Veterans Memorial Wall in 1982 is an important benchmark for anyone whose life was touched by Vietnam. The Wall did a lot to change American perceptions, perhaps not about the war initially, but the edifice was instrumental in fostering new appreciation for soldiers and their families, which in turn enabled the first dialogues about Vietnam since the war ended. Another decade after the Wall began offering real space, the Internet opened virtual space for adult children of Vietnam veterans and relatives (including POW/MIA bracelet families)—estranged for so long—to form emotional and psychological bonds. Many web-based social networks provide resource and support materials, advocacy, instructions for receiving veteran's benefits (especially for their fathers' PTSD and Agent Orange issues), and storytelling forums. There is clearly a profound need to recognize themselves and by extension others affected by war, including veterans, and that drive is an animating principle inherent to these online communities.

For Americans whose only personal experience with Vietnam remained the vicarious sacrifice of "their guy" engraved on POW/MIA bracelets, it was his name they rubbed from the Wall and his bracelet they laid solemnly at its base when visiting Washington. In one typical case, a woman rediscovered her long-forgotten bracelet rummaging through "old love beads and other regalia of the era" for a son wanting to be a hippie for Halloween. Once reawakened, curiosity over finally knowing what happened to him led thousands to search the Internet—on sites such as the POW Network or the Defense Department's Prisoner of War/Missing Personnel Office—where previously tedious and frustrating challenges to determining his status were overcome rather easily. The Internet perpetuated renewed interest in bracelets and in reconnecting with the servicemen, not altogether unlike an adopted child's quest to find a birth parent. Wearers, past and present, began reaching out to make virtual connections and build communities.[9]

In the most gratifying cases, a bracelet wearer learned the serviceman was still alive, and *found* him. Californian Linda Oskins's quest began after she was unable to locate her soldier's name, Mike O'Connor, on the Vietnam Veterans Memorial during a 1996 visit with her husband and two sons. The unanticipated omission raised the distinct possibility that O'Connor in fact survived captivity. Eventually Oskins tracked him down through information from the Richard Nixon Presidential Library. "I would be very, very honored to present you with your POW bracelet if you are receptive to the idea," she anxiously wrote him the next year. "I didn't know a great deal about the Vietnam War since I was just 12 or 13 years old, but now as an adult there are so many questions. I have even more respect for you as my mind creates images of what you experienced. If by any way I have offended you by this letter," she concluded, "please accept my deepest apology." As it turned out, Oskins's introduction began a fruitful correspondence and friendship with O'Connor—who had been shot down in February 1968 and was not released until March 1973—including regular Christmas cards, Veterans Day wishes, and family vacation photographs.[10]

Unlike dozens of other bracelets O'Connor has regularly received from complete strangers, Oskins's holds a particularly special place. "Most people just want to know if they can send back the bracelet," he explained. "Linda has kept in touch. People like Linda who still remember us—all I can say is it's overwhelming. I know they are busy with their lives and they have other things going on, so to take the time to show they appreciate the soldiers who served, I just am very appreciative." For her part Oskins believes the journey with O'Connor's bracelet has made her more patriotic and empathetic to the new generation of Gulf War veterans, values she models for her own children. Here, in separating war from warrior, is the clearest sense of the bracelet's impact in forming those first metaphorical layers of our cognitive and moral onion, the developmental foundation on which future worldviews are built. "My kids were so excited when I found him," Oskins continued. "It's not like we weren't patriotic before, so I just wanted this to be about thanking our veterans, taking your hat off in stadiums, being a responsible citizen. There are all kinds of ways to be patriotic." It is about "the sacrifice he has made," she underscored when contemplating O'Connor's place in her life. "When I think about what I was doing when he was in that prison, I was just out being a kid."[11]

A consistently striking feature of finding your guy is the revelation you actually shared him. Since roughly 2,600 Americans were designated POWs or MIAs, hypothetically Voices in Vital America (VIVA), who made about five million bracelets, produced some 1,900 for every serviceman. Among former POWs and wearers, those who had bracelets are known as "bracelet families." "A lot of them thought they were the only person who had my name on a bracelet," James Hivner, a former POW in Texas, pointed out. He maintains a relationship with more than thirty "adopted" bracelet family members, following their family cycles through marriage, children, and now grandchildren. In turn, wearers got to know his wife and two daughters, who were six and eight years old when he was taken prisoner in 1965. After a bracelet family member died several years ago, Hivner kept in contact with his widow until her Christmas cards stopped coming as well. He then reached out to the couple's daughter and now continues a second-generation relationship after her parents' death. "We talk about the kind of stuff you would with any friend," another of Hivner's bracelet family members said, still remembering the connection she felt in 1970 because the date he was taken prisoner—October 5—is also her birthday. "I've never met the man, but he is part of my family."[12]

More often, widows and surviving relatives preside over these bracelet families. Sue Bailey, born in 1958, shared her particular story about finally reaching out after watching a Vietnam documentary on the History Channel. The program's portion on POWs brought back memories of the silver POW bracelet she wore as a youth, and of her guy, Cole Black, which motivated her to email his wife, Karen Black. She wrote to Mrs. Black,

> Not thinking I would find anything, but figuring it was worth a try, I decided to do a Google search for "Vietnam Cole Black POW," and sure enough, I found information about your husband (and thereby you). I'm sorry to hear of his passing . . . and I'm not sure why I felt compelled to write to you. The experiences of his life and yours must be more than I could ever begin to imagine. But please know that in a small town in New Jersey, a little girl wore your husband's name proudly and hoped every day for his safe return. And now, these many years later, a middle aged woman watches a show about the war and still remembers his service and sacrifice.

Eventually, Mrs. Black responded, politely solidifying the connection. "I very much appreciate the time you took to look up the information about Cole and to write me, and I very much appreciate the patriotism you showed as a young woman wearing that bracelet."[13]

On the West Coast, Kathy Strong, who found James Moreland's bracelet in her Christmas stocking as a twelve-year-old in 1972, did not remove the band until returning it to his sisters. "I just wanted to keep the promise," Strong emphasized, which meant remaining faithful to the bracelet's original purpose for almost forty years. "I knew there was family out there who was waiting for word, and I was just going to wait along with them." Over the years, she thought about Moreland every day. "It's usually when I have my hands out in front of me," she said, "maybe driving a car or typing on the keyboard and I just think I wonder when he's coming home." Unlike most bracelet families, though, Moreland's two sisters, Anita and Linda, sought Strong out and initiated a friendship. "To have worn his bracelet for so long," Anita told a reporter about discovering Strong's perseverance, "we just love her to death." "She did care," Linda added, "and she still does care." So much so that when Moreland's remains were returned to the United States in 2011, Strong was included in his full military funeral. At her insistence, she laid the bracelet to rest with him.[14]

Since spontaneously contacting veterans or families can be intimidating, and sensitive considering that some prefer privacy, wearers still commonly seek community online, sharing messages on veterans' and POW websites or blogging with recollections and testimonies. In essence, they look for some closure by maintaining virtual bracelet families. Posts on the site "Letters and Notes from Those That Wear the Bracelets," for example, tell therapeutic stories of the bracelet's centrality in finally making their little peace with Vietnam. "For me, the significance of the bracelet has increased in time," a woman posted in 1998. "It reminds me that not everyone made it back, and that each POW/MIA has a name, has a family who loves and misses them. It is always an emotional experience for me." "I want you to know," a Georgia woman added, "that I am wearing it now and since I now understand more than I did as a 12 year old, I don't plan to take it off." "I would like to let Maj. Bruce Johnson's family know that he has never been forgotten," another woman disclosed. "My father and I purchased these bracelets when I was a young girl. For years I wore my bracelet and watched for his return. I sit at my computer crying for a man I never met but one whom my family has prayed for, for years. I would like his family to know that his memory will live on."[15]

"Although I was a 10 year old child," a woman commented, "I have carried it with me for what seems like a life time. He has been a part of me for almost 30 years."[16] In hers, and other similar disclosures, are testimonies to the enduring worth of being able to place a tangible person's name on the Vietnam War. "I have possessed a POW bracelet etched with Capt. Robert Kent's name and the date, 12–20–68 since 1973," a California woman posted in 1999.

> At the time I bought the bracelet, I was a 13 year old girl, utterly ignorant of the significance of and meaning behind the bracelet I wore. Because I was so young, I understood little about the Vietnam war. I had no grasp of the ramifications of war, of its horrid reality, or of the very real pain and destruction it caused to so many lives. In truth, my friends and I wore the bracelets because at the time it was the fashionable thing to do. Today, at 38, I can appreciate the life of one man—and of many men—who gave their lives in a thankless war. He belonged to somebody, and sadly, he never came home. Most of all, he was no longer just a name on a 13 year old girl's fashionable bracelet.[17]

In finding a voice to finally communicate to others what her family endured, Christal Presley's book *Thirty Days with My Father: Finding Peace from Wartime PTSD* provides incentive and language for other Vietnam veterans' children suffering with generational PTSD who are still in denial or do not know how to tell their stories. As a catalyst, *Thirty Days* facilitated the belated introduction of many veterans' adult children to each other, and across the post–September 11 Internet landscape their online communities are based on this relatively new recognition of kinship.

Presley finally left home at eighteen and as an adult lived with severe depression and anxiety largely estranged from her family. During college—government funded, ironically, as the daughter of a disabled veteran—she began seeing therapists and psychiatrists who prescribed regimens of sleeping pills, antianxiety medications, and antidepressants. A clear pattern of being subconsciously drawn to older men, whom she recognized as substitute father figures, emerged as well. But when these problematic relationships invariably ended, for years Presley failed to appreciate how the essential drive to fill the void left by not having a father in her life clouded her judgment, superseding a partner's potential compatibility.

Along the way, Presley discovered other veterans' children with generational PTSD, including, to her surprise, one woman with the "same social anxiety, depression meshed with anger, and recurrent nightmares. Like me. She was odd growing up and never fit in," Presley wrote of the revelation. "She can be a hermit, revels in being alone. It's a challenge for her to be social and hard for her to form relationships. Like me." Increasingly uncomfortable pretending the past had not happened and concerned the pleasant memories of childhood were being drowned by the repression of bad ones, she courageously reconnected with her father in a thirty-day experiment on which her book is based. "My whole adult life," she reflected, "had been spent trying not to know what was going on with my father." The basic framework of a truce was laid.[18]

Here again is more powerful evidence of this discernable trend among adult children touched by the Vietnam War, an impulse to finally recognize others and share common cause. What is more, these bonds are extending to embrace the old warriors themselves. "It is the same with war veterans," Presley identified, "the reason my father wears military jackets, belt buckles, and caps embroidered with Vietnam Veteran. It is important to find one another. I am starting to understand this now." Web-based forums such as United Children of Veterans (unitedchildrenofveterans.com), founded by Christal Presley, share PTSD storytelling and resource materials while others, such as Veterans' Children (www.veteranschildren.com) or Soldier's Heart (www.soldiersheart.net) along with numerous Facebook pages ("Children of Vietnam Veterans" or "Sons and Daughters of Vietnam War Veterans"), promote multigenerational reconciliation and healing for families.

Besides outreach and peer support, virtual social networks likewise reflect a mounting sense of obligation among those uniquely qualified to teach what they know to the next generation of veterans' sons and daughters affected by twenty-first-century wars.[19] "We are the forgotten," reads a 2012 post on Daughters of Vietnam Veterans, an online organization embracing sons, too.

> I admit I feel some solidarity of the Vietnam Veterans who have been presumed by society to be, "crazy." That is what it feels like when trying to talk to someone on the phone, begging for help, begging for answers. Combat trauma has made considerable gains in recent years. Most sites dedicated to healing children of combat veterans are made towards just that, children. We aren't children, anymore. Grown adults left untreated by a man-made disaster that manifested itself in our lives. To rid the torment of childhood? To not remember the physical, emotional, and sometimes sexual abuse in the home. There is no pill for that. The glossy pretty websites dedicated to helping the "kids troops" is a constant reminder that our country will continue not to really see post-traumatic stress as what it really is. When the news gives us pictures of the "welcome reunion," we know the fear. The alcoholism, drug abuse, hiding in your closet, walking on eggshells, your Mom being thrown down the stairs . . . the unwelcome sexual advances of a predator that doesn't remember you as a daughter.
>
> Post traumatic stress cannot be felt in textbooks or in your diagnostic statistical manual. It's felt in homes all over this country. We know the horror and we feel the war all over again, the war at home. We are skipping an entire generation of grown adults that can tell you all what it really means to grow up with post traumatic stress, the illness runs deep . . . as deep as the blade cuts into your skin trying to purge the demons out. We need help. We are not children, anymore.[20]

For Cathi Bond-Drake, whose navy veteran father committed suicide in 1981, it took an ill-fated, abusive marriage right out of high school, professional difficulties working with women, lost jobs, years of therapy, a second marriage, and a nervous breakdown to at last recognize her issues were rooted in generational PTSD. "Honestly, by the time my dad died we did talk about Nam, [and] I understood a lot of his behaviors," but even though "I knew all the trauma I'd suffered I could steer people in the direction I wanted them to go. If I didn't want them to know something I just withheld information. I was always telling them only what I wanted them to know, or what I thought I needed to work on." Her husband

Mark, himself a Vietnam veteran fully disabled by PTSD, has been instrumental in helping Cathi make the necessary connections. "I know now that I married my father," she confirmed, "but I married an overly nice version of my father, thank God. It's crazy, but I think we're the only ones that could have helped us along our own individual journeys, honestly."[21]

With continued therapy and renewed faith, Cathi is finally reconciling with her father's memory, and Vietnam. "I remember the first time he tried to commit suicide," she continued, "he actually was able to become sober, and he was pleased with this therapist who was amazing, a Jesuit priest, and my dad was sober for two years. It was so weird because we had that two years when he was sober, and I got [to] see the dad my mom [knew]. I mean, my dad was fun, he was very musically inclined. When he wasn't drunk he was a blast, you know, listening to sixties music and dancing. He was really a very neat person and loved deeply, he loved children, and that's what showed to my mom." She continued,

> I think a lot of it is guilt, survivor's guilt. They never felt like they deserved to have a family or to be happy. My father felt that way. There would be times when my dad would be really drunk and start confiding in me. He never told me long stories, but he would just let me have it, and here would come the tears, and I would be like, "What are you doin'? Why are you drinkin' so much?" and he would say, "I don't deserve you guys," and I would say, "Well, do we deserve you drunk, for heaven's sake? This is ridiculous." We'd have those kinds of episodes where we'd be extremely close, and he'd be very caring and kind with me. Those memories I adore, I treasure them.

"It's just so bizarre the dichotomy between the terror and the adoration," Cathi highlighted.

> I know now that that has impacted my ability to have relationships with normal people. I haven't had any, until recently, and it's pretty incredible. I don't know exactly when it happened the way it did—I'm just grateful that I'm healing. I mean, I loved my father, and my dad really loved me. I don't excuse what he did, but I understand it better. There's huge healing that has occurred and I've learned a lot about Vietnam and that was part of putting this to bed for me and my dad and I watched everything I could get, documentaries and footage, you know. I was so angry, I couldn't talk to God and there was nothing that I wanted to hear from anybody, not even my husband. I've gotten so much peace now.

And online communities play a major role. "You know, I've found so much comfort in the Facebook pages I've been in. It's really only been this year that I've gotten with the Facebook pages and it's been so cathartic. I mean, those guys are so kind, they're so loving and it's so neat." She had participated in several support groups before, including Adult Children of Alcoholics, yet she never really felt as though she fit in because they could not really relate to the military aspects of her unique perspective. "But finding these people on Facebook has helped heal me a lot. I'm just learning so much, they're so respectful and kind."

"When I think about Vietnam I get really mad, really mad," she reflected. "It was a useless war; we should have never been there. It destroyed, what, fifty thousand died there, but how many have died since? There should be a wall, a memorial, for those who have died since. You know, many of us lost our father to suicide, I don't even know, I haven't seen a stat on that."[22]

Charlotte Duggan's father was shot down on New Year's Eve 1971 when she was in junior high, but the true watershed in her life, she believes, took place during therapy sessions following the "wild rebellion stage" of her twenties. "I finally got therapy . . . [and] it helped break down the wall," the MIA's daughter shared, highlighting specifically one cathartic exercise. "The therapist asked, 'Charlotte, do you have any mementos of your dad?' and I said, 'I've got them all over my house.' He said, 'I want you to gather them all up and I want you to find a table and put it in the corner of your room and I want you to put all your memories on that one table and I want you to pray at it twice a day.' I thought he was crazy." Still, she gathered up a helmet, hat, various father-and-daughter photographs, overseas gifts, and the authentic miniature flight suit Major Duggan had made for her onto the altar and worshipped it as directed. "I remember coming back the next week for my appointment, madder than a wet hen," she said of her discomfort. "'How dare you do this to me! This is ridiculous. I don't know what you're trying to accomplish by doing this.'" But the therapist simply explained, "Charlotte, I wanted you to experience physically what you're doing to yourself emotionally." It worked. "It took that act, worshipping at it twice a day for a week," Charlotte understood, "for me to get mad enough to get through the grieving process."[23]

"You can never really let go," she believes. "You don't let go, you honor them. You can build your life as a monument to their memory." And that is what this professional fund-raiser for the American Cancer Society has recently made a conscious decision to do. After years avoiding the Wall and National League of POW/MIA Families activities, Charlotte Duggan finally attended a memorial event in Washington, D.C., which led directly to her involvement in making the Texas Capitol Vietnam Veterans Monument a reality. "Mom would go with Scott [her brother] to the Wall and I couldn't go. I physically could not bring myself to go. Because to me that was accepting the death and I would not accept the death. For forty years it was inside me," she explained, "but never came out" until work on the Texas memorial at the Austin capitol began in 2013. It was during these efforts that Charlotte struck up a heartfelt collaboration with Luci Baines Johnson, the youngest daughter of the president Charlotte has always blamed for her father's loss. "I'm sitting down and starting to talk to my brother Scott and he says, 'oh, thank God, you're finally coming around,' but it took me forty-six years to get to the point where I could talk."[24]

Being an MIA child definitely changed the trajectory of her life, she believes. "I realized that very early on I was the one, you'd walk into the room and you'd be like, 'Oh, that's the MIA kid,' and you'd be getting special treatment for that even though you didn't want it. People come and fawn over me and that's the last thing I wanted, I didn't want to be, I just wanted to be in the room. I didn't want to be fawned over. I just couldn't take the chance of somebody saying, 'OK everybody, pick up their feet, Charlotte's going to drown us with her tears' again."

Before working on the Texas Capitol Vietnam Veterans Monument, she never sought out or interacted with other MIA and Gold Star children, or anyone connected to the Vietnam War. "It was me and the family against the world." Since 2013, however, Charlotte has embraced a newfound solidarity with others affected by the war. "It was hearing the stories from all the veterans about their experiences and how they were treated that jarred me, and all of a sudden I was like, 'I've got another family.'" Now, every New Year's Eve and May 7 (William Duggan's birthday), Charlotte hosts a party with the loudest fireworks display around. "I've gathered everybody together and our fireworks rattle," she proudly points out, "and if we don't rattle a few houses around here, then we're not doin' our job right. He was the life of the party!"[25]

Seven years after visitors started coming to the Wall, Tony Cordero, whose father died in 1965 when the boy was four years old, founded the group Sons and Daughters in Touch (SDIT) to finally introduce Gold Star children to one another and heal together via the common stories they shared. Writer and Vietnam veteran Al Santoli's 1990 article in *Parade* magazine featuring Cordero and SDIT was likewise an epiphany to many still wondering who other orphans were and where they might be. "The political stuff is something that a previous generation had to contend with," Cordero told Santoli of SDIT's mission. "We are the legacy of the 58,000 men and women who died over there, and the good they represented."[26]

"The reason our organization is called Sons and Daughters in Touch," Cordero clarified, "is because in 1989 when we got started, we didn't know we were Gold Star sons and daughters. That's the simply honest-to-God answer. I knew what Gold Star mothers were. I knew what Gold Star wives were. But no one had ever told us." "Other than my own siblings," recalled Karen Spears

Zacharias, "Terry [McGregor, another member of SDIT] was the first person I met face-to-face whose father had died in Vietnam. Meeting him was like finding a childhood pal after decades of separation, or finding out that you aren't the only green Martian on planet Earth. Terry and I share a history of similar sorrows because our fathers share a history as slain soldiers."[27]

Besides crossing paths at the Wall or connecting through SDIT, many Gold Star children at some point finally engaged their mothers in *the talk* or else somehow came into possession of *the trunk*. These belated conversations in which heretofore reticent mothers abruptly started talking about fathers typically accompanied transitional moments—graduations or other rites of passage—and caught young people completely unprepared. On Zacharias's graduation day from high school, her mother expressed how proud her dad would be, and how much joy she had brought him playing together before Vietnam. Despite tears, Karen, who was ten years old in 1966 when her father died, welcomed such extraordinary openness. "I had waited umpteen thousand days to hear Mama speak Daddy's name again," she described of just listening without interruption, not wanting her mother to stop.

> She could've told me a zillion stories of "Dave this" and "Dave that," and I would never have tired of them. Trouble was, Mama had quit saying Daddy's name once he died. . . . So I'd never asked Mama how she and Daddy met, or when he proposed, or why he wanted to be a soldier or was there something else he longed to do, if only he'd lived. I didn't know where his favorite fishing hole was or what kind of cake he liked best. I wasn't sure if he read books or if he had an author he liked most. Or if he took Mama to the picture show. And I didn't know if my soldier daddy was afraid he'd never live to see any of his children graduate from high school—something he never got the chance to do himself. I really wanted to ask Mama, do you think Daddy was afraid to die?[28]

One of life's biggest regrets for Gold Star children is having never gotten to know their father person to person, never relating to him as your adult self. Conversely, one of the greatest joys seems to be reevaluating childhood recriminations of their mothers through adult eyes. Renewed communication with their mothers, often coupled with becoming parents themselves, affords fresh perspectives on their moms' strength and capabilities in shouldering dual-parenting roles amid unbelievable tragedy. Many also belatedly come to appreciate mothers as influential female role models. "My mom was liberated before anyone ever heard of it," Zacharias now understands. "She, not my dad, bought the only two homes we ever had. She never remarried because no one could match up to the man she lost to Vietnam. . . . I am sure my father is pleased that his death brought out the best in her." "My Mother deserves a medal of her own," Stacy Swenck also believes. "She is an original Super Mom who worked full-time and raised three young girls up into happy, successful adults. The strength of both parents lives on in us."[29]

Either stumbled onto accidently, or more likely presented by mothers in conjunction with the talk, trunks (military footlockers or boxes) filled with fathers' personal effects (uniforms, medals, correspondence, artwork, etc.) are another revelation that fired imaginations. "On Thanksgiving Day 1996, the 25th anniversary of his death, Mom appeared and deposited a heavy blue trunk in my living room," Stacy Swenck, who was twelve years old in 1971, remembers of discovering the sacred objects.

> She firmly announced that these were my father's things and were now mine to keep. She was finished with them. I wasn't so sure I wanted the trunk, and I put it away in the closet. Many months later I opened it. There sat his Air Force hat, the silk band stained with sweat. The musty dress blues, a mysterious black beret, scattered medals, stack of letters tied with yarn, a folded triangle flag. I remembered the casket flag, men with quick white gloves folding the neat bundle, placing it with finality on Mom's lap. Years of silence, all bound up into this one trunk, now airing in my spare room.

The fourteen medals were familiar to Swenck, having been displayed for a time on a basement bookcase, but without any citations she stills tries to fully fathom their meaning: a Silver Star, three Distinguished Flying Crosses, an Airman's Medal for Valor, eight Air Medals, and a Purple Heart. "The Silver Star is the second highest medal an Air Force pilot can earn," she described, "but all I remembered was Dad's joke that he had gotten it by flying a general to use a real latrine. In my little girl mind, I had believed for many years that this story was the truth."[30]

Through dozens of letters from Vietnam to her mom and the Swenck sisters, Stacy learned a helicopter pilot's routines and details about her father's willingness to repeatedly fly dangerous missions with seemingly little regard for his own life. Reading these harrowing personal accounts in his own words to her mom, she said, "took my breath away. Why had no one ever talked about his bravery? Why had I been ashamed of him?" The last letter she received from him just two weeks before he died (although a birthday card mailed prior to his death arrived later) left her equally breathless. "So you continue to be yourself," Major Swenck advised about making friends at school. "Never be phoney. Remember other people's feelings. With your combination of beauty and brains you will find no problem in meeting others. I'll say it again. You are one smart and pretty girl. I am very proud of you and your deeds. You just keep your high ideals and ambition and you will be rewarded by others friendship. You certainly have mine. Love, Dad."[31]

"Since opening the trunk, I have researched the war and asked my mother questions," Swenck continued. "She bravely told me how they met and what kind of husband and father he was. My search for information has intensified since Sept. 11, 2001. Seeing the faces of those who had lost loved ones made me know I could not wait any longer to tell my family's story. I wanted those children to know someone understood their loss."[32] Indeed, 9/11 and the perpetual state of warfare those terrorist attacks sparked in the Middle East—long since surpassing Vietnam as America's longest conflict—serve as catalysts motivating Gold Star children to lend their distinctive voices to others populating virtual Vietnam communities online. In opening that cultural space to form a sense of community between veterans' sons and daughters—together with those dealing with generational PTSD or seeking resolution to the MIA issue, as well as aging veterans—these web-based social networks are both instructive and cathartic.

Sons and Daughters in Touch has started incorporating the latest generation of Gold Star children left from Iraq and Afghanistan into the organization's functions. Karen Spears Zacharias, a particularly recognizable Vietnam-era orphan due to the resonance of *Hero Mama*, likewise reaches out to young people coming to grips with losing a father in another controversial war. Often the most meaningful Internet relationships involve Vietnam veterans, since there are some lingering questions only a comrade-in-arms can answer. On memorial sites such as the Virtual Wall (www.virtualwall.org), families can get in touch with soldiers who may have served with their father, and in opening up about loss, veterans also might cope with their own issues. With each passing year more also make the pilgrimage to Vietnam through SDIT and other organizations to introduce themselves to the landscapes and battlefields their fathers knew.[33]

To many, Cordero and Zacharias included, this pursuit fills in missing pieces, often about actual circumstances surrounding their fathers' death or disappearance. "I guess in a sense this search is a way to have a conversation with my father. . . . I've been able to craft the story my father might have told me had the chopper gotten to him in time that morning." After tracking down her dad's best friend in Vietnam, Zacharias could also empathize with why none of his comrades came forward sooner. "I understand," she wrote, "how the pressures of daily living and the grief over an unpopular war may have kept him from coming alongside our family, but the little girl in me wishes he'd been there to tell me tales of my daddy, to take me fishing in a boat the way Daddy might have."[34]

"I knew I had to make sense of that hidden yet dominating event in my life," Swenck emphasized about the post–September 11 influence.

> My mother and I, together, said, "OK, there's going to be a whole new generation of orphans; we need to do something." And it was through that impulse toward activism the healing really began. So she went and became the regional group head of Gold Star Wives and I found Sons and Daughters in Touch and began to get active and think about ways that I could help and it was through that process that I started thinking I could write. I wrote [an] article that was published in the Louisville paper and that's when I decided I would go back to school and wanted to see if I could make an academic study of it. . . . I began to research, scouring the Internet for information. Slowly information came trickling in. I received emails from men who flew with my father. The man who had pulled my father's body out of the water sent me a detailed description of that day. It was the first time he had ever told anyone. I went to the reunion of my father's squadron and met many kind men who have told me stories. Even the gory details have been soothing to me.[35]

Swenck highlighted that "I've continued to stay in touch with vets and I've been collecting material." She continued, "So I have interviews with them. I have letters from them, emails, pictures, photographs, even videotapes that they took in Vietnam and I've got two or three actually big plastic bins full of artifacts and firsthand accounts. Every few months I will share with someone who found me on the Wall and they will email me and sometimes those conversations turn into actual meetings with people; literally there's at least a couple a year."[36]

It is important, she stresses, to remember that "I did not meet another war orphan until I was 43 years old. My experience—the silence, the shame, the secrets, and the interest in finding out later in life—closely matches the experiences of many others. I cannot express how soothing it has been to meet others like myself and to discover that my experiences were typical. It feels like I've removed a festering thorn." She also concedes, however, that there is disagreement among Gold Star children on the value of establishing these associations, suggesting that developmental age, at least in her family, plays a role. Of the three Swenck sisters, Stacy considers the youngest, Heidi, to have had the least traumatic trajectory through childhood while she, the oldest and the one who knew their father best, stumbles most. "We did meet one soldier who knew my dad." Swenck continued, "That man came to California with his wife to meet us and my youngest sister did participate in that, but she doesn't like it." Stacy believes this is a defense mechanism for Heidi, who was six years old when their father died, whereas Lori, the middle sister who was nine, willingly joins in some of the events. "As a matter of fact, one time, on one of her birthdays," she clarified, "I took the letters that Dad had written to her [Heidi] that basically were no words, basically just scribbles, and put them in a presentation folder, and gave it to her and she sobbed and did not like that I had done that."[37]

Even well into adulthood, one might go months without a second thought of his or her dad, only to be overcome with sadness without warning. Web-based Gold Star support groups, forums, and blogs such as Sons and Daughters in Touch (http://sdit.org), Soldier's Daughter (http://soldiersfirstdaughter.blogspot.com), the 2 Sides Project, which extends to Vietnamese orphans (http://www.2sidesproject.com), and Facebook provide additional online outlets and resources. "Miss you so much," a representative forum post reads. "I was only 6 when you left us. I wonder all the time what life would have been like for me and my sister & brother, and mother." Hundreds of others follow parallel themes:

> I see your face in the face of my son, your grandson. He has your hands and crooked smile too. He's just like you actually, in so very many ways.

> Many years have passed, yet it seems like only yesterday we stood at the airport and watched your plane take to the sky. Little did any of we kids know that it would be the last time we would see you. But we didn't know, so [we] watched that plane until we couldn't see it any longer. We got in the car and Mom drove us all home. To us it was just like the times before, you would go away, Mom would write letters, and you would come home and we would go to the next post. That didn't happen though. You never came back and all of us had to learn a new normal. I don't believe we have figured that out yet. There is still this unspoken gap in all our lives. We do things, we have moments and milestones and we want to share them with you. We wonder what it would be like if you were here. There just always seems to be a someone missing. That someone is you. Your space is there . . . empty . . . and always waiting.

> I was five months old when my dad died. Luckily, he was able to spend a month with me before heading to Vietnam. . . . I was fortunate in that my mom put together all kinds of items to help me learn about my dad when I was ready and she remarried a man who honored the memory of my father. So growing-up seemed "pretty normal" and because of that, I pushed that empty place in me further down. After many years of counseling, I am only just beginning to reach that part of me deep inside that LONGS for the comfort of my daddy. To be held by him, to hear his voice. He was an only child and I was his only child. His parents have long since passed and my mom (my only remaining close connection to his

memory) is struggling with her own memory. I feel lonely and miss my dad, but the emotion is so strange because I miss someone I never knew.

I was 11 when daddy left and the memories I have are fading. But the memories I have made along the way in the search have brought me great friends. I have 3 sisters and a brother. But hundreds by fate from the Vietnam war.[38]

When asked why veterans' children, generally speaking, are now building these communities, Tony Cordero speculated,

I think it's because of the time we were born in. If you think about it, they make heroic movies and write books about the "Greatest Generation" and so our predecessors—the sons and daughters of World War II—they don't need to worry about the Ken Burns–Lynn Novick controversy [co-directors of an eighteen-hour PBS documentary on Vietnam drawing criticism from historians and veterans]. Then you look at us. We were born at a time, and came of age, when this rapid-communication society was starting to evolve, and made it easier. We were curious. We were willing to ask questions. I guess we threw a match at the right can of gasoline and it started.[39]

Cordero reflected,

I don't know what history will say about us, but what I'd like it to say is that we were in that sandwich generation where we found a way to build something for ourselves, because nobody was going to build it for us. We reach to the past and provide some assistance to older Gold Star families from World War II and Korea. We're also reaching to the future and present to engage with the younger Gold Star children, families that have lost loved ones since 9/11, to simply impart on them the very simple notion that when you look at me or anybody else in this organization, this is what those beautiful young kids from the post–9/11 era are going to look like.[40]

NOTES

Introduction

1. Kapell, *Exploring the Next Frontier*, 160, 162; Franklin, "Vietnam, Star Trek," 97–101.

2. The Star Trek Transcripts, http://www.chakoteya.net/StarTrek/45.htm.

3. Franklin, "Vietnam, Star Trek," 101.

4. Anderegg, *Inventing Vietnam*, 2.

5. Quoted in Fass, "Child-Centered Family," 16.

6. See Salkind, *Theories of Human Development*.

7. Marten, *Children for the Union*, 4; Mintz, *Huck's Raft*, 118, 120, 127, 130, 132, 255; Greenstein, *Children and Politics*, 80.

Chapter 1. A Sort of Nebulous Sad Thing Happening Forever and Ever

1. Jessica Wilmarth, email message to author, March 21, 2010; Anna B. Gray, email message to author, January 11, 2010; Carol Bierschwal, email message to author, January 15, 2010; Small, *Covering Dissent*, 1, 17; Rowe and Berg, *Vietnam War and American Culture*, 115; Arlen, *Living-Room War*, xi, 81.

2. Herring, *America's Longest War*, 144–45.

3. Arlen, *Living-Room War*, 8, 109, 111, 113; Klein, *Vietnam Era*, 47, 49, 59.

4. Arlen, *Living-Room War*, 6, 7.

5. Ibid., 116.

6. Barnouw, *Tube of Plenty*, 380, 399, 401; Lesser, *Children and Television*, 81; Arlen, *Living-Room War*, 22, 81, 82, 116; "Television: The First Television War," *Encyclopedia of American Foreign Policy*, American Foreign Relations, http://www.americanforeignrelations.com/O-W/Television-The-first-television-war.html.

7. Mark Button to the President, November 1, 1966, 6M4a, Letters from School Children, Box 1, Roger Park School 4th Grade folder, LBJ Library.

8. Steven Long to the President, November 1, 1966, 6M4a, Letters from School Children, Box 1, Roger Park School 4th Grade folder, LBJ Library; Kathy Cornett Smalley, email message to author, May 29, 2014; Eugster, *Notes from Nethers*, 196; Roberta Niederjohn, email message to author, January 14, 2010.

9. Debbi Goodier, email message to author, April 20, 2010; Bart Greenwalt, email message to author, December 9, 2011; Tolley, *Children and War*, 32–34, 90.

10. Bill Coutirié and Richard Dewhurst, *Dear America: Letters Home from Vietnam*, directed by Bill Coutirié, January 1988, HBO.

11. Eileen Mulvihill Harmon, email message to author, January 14, 2010; Lisa Zhito, email message to author, January 12, 2010; Randy Roth to the President, November 1, 1966, 6M4a, Letters from School Children, Box 1, Ursa Major School 4th Grade folder, LBJ Library; Letter, Anthony Allgood to the President, January 24, 1968, Alley, Box 100, Name File, White House Central File WHCF, LBJ Library; Arlen, *Living-Room War*, 82, 114.

12. Marten, *Children and War*, 5; Tolley, *Children and War*, 39, 128; Richard Friedman to the President, March 28, 1966, Freidman, Marya, Box 267, Name File, and Tina Quick to the President, November 5, 1967, Conn L-R, Box 366, Name File, WHCF, LBJ Library.

13. Julia Kagan, "Peace Comes to the Schools," *McCall's*, September 1972, 32; Rebecca Lukens, "War Is for Children," *PTA Magazine*, October 1972, 20–22; Beverly Bush Smith, "Homework for Peace," *Parents' Magazine*, October 1970, 122; Batman for U.S. Savings Bonds, ca. 1966, https://unwritten-record.blogs.archives.gov/2014/01/28/holy-act-of-congress-batman-equal-pay-for-equal-work/.

14. Marc Richards, "The Cold War World According to *My Weekly Reader*," *Monthly Review*, October 1998, 34, 35, 42; *Weekly Reader: 60 Years of News for Kids*, 7, 136, 141.

15. *Weekly Reader: 60 Years of News for Kids*, 8, 141.

16. Ibid., 141.

17. Ibid., 141, 179, 162.

18. Tolley, *Children and War*, 6, 37, 38, 61, 68, 70, 95, 126, 127.

19. Salkind, *Theories of Human Development*, 208; Tuttle, *"Daddy's Gone to War,"* 114.

20. Karen Wilber to the President, November 1, 1966, 6M4a, Letters from School Children, Box 1, Roger Park School 6th Grade folder; Randy Paul Allgaier to the President, February 28, 1968, Alley, Box 100, Name File, WHCF; Tommy Evans to the President, March 19, 1966, Evans T, Box 135, Name File, WHCF, LBJ Library; Tolley, *Children and War*, 36, 39.

21. Tuttle, *"Daddy's Gone to War,"* 45; Glenn Anderson to the President, February 27, 1968, Anderson, Franka, Box 156, Name File, WHCF, LBJ Library.

22. Karen Cooley, email message to author, June 11, 2010.

23. David Giliam to the President, November 1, 1966, 6M4a, Letters from School Children, Box 1, Roger Park School 5th Grade folder, LBJ Library; Budd Carl Pounds, email message to author, January 14, 2010; Steven Peel, email message to author, January 17, 2010.

24. Alice Lesak to the President, September 1, 1966, Lerner, Box 153, Name File, WHCF, LBJ Library.

25. Tolley, *Children and War*, 63, 75.

26. Barnouw, *Tube of Plenty*, 380, 401, 402; Stark, *Glued to the Set*, 169, 171; Delli Carpini, "U.S. Media Coverage," 58, 59; Mundey, *American Militarism*, 178.

27. Palmer Wilson, email message to author, February 14, 2010; Anna B. Gray, email message to author, January 11, 2010.

28. Robert Finn to the President, March 6, 1968, Finn, Q, Box 97, Name File, WHCF; Richard to the President, March 25, 1966, Freidman, Marya, Box 267, Name File, WHCF; Andrew Sorany to the President, March 14, 1968, Sor, Box 451, Name File, WHCF, LBJ Library.

29. Tolley, *Children and War*, 63–67, 99, 109, 116, 117; Jack Zibluk, email message to author, January 17, 2010.

30. Paul Friedman and Dean Ballard to the President, January 10, 1967, Freidman, Marya, Box 267, Name File, WHCF, LBJ Library.

31. Cara Sroges, email message to author, March 4, 2010; Tina Quick to the President, November 5, 1967, Conn L-R, Box 366, Name File, WHCF, LBJ Library.

32. Tolley, *Children and War*, 41, 42, 67, 72, 74, 87; Gerald F. Goodwin, "Black and White in Vietnam," *New York Times*, July 18, 2017.

33. Barnouw, *Tube of Plenty*, 374, 375; Mundey, *American Militarism*, 10, 40, 133, 164, 178; Franklin, "Vietnam, Star Trek," 107.

34. Kapell, *Exploring the Next Frontier*, 156.

35. Franklin, "Vietnam, Star Trek," 91, 93, 97, 102–4; Kapell, *Exploring the Next Frontier*, 156, 158, 160.

36. Cyndi Fitzpatrick, email message to author, January 18, 2010.

37. Jan Dempsey, email message to author, February 15, 2010; Julie Barker, email message to author, January 20, 2010; Klein, *Vietnam Era*, 84.

38. Cindy Lehto, email message to author, July 15, 2010.

39. Tom Paxton, "What Did You Learn in School Today?" recording, Chrysalis One Music, BMG Rights Management U.S., LLC., 1962.

40. Charlene DeStefano to the President, July 22, 1964, Dest, Box 152, Name File, WHCF, LBJ Library.

41. Mundey, *American Militarism*, 172, 177; Franklin, "Vietnam, Star Trek," 93–99; Kapell, *Exploring the Next Frontier*, 156, 158.

42. Diane McAlpin, email message to author, January 17, 2010; Paula Moomey-Ivey, email message to author, June 26, 2010; Anna B. Gray, email message to author, January 11, 2010; Klein, *Vietnam Era*, 48.

43. Mundey, *American Militarism*, 9, 182; Franklin, "Vietnam, *Star Trek*," 106.

44. Confidential, email message to author, January 31, 2010.

45. Steve Richardet, interviewed by the American Century Oral History Project, Southeast Missouri State University, November 25, 2013.

46. Confidential, email message to author, January 31, 2010.

Chapter 2. Why Couldn't I Fight in a Nice, Simpler War?

1. Elder et al., *Children in Time and Place*, 201, 202; Mundey, *American Militarism*, 11; Wright, "Vietnam War in Comic Books," 427, 439, 441; Wright, *Comic Book Nation*, 233;

Braun, "Shazam!" 36; *The Toy*, NO WAR TOYS newsletter, November 1965, in the author's possession; Grieve, *Little Cold Warriors*, 40.

2. "Pop Goes the War," 66; Scott, "Comics and Conflict," 122, 132; Chapman, "From Vietnam to the New World Order," 47.

3. *Battlefield Action* #48 (1962); *Fightin' Army* #66 (1966); Gravett, "War Comics."

4. *Fightin' Army* #74 (1967); Wright, *Comic Book Nation*, 195, 196.

5. *War Heroes* #24 (1967); Gravett, "War Comics."

6. *Army War Heroes* #27 (1968); Wright, *Comic Book Nation*, 199, 240; Scott, "Comics and Conflict," 129, 132; Wright, "Vietnam War in Comic Books," 439, 441; Mundey, *American Militarism*, 11, 159, 175.

7. *Jungle War Stories* #2 (1963); Wright, "Vietnam War in Comic Books," 431, 432, 434; Wright, *Comic Book Nation*, 189, 191; Scott, "Comics and Conflict," 124.

8. *Jungle War Stories* #11 (1965); Wright, *Comic Book Nation*, 191, 192.

9. "Pop Goes the War," 66.

10. Wright, "Vietnam War in Comic Books," 438; Scott, "Comics and Conflict," 125.

11. *Blazing Combat* #2 (1966); David Kendall, *Mammoth Book of Best War Comics*, 207; Scott, "Comics and Conflict," 130, 131.

12. *Sgt. Fury and His Howling Commandos King-Size Special* #3 (1967); Wright, "Vietnam War in Comic Books," 437, 438, 439.

13. *Superman* #216 (1969); Goodrum, *Superheroes and American Self-Image*, 184, 185; Wright, "Vietnam War in Comic Books," 428, 448.

14. *The Avengers* #18 (1965); Maquire, "'The Avengers,'" 2, 13, 15, 20.

15. *Journey into Mystery* #117 (1965); Wright, "Vietnam War in Comic Books," 429, 430, 440, 441, 446–48; Wright, *Comic Book Nation*, 215, 222, 223, 240, 244.

16. *The Amazing Spider-Man* #83 (1970), #108 (1972); Wright, *Comic Book Nation*, 240, 241; Wright, "Vietnam War in Comic Books," 449, 450.

17. Wright, *Comic Book Nation*, 215, 241; Wright, "Vietnam War in Comic Books," 442–45.

18. *Tales of Suspense* #39 (1963); Goodrum, *Superheroes and American Self-Image*, 193, 194; Wright, *Comic Book Nation*, 241; *The Invincible Iron Man* #60 (1973), #68 (1974).

19. *Captain America* #125 (1970), #175 (1974); *The Avengers* #126 (1974); Goodrum, *Superheroes and American Self-Image*, 205; Wright, "Vietnam War in Comic Books," 447.

20. *The Invincible Iron Man* #78 (1975); Wright, "Vietnam War in Comic Books," 446; Goodrum, *Superheroes and American Self-Image*, 196.

21. *Everything's Archie* #16 (1971); Braun, "Shazam!" 36; Duncan and Smith, *Icons of the American Comic Book*, 36.

22. *Everything's Archie* #16 (1971).

23. *Mad* #126 (1969), #119 (1968), #127 (1969); Reidelbach, *Completely MAD*, 41, 106; Labarre, "Joining the Fray?" 135; St. Onge, "'Comedy before Country,'" 155.

24. *Mad* #119 (1968).

25. *Mad* #124 (1969), #126 (1969).

26. *Mad* #145 (1971).

27. *Mad* #147 (1971); Labarre, "Joining the Fray?" 144, 145.

28. *Mad* #147 (1971), #146 (1971).

29. *Mad* #147 (1971).

Chapter 3. Who Bombed Santa's Workshop?

1. David Kurtz, email message to author, January 18, 2010.

2. Cross, *Kids' Stuff*, v, 4, 52, 168; Mintz, "Changing Face of Children's Culture," 43.

3. Cross, *Kids' Stuff*, 111–12, 156; Regan, "War Toys," 56; Engelhardt, *End of Victory Culture*.

4. Regan, "War Toys," 53.

5. Andreas, "War Toys," 84, 85, 89.

6. Tom Duncan Jenkins, email message to author, January 30, 2010.

7. Regan, "War Toys," 49; Higdon, "Mother Opens Fire," 14.

8. *Sears Christmas 1963*, 170, 174.

9. Ibid., 171.

10. *Sears Christmas 1964*, 365.

11. *Sears Christmas 1963*, 171.

12. *Sears Christmas 1966*, 180, 495, 560; *Christmas 1966 Penneys*, 367.

13. Honan, "Merry Bang," 11–12; *Sears Christmas 1966*, 435; Scott, "Comics and Conflict," 146.

14. *Sears Christmas 1964*, 243; *Sears Christmas 1967*, 498.

15. Brian Williams to the President, July 7, 1967, Williams, Box 324, Name File, WHCF, LBJ Library.

16. O'Brien, *Story of American Toys*, 190–92.

17. Cross, *The Cute and the Cool*, 156, 157.

18. Cross, *Kids' Stuff*, 175, 176; "GI Joe Doll Is Capturing New Market," *New York Times*, July 24, 1965, 10; Engelhardt, *End of Victory Culture*, 176.

19. Strang, "War Talk and War Games," 21; Andreas, "War Toys," 84, 85, 96; Sue Adams, email message to author, February 11, 2010.

20. Ferrari, *Reporting America at War*, 140; Engelhardt, *End of Victory Culture*, 178; J. P. Coulter, email message to author, January 16, 2010.

21. Cross, *The Cute and the Cool*, 157; Judy Dickey, email message to author, November 22, 2011.

22. Cross, *Kids' Stuff*, 177; Richard Register, email message to author, December 28, 2016.

23. Engelhardt, *End of Victory Culture*, 177, 178, 180; Barnouw, *Tube of Plenty*, 441; Andreas, "War Toys," 87; Cross, *The Cute and the Cool*, 157; Cross, *Kids' Stuff*, 177, 187, 191, 203, 205; O'Brien, *Story of American Toys*, 204, 211.

24. Goossen, "Disarming the Toy Store," 330–33, 335, 337.

25. Higdon, "Mother Opens Fire," 13, 15.

26. Goossen, "Disarming the Toy Store," 339.

27. Sue Dremann, "Disarming the Nursery," *Palo Alto Weekly Online Edition*, January 14, 2005, http://www.paloaltoonline.com/weekly/morgue/2005/2005_01_14.sidebar14ja.shtm.

28. "Who Bombed Santa's Workshop?" 87, 98.

29. Higdon, "Mother Opens Fire," 13, 15, 17; "Mothers Protest Arms Race in Toys," 12; *The Toy*, No Death Toys newsletter #5, Winter 1966 and 1967, in the author's possession.

30. Strang, "War Talk and War Games," 20–23; Andreas, "War Toys," 91, 94–96; Spock, "Playing with Toy Guns," 24–32.

31. "I Turned Mine In," 94; Higdon, "Mother Opens Fire," 13.

32. Higdon, "Mother Opens Fire," 13, 15; Goossen, "Disarming the Toy Store," 341, 342; Martin J. Cooper, "Little Play Soldiers," recording, copyright 1964 by Little Darlin' Music Company.

33. "Who Bombed Santa's Workshop?" 98.

34. Goossen, "'Like Entering an Armed Camp,'" 60.

35. Goossen, "Disarming the Toy Store," 341; Higdon, "Mother Opens Fire," 16; Feinsilber, "Peace Women Battle," 4; *The Toy*, No War Toys newsletter #4, Spring 1966, in the author's possession.

36. *The Toy*, No War Toys newsletter #4, Spring 1966, in the author's possession.

37. Mark Spoelstra, "White Winged Dove," recording, copyright 1965 by Nina Music, a division of the Dyna Corp.

38. Tom Paxton, "Buy a Gun for Your Son," recording, copyright 1965 by Deep Fork Music, Inc.

39. Goossen, "'Like Entering an Armed Camp,'" 60; Goossen, "Disarming the Toy Store," 338–40, 345; Higdon, "Mother Opens Fire," 14, 15.

40. Feinsilber, "Peace Women Battle," 4.

41. "Makers of Military Toys Are Picketed by Mothers," *New York Times*, March 8, 1966, 49; Feinsilber, "Peace Women Battle," 4; Higdon, "Mother Opens Fire," 16; "Mothers Protest Arms Race in Toys," 12.

42. Letter, Anti-War-Toy Chairman from Vicki Reiss, Parents for Responsibility in the Toy Industry, October 7, 1968, Swarthmore College Peace Collection, Swarthmore College.

43. Goossen, "Disarming the Toy Store," 342.

44. *The Toy*, No War Toys newsletter #4, Spring 1966, in the author's possession.

45. "Incident at Fort Dix: Picketing of Armed Forces Day War Ceremonies for Children," *Christian Century*, June 19, 1968, 809.

46. Jenkins, *Children's Culture Reader*, 24, 25, 27; Sándor John, interview with author, December 30, 2016.

47. Children's Peace Union, *CPU News*, issue 4, June and December 1966, and issue 5, Fall and Winter 1967, in the author's possession.

48. Sándor John interview; Children's Peace Union flier, n.d., in the author's possession.

49. Children's Peace Union, *CPU News*, December 1965, and issue 6, 1968, in the author's possession.

50. Sándor John interview; Children's Peace Union, *CPU News*, issue 8, 1968, in the author's possession.

51. Children's Peace Union flier; Sándor John interview.

52. "5 Children Picket a Store to Protest Sale of War Toys," *New York Times*, May 15, 1966, 3; *CPU News*, issue 4.

53. *CPU News*, December 1965; Children's Peace Union flier, May 1966; *CPU News*, issues 4, 5, and Children's Peace Union, *CPU News*, 1968

54. Sándor John interview.

55. Ibid.

56. "Children Picket the Knickerbocker Greys," *New York Times*, February 8, 1969, 19.

57. "Children Protest Toy Guns," *New York Times*, July 21, 1968, 56.

58. "Maine Wholesaler Refuses to Sell Any More Toy Guns," *Lewiston (Maine) Daily Sun*, June 27, 1968, 26; Goossen, "Disarming the Toy Store," 340.

59. Anderson, *The Movement and the Sixties*, i.

60. *The Toy*, No War Toys newsletter, November 1965, in the author's possession.

61. Richard Register, interview with author, December 28, 2016.

62. Ibid.

63. Ibid.

64. *The Toy*, No Death Toys newsletter #5, Winter 1966 and 1967, in the author's possession.

65. Ibid.

66. *The Toy*, No War Toys newsletter #4, Spring 1966, and newsletter #5; Richard Register interview.

67. No Death Toys newsletter #5.

68. Richard Register interview.

69. No War Toys newsletter #4.

70. Ibid.

71. No Death Toys newsletter #5.

72. "Contest: Will Yours Be War Toy of the Week?" *Stanford Daily*, February 4, 1966, 4; Andreas, "War Toys," 94.

73. "Failing War Toy Succeeds as Peaceful Adventurer," *New York Times*, March 27, 1969, 65; Regan, "War Toys," 53.

74. No War Toys newsletter #4; *Chicago Tribune*, October 22, 1967, 27; Andreas, "War Toys," 98.

75. Honan, "Merry Bang," 11–12; "I Turned Mine In," 94; Andreas, "War Toys," 92, 95.

76. Eve Merriam, "We're Teaching Our Children That Violence Is Fun," *Ladies' Home Journal*, October 1964, 44; Goossen, "Disarming the Toy Store," 330, 341; "The Toy Battle Is No Game," *Business Week*, February 27, 1971, 38; Lyon, "More Than Child's Play," 54–55, 98; "Nabisco Picketed over Monster Toys," *New York Times*, November 16, 1971, 50; Cross, *Kids' Stuff*, 175, 176, 187, 191.

77. Richard Register interview; Goossen, "Disarming the Toy Store," 332, 341; O'Brien, *Story of American Toys*, 203–4; Cross, *Kids' Stuff*, 188, 205.

78. Goossen, "Disarming the Toy Store," 345.

Chapter 4. One of the Most Agonizing Years of My Life

1. Audio Recordings of the Yorkship School Students (November 1967), http://www.yorkshipvillage.com/school-yorkship/vietnam-penpals/.

2. Gene Moppert to Jerry and kids, January 23, 1968, Letters from Vietnam, 4th Platoon for Jerry Davis, Yorkship Family School Collection, Division of Armed Forces History, National Museum of American History, Smithsonian Institution (hereafter Yorkship Family School Collection).

3. Kutner, "Vietnam War Vets Reconnect"; Kathleen Golden, "4th Graders' Notes Made a Difference to Vietnam War Soldiers," April 17, 2015, http://americanhistory.si.edu/blog/4th-graders-notes-made-difference-vietnam-war-soldiers.

4. Tom Flaherty, "250,000 Children Have Their Say," *Life*, December 29, 1972, 88; Tolley, *Children and War*, 58.

5. Amy Rider, email message to author, February 10, 2010; Bart Greenwalt, email message to author, December 9, 2011; Brenda Burke, email message to author, January 27, 2010.

6. Tolley, *Children and War*, 75.

7. Roberta Niederjohn, email message to author, January 14, 2010.

8. Paula Moomey-Ivey, email message to author, June 26, 2010.

9. John McCosh, email message to author, April 7, 2010.

10. Steven Peel, email message to author, January 17, 2010.

11. Carol Bierschwal, email message to author, January 15, 2011.

12. Joe Mode, email message to author, January 15, 2010.

13. Steve Richardet, email message to author, April 17, 2010.

14. Paula Moomey-Ivey, email message to author, June 26, 2010.

15. Lisa Lehrer, interview with the author, February 17, 2017.

16. Katie Hutton, email message to author, January 17, 2010.

17. Regina and Tom Santoriello to the President, July 20, 1966, Gen PP 15–10, Box 120, President, 1963–1969, LBJ Library.

18. Clark Harris, email message to author, January 11, 2010.

19. J. P. Coulter, email message to author, January 16, 2010.

20. Clark Harris, email message to author, January 11, 2010.

21. Rowley, "Pen Pal."

22. Kutner, "Vietnam War Vets Reconnect."

23. Carol Comegno, "A Pen Pal's Memory of Soldiers Adds to History," *Courier-Post*, October 6, 2014, 3A; Kutner, "Vietnam War Vets Reconnect."

24. Platoon Sergeant to Mrs. Robert David, February 28, 1968, Letters from Vietnam, Yorkship Family School Collection.

25. Kelly Sims to Mrs. Jerry Davis, June 11, 1969, Letters from Vietnam, Yorkship Family School Collection.

26. Letters to Kathie Cromie folder, Letters from Vietnam, Yorkship Family School Collection.

27. Comegno, "Camden School's Vietnam Letters."

28. Kutner, "Vietnam War Vets Reconnect."

29. Comegno, "Camden School's Vietnam Letters."

30. Comegno, "Pen Pal's Memory," 3A.

31. Bill Harrison, interview with author, April 19, 2018.

32. Robert Read to Mrs. Davis, January 17, 1968, Meskaitis to class and Teach, May 20, 1968, Yorkship Family School Collection.

33. Captain Harwood Nichols to Mrs. Davis, April 8, 1968, Yorkship Family School Collection.

34. Brian O'Leary to Kathie Cromie, June 22, 1968; J. P. Meskaitis to Billy Harrison, May 30, 1968; SP4 Nick Dandrea to Mrs. Jerry Davis, January 11, 1967, Yorkship Family School Collection.

35. J. P. Meskaitis to Billy Harrison, April 29, 1968, Letters to Bill Harrison folder; Brian O'Leary to Kathie Cromie, March 18, 1968; Meskaitis to class and Teach, May 20, 1968, Yorkship Family School Collection.

36. First Lieutenant Robert H. Smith to Students c/o Mrs. Jerry Davis, October 8, 1969, Yorkship Family School Collection.

37. 4th Platoon Sergeant to Mrs. Robert Davis, April 25, 1968, Yorkship Family School Collection. Kathy Gabriel's pen pal, Brian O'Leary, also visited the class after returning home from Vietnam. Rowley, "Pen Pal."

38. Comegno, "Camden School's Vietnam Letters."

39. Rowe and Berg, *Vietnam War and American Culture*, 4.

40. Robin Machiran, email message to author, December 6, 2010.

41. Colleen Foster, email message to author, January 17, 2010.

42. Julie Ann Kienitz, email message to author, December 7, 2010.

43. Robin Machiran, email message to author, December 6, 2010.

44. Steve Richardet, interviewed by the American Century Oral History Project, Southeast Missouri State University, November 25, 2013.

45. Marion S. DeFazio, letter to author, January 27, 2010; Lisa Lehrer, interview with author, February 17, 2017; Daniel P. Gmyrek, email message to author, January 15, 2010.

46. Laura Rexroat, email message to author, December 5, 2010.

47. Jan Allman, email message to author, June 23, 2010.

48. Cindy Lehto, email message to author, July 15, 2010.

49. Connie Clairday Johnston, email message to author, February 10, 2010.

50. Denise Glastetter, email message to author, May 11, 2010; Gail Anderson to the President, April 3, 1967, and April 11, 1967, Anderson, Franka, Box 156, Name File, WHCF; Cathy to the President, December 16, 1967, Catholica, Box 141, Name File, WHCF, LBJ Library.

51. Jan Allman, email message to author, June 23, 2010.

52. Brian Atchison, email message to author, February 13, 2012; Marion S. DeFazio, letter to author, January 27, 2010.

53. Florence D. Shipley, "Chris Hits Jackpot with Order from Vietnam," *Dubuque Telegraph-Herald*, 1968, posted at http://joyofdesserts.blogspot.com/2011/03/girl-scouts-celebrate-99th-anniversary.html.

54. Lisa Lehrer interview; Aslanian and Eichten, "Transcript of the Vietnam Tapes."

55. Lisa Lehrer interview.

56. Aslanian and Eichten, "Transcript of the Vietnam Tapes."

57. Ibid.

58. Lisa Lehrer interview.

59. Aslanian and Eichten, "Transcript of the Vietnam Tapes."

60. Susan Doyle, email message to author, June 22, 2010.

61. Lisa Lehrer interview.

62. Ibid.

63. Sandra Carolyn LaMunion, email message to author, September 16, 2011.

64. Berg, *Regret to Inform You*, 109, 120.

65. Cyndi Fitzpatrick, email message to author, January 18, 2010; Peter Seeger, "Where Have All the Flowers Gone?" recording, copyright 1961, Sony/ATV Music Publishing LLC, Universal Music Publishing Group, Peermusic Publishing, Bicycle Music Company.

66. Lassonde, "Ten Is the New Fourteen," 59; Lisa Lehrer interview.

67. Carol Bates Brown, "History of the POW/MIA Bracelet," http://thewall-usa.com/bracelet.asp; Siegfried, *Six Degrees of the Bracelet*, xvi; Anton, "Vietnam War Bracelets"; "The History of the POW/MIA Bracelet . . . and SGT. Kenneth Lancaster," http://militarybratlife.com/the-history-of-the-pow-mia-bracelet-and-sgt-kenneth-lancaster/.

68. Bates Brown, "History of the POW/MIA Bracelet"; Anton, "Vietnam War Bracelets."

69. Anton, "Vietnam War Bracelets."

70. Anton, "Vietnam War Bracelets"; Morris, "Bracelet That Stands for a Cause," 16.

71. Ami Partin Brandes, interview with author, January 23, 2017.

72. Kim Kristic, interview with author, February 27, 2017.

73. Roxan Drimmer-Chen, email message to author, March 19, 2017.

74. Susan Doyle, email message to author, June 22, 2010.

75. Anton, "Vietnam War Bracelets"; Paula Moomey-Ivey, email message to author, June 26, 2010.

76. Martindale, "O.C. Woman"; Morris, "Bracelet That Stands for a Cause."

77. Kenneth R. Slavin, December 29, 1998, "Letters and Notes from Those That Wear the Bracelets," http://www.pownetwork.org/tletter1.htm. Hereafter cited as "Letters and Notes."

78. Anton, "Vietnam War Bracelets Come Full Circle."

79. Barbara Layne, October 12, 1998, Angie Pontius, January 13, 1999, Ami Partin Brandes, November 12, 1998, "Letters and Notes."

80. Sue Bailey, email message to author, August 7, 2014.

81. Sue Bailey, interview with author, March 13, 2017.

82. Martindale, "O.C. Woman."

83. Roxan Drimmer-Chen, email message to author, March 19, 2017.

84. Hartman, "Woman Wears POW/MIA Bracelet."

85. Siegfried, *Six Degrees of the Bracelet*, xvi; Hartman, "Woman Wears POW/MIA Bracelet."

Chapter 5. Mom Tried to Make It for Us Like He Wasn't Even Gone

1. Cheryl Hunsell, email message to author, December 7, 2012.

2. Baskir and Strauss, *Chance and Circumstance*, xi, 7; Jones, *Great Expectations*, 106–11; Bitler and Schmidt, "Birth Rates and the Vietnam Draft," 102, 566.

3. Baskir and Strauss, *Chance and Circumstance*, 6, 9, 15, 22, 23.

4. Kutinova, "Paternity Deferments," 351, 352, 359, 361, 364; Baskir and Strauss, *Chance and Circumstance*, 22, 30, 31, 33, 282; Bitler and Schmidt, "Birth Rates and the Vietnam Draft," 566–69; Jones, *Great Expectations*, 108.

5. Lieberman, "American Families," 709; Tolley, *Children and War*, 72.

6. Thorsen, "Campaign," 38.

7. "Celebration of Men Redeemed," 15.

8. McCubbin et al., *Family Separation and Reunion*, 50, 66; Whitbread, "Families," 53.

9. Dahl et al., "War-Induced Father Absence," 100.

10. Whitbread, "Families," 54, 55.

11. Judy Holley, interview with author, May 4, 2017.

12. McCubbin et al., *Family Separation and Reunion*, 66; Tuttle, *"Daddy's Gone to War,"* 216, 217, 226, 237; Zaretsky, *No Direction Home*.

13. Lieberman, "American Families," 716; McCubbin et al., *Family Separation and Reunion*, 28, 29, 41.

14. Diane Blankenship, email message to author, May 13, 2010.

15. Lieberman, "American Families," 716.

16. Swenck, "Emergent Voices."

17. Wade Hall, interview with author, Cape Girardeau, Mo., April 12, 2017.

18. Whitbread, "Families," 114.

19. "Celebration of Men Redeemed," 14; McCubbin et al., *Family Separation*, 28, 29; Whitbread, "Families," 54, 55.

20. Whitbread, "Families," 115.

21. Ibid., 113.

22. McCubbin et al., *Family Separation*, 28, 29, 41, 211; Whitbread, "Families," 115.

23. Dahl et al., "Second Generational Effects," 150; McCubbin et al., *Family Separation*, 34, 40, 67.

24. Lieberman, "American Families," 716; Cathi Bond-Drake, interview with author, Cape Girardeau, Mo., April 10, 2017.

25. Whitbread, "Families," 114; Stacy Swenck, interview with author, Cape Girardeau, Mo., May 21, 2017.

26. Lieberman, "Statement," 197; Karen Cordell, email message to author, February 6, 2010.

27. Stacy Swenck interview.

28. Wade Hall interview.

29. Stacy Swenck interview.

30. Whitbread, "Families," 114, 115.

31. Zacharias, *Hero Mama*, 7, 8.

32. Ibid., 11, 12, 13.

33. Whitbread, "Families," 114; Wade Hall interview.

34. McCubbin et al., *Family Separation*, 50; R. J. Coulter to J. P. Coulter, July 9, 1970, in possession of author; J. P. Coulter, email message to author, January 16, 2010.

35. Cheryl Hunsell, email message to author, December 7, 2012; McCubbin et al., *Family Separation*, 40, 44, 67, 68, 70, 154.

36. Wade Hall interview; "Celebration of Men Redeemed," 14.

37. Thorsen, "Campaign," 38; Susan Hammond, email message to author, February 18, 2010.

38. Wade Hall interview.

39. Karen Cordell, email message to author, February 6, 2010.

40. Thorsen, "Campaign," 38; McCubbin et al., *Family Separation*, 50; Cheryl Hunsell, email message to author, December 7, 2012; J. P. Coulter, email message to author, January 16, 2010.

41. Theresa Conrath to the President, November 1, 1966, 6M4a, Letters from School Children, Box 2, John F. Kennedy School—4th grade folder; Charles Callahan to the President, November 1, 1966, 6M4a, Letters from School Children, Box 2, Ursa Major School—5th grade folder; Patricia Finnell to the President, February 10, 1965, Finn, Q, Box 97, Name File, WHCF, LBJ Library.

42. Melvin Merchant, email message to author, March 14, 2010.

43. Judy Holley interview; Karen Cordell, email message to author, February 6, 2010.

44. Stacy Swenck interview.

45. R. J. Coulter to J. P. Coulter, July 16, 1970, July 26, 1970, in possession of author.

46. R. J. Coulter to J. P. Coulter, March 15, 1971, July 26, 1970, in possession of author.

47. Whitbread, "Families," 113; R. J. Coulter to J. P. Coulter, July 16, 1970, July 26, 1970.

48. Tony Cordero, interview with author, November 28, 2017; Whitbread, "Families," 113.

49. Diane Blankenship, email message to author, May 13, 2010.

50. Susan Hammond, email message to author, February 18, 2010; R. J. Coulter to J. P. Coulter, July 26, 1970, March 15, 1971.

51. Melvin Merchant, email message to author, March 14, 2010; Karen Cordell, email message to author, February 6, 2010.

52. Susan Hammond, email message to author, February 18, 2010; Karen Cordell, email message to author, February 6, 2010; "Celebration of Men Redeemed," 15.

53. Sons and Daughters in Touch, http://sdit.org/.

54. McCubbin et al., *Family Separation*, 40, 44; Lieberman, "American Families," 709, 716; McCubbin et al., "Prisoner of War," 29.

55. Tuttle, *"Daddy's Gone to War,"* 89, 218, 220; "Celebration of Men Redeemed," 19.

56. Wade Hall interview.

57. Karen Cordell, email message to author, February 6, 2010; Tuttle, *"Daddy's Gone to War,"* 89, 215, 217, 218, 237.

58. "Celebration of Men Redeemed," 19; Judy Holley interview; Tuttle, *"Daddy's Gone to War,"* 218.

59. Sons and Daughters in Touch, http://sdit.org/tributes/robert-b-swenck/.

60. Lieberman, "American Families," 715.

61. Karen Cordell, email message to author, February 6, 2010.

62. Jones, *Great Expectations*, 214, 216.

63. Monthly Vital Statistics Report, Advance Report, Final Divorce Statistics, 1976, from the National Center for Health Statistics, http://www.cdc.gov/nchs/data/mvsr/supp/mv27_05sacc.pdf; Josef E. Garai, "Children of Divorce," *Parents' Magazine*, March 1973, 47; Waldman and Whitmore, "Children of Working Mothers," 50, 55; Zaretsky, *No Direction Home*, 11; Jones, *Great Expectations*, 247; Coontz, *Way We Never Were*, 166, 167, 182, 183; Skolnick, *Embattled Paradise*, 121.

64. Doug Tarwater, email message to author, March 19, 2010.

65. Cheryl Hunsell, email message to author, December 7, 2012.

66. J. P. Coulter, email message to author, February 11, 2010.

67. Daughters of Vietnam Veterans, "We Are Not Children Anymore," October 10, 2012, http://dovv.weebly.com/blog/we-are-not-children-anymore.

68. Tucker, *Encyclopedia of the Vietnam War*, 334–35; Figley and Leventman, *Strangers at Home*; Hendin and Pollinger Haas, *Wounds of War*.

69. Cathi Bond-Drake interview; Daughters of Vietnam Veterans, "Secondary Traumatization," October 10, 2012, http://dovv.weebly.com/blog/secondary-traumatization; Ochberg, "Letter to Children of Veterans."

70. Presley, *Thirty Days with My Father*.

71. Ibid.

72. Ibid.

73. Ibid.

74. Wade Hall interview.

75. Cathi Bond-Drake interview.

76. Ibid.

Chapter 6. God Bless Dad Wherever You Are

1. McCubbin et al., *Family Separation*, 46, 47; Zaretsky, *No Direction Home*, 43; "Celebration of Men Redeemed," 15.

2. Berg, *Regret to Inform You*, 109, 120; McCubbin et al., *Family Separation*, 79.

3. "Memories of Divided Families," 36–43.

4. "Living with Uncertainty," 18.

5. Wylie, "At Least I Know Jim's Alive," 79, 215, 218, 219.

6. "Living with Uncertainty," 18.

7. "Memories of Divided Families," 40, 41.

8. Thorsen, "Campaign," 42; "Memories of Divided Families," 39, 41.

9. Kane, "Life without Father," 24; Thorsen, "Campaign," 38; McCubbin et al., "Coping Repertoires of Families," 464.

10. "Memories of Divided Families," 41.

11. Hunter, "Vietnam POW Veteran," 196; Hunter, "Families in Crisis," 7, 8, 9; McCubbin et al., "Prisoner of War," 33, 34.

12. Thorsen, "Campaign," 42.

13. McCubbin et al., "Coping Repertoires of Families," 465, 466, 467.

14. "POW Dad."

15. Tony Cordero interview; "Memories of Divided Families," 40.

16. McCubbin et al., "Coping Repertoires of Families," 465, 466, 467; Thorsen, "Campaign," 42; McCubbin et al., *Family Separation*, 53, 159.

17. Hunter, "Long-Term Effects," 315, 316; McCubbin et al., "Coping Repertoires of Families," 461; "Memories of Divided Families," 40.

18. McCubbin et al., *Family Separation*, 13, 46, 47, 68; Zaretsky, *No Direction Home*, 52, 55; Hunter, "Long-Term Effects," 317.

19. "POW Dad."

20. "Memories of Divided Families," 39; Wren, "What Is Christmas?" 40.

21. McCubbin et al., *Family Separation*, 68, 70, 74, 75, 92; "Memories of Divided Families," 36–43; Thorsen, "Campaign," 32; Berg, *Regret to Inform You*, 109.

22. "Celebration of Men Redeemed," 13, 14.

23. "Memories of Divided Families," 39; Berg, *Regret to Inform You*, 89.

24. Wren, "What Is Christmas?" 36, 37.

25. Thorsen, "Campaign," 38.

26. Wylie, "At Least I Know Jim's Alive," 215.

27. Wren, "What Is Christmas?" 36; "Memories of Divided Families," 41.

28. McCubbin et al., "Coping Repertoires of Families," 461.

29. Herring, *America's Longest War*, 302; "Memories of Divided Families," 37; Wylie, "At Least I Know Jim's Alive," 222; Thorsen, "Campaign," 32.

30. Zaretsky, *No Direction Home*, 32, 38, 43, 52, 54, 55; "Living with Uncertainty," 18.

31. Herring, *America's Longest War*, 323; Berg, *Regret to Inform You*, viii; "Celebration of Men Redeemed," 13.

32. "POW Dad."

33. "Celebration of Men Redeemed," 19; McCubbin et al., *Family Separation*, 196; Hunter, "Vietnam POW Veteran," 194, 195; Hunter, "Families in Crisis," 8.

34. Hunter, "Families in Crisis," 8; Zaretsky, *No Direction Home*, 52; McCubbin et al., *Family Separation*, 153.

35. McCubbin et al., "Prisoner of War," 33, 34; Hunter, "Families in Crisis," 12.

36. McCubbin et al., *Family Separation*, 153; Hunter, "Vietnam POW Veteran," 196; Hunter, "Families in Crisis," 9, 12.

37. Hunter, "Long-Term Effects," 322; "Celebration of Men Redeemed," 19; McCubbin et al., *Family Separation*, 92; Thorsen, "Campaign," 42.

38. "Memories of Divided Families," 40, 41.

39. Mike McGrath, email message to author, July 20, 2017.

40. Philip Taubman, "Life with Father," *Time*, June 11, 1973, 23, 24.

41. Ibid., 23.

42. Ibid., 24.

43. Mike McGrath, email message to author, July 20, 2017.

44. Hunter, "Families in Crisis," 13, 14; Hunter, "Long-Term Effects," 324.

45. McCubbin et al., "Prisoner of War," 33, 34.

46. Dahl et al., "War-Induced Father Absence," 99; Hunter, "Families in Crisis," 11.

47. Hunter, "Long-Term Effects," 317; Dahl et al., "Second Generational Effects," 151; Nice, "Children of Returned Prisoners of War," 8; Hunter, "Families in Crisis," 9; Dahl et al., "War-Induced Father Absence," 99, 100, 104–6.

48. Mike McGrath, email message to author, July 20, 2017.

49. Kane, "Life without Father," 24.

50. Herring, *America's Longest War*, 362.

51. Ibid., 327, 360, 362, 363.

52. Charlotte Duggan Priest, interview with author, July 19, 2017.

53. Dahl et al., "Second Generational Effects," 150; Dahl et al., "War-Induced Father Absence," 105; Charlotte Duggan Priest interview.

54. Kane, "Life without Father," 20, 24.

55. Elizabeth York Enstam, "Women and the Law," Texas State Historical Association, June 15, 2010, modified August 28, 2017, https://tshaonline.org/handbook/online/articles/jsw02; Relating to the Presumption of Date of Death According to a Certificate of Death Issued by the Armed Services, Acts 1973, 63rd R.S., ch. 420, General and Special Laws of Texas; Kane, "Life without Father," 24.

56. Charlotte Duggan Priest interview.

57. Hunter, "Vietnam POW Veteran," 191; Charlotte Duggan Priest interview.

58. Charlotte Duggan Priest interview.

59. Kane, "Life without Father," 24.

60. Charlotte Duggan Priest interview.

61. Dahl et al., "Second Generational Effects," 151; Hunter, "Long-Term Effects," 318; Dahl et al., "War-Induced Father Absence," 99, 105, 106.

62. Charlotte Duggan Priest interview.

Chapter 7. How Come the Flags around Town Aren't Flying at Half-Mast?

1. Lieberman, "American Families," 710; Lieberman, "Statement," 197; *Gold Star Children*; Zacharias, *Hero Mama*, 14.

2. Michael Ellinger, interview with author, May 8, 2015.

3. Swenck, "Emergent Voices," 1.

4. Tony Cordero interview.

5. Zacharias, *Hero Mama*, 6, 7.

6. Michael Ellinger interview; Zacharias, *Hero Mama*, 13.

7. Stacy Swenck interview.

8. Zacharias, *Hero Mama*, 23, 25, 48.

9. Michael Ellinger interview; Zacharias, *Hero Mama*, 56.

10. Swenck, "Emergent Voices," 1.

11. Zacharias, *Hero Mama*, 31.

12. Lieberman, "Statement," 197; Lieberman, "American Families," 712; *Gold Star Children*.

13. Zacharias, *Hero Mama*, 189.

14. Swenck, "Emergent Voices," 15; Zacharias, *Hero Mama*, 68, 154.

15. Zacharias, *Hero Mama*, 26, 27.

16. Ibid., 27, 69.

17. Ibid., 69, 121, 292.

18. Swenck, "Emergent Voices," 19; Zacharias, *Hero Mama*, 121.

19. Roberta Niederjohn, email message to author, January 14, 2010; Swenck, "Emergent Voices," 2, 17.

20. Tony Cordero interview.

21. Swenck, "Emergent Voices," 1; Stacy Swenck interview.

22. Swenck, "Emergent Voices," 19; Zacharias, *Hero Mama*, 192; *Gold Star Children*.

23. Zacharias, *Hero Mama*, 121.

24. Ibid., 155, 156.

25. Swenck, "Emergent Voices," 1.

26. *Gold Star Children*.

27. Tony Cordero interview.

28. *Gold Star Children*; Swenck, "Emergent Voices," 23; Stacy Swenck interview.

29. Santoli, "We Never Knew Our Fathers," 22; *Gold Star Children*.

30. Swenck, "Emergent Voices," 23; *Briscoe*, "Children of the Fallen," 53; Tony Cordero interview; Santoli, "We Never Knew Our Fathers," 21.

31. Zacharias, *Hero Mama*, 109.

32. McCubbin et al., *Family Separation*, 165, 215; Leonard Zunin, "Second Life for War Widows," *Time*, July 25, 1969, 54–55.

33. Michael Ellinger interview.

34. Ibid.

35. Zacharias, *Hero Mama*, 121; Stacy Swenck interview.

36. Tony Cordero interview.

37. Stacy Swenck interview.

38. Zacharias, *Hero Mama*, 348.

Chapter 8. Yes, I Am My Lai, but My Lai Is Better Than Viet Cong!

1. Luce, "Amer-Asian Children in Vietnam," 996.

2. Yarborough, *Surviving Twice*, x; Callery, "Children of War," 8; Sachs, *Life We Were Given*, 137; Peck-Barnes, *War Cradle*, 124.

3. Yarborough, *Surviving Twice*, 270.

4. Herring, *America's Longest War*, 327, 331, 333, 337, 360; Callery, "Children of War," 5, 6; Loren Jenkins, "Vietnam's War-Torn Children," *Newsweek*, May 28, 1973, 52; Peck-Barnes, *War Cradle*, 58, 67.

5. Callery, "Children of War," 7, 8; Sachs, *Life We Were Given*, 54; Paley, "Other People's Children," 69, 95.

6. Peck-Barnes, *War Cradle*, 65, 66, 107, 121.

7. Catherine Pomeroy Collins and Leslie Aldrich Westoff, "My Search for Nobody's Child," *McCall's*, April 1973, 67, 92; Callery, "Children of War," 7.

8. Cummings, "Meet Melissa: Adopted Vietnamese Child," *Parent's Magazine*, February 1973, 52; Jane Cary Peck, "Of Politics and Vietnamese Orphans: A Call for Vigilance," *Christian Century*, July 3, 1974, 704, 705; Callery, "Children of War," 10, 11.

9. Callery, "Children of War," 22, 24, 25; Cummings, "How Ngoc-Lon Became Melissa," 44; Paul Brinkley-Rogers, "A New Family for Duong Muoi," *Newsweek*, May 28, 1973, 54.

10. Cummings, "How Ngoc-Lon Became Melissa," 45; Callery, "Children of War," 21.

11. Peck-Barnes, *War Cradle*, 55, 56; Callery, "Children of War," 19, 20, 28.

12. Callery, "Children of War," 22, 24; USAID, *Operation Babylift Report*, 2, 3.

13. Peck-Barnes, *War Cradle*, 23, 84, 85, 113.

14. Herring, *America's Longest War*, 333, 336, 337, 360.

15. Peck-Barnes, *War Cradle*, 171; G. Emerson, "Operation Babylift: Airlift of Vietnamese Children," *New Republic*, April 26, 1975, 8; USAID, *Operation Babylift Report*, 1, 2, 5; Sachs, *Life We Were Given*, xiv, 130, 163.

16. Lifton, "Orphans in Limbo," 20; Sachs, *Life We Were Given*, xiv, 8, 103, 130; Desmond Smith, "Second-Hand Babies: Vietnamese Orphans," *The Nation*, April 19, 1975, 454; Paley, "Other People's Children," 69; "Rescuing Vietnam Orphans: Mixed Motives," *Christian Century*, April 16, 1975, 374; "Sentimental Binge: Operation Baby Lift," *Newsweek*, April 28, 1975, 88; "Too Little, Too Late," *New Republic*, April 19, 1975, 9.

17. Sachs, *Life We Were Given*, 31, 64; "Orphans of the Storm," *Newsweek*, April 14, 1975, 28; "Orphans Hard Passage," *Newsweek*, April 21, 1975, 40; "Orphans Saved or Lost," *Time*, April 21, 1975, 11; Peck-Barnes, *War Cradle*, 168; Johnston, "Torment over the Viet Non-Orphans," 14; USAID, *Operation Babylift Report*, 7.

18. USAID, *Operation Babylift Report*, 2, 3; Sachs, *Life We Were Given*, 61, 123, 134, 186.

19. Sachs, *Life We Were Given*, 32, 62, 66, 128.

20. Peck-Barnes, *War Cradle*, 125; "Bitter Legacy of the Baby Lift," 17.

21. Sachs, *Life We Were Given*, 132.

22. Ibid., 58, 90, 93, 97.

23. "Bitter Legacy of the Baby Lift," 17; Sachs, *Life We Were Given*, 54, 62, 98; Peck-Barnes, *War Cradle*, 137; Johnston, "Torment Over the Viet Non-Orphans," 14.

24. USAID, *Operation Babylift Report*, 4; Peck-Barnes, *War Cradle*, 171.

25. Peck-Barnes, *War Cradle*, 60, 61, 176; Sachs, *Life We Were Given*, 60; USAID, *Operation Babylift Report*, 5, 6.

26. Sachs, *Life We Were Given*, 65, 79, 132, 165.

27. Peck-Barnes, *War Cradle*, 232, 241; Sachs, *Life We Were Given*, xviii, 98, 136.

28. "Where They Go: South Vietnamese Orphans," *Time*, April 14, 1975, 14–15; Cummings, "Meet Melissa," 41; *Operation Babylift: The Lost Children of Vietnam*, Against the Grain Productions, 2009, DVD.

29. Peck-Barnes, *War Cradle*, 266.

30. Sachs, *Life We Were Given*, 132, 164; Peck-Barnes, *War Cradle*, 60, 236, 237; USAID, *Operation Babylift Report*, 4.

31. Johnston, "Torment over the Viet Non-Orphans," 15, 86; Cummings, "Meet Melissa," 41.

32. Cummings, "How Ngoc-Lon Became Melissa," 78; "Culture Shock for Orphans," *Science Digest*, August 1975, 21; Sachs, *Life We Were Given*, 120.

33. Cummings, "Meet Melissa," 42, 43; "You Have a New Brother! 5 Year Old Vietnamese Child," *McCall's*, May 1976, 18.

34. Peck-Barnes, *War Cradle*, 265.

35. Cummings, "Meet Melissa," 40, 41, 43.

36. Peck-Barnes, *War Cradle*, 237; Cummings, "Meet Melissa," 43.

37. "Clouds Over the Airlift," *Time*, April 28, 1975, 20; Sachs, *Life We Were Given*, 198, 208.

38. Lifton, "Orphans in Limbo," 22.

39. Lifton, "Orphans in Limbo," 20; Sachs, *Life We Were Given*, 198, 202, 203, 206.

40. Sachs, *Life We Were Given*, 204, 208, 209.

41. Callery, "Children of War," 19, 20; Yarborough, *Surviving Twice*, 205; Sachs, *Life We Were Given*, 213, 214.

42. Peck-Barnes, *War Cradle*, 276, 277.

43. Sachs, *Life We Were Given*, 209, 214.

44. Sachs, *Life We Were Given*, xv; Peck-Barnes, *War Cradle*, 285.

45. Peck-Barnes, *War Cradle*, 259, 287; Nwadiora and McAdoo, "Acculturative Stress," 481; Olmsted, "Bui Doi," 144.

46. Sachs, *Life We Were Given*, xix, xvi, xvii, 107, 214.

47. Peck-Barnes, *War Cradle*, 275.

48. Sachs, *Life We Were Given*, 64, 130; Shana Alexander, "Amnesty, Agony, and Responsibility: Illegitimate Children of American Soldiers," *Newsweek*, March 19, 1973, 34; Yarborough, *Surviving Twice*, 98.

49. Bass, *Vietnamerica*, 22, 27; DeBonis, *Children of the Enemy*, 3; Olmsted, "Bui Doi," 128; Peck-Barnes, *War Cradle*, 44.

50. Callery, "Children of War," 8; Yarborough, *Surviving Twice*, 14; Luce, "Amer-Asian Children in Vietnam," 996.

51. Leong and Johnson, *Vietnamese Amerasian Mothers*, 31, 34; McKelvey, *Dust of Life*, 45.

52. DeBonis, *Children of the Enemy*, 8; Yarborough, *Surviving Twice*, 18.

53. Yarborough, *Surviving Twice*, 18; DeBonis, *Children of the Enemy*, 228.

54. Callery, "Children of War," 5; Lacey, *In Our Fathers' Land*, 6.

55. "Honorable Estate: Boom in U.S.-Vietnamese Marriages," *Newsweek*, August 8, 1966, 31; Olmsted, "Bui Doi," 86, 88; DeBonis, *Children of the Enemy*, 228, 267.

56. Yarborough, *Surviving Twice*, 11, 58.

57. Ibid., 28.

58. Felsman et al., *Vietnamese Amerasians*, 7; Nguyen, "Vietnamese Amerasians," 27, 31.

59. United States General Accounting Office, *Vietnamese Amerasian Resettlement*, 4; Callery, "Children of War," 5; Yarborough, *Surviving Twice*, 12; Lacey, *In Our Fathers' Land*, 33; Nguyen, "Vietnamese Amerasians," 31.

60. Yarborough, *Surviving Twice*, 61, 62.

61. Callery, "Children of War," 5; Nguyen, "Vietnamese Amerasians," 25; Murray Polner, "Half and Half and Unwanted: Half Black Children of American GIs," *Commonweal*, March 24, 1972, 52, 53; DeBonis, *Children of the Enemy*, 99.

62. Lacey, *In Our Fathers' Land*, 8; Yarborough, *Surviving Twice*, 45, 47.

63. DeBonis, *Children of the Enemy*, 9; Yarborough, *Surviving Twice*, 39, 43; Olmsted, "Bui Doi," 103.

64. DeBonis, *Children of the Enemy*, 9; Nguyen, "Vietnamese Amerasians," 23, 24; Yarborough, *Surviving Twice*, 45, 49; Lacey, *In Our Fathers' Land*, 11.

65. Olmsted, "Bui Doi," 100; Lacey, *In Our Fathers' Land*, 14; McKelvey, *Dust of Life*, 71, 83, 85, 88; Nguyen, "Vietnamese Amerasians," 25.

66. DeBonis, *Children of the Enemy*, 212.

67. Yarborough, *Surviving Twice*, 58; Lacey, *In Our Fathers' Land*, 14.

68. McKelvey, *Dust of Life*, 10, 11, 85; Lacey, *In Our Fathers' Land*, 14; Yarborough, *Surviving Twice*, 74, 76, 77.

69. Herring, *America's Longest War*, 327, 342, 360; Yarborough, *Surviving Twice*, 39, 45, 58.

70. Lacey, *In Our Fathers' Land*, 15.

71. McKelvey, *Dust of Life*, 4, 21, 25, 52; DeBonis, *Children of the Enemy*, 3; Felsman, *Vietnamese Amerasians*, 47.

72. Felsman, *Vietnamese Amerasians*, 48; DeBonis, *Children of the Enemy*, 74, 94, 95.

73. DeBonis, *Children of the Enemy*, 147.

74. Felsman, *Vietnamese Amerasians*, 50; DeBonis, *Children of the Enemy*, 103.

75. Yarborough, *Surviving Twice*, 14.

76. Lacey, *In Our Fathers' Land*, 58; McKelvey, *Dust of Life*, 10; Olmsted, "Bui Doi," 80, 148; Nwadiora and McAdoo, "Acculturative Stress," 479, 480; Bass, *Vietnamerica*, 170; Lacey, *In Our Fathers' Land*, 28, 62, 64; DeBonis, *Children of the Enemy*, 99.

77. Bass, *Vietnamerica*, 189; McKelvey, *Dust of Life*, 5, 22; Yarborough, *Surviving Twice*, 9, 10, 50, 159.

78. Bass, *Vietnamerica*, 37, 38; Yarborough, *Surviving Twice*, 65.

79. Callery, "Children of War," 17; Olmsted, "Bui Doi," 120; Yarborough, *Surviving Twice*, 94, 95; DeBonis, *Children of the Enemy*, 3; Lamb, "Children of the Vietnam War," 3–5.

80. Callery, "Children of War," 15, 17.

81. Bass, *Vietnamerica*, 3, 13; McKelvey, *Dust of Life*, 33; Yarborough, *Surviving Twice*, 101, 102, 103.

82. Bass, *Vietnamerica*, 42, 46; Yarborough, *Surviving Twice*, 94, 103, 118; McKelvey, *Dust of Life*, 97; United States General Accounting Office, *Vietnamese Amerasian Resettlement*, 33.

83. Yarborough, *Surviving Twice*, 103; DeBonis, *Children of the Enemy*, 11, 12.

84. Nguyen, "Vietnamese Amerasians," 36.

85. Yarborough, *Surviving Twice*, x, 107, 112, 114.

86. Nguyen, "Vietnamese Amerasians," 36; Bass, *Vietnamerica*, 164.

87. Yarborough, *Surviving Twice*, xi; Nguyen, "Vietnamese Amerasians," 40; DeBonis, *Children of the Enemy*, 14; Yarborough, *Surviving Twice*, 62; Nancy Cooper, "Go Back to Your Country: Amerasians Head for Their Fathers' Homelands," *Newsweek*, March 14, 1988, 31.

88. Lamb, "Children of the Vietnam War," 5; Lacey, *In Our Fathers' Land*, 50, 51; Yarborough, *Surviving Twice*, 154; United States General Accounting Office, *Vietnamese Amerasian Resettlement*, 80.

89. Lacey, *In Our Fathers' Land*, 21, 31, 32, 33, 45; McKelvey et al., "Premigratory Expectations," 141–48; Felsman, *Vietnamese Amerasians*, 7; DeBonis, *Children of the Enemy*, 225; Anis, "Psychosocial Adjustment of Vietnamese-Americans," 59–60; McKelvey, *Dust of Life*, 102.

90. Yarborough, *Surviving Twice*, 138; Nguyen, "Vietnamese Amerasians," 46, 47; Bass, *Vietnamerica*, 190, 191, 272.

91. Yarborough, *Surviving Twice*, 151; DeBonis, *Children of the Enemy*, 136, 225; Lacey, *In Our Fathers' Land*, 27.

92. DeBonis, *Children of the Enemy*, 15; McKelvey, *Dust of Life*, 102; Nguyen, "Vietnamese Amerasians," 47; Yarborough quoted in Nguyen, "Vietnamese Amerasians," 48.

93. Bass, *Vietnamerica*, 267; Lamb, "Children of the Vietnam War," 2; Olmsted, "Bui Doi," 160, 161.

94. McKelvey, *Dust of Life*, 112.

Aftermath

1. Comegno, "Pen Pal's Memory," 3A; Bill Harrison interview; "Camden School's Vietnam Letters"; "Cherry Hill Vietnam KIA, Sgt Glen Williams, Memorabilia in Smithsonian," December 5, 2014, http://www.alch372.com/2014/12/05/glenwilliams/.

2. Anna B. Gray, email message to author, January 11, 2010.

3. Elder et al., *Children in Time and Place*, 45, 242; 249; Jones, *Great Expectations*, 7, 104, 164.

4. Cindy Lehto, email message to author, July 15, 2010.

5. Melvin Merchant, email message to author, March 14, 2010.

6. Cindy M. Sigmon, email message to author, January 26, 2010.

7. Karen Cordell, email message to author, February 6, 2010.

8. Steven Craig, email message to author, January 18, 2010.

9. Cheryl Matthews, November 16, 1998, Keri Bowers, February 2, 1999, "Letters and Notes."

10. Martindale, "O.C. Woman."

11. Ibid.

12. Ibid.; Anton, "Vietnam War Bracelets."

13. Sue Bailey, email message to author, March 3, 2012.

14. Hartman, "Woman Wears POW/MIA Bracelet."

15. Barbara Layne, October 12, 1998, Ami Partin, November 12, 1998, Kathy Mianecki, March 19, 1999, "Letters and Notes."

16. Kathy Becker, March 28, 1999, "Letters and Notes."

17. Keri Bowers, February 2, 1999, "Letters and Notes."

18. Presley, *Thirty Days with My Father*.

19. Ochberg, "Letter to Children of Veterans."

20. Daughters of Vietnam Veterans, "We Are Not Children Anymore," October 10, 2012, http://dovv.weebly.com/blog/we-are-not-children-anymore.

21. Cathi Bond-Drake interview.

22. Ibid.

23. Charlotte Duggan Priest interview.

24. Ibid.

25. Ibid.

26. *Gold Star Children*; Santoli, "We Never Knew Our Fathers," 21, 22.

27. Tony Cordero interview; Zacharias, *Hero Mama*, 324.

28. Zacharias, *Hero Mama*, 274, 275.

29. *Gold Star Children*; Zacharias, *Hero Mama*, 286; Sons and Daughters in Touch, http://sdit.org/tributes/robert-b-swenck/.

30. Sons and Daughters in Touch, http://sdit.org/tributes/robert-b-swenck/; Swenck, "Emergent Voices," 2.

31. Robert B. Swenck to Stacy Swenck, November 4, 1971, in the author's possession.

32. Sons and Daughters in Touch, http://sdit.org/tributes/robert-b-swenck/.

33. Briscoe, "Children of the Fallen," 53; Santoli, "We Never Knew Our Fathers," 22; Zacharias, *Hero Mama*, 331.

34. Zacharias, *Hero Mama*, 292, 317.

35. Stacy Swenck interview.

36. Ibid.

37. Swenck, "Emergent Voices," 3; Stacy Swenck interview.

38. Sons and Daughters in Touch, http://sdit.org/tributes/david-e-benson/;
http://sdit.org/tributes/carroll-wayne-spragins/;
http://sdit.org/tributes/everett-d-keaton/;
http://sdit.org/tributes/john-lance-geoghegan/;
http://sdit.org/tributes/thomas-moore-2/.

39. Tony Cordero interview.

40. Ibid.

BIBLIOGRAPHY

Anderegg, Michael, ed. *Inventing Vietnam: The War in Film and Television*. Philadelphia: Temple University Press, 1991.

Anderson, Terry. *The Movement and the Sixties: Protest in America from Greensboro to Wounded Knee*. New York: Oxford University Press, 1995.

Andreas, Carol. "War Toys and the Peace Movement." *Journal of Social Issues* 25, no. 1 (January 1969): 83–99.

Anis, Joyce. "Psychosocial Adjustment of Vietnamese-Americans." PhD dissertation, University of Minnesota, 1996.

Anton, Mike. "Vietnam War Bracelets Come Full Circle." *Los Angeles Times*, November 4, 2010.

Appy, Christian G. *Patriots: The Vietnam War Remembered from All Sides*. New York: Penguin, 2004.

———. *Working-Class War: American Combat Soldiers and Vietnam*. Chapel Hill: University of North Carolina Press, 1993.

Arbuckle, Les. *Saigon Kids: An American Military Brat Comes of Age in 1960s Vietnam*. New York: AP Editions, 2017.

Arlen, Michael J. *Living-Room War*. Syracuse, N.Y.: Syracuse University Press, 1997.

Aslanian, Sasha, and Gary Eichten. "Transcript of the Vietnam Tapes." Minnesota Public Radio, July 2, 2008, www.mprnews.org/story/2008/07/02/vietnamtranscript.

Aune, Regina Claire, and Aryn Lockhart. *Operation Babylift: Mission Accomplished: A Memoir of Hope and Healing*. Denver: Blueline, 2015.

Barnouw, Erik. *Tube of Plenty: The Evolution of American Television*. 2nd rev. ed. New York: Oxford University Press, 1990.

Baskir, Lawrence M., and William A. Strauss. *Chance and Circumstance: The Draft, the War, and the Vietnam Generation*. New York: Vintage, 1978.

Bass, Thomas A. *Vietnamerica: The War Comes Home*. New York: Soho, 1996.

Beidler, Philip. *American Literature and the Experience of Vietnam*. Athens: University of Georgia Press, 1982.

Berg, Norman E. *Regret to Inform You: Experiences of Families Who Lost a Family Member in Vietnam*. Central Point, Ore.: Hellgate, 1999.

Bitler, Marianne P., and Lucie Schmidt. "Birth Rates and the Vietnam Draft." *American Economic Review: Papers and Proceedings* 102, no. 3 (2012): 566–69.

"Bitter Legacy of the Baby Lift." *Time*, May 24, 1976, 17.

Braun, Saul. "Shazam! Here Comes Captain Relevant." *New York Times*, May 2, 1971, 36, 37.

Briscoe, Daren. "Children of the Fallen." *Newsweek*, March 20, 2005, https://www.newsweek.com/children-fallen-114393.

Bruegman, Bill. *Toys of the Sixties: A Pictorial Guide*. Akron, Ohio: Cap'n Penny, 1992.

Callery, T. Grant. "Children of War: The Problems of Amerasian Children in Vietnam." *Case Western Reserve Journal of International Law* 6 (1973): 4–32.

"A Celebration of Men Redeemed." *Time*, February 19, 1973, 13–19.

Chapman, Roger, ed. *Culture Wars: An Encyclopedia of Issues, Viewpoints, and Voices*. New York: M.E. Sharpe, 2010.

———. "From Vietnam to the New World Order: The GI Joe Action Figure as Cold War Artifact." In *The Impact of the Cold War on American Popular Culture*, edited by Elaine McClarnand and Steve Goodson. Carrollton: State University of West Georgia, 1999.

Clark, Cherie. *After Sorrow Comes Joy*. New York: Lawrence & Thomas, 2000.

Comegno, Carol. "Camden School's Vietnam Letters among Items Headed to Smithsonian." *Courier-Post (Camden, N.J.)*, October 5, 2014, http://www.courierpostonline.com/story/news/local/south-jersey/2014/10/05/camden-schools-vietnam-letters-among-items-headed-smithsonian/16676461.

———. "A Pen Pal's Memory of Soldiers Adds to History." *Courier-Post (Camden, N.J.)*, October 6, 2014, 3A.

Coons, Hannibal. *Dear Mr. President: The Hilarious Letters Kids Write to the President*. New York: Doubleday, 1971.

Coontz, Stephanie. *The Way We Never Were: American Families and the Nostalgia Trap*. New York: Basic Books, 1992.

Cossen, M. J., and Winson Trang. *A Dream Come True: Coming to America from Vietnam, 1975*. Logan, Iowa: Perfection Learning, 2001.

Cross, Gary S. *The Cute and The Cool: Wondrous Innocence and Modern American Children's Culture*. New York: Oxford University Press, 2004.

———. *Kids' Stuff: Toys and the Changing World of American Childhood*. Cambridge, Mass.: Harvard University Press, 2001.

Cummings, Susan, as told to Elizabeth Mulligan. "How Ngoc-Lon Became Melissa." *Parents' Magazine*, April 1971, 44.

———. "Meet Melissa: Adopted Vietnamese Child." *Parents' Magazine*, February 1973, 40, 41.

Dahl, Barbara B., and Hamilton I. McCubbin. "Children of Returned Prisoners of War: The Effects of Long-Term Father Separation." Paper presented at Annual Meeting of the American Psychological Association, Chicago, August 1975.

Dahl, Barbara B., Hamilton I. McCubbin, and Gary R. Lester. "War-Induced Father Absence: Comparing the Adjustment of Children in Reunited, Non-reunited and Reconstituted Families." *International Journal of Sociology of the Family* 6, no. 1 (Spring 1976): 99–108.

Dahl, Barbara B., Hamilton McCubbin, and K. Ross. "Second Generational Effects of War-Induced Separations: Comparing the Adjustment of Children in Reunited and Non-reunited Families." *Military Medicine* 141 (1977): 146–51.

Darowski, Joseph J. *The Ages of The Avengers: Essays on the Earth's Mightiest Heroes in Changing Times*. Jefferson, N.C.: McFarland, 2014.

DeBonis, Steven. *Children of the Enemy: Oral Histories of Vietnamese Amerasians and Their Mothers*. Jefferson, N.C.: McFarland, 1995.

Delli Carpini, Michael X. "U.S. Media Coverage of the Vietnam Conflict in 1968." In *The Vietnam Era: Media and Popular Culture in the U.S. and Vietnam*, edited by Michael Klein. Winchester, Mass.: Unwin Hyman, 1990.

Duncan, Randy, and Matthew J. Smith, eds. *Icons of the American Comic Book: From Captain America to Wonder Woman*. Santa Barbara, Calif.: Greenwood, 2013.

Egendorf, Arthur. *Healing from the War: Trauma and Transformation after Vietnam*. Boston: Houghton Mifflin, 1985.

Elder, Glen H., John Modell, and Ross D. Parke, eds. *Children in Time and Place: Developmental and Historical Insights*. New York: Cambridge University Press, 1994.

Emerson, Gloria. *Winners and Losers: Battles, Retreats, Gains, Losses, and Ruins from the Vietnam War*. New York: W. W. Norton, 1985.

Engelhardt, Tom. *The End of Victory Culture: Cold War America and the Disillusioning of a Generation*. New York: Basic Books, 1995.

Eugster, Sandra. *Notes from Nethers: Growing Up in a Sixties Commune*. Chicago: Academy Chicago Publishers, 2007.

Fass, Paula S. "The Child-Centered Family? New Rules in Postwar America." In *Reinventing Childhood after World War II*, edited by Paula S. Fass and Michael Grossberg. Philadelphia: University of Pennsylvania Press, 2012.

Feinsilber, Myron. "Peace Women Battle against War Toys." *Daily Independent Journal* (San Rafael, Calif.), December 18, 1965, 4.

Felsman, J. Kirk, Mark C. Johnson, Frederick T. L. Leong, and Irene C. Felsman. *Vietnamese Amerasians: Practical Implications of Current Research*. Washington, D.C.: Office of Refugee Resettlement, 1989.

Ferrari, Michelle. *Reporting America at War: An Oral History*. New York: Hachette, 2003.

Figley, Charles R., and Seymour Leventman, eds. *Strangers at Home: Vietnam Veterans since the War*. New York: Routledge, 1990.

Franklin, H. Bruce. *The Vietnam War in American Stories, Songs, and Poems*. Boston: Bedford Books of St. Martin's Press, 1996.

———. "Vietnam, Star Trek, and the Real Future." In *Star Trek and History*, edited by Nancy R. Reagin. Hoboken, N.J.: Wiley, 2013.

Gold Star Children: Two Generations Share Loss and Healing. JRB Communications, LLC, 2013. DVD.

Goodrum, Michael D. *Superheroes and American Self-Image: From War to Watergate*. Farnham, Surrey, UK: Ashgate, 2016.

Goossen, Rachel Waltner. "Disarming the Toy Store and Reloading the Shopping Cart: Resistance to Violent Consumer Culture." *Peace and Change* 38, no. 3 (July 2013): 330–54.

———. "Like Entering an Armed Camp': Christian Peacemaker Teams and the Language of Violent-Toy Protests." *Mennonite Quarterly Review* 86 (January 2012): 60.

Gravett, Paul. "War Comics: Reinforcing the Military's Propaganda Machine?" July 4, 2010. http://www.paulgravett.com/articles/article/war_comics.

Greenstein, Fred I. *Children and Politics*. New Haven, Conn.: Yale University Press, 1969.

Grieve, Victoria M. *Little Cold Warriors: American Childhood in the 1950s*. New York: Oxford University Press, 2018.

Hammond, William M. *Reporting Vietnam: Media and Military at War*. Lawrence: University Press of Kansas, 1998.

Hartman, Steve. "Woman Wears POW/MIA Bracelet for Nearly 40 Years." CBS News, May 16, 2011, http://www.cbsnews.com/news/woman-wears-pow-mia-bracelet-for-nearly-40-years/.

Hawley, Thomas M. *The Remains of War: Bodies, Politics, and the Search for American Soldiers Unaccounted for in Southeast Asia*. Durham, N.C.: Duke University Press, 2005.

Hendin, Herbert, and Ann Pollinger Haas. *Wounds of War: The Psychological Aftermath of Combat in Vietnam*. New York: Basic Books, 1984.

Herring, George C. *America's Longest War: The United States and Vietnam, 1950–1975*. New York: McGraw-Hill, 2014.

Higdon, Hal. "A Mother Opens Fire on War Toys." *Pageant*, January 1966, 14.

Holland, Thomas W., ed. *Boys' Toys of the Fifties and Sixties: Memorable Catalog Pages from the Legendary Sears Christmas Wishbooks, 1950–1969*. Sherman Oaks, Calif.: Windmill, 1997.

Holsinger, M. P. *War and American Popular Culture: A Historical Encyclopedia*. Westport, Conn.: Greenwood, 1999.

Holt, Marilyn Irvin. *Cold War Kids: Politics and Childhood in Postwar America, 1945–1960*. Lawrence: University Press of Kansas, 2014.

Honan, William H. "Merry Bang, Bang (and Happy New Year) War Toys." *New Republic* 153 (December 25, 1965): 11–12.

Hunter, Edna J. "Families in Crisis: The Families of Prisoners of War." San Diego, Calif.: Center for Prisoner of War Studies, Naval Health Research Center, December 1977.

———. "Long-Term Effects of Parental Wartime Captivity on Children: Children of POW and MIA Servicemen." *Journal of Contemporary Psychotherapy* 18, no. 4 (Winter 1988): 312–28.

———. "The Vietnam POW Veteran: Immediate and Long-Term Effects of Captivity." San Diego, Calif.: Center for Prisoner of War Studies, Naval Health Research Center, April 1977.

Indochina Evacuation and Refugee Problems. Hearing Before the Subcommittee to Investigate Problems Connected with Refugees and Escapees of the Committee on the Judiciary, United States Senate, Ninety-fourth Congress, First Session, April 8, 1975.

"I Turned Mine In." *Time*, September 6, 1968, 94.

Jenkins, Henry, ed. *The Children's Culture Reader*. New York: New York University Press, 1998.

Johnston, Tracy. "Torment over the Viet Non-Orphans." *New York Times Magazine*, May 9, 1976, 14–15, 76–78, 83, 86, 87.

Jones, Landon Y. *Great Expectations: America and the Baby Boom Generation*. New York: Ballantine, 1981.

Kane, Joseph J. "Life without Father." *Time*, June 11, 1973, 24.

Kapell, Matthew Wilhelm. *Exploring the Next Frontier: Vietnam, NASA, Star Trek and Utopia in 1960s and 1970s American Myth and History*. New York: Routledge, 2016.

Katz, Harry L. *Cartoon America: Comic Art in the Library of Congress*. New York: Abrams, 2006.

Kelley, William E., ed. *Post-Traumatic Stress Disorder and the War Veteran Patient*. New York: Brunner/Mazel, 1985.

Kendall, David. *The Mammoth Book of Best War Comics*. New York: Running Press, 2007.

Klein, Michael, ed. *The Vietnam Era: Media and Popular Culture in the U.S. and Vietnam*. Winchester, Mass.: Unwin Hyman, 1990.

Kline, Stephen. *Out of the Garden: Toys and Children's Culture in the Age of TV Marketing*. London: Verso, 1993.

Kutinova, Andrea. "Paternity Deferments and the Timing of Births: U.S. Natality During the Vietnam War." *Economic Inquiry* 47, no. 2 (April 1, 2009): 351–64.

Kutner, Max. "Vietnam War Vets Reconnect with Their 1960s Pen Pals for a Museum Donation." *Smithsonian Magazine*, November 17, 2014, http://www.smithsonianmag.com/smithsonian-institution/vietnam-war-vets-reconnect-their-1960s-pen-pals-museum-donation-180953343/.

Labarre, Nicolas. "Joining the Fray? *Mad* on Richard Nixon and Spiro Agnew." *Studies in American Humor* 30 (2014): 135–54.

Lacey, Marilyn. *In Our Fathers' Land: Vietnamese Amerasians in the United States*. Washington, D.C.: Migration and Refugee Services, United States Catholic Conference, 1985.

Lamb, David. "Children of the Vietnam War." *Smithsonian Magazine*, June 2009, https://www.smithsonianmag.com/travel/children-of-the-vietnam-war-131207347/.

Lassonde, Stephen. "Ten Is the New Fourteen: Age Compression and 'Real' Childhood." In *Reinventing Childhood after World War II*, edited by Paula S. Fass and Michael Grossberg. Philadelphia: University of Pennsylvania Press, 2012.

Leong, Frederick T., and Mark C. Johnson. *Vietnamese Amerasian Mothers: Psychological Distress and High Risk Factors*. Washington, D.C.: Office of Refugee Resettlement, Department of Health and Human Services, 1992.

Lesser, Gerald S. *Children and Television: Lessons from Sesame Street*. New York: Random House, 1974.

"Let's Not Kid the Kids about Vietnam." *Reader's Digest*, July 1965, 56–57.

Lieberman, James E. "American Families and the Vietnam War." *Journal of Marriage and the Family* 33, no. 4 (November 1971): 709–21.

———. "Statement on the Effects of U.S. Casualties in Viet Nam on American Families." *Journal of Marriage and the Family* 32, no. 2 (May 1970): 197–99.

Lifton, Betty Jean. *Children of Vietnam*. New York: Scribner, 1972.

———. "Orphans in Limbo." *Saturday Review*, May 1, 1976, 20.

Lifton, Robert Jay. *Home from the War: Vietnam Veterans: Neither Victims nor Executioners*. New York: Simon & Schuster, 1973.

Lipman, Jana K. *Mixed Voices, Mixed Policies: Vietnamese Amerasians in Vietnam and the United States*. Providence, R.I.: Wayland Press, 1997.

"Living with Uncertainty: The Families Who Wait Back Home." *Time*, December 7, 1970, 18.

Luce, Don. "Amer-Asian Children in Vietnam." *Christian Century*, August 25, 1971, 996–97.

Lyon, Nancy. "More Than Child's Play." *Ms.*, December 1972, 54–55, 98.

———. *Twice Born: Memoirs of an Adopted Daughter*. New York: Other Press, 2006.

Mabry, Philip James. "'We're Bringing Them Home': Resettling Vietnamese Amerasians in the United States." PhD dissertation, University of Pittsburgh, 1996.

Maquire, Lori. "'The Avengers Always Stand Ready to Do Their Part': *The Avengers* and the Vietnam War." In *The Ages of the Avengers: Essays on the Earth's Mightiest Heroes in Changing Times*, edited by Joseph J. Darowski. Jefferson, N.C.: McFarland, 2014.

Marten, James, ed. *Children and War: A Historical Anthology*. New York: New York University Press, 2002.

———. *Children for the Union: The War Spirit on the Northern Home Front*. New York: Ivan R. Dee, 2004.

Martindale, Scott. "O.C. Woman Seeks, Finds 'Her' Vietnam POW." *Orange County (Calif.) Register*, January 20, 2012. http://www.ocregister.com/articles/oskins-336617-connor-bracelet.html.

May, Elaine Tyler. *Homeward Bound: American Families in the Cold War Era*. New York: Basic Books, 2008.

McCubbin, Hamilton I. "Longitudinal Research of Families of Returned Prisoners of War and of Servicemen Missing in Action: A Review of the Findings." In *Proceedings, Third Annual Joint Medical Meeting Concerning POW/MIA Matters*. San Diego: Center for Prisoner of War Studies, Naval Health Research Center, November 1976.

McCubbin, Hamilton I., Barbara B. Dahl, Gary R. Lester, Dorothy Benson, and Marilyn L. Robertson. "Coping Repertoires of Families Adapting to Prolonged War-Induced Separations." *Journal of Marriage and Family* 38, no. 3 (August 1976): 461–71.

McCubbin, Hamilton I., Barbara B. Dahl, Gary R. Lester, and Beverly Ross. "The Prisoner of War and His Children: Evidence for the Origin of Second Generational Effects of Captivity." *International Journal of Sociology of the Family* 7, no. 1 (January–June 1977): 25–36.

McCubbin, Hamilton I., Edna J. Hunter, Philip J. Metres Jr., Edna J. Hunter, and John A. Plag, eds. *Family Separation and Reunion: Families of Prisoners of War and Servicemen Missing in Action*. Washington, D.C.: U.S. Government Printing Office, 1974.

McKelvey, Robert S. *The Dust of Life: America's Children Abandoned in Vietnam*. Seattle: University of Washington Press, 1999.

McKelvey, Robert S., Alice R. Mao, and John A. Webb. "Premigratory Expectations and Mental Health Symptoms in a Group of Vietnamese Amerasian Youth." *Journal of the American Academy of Child and Adolescent Psychiatry* 32, no. 2 (March 1993): 141–48.

"Memories of Divided Families." *Life*, December 4, 1970, 36–43.

Mintz, Steven. "The Changing Face of Children's Culture." In *Reinventing Childhood after World War II*, edited by Paula S. Fass and Michael Grossberg. Philadelphia: University of Pennsylvania Press, 2012.

———. *Huck's Raft: A History of American Childhood.* Cambridge, Mass.: Harvard University Press, 2006.

Morris, Bernadine. "Bracelet That Stands for a Cause." *New York Times*, June 17, 1972.

"Mothers Protest Arms Race in Toys." *Toledo (Ohio) Blade*, March 9, 1966, 12.

Mundey, Lisa M. *American Militarism and Anti-Militarism in Popular Media, 1945–1970.* Jefferson, N.C.: McFarland, 2012.

Nguyen, Ky-Giao C. *Vietnamese Amerasians: A Study of Identity Construction.* MA thesis, University of Texas–Arlington, 2010.

Nice, D. Stephen. "Children of Returned Prisoners of War: Are There Really Second Generational Effects?" San Diego, Calif.: Center for Prisoner of War Studies, Naval Health Research Center, May 1978.

Nwadiora, E., and H. McAdoo. "Acculturative Stress among Amerasian Refugees: Gender and Racial Differences." *Adolescence* 31, no. 122 (Summer 1996): 477–87.

O'Brien, Richard. *The Story of American Toys: From the Puritans to the Present.* New York: Abbeville, 1990.

Ochberg, Frank M. "Letter to Children of Veterans." United Children of Veterans, http://unitedchildrenofveterans.com/letter-to-children-of-veterans/.

Olmsted, Elizabeth. "Bui Doi: Vietnamese Amerasian Experiences in Vietnam and the United States." MA thesis, Texas Women's University, 2004.

Olson, James S., ed. *The Vietnam War: Handbook of the Literature and Research.* Westport, Conn.: Greenwood, 1993.

Ossian, Lisa. *The Forgotten Generation: American Children and World War II.* Columbia: University of Missouri Press, 2011.

Paley, Grace. "Other People's Children: The 'Young Shoots' of Vietnam." *Ms.*, September 1975, 69.

Peck-Barnes, Shirley. *The War Cradle: The Untold Story of "Operation Babylift."* Denver: Vintage Pressworks, 2000.

Polner, Murray. "Half and Half and Unwanted: Half Black Children of American GIs." *Commonweal*, March 24, 1972, 52, 53.

"Pop Goes the War." *Newsweek*, September 12, 1966, 66.

"A POW Dad and His Family's Fierce, Loving Allegiance." National Public Radio/StoryCorps, May 27, 2016, https://www.npr.org/templates/transcript/transcript.php?storyId=479507187.

Presley, Christal. *Thirty Days with My Father: Finding Peace from Wartime PTSD.* Deerfield Beach, Fla.: Health Communications, 2012. E-book.

Reagin, Nancy R., ed. *Star Trek and History*. Hoboken, N.J.: Wiley, 2013.

Regan, Patrick M. "War Toys, War Movies, and the Militarization of the United States, 1900–85." *Journal of Peace Research* 31, no. 1 (February 1994): 45–58.

Reidelbach, Maria. *Completely MAD: A History of the Comic Book and Magazine*. Boston: Little, Brown, 1991.

Rhodes, Joel P. *Growing Up in a Land Called Honalee: The Sixties in the Lives of American Children*. Columbia: University of Missouri Press, 2017.

Rowe, John Carlos, and Rick Berg, eds. *The Vietnam War and American Culture*. New York: Columbia University Press, 1991.

Rowley, Kathleen A. "A Pen Pal Calls on 'His Kids.'" *Courier-Post* (Camden, N.J.), March 15, 1969, http://www.alch372.com/wp-content/uploads/2014/11/CourierWknd1968.pdf.

Sachs, Dana. *The Life We Were Given: Operation Baby Lift, International Adoption, and the Children of War in Vietnam*. Boston: Beacon, 2010.

Salkind, Neil J. *Theories of Human Development*. New York: Van Nostrand, 1981.

Santoli, Al. "We Never Knew Our Fathers." *Parade*, May 27, 1990, 21.

Scott, Cord A. "Comics and Conflict: War and Patriotically Themed Comics in American Cultural History from World War II through the Iraq War." PhD dissertation, Loyola University Chicago, 2011.

Siegfried, John. *Six Degrees of the Bracelet: Vietnam's Continuing Grip*. Bloomington, Ind.: Xlibris, 2011.

Skolnick, Arlene. *Embattled Paradise: The American Family in the Age of Uncertainty*. New York: Basic Books, 1991.

Small, Melvin. *Covering Dissent: The Media and the Anti-Vietnam War Movement*. New Brunswick, N.J.: Rutgers University Press, 1994.

Spock, Benjamin. *The Common Sense Book of Baby and Child Care*. New York: Duell, Sloan & Pearce, 1946.

———. "Playing with Toy Guns: Effects of Warlike Games and Toys on Children." *Redbook*, November 1964, 24–32.

———. *Raising Children in a Difficult Time*. New York: W. W. Norton, 1974.

Stark, Steven D. *Glued to the Set: The 60 Television Shows and Events That Made Us Who We Are Today*. New York: Free Press, 1997.

St. Onge, Jeff. "'Comedy before Country': Engaged Levity and Absurdist Critique in *Mad* Magazine." *Studies in American Humor* 30 (2014): 155–67.

Strang, Ruth. "War Talk and War Games." *PTA Magazine*, January 1968, 20–23.

Swenck, Stacy. "Emergent Voices: Three Memoirs from American War Orphans." MA thesis, California State University–San Marcos, 2007.

Taylor, Ella. *Prime-Time Families: Television Culture in Postwar America*. Berkeley: University of California Press, 1991.

Taylor, Rosemary. *Orphans of War*. New York: HarperCollins, 1988.

Thomas, Roy W. "American Comic Books and the Reflection of Cold War Attitudes, 1945–1970: A Study of the Depiction of Communism and of Communist Nations in U.S. Comic Books from the End of World War II through the Height of the Vietnam War." MA thesis, California State University–Dominguez Hills, 2005.

Thorsen, Karen. "A Campaign to Get a Husband Home." *Life*, September 29, 1972, 32–42.

Tolley, Howard, Jr. *Children and War: Political Socialization to Internal Conflict*. New York: Teachers College Press, 1973.

Tucker, Spencer C., ed. *The Encyclopedia of the Vietnam War: A Political, Social, and Military History*. New York: Oxford University Press, 1998.

Tuttle, William M. *"Daddy's Gone to War": The Second World War in the Lives of America's Children*. New York: Oxford University Press, 1993.

Umansky, Lauri. *Motherhood Reconceived: Feminism and the Legacies of the Sixties*. New York: New York University Press, 1996.

Valverde, Kieu-Linh Caroline. "From Dust to Gold: The Vietnamese Amerasian Experience." In *Racially Mixed People in America*, edited by Maria P. Root. Newbury Park, Calif.: Sage, 1992.

United States Agency for International Development. *Operation Babylift: Report, Emergency Movement of Vietnamese and Cambodian Orphans for Intercountry Adoption, April–June, 1975*. Washington, D.C.: United States Agency for International Development, 1975.

United States General Accounting Office. *Amerasian Resettlement*. United States General Accounting Office, Program Evaluation and Methodology Division, 1992. Washington, D.C.: General Accounting Office, 1992.

———. *Vietnamese Amerasian Resettlement: Education, Employment, and Family Outcomes in the United States, Report to Congressional Requesters*. Washington, D.C.: General Accounting Office, 1994.

Waldman, Elizabeth, and Robert Whitmore. "Children of Working Mothers, March 1973." *Monthly Labor Review*, May 1974, 50, 55.

Warren, Andrea. *Escape from Saigon: How a Vietnam War Orphan Became an American Boy*. New York: Farrar, Straus & Giroux, 2004.

Weekly Reader: 60 Years of News for Kids, 1928–1988. New York: World Almanac, 1988.

Weitzman, Lenore J. *The Divorce Revolution: The Unexpected Social and Economic Consequences for Women and Children in America*. New York: Free Press, 1985.

Whitbread, Jane. "The Families of the Men in Vietnam." *Parents' Magazine*, October 1967, 53–55, 113–15.

Whitfield, Stephen. *The Culture of The Cold War*. Baltimore: Johns Hopkins University Press, 1996.

"Who Bombed Santa's Workshop? Should War Toys Be Banned? Panel Discussion at Edgewood Elementary School." *New York Times Magazine*, December 12, 1965, 87, 98.

Wiest, A. A., M. Barbier, and G. Robins. *America and the Vietnam War: Re-Examining the Culture and History of a Generation*. New York: Routledge, 2010.

Wren, Christopher S. "What Is Christmas to the P.O.W. Wives?" *Look*, December 15, 1970, 36–40.

Wright, Bradford W. *Comic Book Nation: The Transformation of Youth Culture in America.* Baltimore: Johns Hopkins University Press, 2001.

———. "The Vietnam War in Comic Books." In *The Vietnam War: Handbook of the Literature and Research,* edited by James S. Olson. Westport, Conn.: Greenwood, 1993.

Wylie, Evan McLeod. "At Least I Know Jim's Alive." *Good Housekeeping,* February 1970, 79, 214–19.

Yarborough, Trin. *Surviving Twice: Amerasian Children of the Vietnam War.* Washington, D.C.: Potomac, 2005.

Zacharias, Karen Spears. *Hero Mama: A Daughter Remembers the Father She Lost in Vietnam—and the Mother Who Held Her Family Together.* New York: HarperCollins, 2005.

Zaretsky, Natasha. *No Direction Home: The American Family and the Fear of National Decline, 1968–1980.* Chapel Hill: University of North Carolina Press, 2007.

INDEX